Fiction and the Shape of Belief

Sheldon Sacks

Fiction and the Shape of Belief

A Study of
Henry Fielding

With Glances at
Swift, Johnson
and Richardson

The University of Chicago Press
Chicago & London

The University of Chicago Press, Chicago 60637
The University of Chicago Press, Ltd., London

83 82 81 80   5 4 3 2 1

ISBN: 0-226-73337-8
LCN: 79-24436

For Arthur Friedman

Preface

With a few exceptions, friends who have read the manuscript of this book seem to fall into two classes: those who dislike the first and last chapters, and those who dislike the chapters in between. The latter confined their criticisms primarily to the notion that Fielding's novels were not worth such detailed attention; since we wish nothing but good things for friends, I may only acknowledge their objections with a profound hope for the radical amelioration of their taste.

The objections of the first class, though, cannot be set aside so lightly, especially as other readers of this book will, I fear, share them. These are objections to intricate enquiries, no matter how well-intentioned, into what they consider the barren area of literary theory. Though I very much hope and, in my more optimistic moments, believe that such arguments as I advance in the first and last chapters are the most fruitful parts of this book, it is as well to admit at the outset that they are intricate indeed and may tax the patience of readers interested only in criticism which illuminates a particular literary work. Of such readers it is not unfair, I believe, to ask only that degree of tolerance necessary for reserving judgment about the fruitfulness of the enquiry until they have completed the book.

No one can be more aware than I am that the very terms "theory," "formulate," "subtype" are remote from any form of poetic activity, nor that the prosaic tedium consequent on committing an act of classification seems at odds with a humanistic concern for literary works that have moved generations of men to laughter or to tears. It was Imlac who, wherever he went, "found that Poetry was considered as the highest learning, and regarded with a veneration somewhat approaching to the Angelick Nature." But if this is true, as I firmly believe, nothing that contributes to even a purely intellectual understanding of the relationship of poets to poetry; of novelists to novels; of one vital form of human concern, ethics, to another, literary works, can be trivial. An eloquent expression of the intuitive recognition of the causes of a poem's excellence is one way of fostering such understanding, but it is only one of many and, though more palatable than most, it has its own limitations.

Since this book, whatever its faults, is a serious enquiry into a complex subject, the relation between ethical belief and literary form, I did not eschew

the use of such tools as general propositions about the nature of inferences, the
relevance of taxonomic activity to the nature of a theory, or other seemingly
remote concerns which have been traditionally of value in advancing human
knowledge about matters less ethereal than literary works.

I have been materially aided and abetted in writing this book by so many
friends—albeit sometimes against their better judgment—that the following
acknowledgments are mere tokens of very special indebtedness. The final
statement of every important concept in this book reflects the generous advice
and criticism of Professor Ralph Wilson Rader, who, in addition, put at my
disposal his own extensive knowledge of Fielding's life and works. Professors
Bertrand H. Bronson and James Sledd, who read the MS at various stages in
its development, not only offered encouragement essential for its completion,
but criticism that seriously influenced its form. For crucial kindnesses of a different order, I am indebted to Professors Mark Schorer and David Reed.

From my wife, Marjorie Hamilton Sacks, I have stolen ideas without acknowledgment, accepted assistance without sufficient thanks, and borrowed
inspiration without measure. Finally, as a thoroughly inadequate expression of
gratitude to my teacher, critic, and friend for more than a decade, I have ded-
icated this book to Professor Arthur Friedman.

Contents

Chapter One

Toward a Grammar
of the Types of Fiction

'I suppose,' [William] said
suddenly, 'it's not what you say
but the way you say it that you
think matters. Do your plays have plots?'
'They have themes.'
'What's the difference?'

. . .

Hersey went to him and took his
hands in hers. 'Nick,' she said,
'he's killed William.' [1]

Satires and Apologues

Coleridge wrote that one cannot emerge from a reading of
Fielding's novels "without an intense conviction that he could not be guilty of
a base act." Fielding, who had asserted that his "sincere endeavor" in *Tom
Jones* was "to recommend goodness and innocence," would certainly have
been pleased to learn that so sensitive and intelligent a critic had testified to the
success with which he had embodied his moral purpose in a "history"—that is,
what we now call a novel. But no novelist—even of an age resolutely determined to differentiate moral and aesthetic values—could be more aware than
Fielding was that he was not writing a "system," and that he did, in fact, have
to write a good "history" in order to implement his moral intention. The generations of intelligent and sensitive men that have read and still continue to
read Fielding with pleasure provide strong, if partial, testimony that he somehow did include his moral beliefs, opinions, and prejudices in works coherently
organized as novels without seriously detracting from their artistic effect.
How? Or, more generally, how can any novelist embody his beliefs in novels?
The impetus for the whole of this book derives from a desire to answer these
questions.

Though there have been nearly as many ostensible answers to the former
question as there have been critics of Fielding's writing, the disagreements

[1] Ngaio Marsh, *Death and the Dancing Footman* (London and Glasgow: Fontana
Books, 1958), pp. 28 and 137.

have been concerned with the substance of Fielding's beliefs rather than with how they are embodied in his novels. Indeed, some of the favorite critical languages of our own day, useful as they may be for answering some kinds of questions about literary works, prevent the question "how" from ever being asked. Those systems with which we seem most enamoured presume, as an unarticulated article of faith, that the answer to the question "how" is a self-evident proposition applicable with only minor variations to all kinds of prose fiction or even to all forms of literature.[2]

One might be hard-pressed to find an undergraduate English major in an American university who, if asked to contrast the forms of *Rasselas*, *Gulliver's Travels*, and *Pamela* in an essay, would not immediately hunt for organizing themes and then proceed to show how they are variously exploited by Johnson, Swift, and Richardson. The hypothetical student might label one an Oriental tale, one a satire, and the third a novel, but the enormous discrepancy between the ascription of the different labels and the single thematic approach to the three forms would not become apparent. The very facility with which the themes may be ferreted out—in a pinch, illusion versus reality may be applied with telling effect to the most stubborn literary case—seems adequately to justify the general popularity of such an approach to all problems of literary form. But one of its unfortunate side-effects is that it reduces all forms of prose fiction to one: they are all fictional examples of the truth of some universal-or-particular, subtle-or-simple, buried-or-apparent but always formulable statement about a specifiable though possibly obscure subject.

---

[2] I in no sense mean to imply that all critics make such a presumption. My own attempt to answer the question is heavily indebted to critics—to consider only those whose native tongue is English—ranging from David Hume to Wayne C. Booth. About Booth's impressive book, *The Rhetoric of Fiction* (Chicago: University of Chicago Press, 1961), a special word is in order. Mr. Booth might disagree with many of the statements in the following pages, especially with those which relate rhetorical signals to novelists' beliefs, but many of our theoretical commitments are similar, and, indeed, we are mutually indebted to many of the same contemporary critics. Though my indebtedness to Mr. Booth's earlier publications is acknowledged in the text, the present work was completed before *The Rhetoric of Fiction* was published and it has proved impracticable to discuss, even in footnotes, all points of agreement and disagreement. Perhaps such discussion is unnecessary since, despite some obvious similarities, *The Rhetoric of Fiction* and the present work are attempts to answer different critical questions. In general I have referred only to those works from which I have borrowed ideas central to the argument advanced in this book, and have explicitly disagreed with other critics only when argument might serve to clarify the explication of the relation of fiction to ethical belief. One result of this procedure is that some of my own favorite works about the novel, Fielding, Swift, and others are not cited.

Either the statement or, more frequently and impressively, the one- or two-word subject about which the book makes an ineffable statement (appearance-reality; being-becoming; darkness-light; chaos-order) is the organizing theme of the work.

If we begin with such a framework of critical terminology, we need not bother to read Fielding at all to discover in a general way *how* he embodied his ethical beliefs in *Tom Jones;* we answered the question before we ever asked it. Fielding's ethical beliefs, opinions, prejudices, must take the shape of fictional examples—possibly obvious, possibly so obscure as to need historical elucidation—of the truth of a statement about a subject. As devotees of close readings of texts, of course, we would not be content to explain Fielding without reading him; we would diligently uncover the prominent themes in his work and his characteristic modes of embodying those themes. But no matter what degree of love, care, intelligence, and sensitivity we, as critics, bring to this task, what we can discover is almost startlingly limited by the frame of reference implicit in the terms we have adopted.[3] If we have started out to find themes, themes we shall find; it is impossible not to. If we are sensitive and intelligent enough our perceptions may give us incidental but invaluable insight into Fielding's art, but the kinds of critical discriminations we can make are nevertheless rigidly controlled by our initial preconceptions. Using the aesthetically acceptable word "theme," with its musical overtones, for "subject" or "statement" and carefully cultivating the ability to discover in the most poetically suggestive or abstruse of terms the particular themes of particular works, we are likely to disguise from ourselves the fact that we are treating *Tom Jones* as a species of apologue, which differs from the conventional moral tale only in that its themes are more inaccessible and the relationship of its parts to its controlling ethical statements so tenuous that to describe it demands the highest degree of ingenuity. We sometimes seem doomed, in discussing the relation between Fielding's beliefs and his novels, to treat the latter as if they were organized as apologues, like Johnson's *Rasselas,* though always with the proviso that Fielding, since he was actually writing a novel, embodied his themes more subtly—so subtly that experienced critics can sometimes infer diametrically opposed ethical beliefs from the novels. But to praise Fielding as a writer of fiction because of his obscurity may be as unfair to him as it is to condemn Johnson as a writer of fiction because of his clarity. For if Fielding's novels are not organized as fictional examples of the truth of a

---

[3] What I should regard as the definitive treatment of this problem is R. S. Crane's *The Languages of Criticism and the Structure of Poetry* (Toronto: University of Toronto Press, 1953).

statement, or a series of such statements, when we do regard them for special purposes as if they were apologues we may well miss the subtlety and dexterity with which Fielding has, in fact, expressed his beliefs and opinions; we will have ignored the extremely important task Fielding had to perform in making those opinions an integral part of his novels.

Conversely, if we examine *Rasselas* as fiction with the expectation of finding in it the virtues of character portrayal, probability, and subtlety of action that we discover in a novel, we are bound to conclude that, despite the matchless resonance of Johnson's sentences and the profundity of his message, he is a poor novelist. Indeed he is. But it would be a serious error if we should conclude that he was therefore an inept writer of prose fiction.

If we examine *Rasselas* as if it were organized as a novel like *Tom Jones*, we must surely miss the subtlety and dexterity with which Johnson has exploited all the relevant techniques of fiction to give us a convincing example of the truth of his ethical burthen; we will have ignored the extremely important and demanding task Johnson had to accomplish to create what may well be the most impressive apologue—not essay—in the English language. The task we face, then, in trying seriously to investigate the relationship between a writer's moral beliefs and the literary works he has created is not limited to answering the questions that puzzle us; like Pamela's, our most serious problem is first to get the question asked in a legitimate manner so that our answers will testify to something more than the sincerity and respectability of our desires.

To ensure even minimal significance for the answer, we may not ask the question in a manner that prevents our enquiry into the different principles of coherence of variant forms of prose fiction. Such an enquiry is a prerequisite for investigating the possibility that, in writing a work organized like *Tom Jones*, Fielding could *not* have embodied his moral beliefs as fictional examples of ethical statements without destroying the novel's coherence; to reverse the coin, it is also a prerequisite for exploring the possibility that, in writing a work like *Rasselas*, Johnson could *not* have employed the techniques which would constitute the minimal virtues of any novel without destroying both the coherence and effectiveness of his apologue. Any question so formulated that it identifies the principles of organization of the two works simply on the grounds that they are both prose fictions (e.g., What are the organizing themes of *Rasselas* and *Tom Jones?*) prevents such an enquiry. Investigation might lead to the conclusion that all works of prose fiction do, in fact, have the same general principle of coherence—for example, they are all fictional exploitation, more or less subtle, of identifiable themes. But we cannot investigate even this possibility if our initial question excludes alternative solutions.

What makes the problem peculiarly intricate is that a relatively slight lapse of consciousness about the critical propositions to which adoption of even the most conventional literary distinctions commits us may obscure the critical question we wish to answer.

It would be widely acknowledged as a sign of critical vulgarity to blame a sensitive critic interested primarily in providing his reader with a spanking new reading of an old masterpiece for relying solely on a delicately nurtured intuition. To achieve an insight is infinitely more poetical than to examine an assumption. If the reading is sufficiently sensitive and novel, there is little to be gained by insisting that the terminology the critic customarily adopts in dealing with literary works limits his intuitive discriminations with the same degree of rigidity self-imposed by the most arrant foe of eclecticism. For this reason, perhaps, one of the truly eminent critics of our day tells us with approbation that "no literary critic of any experience will make much effort to define his terms";[4] the results of such an effort might be uselessly disconcerting.

There is no doubt, though, about the results of the mundane task attempted in this book if performed without such an effort; they would be disastrous. I think this may be shown clearly, though, I fear, only by a discussion of considerable length, if we turn from consideration of the problematic results of a problematic confusion between *Tom Jones* and *Rasselas* to speculation about *Gulliver's Travels*. Possibly no literate man in the western world would hesitate for a moment if asked what sort of a work *Gulliver's Travels* is: it is a satire. None but an irretrievable Pyrrhonist would challenge this, or, even more relevant at the moment, would doubt that there is a class of literary creations which, like *Gulliver's Travels*, are satires. That there is a class called satire is a literary fact. But much like "tragedy," the term "satire" ages ago broke from its confinement as the discriminator of a literary type to escape into the freer verbal universe of everyday English with occasional forays into the unbridled world of journalese; Marilyn Monroe's death is "tragic" in somewhat the same way in which Nikita Khrushchev is said to have a "harsh, satiric personality."

When we call *Gulliver's Travels* a satire, we are clearly using the term in the first rather than in the more general of these senses. But satire exists as literary fact, not in the same sense as a whale exists, or even as all whales exist, as biological fact, but, rather, as the existence of mammals is a "fact"

---

[4] Northrop Frye, *Fearful Symmetry* (Princeton: Princeton University Press, 1947), p. 316.

of the physical world. Though whales suckle their young and grow hair, they have at least as many traits in common with sailfish as they do with men; our selection of the particular similarities to define a class called mammals is justified only because, when we lump whales together with elephants, hyenas, and men, we facilitate the knowledge of the biological universe, contained, for example, in Darwin's theories. Since "mammal," like satire, is also a relatively commonplace word in English, it may, of course, be used by persons who never heard of Darwin and who might consider his theories nonsensical or even morally evil.

To say that *Gulliver's Travels* is a satire is, justifiably, to lump it with *Colin Clout* and *Macflecknoe* instead of with *Tom Jones, Pride and Prejudice,* and *The Catcher in the Rye.* That it shares other traits (e.g., it is a work of prose fiction) with the last three would in no sense be irrelevant to a discussion of its effectiveness as satire. We should expect even the most elementary book on the development of English satire both to include a discussion of *Gulliver's Travels* and to differentiate it as a work of prose fiction. But the "fact" that it is prose fiction is completely irrelevant to its inclusion in such a book, i.e., to its being classified as satire, since *Colin Clout* and *Macflecknoe* are verse creations.

On the other hand, we should expect the most elementary text purporting to describe the development of techniques of prose fiction in England both to include a discussion of *Gulliver's Travels* and to differentiate it as a satire. In this instance, the fact that it is satire is irrelevant to its inclusion with works like *Tom Jones* and, say, *Pamela* in the class of prose fiction.

As long as we are using the label "satire" in connection with *Gulliver's Travels* the only real risk of confusion—though it is a serious one—derives from a failure to understand the kind of similarity we have selected, intuitively or otherwise, as the criterion for distinguishing the genre from others. For example, we might have classified *Gulliver's Travels* with *Colin Clout* and *Macflecknoe* because they share some single quality—perhaps some defined "tone"—which, for a given end, we regard as the distinguising mark of all such works; if we do so, the quality or qualities, element or elements of similarity we have used to define "satire" could themselves be subordinated qualitative parts of works with very different principles of coherence. Or, more in keeping with the usual notion we attach to the term "genre" or "type," we might have established the class accordingly only to some similar principle of coherence without regard to similarities of the parts of the different works; in this instance qualities and elements might vary considerably among the several works, but, in each, the relationship of its parts to the whole work would be *definably* similar to the relationship that the parts of other satires have to the whole work in which they appear.[5]

To judge which kind of procedure would result in the more useful class is, of course, impossible without considering the kind of knowledge that the classification system is meant to facilitate. But for the purpose of this study, only the latter is relevant, since our attempt, at this point, is to explore the possibility that the variant principles of organization of coherent prose fictions limit the way in which a writer may embody his ethical beliefs, opinions, or prejudices in them.

Let us assume tentatively that satires are works which ridicule particular men, the institutions of men, traits presumed to be in all men, or any combination of the three.[6] But they do not do this incidentally; all their parts are designed to this end and, indeed, can only be understood *as* parts of a whole to the extent that they contribute to such ridicule. In other words, this is the principle that actually informs the work. Unless all the elements of a work make such a contribution, we will temporarily refuse to classify it as a coherent satire. If we assume also that *Gulliver's Travels* is a coherent satire, then all the elements of fiction it contains—the traits ascribed to the created characters, the actions portrayed, the point of view from which the tale is told—will have been selected, whether consciously or intuitively, to maximize the ridicule of some combination of the three objects of satire. If this is true, there are some obvious consequences to our description of the form. One consequence is that none of the fictional creations in *Gulliver's Travels* can ever themselves be satirized; since all three objects of satire are extant only *outside* the fictional world created in the book, any ridicule which attaches to Gulliver, the Houyhnhnms, or the Lilliputians, or disgust which attaches to the Yahoos, can be understood, in relation to the whole work, only as an attempt to facilitate the ability of the fictional creations to ridicule the objects, of whatever sort. Similarly, any virtues which attach to the fictional creations

[5] I use the expression "definably similar" advisedly; elements from different works are unlikely to make precisely the same contributions to the works of which they are parts even when the two works belong to the same class. Even within a single work no two parts make precisely the same contribution to the whole work, but their relationship to the whole work shares a defined and significant similarity common to the relationship of the parts of any prose fiction to the works of a single class.

[6] Though I am sure that Professor E. W. Rosenheim would disagree with many of my remarks in this chapter, my notions about satire derive in part from his extremely suggestive doctoral dissertation, *Swift's Satire in a Tale of a Tub* (University of Chicago, 1953).

within the book can be understood only as traits which enable Swift to maximize the ridicule directed at the external world.

Let us assume also that there is another class of prose fiction, of which
Rasselas is a perfect example, which we will call "apologues." The informing
principle of all such works is that each is organized as a fictional example of
the truth of a formulable statement or closely related set of such statements.
Again, since we are interested in establishing classes of literary creations—in
this case, classes of works of prose fiction differentiated according to variant
principles of coherence—all the parts of any apologue, including all the
techniques of prose fiction, can be understood as parts of the whole only
to the extent that they contribute to the effectiveness with which the fiction
illustrates the truth of the statement.[7]

It should be immediately evident that the form of satire and the form of
apologue, as they have been defined, can in no sense overlap; even though
some episodes of the works may contain similar elements, as *parts* of *Gulliver's
Travels* or *Rasselas* they will not have the same relationship to the whole work
in which they appear.

If Swift had wished to attack gluttony, he might very well have included
an episode in which skinny men are represented as virtuous and wise while fat
men are shown to be foolish and wicked. This would in no sense indicate that
Swift admired skinny men, since, if gluttony is an object of satire, all fictional elements, including the virtue attaching to skinny men, must be subordinated to an effective attack on gluttony. It is barely conceivable that Swift did
admire skinny men, but nothing in the work tells us this. To interpret the
preferential depiction of skinny men as, in its own right, an exemplary portrait,
a fictional example of the truth of the statement that skinny men are admirable, is to forget that *Gulliver's Travels* is a satire.[8] It is to treat *Gulliver's
Travels as if* it were organized like *Rasselas*.

To take a less trivial but more complicated example, if *Gulliver's Travels*
is organized as a satire in the sense defined above, then, no matter how many
virtues are ascribed by Swift to the Houyhnhnms, it is unreasonable to interpret his rational horses as portraits of Swift's ideal of rationality or, for that
matter, of any other ideal. Knowing Swift's religious beliefs, we should cer-

---

[7] For the moment it is useful to insist that all elements of any one work must share
the defined similarity to the whole if we are to regard it as coherent. This notion is
considerably modified in this chapter and in chapter five.

[8] It is important to note that the organizing principle of a satire is not the same as
that of a negative apologue—i.e., of a work organized as the fictional example of a
negative statement.

tainly make at least a working assumption that he is attacking what an advocate of his brand of Christianity could be expected to deplore in mankind; but
the virtues of such fictional creations as the Houyhnhnms have not been selected with a view—intuitive or otherwise—toward creating a fictional example of a virtuous society. The virtues ascribed to the Houyhnhnms have
been chosen according to how well they facilitate the ridicule of certain of the
traits, manners, and institutions of men. If this is indeed so, when we discover
striking discrepancies between virtues ascribed to the Houyhnhnms and what
Swift would probably have considered virtues in an ideal society, we have no
justification for a *prima facie* case that the Houyhnhnms themselves are *objects* of satire or even of ridicule. Not only is it true that the fictional creations in *Gulliver's Travels* cannot themselves be "satirized," but, if the work
is organized as satire, we would expect to find that some of the virtues ascribed to his fictional creations are virtues Swift would wish for in an ideal
society and others are not. It is obvious, for example, that the approbation of
the Brobdingnag rules that no "law of that country must exceed" twenty-two
words and that "to write a commentary upon any law is a capital crime" provide excellent platforms from which to hurl appropriate ridicule at the ob-
scurantist deficiencies of English law. But one can hardly entertain the notion
that Swift at his most misanthropic would literally approve an English government which tried to hang a man because he had written a commentary on
the law.[9] And yet it would be patently fallacious to infer from this observation that Swift is "satirizing" or even ridiculing the Brobdingnagian rules. He
is doing only what we would expect him to do if he were satirizing English
law and lawyers: ascribing those virtues to his fictional creations which will
facilitate the ridicule of what he finds reprehensible in the external object of
satire. Swift is hardly a nudist because the Houyhnhnms don't wear clothes
and Gulliver finds it impossible to explain to his "master" "why nature should
teach us to conceal what nature had given." [10]

The reverse of the coin is apposite also. In *Rasselas*, ridicule is leveled
against the pretentious inventor of the flying machine. And a very strong
argument has been advanced that Johnson was familiar with John Wilkins'

[9] Swift is notorious for his virulent dislike of lawyers. But one of the signs of satire
is that when we interpret elements which appropriately ridicule an external object as
if they were the author's positive suggestions about how to deal with the objects he
dislikes, the satirist will inevitably appear a fool or a monster. Swift, of course, was
neither.

[10] Jonathan Swift, *Gulliver's Travels*, ed. Arthur E. Case (New York: The Ronald
Press Co., 1938), p. 256.

Mathematical Magic and drew heavily on parts of it in the "Dissertation on Flying." [11] Had a similar incident appeared in *Gulliver's Travels*, with many elements derived directly from Wilkins, we should not be able to rest content even with the observation that Swift was ridiculing the experiments of the "new science." If the elements taken from John Wilkins were obvious enough to identify the *Mathematical Magic* to knowledgeable contemporaries of Swift, a failure to recognize the ridicule of Wilkins would be a failure to comprehend one of the particular objects of the satire and therefore its full force. We can learn a great deal about Johnson's methods of composition from the discovery of the connection between his and Wilkins' work; we can see how Johnson wrestled with his material, how he altered, selected, modified his source to create an episode which contributes greatly to the fictional exploitation of the organizing theme of *Rasselas*. But interesting as a study of Wilkins as one of Johnson's sources may be, the complete lack of this information could modify our understanding of *Rasselas* only to the extent that ignorance of the fact that the character of Brett Ashley was suggested to Hemingway by a lady whom F. Scott Fitzgerald disliked would alter our view of *The Sun Also Rises*; Brett Ashley's role in the novel is defined without reference to the little-known lady, and the role of Johnson's would-be Daedalus is defined in the apologue without reference to Wilkins.

To sum up, no part of a coherent apologue can be organized as satire and no part of a coherent satire can be organized as apologue, except in works which contain digressions—i.e., in works in which the informing principle is temporarily in abeyance or ceases permanently to function.[12] Apologue and satire are mutually exclusive forms when considered from the point of view of their informing principles. The task that any episode must perform in the one differs radically from that which any episode must perform in the other.

---

[11] Gwin J. Kolb, "Johnson's 'Dissertation on Flying' and John Wilkins' *Mathematical Magic*," MP, XLVII (1949), 24-31. For many of my subsequent remarks about *Rasselas* I am heavily indebted to Kolb's published works about Johnson, particularly to "The Structure of *Rasselas*," PMLA, LXVI (1951), 698-717.

[12] The problem of what constitutes a digression in an otherwise coherent work is intricate and, to myself, fascinating, both because of the insight into artistic coherence afforded by investigating the problem and because of the subtlety with which eighteenth-century novelists have been able to employ digressions to achieve special effects. (For a detailed discussion see chap. five.) A perfectly coherent literary work may, of course, be a bad one, and a work containing many digressions may be a very good one. Indeed, some of the more interesting works of English fiction, both before and during the eighteenth century, do not depend for their effects upon a strong principle of coherence at all. (For a brief discussion of a work of this sort see my remarks on *Moll Flanders* in chap. six.)

But since the capacity of men to make inferences from any sample of language is almost infinite, if we ask irrelevant questions about *Gulliver's Travels* or *Rasselas* we will find some sort of answers. If we start to find the organizing themes of *Gulliver's Travels* we will find them as surely as we find them in *Rasselas*. But if we do so—still assuming that *Gulliver's Travels* is organized in the manner described—our answers will be valid only on the supposition that it is an apologue. Such answers dangerously distort our view of its form if it is not organized as apologue. Only by considering it a satire may we legitimately ask how Swift might have embodied his beliefs, opinions, prejudices, in it. Take, for example, a deceptively simple question which, I believe, underlies much of the recent controversy about the fourth book of *Gulliver's Travels:* Are the Houyhnhnms represented as Swift's ethical ideal for humanity or are they satirized? No question is more susceptible of producing equally persuasive but contradictory answers; it depends upon a dichotomy which obscures the task of both critical enquiry and historical research. If the informing principle of *Gulliver's Travels* is something like the one we have assumed, the only relevant answer to the question must be *neither*. The Houyhnhnms cannot be a representation of Swift's ethical ideal, since all parts of the work, including the virtues ascribed to the rational horses, have been selected to facilitate ridicule of the external objects of the satire, not to create fictional examples of ethical truths.[13] They cannot themselves be "satirized," since one of the conditions of such a work is that the objects of satire are external. It is possible that they are represented as ridiculous in part, but, if so, such ridicule must be obvious enough to maximize the attack on one of the external objects; if the ridicule is so evanescent that we may argue about its very existence, it is unlikely to be present in a satire.[14] In any event, however convincingly we argue that a theologian of Swift's time, persuasion, personality, would consider the graceless world of Houyhnhnmland unchristian or otherwise undesirable, the information has no bearing on whether the Houyhnhnms are meant to be ridiculous. Such discrepancy is precisely what

[13] It is simple enough to imagine a work constructed so that it represents in its initial stages a completely virtuous world and demonstrates in the last part, with many particular references, how the writer's age falls short of ethical perfection. But such a work, though it very well might ridicule, would be coherent not as satire but as apologue: a fictional example illustrating the truth that men do not live up to the ideal.

[14] The ways in which Swift employs ridicule are sometimes incredibly subtle, but that subtlety itself depends on almost a blatant assurance of the presence of ridicule where it is intended. After the first four or five chapters of *Gulliver's Travels*, it would have been difficult for Swift to include an episode which did not ridicule an external object.

one would expect to find in a work organized to ridicule external objects.

The term "satire" is used not only to discriminate among literary forms, but in a far more general sense even when it is applied to literary works. When we speak of "elements of satire" in a literary work we normally refer either to elements ridiculed within the work which have some sort of an identifiable counterpart external to the created fictional world, or simply to elements ridiculed within the work without consideration of an external counterpart. In the first sense we may justifiably call the episode in *Rasselas* which deals with the Stoic who loses his daughter "satiric," since the character is ridiculed and the brand of Stoicism he professes is an identifiable philosophic position maintained in eighteenth-century England. In the second sense we may say that Imlac is satirized when, in a fit of enthusiasm, he defines a poet's qualifications in impossibly grandiose terms. Or, to turn from apologue to an as yet undefined form, it is in the first sense that we can call Jane Austen's Sir Walter Eliot, with all his displayed and unwarranted pride of birth, an element of satire in *Persuasion*, but in the second sense that the incessantly chattering Miss Bates is satirical in *Emma*. But the two uses easily overlap: we have all, I suspect, known people who define their own professions in grandiose terms, and chattering women are always with us. Any writer of fiction with a moderate share of human antipathies is likely to ridicule some character, action, or social attitude in his work, and a critic would have to be very limited indeed who could not discover in the external world a counterpart to the object of ridicule in the fictional world.

It is only mild hyperbole to assert that any fiction writer of prominence who exhibits social awareness may look forward with assurance to an article, thesis, or book purporting to describe the elements of satire in his work. If we are aware that the term "satire" is being used in a flexible sense, such critiques may prove illuminating. But from the moment that we confuse the everyday use of the term with its use in discriminating a literary type according to an informing principle, chaos results. At the moment we claim that Johnson embodied one of his beliefs in *Rasselas* as a satire on Stoicism, or that Jane Austen embodied hers in *Persuasion* as a satire on pride of birth, we have advanced halfway to irretrievable confusion. The ridicule attached to Miss Bates, for example, is not included in *Emma* to facilitate a scornful attack on chattering women: the ridicule not only has its own role to play as part of a work whose informing principle is different from that of satire, but, in addition, an examination of the principle of selection of elements may show us that the ridicule attached to Miss Bates' inconsequential volubility achieves an end opposed to that of satire. That is, in fact, the situation in *Emma*, when the annoying chatter of Miss Bates leads the heroine gratuitously to mock her at the Box Hill outing. This, the most obviously culpable social act performed by Emma, leads to her verbal castigation by the "hero" and to her own recognition of the unworthiness of her action. Throughout the early stages of the novel, Jane Austen has represented Miss Bates' aimless conversation at sufficient length to justify Emma's irritation, but has been careful to include just enough indications of the character's good nature and freedom from malice so that we are shocked at Emma's callous act. The partial justification for her irritation is one of the elements that leads us to desire the heroine's reformation rather than her serious punishment. If we can infer anything at all from such a state of affairs about Jane Austen's attitude toward chattering women outside the fictional world she created, it is surely that they merit tolerance, not ridicule.

Oddly enough, the confusion of the two uses of the term "satire" has unfortunate consequences not merely for an enquiry into how novelists' beliefs are embodied in their novels, but also for our more general critical concerns: if we interpret part of a work organized by another principle as if it were part of a satire, we cannot discuss the artistic choices which have, in fact, made the work effective, though we may well have experienced aesthetic pleasure only because of their inclusion. If we interpret the portrait of Miss Bates as if it were part of a satire, it is all too easy to describe those stylistic elements which delightfully ridicule that voluble lady. But it is unlikely that we will recognize the adeptness with which Jane Austen has revealed, with exquisitely appropriate understatement, Miss Bates' essential good nature and freedom from malice, so that, when Emma errs, the extent of her culpability is precisely defined. Any conscious recognition we may have of the virtuous traits revealed in Miss Bates' meanderings might well be interpreted as a flaw in a satire to the extent that it prevents maximizing the ridicule of the external object—in this case the chattering woman.

An inability to explain the artistic virtues that have made us feel that a work is excellent is a probable consequence of considering parts of works which are not satires as if they were, even when no serious distortion of a writer's beliefs results.[15]

Possibly, interpreting Johnson's ridicule of the Stoic in *Rasselas* as a satire on Stoicism would not lead to a distortion of his attitude toward that philosophic school. But, leaving aside the many subtly rendered elements in the relevant episode, Johnson's choice of the death of the Stoic's daughter as the

[15] We may expect similar results from a confusion of any of the three types of prose fiction discussed in this chapter.

instrument to reveal the inadequacy of Stoicism in preventing human misery would alone mark him as an inept satirist, had he indeed been writing satire. To select as an instrument for such a revelation an event which, if anything does, justifies passionate misery is perfectly comprehensible in a work which demonstrates by fictional example that human activity—including conscious commitment to a philosophy—can never prevent earthly unhappiness. The very choice of the episode, as well as its masterful portrayal, testifies to the excellence of the apologue, though the merest novice could show Johnson that, if he wished to facilitate ridicule of Stoicism as an external object of satire, he could hardly have made a worse choice. The more trivial the cause that motivates the Stoic's despair, the greater the possibilities for ridiculing Stoicism. As a matter of fact, Johnson's selection—perfect as it is for *Rasselas* —must have presented him with some difficult artistic problems. The death of the Stoic's daughter and his consequent misery had to be represented with at least enough plausibility to make the episode a convincing fictional example. And yet, had Johnson invested the Stoic with one grain more of individuality or had he removed a single mocking reference to the countenanced blackmail by the Stoic's servants, Rasselas' dispassionate reaction to the death of an admired teacher's only child must certainly have branded him as a character worthy of condemnation, despite the revealed discrepancy between Stoical pretensions and human practices. Without a single remark to indicate compassion for the intense suffering expressed by the Stoic, Rasselas, whose humanity admittedly "would not suffer him to insult misery with reproof," [16] does refrain after a while from argument with the mourner. But his sole reaction to the misery of the former Stoic is to understand "the emptiness of rhetorical sound, and the inefficacy of polished periods and studied sentences." [17] Surely this is a rationalistic monster who must either be punished severely for insensibility to human suffering or undergo strenuous reformation. But this callous recognition of "the emptiness of rhetorical sound" actually constitutes the desired "reformation" in Rasselas: comprehension of Imlac's warnings that teachers of morality "discourse like angels, but they live like men." [18] The truth of the matter is, of course, that Rasselas is no monster, but rather the main character in an apologue. Johnson's fiction, from beginning to end, has been organized so that it prevents the reader from even considering the possibility that Rasselas' reaction to misery was unfeeling. Each episode is repre-

---

[16] *Samuel Johnson: Rasselas, Poems, and Selected Prose,* ed. Bertrand H. Bronson (New York: Rinehart and Co., 1958), pp. 546-547.

[17] *Ibid.,* p. 547.

[18] *Ibid.,* p. 546.

sented so that interest in what will happen to any characters, or to the altering relationships among a group of characters, has been deftly subordinated to consideration of the thematic statement which dictated their inclusion in the first place. If we become more interested in Rasselas' emotional reaction to the Stoic's misery than we are in his recognition of the futility of achieving earthly happiness by the acquisition of "invulnerable patience," [19] the apologue has failed: all elements of the fiction have not been subordinated to the creation of an example of the truth of a formulable statement. The episode, no matter how interesting in itself, would obscure the theme it is to help exemplify. It would not, in such a case, be a coherent part of an apologue, nor, obviously, of a satire; it might well constitute a coherent part of a work informed by still a third principle.

Represented Actions

Let us assume, then, that there is a third class of prose fiction, "represented action," which is organized neither as satire nor apologue nor even as a complicated reconciliation of the two. In any work which belongs to this class, characters about whose fates we are made to care[20] are introduced in unstable relationships which are then further complicated until the complications are finally resolved by the complete removal of the represented instability.

If it was important to emphasize that all the elements of a satire or an apologue could be understood as parts only as they are governed by the informing principles of their respective classes, it is crucial to insist that a work is a represented action only if every element—including any formulated ethical statement or ridiculed object—is subordinate to the artistic end just described. Parts of any work of prose fiction will consist of represented characters portrayed in some sort of relationship with other characters: in *Rasselas* the Stoic does lose a daughter and his reactions to that loss do alienate his former disciple, Rasselas. In *Gulliver's Travels* Gulliver's Houyhnhnm master initially regards

---

[19] *Ibid.,* p. 545.

[20] It would undoubtedly be more accurate to say something like "characters who are evaluated by devices of disclosure in a manner consonant with the artistic end to which all elements of the work contribute" rather than "characters about whose fates we are made to care." But it would be terribly inconvenient to do so. Elsewhere, too, it has proved more convenient to use psychological rather than formal terms and I have not hesitated to do so when there was no chance of misunderstanding. I believe it is clear enough here that in any given represented action the author may have failed to make anyone care about his characters one way or the other, but that the work would still be identifiable as an action.

him as a startling member of a loathsome species of cattle, but his good traits
so alter the rational horse's relationship to him that, on Gulliver's enforced
departure, it condescends to bid him *bon voyage* and does him the "honour to
raise it [his hoof] gently" to Gulliver's mouth. Even in a form so remote
from an action as a philosophical dialogue—Hume's *Dialogues Concerning
Natural Religion*, for example—Philo and Cleanthes draw closer together at
the very end when they achieve at least ostensible agreement on the evi-
dences of design in God's works. In other words, characters represented with
at least a modicum of traits in some sort of relationship with other characters
are necessarily present in any work of fiction even when, as in philosophical
dialogues, the fiction makes only a casual contribution to a rhetorical end.

But in works like *Emma, Pamela,* and *Tom Jones,* or, for that matter, in
The Sun Also Rises or *The Sound and the Fury,* ethical statements and ridicule of character traits—central to the informing principles of apologue and
satire, respectively—are always subordinated to the informing principle of
represented action.

We have seen an example of this in *Emma*. Miss Bates' volubility is represented in such a manner that Emma's single act of gross discourtesy to her
chattering acquaintance is seen as at once understandable and culpable. The act
brings down upon Emma's head severe reproof from Knightley; her consequent self-reproach is an indication of her essential moral soundness and, in
addition, reveals that the heroine's relationship to her future husband is considerably less avuncular than she imagines. Such revelation—suitably quiet
during that part of the action which develops the unstable relationships to
their most complicated degree—has been subtly implemented almost from the
beginning. Before Frank Churchill has actually met Emma, for example,
Knightley, in contrast to his usual rational and dispassionate manner of disagreeing with Emma, displays, in an otherwise warranted objection to
Emma's anticipatory flattering portrait of the awaited Churchill, the emotions
of a jealous man. Nevertheless, since Emma is the most important character
and her recognition of her mistaken views and actions constitutes the most important internal change in the book, we may be tempted to view its organizing
principle as a representation of that internal change, and her relationship with
Miss Bates as an index to the change. If this were true, Emma's recognition
of her true feelings for Knightley must be regarded primarily as an index to
her improving moral state, and the role of each of the characters as delimited
by how he contributes to, reveals, or explains Emma's change. Such a principle
cannot, however, account for all the elements of the fiction. We may use a
sort of shorthand device to clarify the sense in which all elements are subordi-

nated to the principle described as informing works which are actions. If *Emma* were organized as a representation of the heroine's internal change, a just representation of Emma at the highest point of her moral development would provide a satisfactory conclusion to the action. Assuming, with considerable justification, that the way in which Jane Austen concluded the book is, at the very least, satisfactory, we discover that she has included a representation of events which are irrelevant to any further development of Emma's moral consciousness. A representation of such events was necessary, however, if the action were to be concluded satisfactorily.

After the revelation of the secret engagement of Jane Fairfax to Frank Churchill, the future relationship between them does not affect Emma's moral development in any significant way.[21] Yet not only does that relationship receive extended treatment toward the end of the book, but Emma, as well as the reader, peruses Churchill's explanatory letter in detail. The letter is further discussed at length between Emma and Knightley some time after they have revealed their love for each other; though there is disagreement about the degree to which Churchill's actions are excused by the letter, even Knightley perceives Churchill's real affection for Jane Fairfax and envisages a probable satisfactory future for the engaged couple. Without effecting a single change in Emma's moral awareness, now nearly complete, Jane Fairfax might have been represented as finally spurning Frank Churchill; she might have become a governess, though that has previously been regarded as an undesirable fate for her. Or she could have married Churchill, and the explanatory letter with Emma's and Knightley's comments upon it might have been omitted. Either way, though, the ending would have been unsatisfactory. Apart from Emma's moral development, we have been led to desire and expect a reasonably happy fate, in keeping with her moral deserts, for Jane Fairfax; only marriage to Churchill *and* the assurance contained in the comments on Churchill's letter accomplish this end.

We might also ask whether the present ending would be satisfactory if it were kept exactly the same but excluded the momentary delay in the wedding

---

[21] After she reads Churchill's explanatory letter, Emma recognizes the value of directness and the danger of subterfuge in human relationships. But alteration of her moral consciousness could have resulted equally—perhaps even more forcefully—from the altered versions of the novel's end postulated in this discussion. If, for example, Jane Fairfax had not married Churchill but determined to spend her life as a governess in the home of one of Mrs. Elton's vulgar friends, Churchill's letter explaining what had led to Jane's unhappiness might be seen as clearly motivating Emma's recognition of the dangers of subterfuge. Such an ending would have been unsatisfactory for reasons extraneous to Emma's internal change.

plans caused by Emma and Knightley's mutual concern for Mr. Woodhouse's well-being. Emma's concern for her father's welfare in no way constitutes an element of moral change, since it has been one of the constants of their relationship from beginning to end. Despite Mr. Woodhouse's hypochondria, xenophobia, and other quirks, the elements of his personality which might prevent Emma's marrying during his lifetime, unreasonable as they may seem to a modern reader, have not been regarded in the action as meriting unhappiness. He is represented as incapable of enduring an existence apart from his own home or apart from Emma. Since Mr. Knightley has been shown to possess exactly those traits which would enable him to understand the dilemma of both father and daughter and also to possess sufficient elasticity to forego some connubial privileges, he solves the problem neatly by his decision that "so long as her father's happiness . . . required Hartfield to continue her home, it should be his likewise." To end *Emma* without devising a satisfactory fate for Mr. Woodhouse would be a failure to complete one of the expectations aroused throughout the work.

In the final paragraph of *Emma*, note the effect of leaving out the phrase I have italicized:

> The wedding was very much like other weddings, where the parties have no taste for finery or parade; and Mrs. Elton, *from the particulars detailed by her husband*, thought it all extremely shabby, and very inferior to her own. "Very little white satin, very few lace veils; a most pitiful business! Selina would stare when she heard of it." But, in spite of these deficiencies, the wishes, the hopes, the confidence, the predictions of the small band of true friends who witnessed the ceremony, were fully answered in the perfect happiness of the union.[22]

Emma, had she wished to, could not have contrived a more fitting punishment for Mrs. Elton than her own marriage to Knightley. Though it would be absurd to rest the case for the effectiveness of the conclusion of any literary work on a few words, the single prepositional phrase informing us that Mrs. Elton's information about the wedding comes second-hand is a brilliant stroke. Her vicious attempt to humiliate Harriet, her vulgar attempt to run Knightley's social affairs, her irritating patronization of the socially and ethically superior Jane Fairfax—all these require that some special fate be reserved for Mrs. Elton, and yet it must not detract from the happiness surrounding the long-awaited union of Emma and Knightley. The single phrase vividly places Mrs. Elton in a social limbo where the consequences of her acts are

[22] Jane Austen, *Emma* (Cambridge, Mass.: Houghton Mifflin Co., 1957), p. 381.

nevertheless not so serious as forever to preclude the dubious comforts afforded by Selina.

Of the three examples discussed as necessary or particularly effective for the conclusion of the work, none is dictated by a need to represent a final stage of Emma's moral growth. But the necessity for and the excellence of these parts can easily be understood as a consequence of the final satisfactory stabilization of very complicated relationships among characters about whom we have been made to care. Emma's change is not, therefore, to be regarded as unimportant. Every stage of that change affects every important relationship in the book and, in turn, that change itself is seriously affected by the relationship of Emma to other characters, and by the relationships of other characters considered without direct regard to Emma. During the long period of her intransigent faith in her abilities to control the amorous destinies of others, Emma's influence upon Harriet directly alters the latter's relations with Robert Martin, Elton, Churchill, and, finally, Knightley. But the final relationship between Harriet and Knightley—Harriet, partly as a result of Emma's meddling, aspires to marry Knightley—brings Emma to an awareness of the terrible consequences of her meddling, to a consciousness of the nature of her own feelings for Knightley, and, at last, as an appropriate form of punishment, to a temporary state of anguish in anticipation of Harriet's possible success. Yet these consequences are not contingent only upon the relations between Emma and Harriet. The decency and alacrity with which Knightley rescues Harriet from humiliation at the ball is prerequisite both for Harriet's aspirations and for Emma's fear. In turn, Knightley's gallantry is made necessary only because of the rudeness displayed by the Eltons. Again in turn, traits revealed earlier in both the Eltons have prepared us to accept such rudeness as a probable consequence of Emma's ill-starred attempt to marry Harriet to the clergyman.

Emma's change is vital to the changing relationships in the novel, but in other works which conform to the definition of action there may be no internal change in any character. In *Treasure Island*, *The Hound of the Baskervilles*, and any number of mystery tales, characters about whom we are made to care are introduced in unstable relationships which are then further complicated, and the complication is eventually resolved by the removal of the represented instability, even though no character undergoes internal change. Works which belong to the class of actions differ as greatly from each other and from *Emma* as, say, *Rasselas* differs from *Pilgrim's Progress*. The latter two are clearly apologues and are distinguished from all satires and represented actions by virtue of their organizing principle. But otherwise the differences between the two works are vast. A critique of *Pilgrim's Progress* which failed to note that its fictional examples are allegorical would be absurd. Further, in a complete discussion of Bunyan's artistry we should expect the critic to discriminate between *Pilgrim's Progress* and any other allegory—to isolate the qualities which make it unique. But during an investigation of the qualities which distinguish Bunyan's apologue from all others, we would find ourselves answering many questions that we would ask about *Rasselas* also. The answers would differ considerably, but the questions would be applicable to both (e.g., What elements in this episode make it a particularly persuasive example?). The same questions, however, when applied to satires or to represented actions, are either palpably irrelevant or, alas, lead to ostensible answers which would be significant only if the satire or action were in fact an apologue.

We do not wish to "reduce" the complexity or the merit of any work that falls into one of the three classes to the similarity which defines that class. The classes contain a full range of good, bad, and horrible examples of satires, apologues, and actions. In this the system of classification may be compared to a grammar of the English language which isolates the principles by which English sentences are formulated. As such, the latter will differentiate the principles by which all English sentences may be formulated from the principles by which all Italian sentences may be formulated. It will not discriminate between a sentence written by Samuel Johnson and one written by an advertising copywriter; though both have employed English and not Italian grammar, and any discussion of the excellence of Johnson's style or the copywriter's would have to take cognizance of the choices afforded by English, not Italian, grammar, we should hardly confound the two.

From Type to Form:
Variants of Actions

Actions differ from each other in so many particulars that it would be impossible to list even the important ones. There are, however, three variables directly relevant to problems discussed below which need clarification at this point. These three variables are useful only in further discriminating among works which are actions; they are irrelevant to a discrimination among action, satire, and apologue; and, as we will see, they are irrelevant also to the problem of formulating a meaningful question about the relation of a novelist's beliefs to the novels he writes. Nevertheless, they have a bearing upon the answers we get to the question, as will be apparent from later chapters dealing with Fielding.

In considering the ending to *Emma*, I made use of the notion that, in order to satisfy expectations aroused in the work, the final stabilization of relationships had to ensure for each character a fate that was commensurate with his moral desert. But, while this is true of works like *Emma*, *Tom Jones*, and *The Egoist*, it is not true of all actions. In such works—which I shall simply call "comic" from now on—all the techniques of representation from beginning to end lead us to expect that all the "good guys" and the "bad guys" will receive their ethical deserts. For example, to postulate the changes that would be necessary to make acceptable an ending in which Tom Jones was hanged and Sophia married Blifil, we should have to go back to the first chapter, and from the number and variety of alterations we should have to make on each page we should soon realize that we had undertaken an impossible task; it would be much simpler to write a new novel. Even among works which are comic in the sense defined, it would be necessary for a complete criticism to make many further distinctions among the kinds of comic action. In slightly different terms, a distinguished critic has been able to show that *Tom Jones* differs from mere amiable comedy in that, though we constantly expect good things to happen to the deserving, we are forcibly made aware that things need not have turned out so well as they do.[23]

There are, obviously, works in which almost—though not quite—the opposite is true: the characters with whose fates we are most concerned, frequently those whom we are made most to admire, are doomed almost from the outset and make choice after choice which leads to their inevitable misery as well as to the unhappiness of all those related to them positively. Examples are found in *An American Tragedy* and *The Return of the Native*. I can see no real objection to calling "tragic" all actions in which expectations are aroused from the outset that the complication of relationships among the characters can be resolved only in a state of misery. But to do this safely we must keep in mind three qualifications. First, we are dealing with works of prose fiction and should not expect or necessarily desire our definition to coincide exactly with definitions derived from drama, or with the general use of the term apart from literature. Second, the word "tragic," when used in the sense defined, is not necessarily honorific, and our list may include very bad tragic actions. Finally, and most important for the purpose of the present book, we must not regard comic and tragic actions as elements in a dichotomy; though no action may be both comic and tragic in the sense defined above, they may indeed be neither. Though we should expect more frequent at-

[23] R. S. Crane, "The Concept of Plot and the Plot of *Tom Jones*," *Critics and Criticism* (Chicago: University of Chicago Press, 1952), pp. 614-647.

tempts at evoking laughter in comic actions, the presence or absence of such an attempt does not necessarily indicate whether an action is comic or tragic (this is, however, important in making further discriminations among different sorts of comic actions). To borrow examples from works which are not prose fictions, the fool in *King Lear* is indeed a wit, the porter in *Macbeth* is quite amusing, and the gravedigger in *Hamlet* is uproarious; any laughter they evoke does not alter a groatsworth our expectations about the destiny of Lear, Macbeth, or Hamlet.

Many novels, including some of the most admired, consist of actions which are neither comic nor tragic, but which we should certainly not wish opprobriously to dub "melodramatic." For convenience, I shall simply refer to them as "serious actions." In such works the final stabilization of relationships may result either happily or unhappily for the characters with whom we are most in sympathy. If we were contrary enough to wish to conclude *Tom Jones* with the hero's hanging or to conclude *The Return of the Native* with a pleasant picture of Clym and Eustacia presenting Mrs. Yeobright with her first grandchild, such conclusions could be made acceptable only by impossibly vast alterations beginning at the initial stages of the novels. But in serious as opposed to comic or tragic actions, such reversals are possible with alterations beginning no further back than the final complication of relationships among the major characters; frequently, such alterations may satisfactorily be made at a point after the final complication of relationships, though before the first stage of the resolution. Examples of this sort of work are numerous and would include such very different actions as *Pamela, Bleak House, Great Expectations,* and, despite the convenient cloud hovering about his head, *Lord Jim.* Such works do not involve "trick" endings, nor does the facility with which their conclusions may be altered indicate that the novelist has some deficiency which prevented his writing a comic or a tragic action; they are not comedies or tragedies which have failed. They are, instead, actions in which the choices made by the characters have been represented with a view toward emphasizing the ambiguous consequences to their shifting relations with other major characters in the novel.

In a comedy like *Tom Jones* the effectiveness of the work depends largely upon Fielding's ability to create an illusion that Tom is in serious difficulties while at the same time reassuring us, by every comic device at his command, that Tom will extricate himself or be extricated from those difficulties. Our interest is always centered on how Tom will do it, not on whether he will do it. We know before Tom ever leaves Paradise Hall that he will be reconciled with Allworthy, marry Sophia, and foil Blifil, but we cannot know how. The purely narrative signals that suggest he may not succeed in doing any of the three nevertheless keep us interested in what is going to happen to Tom Jones next. What is going to happen next is still a mystery, since the comic devices themselves can never assure us of more than that eventually, somehow, all will turn out well. But it is clear that, had Fielding chosen to do so, he could have written something other than comedy—something more akin to an adult *Oliver Twist*. Instead of maximizing the comic elements from the beginning, he might have written a work in which, though we would not see Tom as foredoomed, we had no reassuring indication that Allworthy would not remain deceived, that Sophia would not submit to her father's will (the character of Western would need considerable alteration), that Blifil would not emerge victorious. The center of our interest, then, would shift from *how* Tom will emerge from his difficulties to a concern with *whether* he will emerge from his difficulties at all; we can at least conceive of a work in which the hero might end up either hanged by the neck or married to Sophia— though I presume that no one would be so ill-advised as to desire the sacrifice of *Tom Jones* for such a work.

To reverse the coin, Richardson neither makes use of reassuring comic devices nor does he attempt to maximize the feeling that Pamela is inextricably doomed to rape; instead, she and Mr. B. are each presented with a constant choice of evils in which one always leads to the possibility of future good as well as future evil, while the other leads only to an unsatisfactory end to their relationship. Early in the novel, Pamela might have returned to share her parents' poverty, an alternative represented as undesirable for her then; or remained with the hope of a transfer to another domestic position, an alternative represented as more desirable for her, but leading to the danger of her being raped, which danger, of course, she must brave frequently if the relationship with Mr. B. is to be stabilized by her marriage. Though the tale is represented from Pamela's point of view, the heroine's choices themselves are possible only as a part of the sequence of choices made by most of the characters concerned in the complex relationships. The choices are represented as plausible consequences of their revealed traits. In the instance above, Mr. B. himself might have elected to find Pamela another situation instead of trying to rape her. His decision, in turn, is partially conditioned by Mrs. Jarvis' urging Pamela to appear before him in her country clothes. A "sequence of choices" is common to all actions. It is a mark of the serious action that any one choice may either assist or prevent a major character from receiving his ethical desert. And, as opposed to comic action, the emphasis is always upon whether it *will* assist or prevent the appropriate reward.

Perhaps as a result of a saturnine temperament, or because I share some predilection of my day for regarding gloom as more significant than mirth, or because there are good critical reasons for it, I prefer Dickens' original ending to the altered form of *Great Expectations*. But however cogent the critical reasons may be for preferring a conclusion in which Pip and Estella spend moderately unhappy lives irrevocably separated from each other, there is little convincing evidence that, in allowing Pip to see no shadow of another parting from Estella, Dickens has attached an irrelevant ending to his tale. Nor, I think, is it impossible to conceive of an ending even more gloomy than the original which would still provide a satisfactory conclusion. What is relevant to this discussion is not that one ending might be preferable to another, but only that alternate endings were possible. Had a well-meaning friend asked Fielding to prevent the marriage of Tom and Sophia at the end, Fielding could have obliged only by rewriting his whole novel. Had an equally well-meaning but ill-advised friend expressed a desire to see the Yeobright grandchild christened, Hardy could have played godfather only by scrapping his novel. Since Dickens had written a work neither comic nor tragic but serious, whether ill-advised or not, he could oblige his friend by allowing Estella and Pip to wander hand in hand to at least the mixed critical applause of generations of readers.

Actions, then, are works in which characters about whose fates we are made to care are introduced in unstable relationships which are then further complicated until the complication is finally resolved by the complete removal of the represented instability. We may ask, with relevance, whether any given action is comic, tragic, or serious, though such a question is irrelevant to all satires and apologues.

Actions may significantly differ also according to whether they are episodic or continuous; this distinction rests primarily on the way in which minor characters contribute to the controlling action in which they are agents. In the works to which we have referred casually by way of example, there are only a few characters who exhaust their function almost immediately after their introduction. But in *Joseph Andrews* a considerable number of minor characters are introduced, perform their roles, and disappear from the remainder of the action within a single episode or so;[24] Trulliber, the coach passengers, the sailor-turned-innkeeper, the man of false courage, are characters of this sort.

Initially, characters like Joseph, Lady Booby, Adams, and Slipslop are rep-

[24] See chapter two.

resented in a highly unstable relationship which becomes still further complicated with the later arrival of Fanny on the scene. The resolution of these
relationships is, in the middle section of the action, temporarily impeded or
advanced, or even ethically defined, by Adams' and Joseph's encounters with
a series of characters who appear, act, and disappear from the novel. We are
always reminded so strongly of the unresolved instability that even if a minor
character is shown to hinder the resolution only slightly, or if his sole contribution to the action is merely to create in us a stronger desire for one final resolution rather than another, his role is relevant; the episode in which he
appears will not seem a digression.[25] In the hands of a comic master like Fielding, the elasticity of such an action permits a wide variety of characters, incidents, stylistic variants, and change of tone in a yet perfectly coherent work.
Joseph Andrews, almost the first of English novels, is not only one of the
best but may also be regarded as the crystallization of a type of fiction whose
special effects were not again so fully exploited until Mark Twain set Huck
Finn adrift on a raft and, still later, Joyce invested Stephen and Bloom and
Molly with twenty-four hours of perpetual life.[26]

In distinguishing any action from others it will prove useful to ask if it is
episodic, continuous, or if, as with *Tom Jones*, it achieves its special effect
through a combination of the two. This further distinction among actions
may also have important consequences for the answers we get to questions
about the relation of belief to literary works, but will not affect the formulation of the relevant general questions. Other important variants for discriminating among actions are discussed as the need for them arises.

In pursuing the enquiry into the relationship between a novelist's moral
beliefs, opinions, and prejudices and the work he creates, I have advanced the
theory that all relevant works of prose fiction are organized according to one
of three mutually exclusive types: satire, apologue, or action.[27] Further divi-

---

[25] See chapter five.

[26] It is important to distinguish such actions from works with episodes loosely united
by the appearance in each of a single character. For a brief discussion of *Moll Flanders*
as one example of the latter type of fiction see chapter six.

[27] The three "types" classified according to a defined similarity of relationship of
parts are, for general critical questions, only elementary distinctions, which are sufficient for formulating a relevant question about the relationship between novelists'
beliefs and novels. But the three types must not be identified with what we would normally call the forms of fiction. A comic action does not have the same "form" as a
serious action. A comic action whose major characters undergo internal change does
not have the same form as a comic action in which all the characters are static, though
they share the similarities which define the type "action" and the similarities which define the type "comic action." The forms of the novel alone are numerous, and may

sions among the types are not only possible but necessary. If the distinctions are refined enough, we will no longer be discussing "types" at all, since our prime concern in a full critique would be to discover the peculiar effectiveness of a single work, that is, how it differs from all other members of its class; we should be unlikely to consider information that a particular biological specimen is a mammal, Homo sapiens, female, and blonde constitutes adequate reason for marrying her, though the fact that she is not a whale, a man, or bald would presumably affect our decision. Probably we would want to know those things about her which distinguish her from other women. If she were in fact a human blonde female it is unlikely that we should ask, in swinging from tree to tree does she employ prehensible toes or a tail? It is devoutly to be hoped that the question would prove irrelevant.

At this point it may be useful to repeat, with minor alterations, the organizing principles of the three types:

A satire is a work organized so that it ridicules objects external to the fictional world created in it.

An apologue is a work organized as a fictional example of the truth of a formulable statement or a series of such statements.

An action is a work organized so that it introduces characters, about whose fates we are made to care, in unstable relationships which are then further complicated until the complication is finally resolved by the removal of the represented instability. I shall now substitute the term "novel" for "action."[28]

---

most conveniently be classified according to their use of defined variables which distinguish among actions. At some point in an adequate criticism of a single literary work, we will inevitably be discussing those variations which distinguish a particular literary work from all other literary works of its class, even if that class has been defined according to the most subtle and intricate combination of variables possible. *Emma* and *Pride and Prejudice*, for example, would probably be classified as having the same form according to any distinctions likely to be useful in discussing forms of literary works. They are nevertheless very different works, each with a unique effect. Possibly it is the dual recognition of the uniqueness of any literary work and the utility of regarding it as a member of a class that leads some critics, who would reject platonic notions of ideal forms, to discuss the virtues of a literary work according to the degree to which it fulfills the conditions of a type and, at the same time, to insist that every work is *sui generis*. Viewed in this way, there is no contradiction between the notions that each literary work belongs to a class of literary works and is, at the same time, *sui generis*.

[28] The novel is not a single form, but rather the whole set of quite different forms which can be described according to the many variables possible in actions. (See note 27.) For some critics, my statement that all novels are actions will seem unduly restrictive. There is the possibility that, while all works usefully classified as novels must contain characters introduced in unstable relationships which are later resolved, the

The primary justification for establishing three classes—obviously others equally "correct" are possible—is to formulate a meaningful general question, or possibly questions, about the relation between a novelist's beliefs and the forms of his novels; the questions would be relevant to all novelists and novels; the answers would differ appreciably, but there would always be answers. To put this in different terms, this book attempts to formulate a theory about a constant and necessary relationship between the ethical beliefs of novelists, whatever the content of those beliefs, and novels.

If the three types of prose fiction are organized as they have been described, or even something like the way in which they have been described, certain apposite critical problems emerge. In contrast with those of satire and apologue, the organizing principle of actions offers no convenient access to consideration of ethical questions in novels. It would at first, or even second, glance seem actually to preclude such concerns on the part of both critic and novelist. Certainly it seems to preclude even the remote possibility that a writer of prose fiction whose primary concern is the inculcation of moral virtues could write a coherent novel. This would mean that a great many novelists, especially though not exclusively of a time previous to our own, were liars or fools or possibly both. Not least among such reprobates we must list both Henry Fielding and Samuel Richardson. Then, too, some of our most distinguished critics, ranging in time from Johnson to Leavis, were not merely wrong, but even their concerns were absurdly irrelevant to most literary works.

Surely our own experience with novels must lead us intuitively to rebel against such far-fetched conclusions. There is probably no reader of novels who has not at times disagreed violently with the views of a given novelist, even when he had no knowledge of such views other than that afforded by reading his novel. The very question, *what is the man saying*, occurs so universally that, no matter how we should want to re-formulate it for the purpose of precise inquiry into the role of ethics in novels, to ignore it is both foolhardy and critically irresponsible.

---

development of these relationships may more accurately be described as subordinate to the change in a single character—i.e., the work is organized as a representation of a character rather than an action. I am inclined to believe that we can best understand even such a work as Joyce's *Portrait of the Artist* as an action in which—as one of the variables possible in actions—the internal change of a major character is extremely prominent. There are difficulties attendant on this view, but the consequences of its being wrong are not terribly significant for the present work, since, even if we were to include representations of character, action, or thought as novels, the general statements about the shape of belief in novels, as opposed to satires or apologues, would remain unchanged.

Under these circumstances it is natural, almost inevitable, for us to continue to discuss the ethical content of novels and to do so in two ways: as fictional exemplifications of moral truths or, if we boggle at reducing art to morality, as exemplifications of *ineffable* moral truths; and as ridiculed fictional counterparts of external objects that the novelist dislikes. In other words, to regard novels as part apologue and part satire. And yet, if our description, or something like our description, of the organizing principle of novels is valid, they cannot be part apologues and part satires.

The problem is reversible. The ease with which our description of the organizing principle of apologues enables us to investigate their ethical content is almost matched by the obstructions it offers to any consideration of them as prose fictions. A sensible temptation is to treat a work like *Rasselas* either as an intellectual document or as an ordinary work of rhetoric employing as one of its persuasive devices elements of prose fiction. Yet if we succumb to the first of these temptations we will be forced to recognize almost immediately that the work does not contain a single new idea and that hardly a line qualifies it as a disinterested inquiry into the possibility of human happiness. We may, of course, fruitfully investigate the way in which ideas implemented in the work are or are not derived from doctrine current in the eighteenth century. But this is to beg the issue; unless we believe that *Rasselas'* only claim to importance is that it was written by Johnson, any justification for such an investigation must include the notion that the ideas we traced to their source have been embodied in a work with significance and merit apart from the sources to which we have traced it.

To treat it as a subtype of rhetoric offers still greater temptation, since it undoubtedly shares some of the aims and even some of the techniques of works organized to persuade a given audience to a given course of action. Such treatment would seem even further warranted, since it would not be difficult to show that one of Johnson's moral intentions, in addition to making enough money to bury his mother properly, was to persuade his readers to turn their eyes toward heaven. To explore the relation between an author's moral intention and the form in which he embodies that intention presents a difficult problem, but some solution is crucial for the purposes of this work; it is discussed in detail in a separate chapter below.[29] At this point we must be content to note that even a direct statement of moral intention is crucial evidence only of moral intention and not of the form in which it is implemented. There was nothing to prevent Johnson from implementing his intention in a

[29] See chapter six.

work organized as a satire or as a represented action, since both have moral effects at least as likely to turn our eyes toward heaven as an apologue. Our experience with apologues, though possibly more limited than with novels, must lead us intuitively to rebel against the conclusion that they are works organized to persuade a given audience to a given course of action, at least in anything like the sense that a very good sermon or one of Burke's speeches is organized to do so. Even readers for whom the idea of turning one's eyes to heaven seems silly, or to whom the exhortations of puritanical Christianity seem exaggerated, have read and continue to read *Rasselas* and *Pilgrim's Progress* with a kind of pleasure that seems in no way akin to the pleasure we may derive from the deftness with which a Barrow or a Burke attempts to persuade us to a course of action with which we are not in sympathy. To digress for a moment from prose to verse fictions, were we to add to the list *The Divine Comedy* and the *Faerie Queene,* both apologues though in verse, the intuitive rebellion would, I suspect, be almost universal. It may be that our failure to determine the independent and artistically meritorious task that a writer must perform in creating a great apologue makes us reluctant to treat it as other than an action with additional metaphorical virtues.

In an age of novels, nothing is more natural than to seek an explanation for the artistic merits of all works of fiction that we admire in the familiar virtues to which we have become accustomed in good actions. The long history of criticism of the drama and epic which precedes the novel provides us with convenient questions and a familiar language for dealing with some of the artistic virtues possible to actions: subtlety and psychological depth of characterization; a discernible connection between the traits revealed about characters and the choices they make; a flexibility of characterization that permits the representation of emotional changes in characters as the plausible result of their fictional experiences; a representation of these changes in such a manner that they seem motivated and significant, not merely the described alterations of useful puppets. If, as with Johnson's work, the apologue considered and found wanting in these respects has only a limited popularity and a prestige deriving largely from an author whose literary reputation does not rest in any significant measure on the artistic merit of a prose fiction, we are likely to be content with treating it as a type of intellectual discourse. That is to say, we are likely to ignore it *as* a work of prose fiction altogether.

But we would never rest content with such treatment of *Gulliver's Travels,* though the organizing principle of satire shares with that of apologue an apparent incompatibility with the only *fictional* virtues for which our traditional critical language provides adequate discriminations. Too many readers for too many generations have reaped delight from the adventures of Gulliver to permit any critical pretense that the prose fiction is incidental and can be ignored. Moreover, Swift's literary reputation is too closely dependent on the prestige of *Gulliver's Travels* to permit a critic who finds the work wanting in novelistic virtues to condemn it even *as* a work of prose fiction.

Many of the particular satiric virtues of *Gulliver's Travels* can be, and have been, isolated by descriptions of how Swift exploits devices such as the *reductio ad absurdum* and other rhetorical implements for ridicule which are as appropriate for exploitation in a satirical essay as in a satirical prose fiction. Some matters relevant to fiction can be explored in a limited way by such a conception as the satirical mask, extremely useful in accounting for elements in a short work like Swift's "Modest Proposal," but of dubious utility, possibly even a stumbling block, in investigating a long satire whose narrator does not maintain any consistent pose (i.e., does not wear a single "mask") for more than a page at a time. It is inevitable that, under such circumstances, when we turn to the varied and delightful adventures of Lemuel Gulliver, we will actually *find* in them the qualities of organized actions; we will find such qualities since a prose fiction of any length will by virtue of its *being* a prose fiction represent characters in some fashion, in some kind of relationship with others.

In any given episode in *Gulliver's Travels* we need only ignore some elements and pretend that others are there to treat it as an action. We may say that, "as a result of his trying adventures, Gulliver has at this point in the fourth book gone mad." To defend this interpretation we need only ignore the fact that Gulliver has earlier in the work, during the time of presumed sanity, frequently displayed precisely the same qualities for similar satiric ends as those on which we are now predicating his madness; we need only add, mentally, a series of parts not contained in the work which would show us that his hardships in some more-or-less consistent manner so alter Gulliver's "character" that his internal change plausibly culminates in madness. But in so doing, merely to account for a particular effect in a part of the work, we have rewritten *Gulliver's Travels*; we have taken a few accurate observations of qualitative parts (e.g., Gulliver has had trying adventures; he is represented as in some sense a character) and treated them as if they were parts of another work to account for an effect that we admire in the satire.

The objection to this procedure is in no sense predicated on the notion that it leads to a "misreading" of the satire, or that a possible critical solution to some of the problems raised above will result in a "new reading" of this or any other literary work. There seems to me nothing more absurd than a new "key" to a work read by generations of readers who have reacted with pleasure to all its parts. For them to have "misunderstood" the work implies that the readers, the author, or the critic is insane, and if one is performing a critical task it is only decent to assume that the first two have their wits about them. The assumption in this book, then, is that the greater part of any group of readers who are pleased by a whole novel, apologue, or satire must have reacted appropriately to all its parts. Confusion arises only when we make the terribly complex attempt to explain the formal properties of the work which might account for its effectiveness.

We begin with certain apparent facts: many generations of readers have been pleased by all of *Gulliver's Travels;* the same is true of *Rasselas,* and appreciative readers include some with no belief in an afterlife; at least some intelligent and sensitive readers who have enjoyed a novel like *Tom Jones* insist that it has a strong moral effect. Add to these facts a supposition: the organizing principles of *Gulliver's Travels, Rasselas,* and *Tom Jones* are those ascribed above respectively to satire, apologue, and action. We may now make some inferences: no explanation of the pleasure that readers derive from the whole of *Gulliver's Travels* or *Rasselas* can be correct if it assigns to elements of prose fiction in those works functions they could perform only in an action; no explanation of the moral effect of *Tom Jones* can be correct if it presumes that the moral content of the novel has a "shape" possible only to the moral content either of satire or of apologue. To explain the facts, retain the supposition, and solve the problems raised by the inferences, we must show that fictions which are satires and fictions which are apologues must meet special demands different from those of actions and that, if those demands are met, the pleasure that generations of readers have derived from them *as* prose fictions is comprehensible. We have also to show that a novel may have an ethical content at least compatible with a work organized as an action. It would be still more desirable if we could show that some ethical content is a necessary part of any action.

The Peculiar Demands of Satire:
Gulliver's Travels

A closer examination of the description of the organizing principle of satire will show that Gulliver, other agents of ridicule, and the events in which they take part had to meet very exacting demands if *Gulliver's Travels* were successfully to accomplish the artistic end of satire. In this work a single character narrates his own adventures for some four hundred pages. The contributions he can make toward achieving the artistic end of a satire are directly proportionate to the degree to which, as a fictional construct, he may be exploited to ridicule the external objects of the satire. Any qualities which increase the effectiveness with which Swift can employ his services as an implement for successful ridicule augment his virtues as the main character of the lengthy satire. Swift, then, might easily have shown Gulliver as constantly foolish and identified his foolishness with the undesirable element in the external world, while ascribing to the "people" among whom Gulliver finds himself precisely those traits which would best display Gulliver's foolishness. That is, Gulliver might have been shown throughout his travels as he is when he tries to introduce gunpowder into Brobdingnag and then interprets the king's horror at the thought of brutally blowing up his enemies as a sign of "narrow principles." Or Swift might have elected to portray Gulliver as a constantly superior figure, identified the culpable traits of the people Gulliver is among with the external object of ridicule, and heaped scorn upon *them*. That is, Gulliver might have been shown consistently as he is when he refuses to enslave the Blefuscudians to satisfy the ambitions of a Lilliputian king. Clearly, though, if Swift were able to exploit Gulliver now in one way, now in another, without confusion, he would more fully have exploited his artistic medium. If we could show that he had succeeded in going still farther to create a character who could be used in both ways on the same page of the work, that he had devised the same degree of flexibility for his minor fictional creations, and that he had exploited not two but *four* possible relationships between the main character, the creatures in the lands in which he sojourns, and the external objects of satire, we might indeed begin to understand the degree of artistry that entered into the creation of one of the great satires of all time.

We might well ask whether Swift, in order to create a character appropriate for such a role in a satire, might not have been forced to endow Gulliver with contradictory traits and attitudes. But the description of the organizing principle of satire suggests that, no matter how minimal a virtue consistency may be in a work organized as an action, it is not relevant to the artistic end of satire. In the latter the artistic problem is not to make a character consistent but to make certain that the question of consistency never arises in the course of a normal reading of the work. Of course, the fictional creations must convince us that they have a kind of existence or the ridicule itself fails. Unless Swift manages to create an illusion that a giant king is engaging in a dispute with a character named Gulliver, the gunpowder episode loses much of its force. Unless we can visualize the breasts of the Brobdingnag maidens as parts of gigantic women, Gulliver's disgust is senseless and the attack upon human pride in its own species loses its bite. But the demands for creating such an illusion are in no sense the same as those for creating an illusion in an action.

One way to help create an illusion of reality in a character is to represent him performing actions, revealing thoughts, reacting to other characters in a way consistent with his revealed traits. In any work in which a character is represented as undergoing a motivated internal change or in any work which depends heavily upon keeping us interested in the future destiny of characters, such consistency is a minimal demand. To create an illusion of reality about Gulliver, Swift could conceivably have made use of such consistency, though only at the sacrifice of a good deal of Gulliver's satiric versatility. But if Swift could circumvent the demand for consistency and still succeed in creating for his character an illusion of life sufficiently strong to accomplish his satiric purpose, this would be clearly preferable. To do so he might have included an inordinate number of facts about Gulliver which committed him to almost nothing in the way of future action.[30] That is, we would be unable to predict from any of the traits revealed in the included facts the alternative the character might select when faced with a serious choice. We should then expect to learn a good many external details about his grandmother, and about where he lived and studied. He may safely be given a profession and even some generalized moral traits (e.g., honesty) susceptible of so broad an interpretation that scarcely any act less than stealing need be regarded as inconsistent with it. He may even participate in an occasional exciting adventure—he may have to swim to shore after a shipwreck which has been shown to occur at such a precise latitude that no skeptic can doubt its existence. He is, nevertheless, committed to practically no particular course of action in the future. If Swift were then to use the very first subsequent ethical opinion expressed by Gulliver in combination with obvious rhetorical devices clearly for purposes of ridicule and to continue to couple any evaluative statement Gulliver makes with such rhetorical devices, the ridicule would adequately override any concern with what, in another type of fiction, would be revealed traits. Once such a pattern emerged, Gulliver could make far-reaching ethical pronouncements even if they contradicted other pronouncements. In doing so he will not be an inconsistent character; consistency has played no part in creating for him a vivacious life which already spans three centuries and shows no hint of permanent decline.

The degree to which the requirements for creating an effective agent of

---

[30] If this were to prove useful in ridiculing contemporary travel books, so much the better for the end of the satire.

satire differ radically from those for creating an agent of action may seem more striking if we note the consequences of a choice limited to an interpretation of Gulliver as Swift's spokesman and an alternative view of him as a fully represented character such as we might expect to find in an action. The alternative view would seem to be preferable; it would be patently absurd to attribute Gulliver's occasional phlegmatic naïveté, frequent insensitivity, and rhetorically deflated opinions to Swift. And yet, though less obviously, the alternative view of Gulliver is scarcely more tenable than the interpretation of him as Swift's spokesman.

One sensitive reader of *Gulliver's Travels* has ascribed the following traits to the book's major character: in all respects an average good man; reasonably intelligent; irritatingly circumstantial and unimaginative; simple, direct, uncomplicated; an example of the bluff, good-natured, honest Englishman.[31] Undoubtedly, each of these traits is displayed, alone or in combination, by Gulliver at many points during his adventures. One might wonder, however, whether Gulliver is unimaginative when he uses his knowledge of Lilliputian history to suggest remedies for defects in the English legal and educational systems, or whether he is reasonably intelligent when he attempts to persuade the Brobdingnagian king of the utility of gunpowder by a description of its effects so bloody that it is obviously calculated to repel any average good man. Short of the presumption of so radical an alteration as that which gradually transforms the moral character of King Lear in the course of a five-act drama, it is difficult to postulate a consistent set of traits which would reconcile Gulliver's eloquent refusal to enslave the Blefuscudians with his obtuse inability to comprehend the Brobdingnag king's reluctance to make himself absolute master of the lives and fortunes of his subjects. We can always explain such discrepancies—and many others that any reader could easily isolate—by the general presumption that any man might change over a period of time filled with various hardships, or by another equally general presumption that characters vary considerably when placed in different circumstances. But since any such general notions would equally well justify a thoroughly inconsistent character in any prose fiction, they can be applied cogently to Gulliver only if we can show in detail the stages of the radical change he has undergone between his last days in Lilliput and his conversation with the king of Brobdingnag and, further, show that such a radical moral change of a major character at this point makes a significant contribution to a specifiable artistic end which

[31] Samuel Holt Monk, "The Pride of Lemuel Gulliver," in *Eighteenth Century English Literature: Modern Essays in Criticism*, ed. James L. Clifford (New York: Oxford University Press, 1959), pp. 116-117.

informs all parts of *Gulliver's Travels*. It is always difficult to prove a negative, but I know of no cogent evidence offered by any critic of *Gulliver's Travels* which indicates that the two general presumptions mentioned above justify Gulliver as a consistent represented character in any greater degree than they might be used to justify the most inconsistent character we can discover, or even purposely create in a prose fiction.

In contrast, the interpretation which conceives of Gulliver not as a character whose effectiveness depends significantly upon consistency, but as a creation whose primary virtue can be measured by the versatility with which he contributes to the stated artistic end common to satires, offers a simple explanation of the apparent inconsistencies; these, in fact, would be expected in any fairly long satire. Such an interpretation may seem more convincing if we note that when Gulliver's opinions diverge most radically from those he has expressed earlier, the consistency of the objects of the satire is most clearly preserved and most forcefully attacked. Gulliver makes his eloquent refusal to enslave a free people at a moment when, by a number of rhetorical means, the intrigues and ignoble aspirations of Lilliputian statesmen—and *not* Gulliver himself—are momentarily identified with the particular and general intrigues and aspirations of the English court. Gulliver, here "an average good man," in refusing the request of the Lilliputian monarch, allows Swift to point a scornful finger at certain politicians of Queen Anne's day.

But when he confronts the Brobdingnag king, Gulliver, through his own reiterated statements, becomes the advocate for and representative of the political institutions of western Europe. His description of the effects of gunpowder, including such recommendations as its ability to "destroy whole ranks of an army at once," to "sink down ships, with a thousand men in each," to "divide hundreds of bodies in the middle, and lay all waste before them," [32] is hardly likely to recommend either gunpowder or the world of "civilized" men to the king. It is the highly obtuse and even bloody-minded Gulliver who now characterizes the external object, and, since he is "our" spokesman, his discomfiture becomes our own; the epithet "little odious vermin" with which the king characterizes Gulliver's "race," attacks, among other things, the inhumane political aspirations of so-called civilized nations with even greater force and more general applicability than Gulliver's earlier eloquent refusal to enslave a free people disparaged England's aspirations. The effectiveness of the later incident in no way depends upon our accepting the giant king as an idealized portrait of a monarch, but is rather increased by *his* being seen as

[32] *Gulliver's Travels*, p. 137.

an average good man who rejects with horror Gulliver's proffered gift; in other words, considering the terms in which Gulliver has described the virtues and potentialities of gunpowder, the king need not be represented as a better man than Gulliver was at moments in Lilliput (or, indeed, in Brobdingnag) to reject it.

But the point is not that Gulliver is an inconsistent character whose inconsistencies are occasionally put to incidental use by Swift, but that the consistency of a character's traits if he is an agent of satire is irrelevant to the effect of the whole work. If Swift had made Gulliver a consistent character he would in no way have improved *Gulliver's Travels* but, instead, might not have been able to write a coherent satire at all. This point is so crucial to the grammar of the types of fiction presented in this chapter that it may be worth further clarification.

Suppose we purposely make some elementary inferences about Gulliver's character from his revealed thoughts, acts, and speeches during the earliest stages of the satire. That is, suppose we actually regard *Gulliver's Travels* as an action and make the kind of inference which would be necessary for even the crudest comprehension of a novel—the kind of inference, for example, which would lead us to be startled if, after the first chapter of *Pride and Prejudice*, Mr. Bennet were to consult his wife about a philosophical problem, and Mrs. Bennet were to solve it by reference to a system of ethics she had written ten years previously.

Gulliver is not represented initally as a character who exhibits strong foibles in his normal state of existence but is, in all respects, at least an average good Englishman. That he is circumstantial and unimaginative is also clear from the outset, and the impression is strengthened by the dispassionate tone of his narrative. Business failure and near drowning he takes in stride and he narrates these events with no indication of emotional distress. Not a single revelation of his state of mind do we get in his dispassionate avowal that "I often let my legs drop, and could feel no bottom." [33] No clue to the sense of relief he must have felt when at last he tells us "I found myself within my depth." [34] So stable a personality is he that to "perceive on his chest a human creature not six inches high, with a bow and arrow in his hands" [35] elicits little comment, though when he feels at least forty more crawling upon him he informs us, still in unimpassioned narrative prose, that he was in the "utmost astonishment, and roared so loud that they all ran back in a fright." [36] It takes but a moment for him to return to his normal calm state, withstand a spate of

[33] *Ibid.*, p. 3.   [35] *Ibid.*
[34] *Ibid.*, p. 4.   [36] *Ibid.*

arrows, and arrange without heroics for nourishment. We accept, as an extension of his "circumstantial and unimaginative" mind, his brief account of what occurs when the Lilliputians eased his bonds and he was "able to turn upon my right [sic], and to ease myself with making water; which I very plentifully did, to the great astonishment of the people, who conjecturing by my motions what I was going to do, immediately opened to the right and left on that side to avoid the torrent which fell with such noise and violence from me." [37] But, considering the great variety of adventures that Gulliver has recounted phlegmatically, we will, if we are interested in the revelation of his character, inevitably attach considerable weight to the first episode in which he displays real concern. And, finally, Gulliver does show concern and, perhaps most surprising for an average good Englishman, he *is* stung to comparative eloquence. In the following passage he is moved and he makes an excellent effort to move us; his struggle between urgency and shame, as opposed to his struggle to escape from drowning, is something we are made to feel. To convince us he creates a little gem of rhetoric with adequate proofs from the speech, the speaker, and the audience:

> I had been for some hours extremely pressed by the necessities of nature; which was no wonder, it being almost two days since I had last disburthened myself. I was under great difficulties between urgency and shame. The best expedient I could think on, was to creep into my house, which I accordingly did; and shutting the gate after me, I went as far as the length of my chain would suffer, and discharged my body of that uneasy load. But this was the only time I was ever guilty of so uncleanly an action; for which I cannot but hope the candid reader will give some allowance, after he hath maturely and impartially considered my case, and the distress I was in. From this time my constant practice was, as soon as I rose, to perform that business in open air, at the full extent of my chain, and due care was taken every morning before company came, that the offensive matter should be carried off in wheelbarrows by two servants appointed for that purpose. I would not have dwelt so long upon a circumstance, that perhaps at first sight may appear not very momentous, if I had not thought it necessary to justify my character in point of cleanliness to the world; which I am told some of my maligners have been pleased, upon this and other occasions, to call in question.[38]

Gulliver has every right to expect that after we have "maturely and impartially considered his case" we will forgive him for performing his natural functions. But he must also expect that when a bluff, good-natured English-

[37] *Ibid.*, p. 9.
[38] *Ibid.*, pp. 13-14.

man, by nature circumstantial and unimaginative, waxes eloquent, we will take special notice. When that eloquence is employed in so dubious a cause, we are justified in believing that even the delusion of grandeur consequent upon his second voyage is less aberrant than his state of mind in Lilliput. Unfortunately, there is little pleasure and less profit to be gained from reading the subsequent adventures in Lilliput and elsewhere as the delusion of a man whose mind has been unhinged by hardship. If we view Gulliver in this way, Swift has made an artistic blunder in suggesting that Gulliver is even slightly unbalanced at the precise moment when his reliability as a reporter must be unquestioned.

But, as generations of readers testify, Swift did not blunder; the attempt to define a consistent set of traits which motivate Gulliver's actions is a critical chimera, not a difficulty for the reader of *Gulliver's Travels* who finds rich food for laughter and for thought in Gulliver's eloquent plea. Food for laughter, because of the disparity between Gulliver's strange circumstances and the attention he devotes to detailing and excusing a trivial natural act. Food for thought, since, no matter how much of our laughter may be directed at travel literature, Gulliver's apology is merely a rhetorically exaggerated expression of our own unwarranted pride in our species, and of our consequent disclination to accept as natural our own animality. When we laugh at Gulliver's appeal to us, it is an aspect of ourselves we have found ridiculous; as he details the relatively intricate arrangements to ensure future cleanliness, we are cogently and bitingly reminded of our natural place in the physical universe which our pride rejects. And we are reminded of this again and again in the course of Gulliver's travels: when a monkey suckles a disgusted Gulliver, when a Yahoo female makes sexual overtures to him, or when he himself, forced to view humans from a perspective not normal to a man, sees in the traditionally lovely act of a mother suckling her child cause for disgust.

Any relevant motivation for Gulliver's eloquent plea is contained in the plea itself, not in the traits we may infer from his adventures in England and on the sea, and no traits that he reveals in that plea commit him to any future course of action as a character, since they are exhausted in the immediate satiric end. It is not his acts that reveal his traits, but those almost explicit statements about himself, before any strong element of ridicule becomes evident in the work, that tell us he is an average good Englishman, and it is only that general definition that he retains throughout *Gulliver's Travels*. When it helps the cause of ridicule, the average good Englishman may be quite good and sensitive and perceptive, as when he rejects the Lilliputian king's order to enslave Blefuscu and thus effects Swift's attack on English politics; or the average good Englishman, while necessarily retaining that definition, may be an obtuse and bloody-minded fool as when he becomes the spokesman for average good men like himself and us to the horrified king of Brobdingnag.

The subsidiary agents need not—though they may—retain even that measure of consistent definition. The Lilliputian court becomes the English court when it suits Swift's purpose, and its courtiers leap over sticks and walk upon tightropes to earn positions and orders embarrassingly similar to those won by Gulliver's countrymen, though Gulliver need not see the similarity; but suddenly they are Lilliputians again and Gulliver could have saved the breath—though we are delighted that he didn't—wasted in his protestation against having had an affair with a female of that country. In Brobdingnag, when Swift can make good use of the size of the Brobdingnagians to attack our pride in our species by identifying their gross physical features with our own, he does so, and this does not prevent him from attacking that same pride by contrasting their physical prowess with ours, or by representing their king as an average good man horrified by an average good Englishman and contrasted to Western monarchs. Indeed, to take the polar instance, the Yahoos do not "represent" men, nor men debased, nor men seen only with their brute attributes. They too are satiric creations which Swift employs with versatility to embarrass us. At one point Swift is able to exploit them by showing them as *superior* to men; so, after having to listen to his master's lengthy identification of some Yahoo traits with human ones, Gulliver informs us: "I expected every moment that my master would accuse the yahoos of those unnatural appetites in both sexes, so common among us. But Nature, it seems, hath not been so expert a schoolmistress; and these politer pleasures are entirely the productions of art and reason, on our side of the globe." [39]

Any of the agents of satire in *Gulliver's Travels*, including its central "average good Englishman," may be placed in any possible relationship with any other agent to effect ridicule of the external object. The critical difficulty which resulted from simple inferences about Gulliver's character resulted only from a critical "trick" of reading the opening chapters as we might if Gulliver's narrative were even potentially the introductory stages of an action —let us say of a purely superficial adventure story. But despite the number of adventures narrated by Gulliver, his early tale does not bear more than a superficial resemblance to the organization of the initial parts of an action. This is made clear by the way in which Swift has treated Gulliver's near

[39] *Ibid.*, p. 286.

drowning before he reaches Lilliput. If one purposely attempted to write an inept narrative of a man struggling to reach a far-away shore, it could not possibly fail, as Swift's narrative does, to arouse some suspense about whether or not the man will reach shore, to make us feel, as Swift's narrative does not, some sense of relief as the swimmer feels land beneath his feet. Swift's description could have resulted only from the attempt of an extraordinarily deft craftsman to create the illusion that a character whom we have watched perform such a particularized feat does somehow exist, while, at the same time, he has carefully suppressed all elements which would make us concerned primarily with the character's fate. Versimilitude alone is the effect that Swift achieves, and verisimilitude is not a product of traits revealed through acts. As a result, we never infer from Gulliver's completely inexpressive narrative that he is an inexpressive "man." He does not in the course of it reveal his own inexpressiveness; the narrative simply does not reveal anything important about him. The very early parts of the chronicle which define him as an average good Englishman, the many briefly recounted events of the sea voyage which give Gulliver a firm toe-hold on fictional existence, provide precisely the right elements for our acceptance of the Lilliputians as, in their own right, fictional products of verisimilitude; but it is only the clever adumbration of the narrative elements that has prevented us from inferring a whole set of additional traits about Gulliver, and it is his existence as a product of verisimilitude that keeps us from feeling cheated when, to effect the first clear ridicule in the book, he acts in a manner which, had he been revealed instead of defined as an average good Englishman, we should have to interpret as inconsistently eccentric.

The effect of the satire depends both upon a constant recognition of Gulliver's fictional existence as a character and upon his absolute freedom to display whatever traits will most powerfully effect ridicule at any moment. The former is sustained by occasional narrative sequences, as when Gulliver swims to capture the Blefuscudian fleet; but here Swift's wisdom in sending Gulliver on four journeys instead of on one satiric voyage is clear. If the episodes analogous to primitive "adventure" narratives were employed too frequently in the strange lands that Gulliver visits, the suppression of our concern with Gulliver's fate would become too difficult to sustain; but if it fails, so does the satire. One step in the wrong directon, and the brilliant satiric passage in which the Brobdingnag monkey carries off the struggling hero, or that in which he intrepidly fights a gigantic insect with his rapier, is transformed into a horror story in which the satiric point is lost. Once we feel about Gulliver as we would about the hero of any adventure story, he instantly becomes tied to a set of revealed traits which, inevitably, we would infer from his acts and thoughts; his satiric versatility would then be seriously compromised. But his three visits home between voyages amply renew his place in the world of Englishmen with considerable economy of means and without danger of destroying the effect of the satire.

In a schematic discussion such as this it is impossible to do justice to the inventiveness of the techniques Swift uses to get us to see ourselves, our institutions, our acts, from points of view which reveal to us the ridiculous inhumanity of our customs and the pathetic shoddiness of our ethical pretensions. But whatever the variety of techniques he employs, Swift effects his satire by utilizing four possible relationships among Gulliver, the creatures he visits, and the external objects of satire. We have noted examples of two of these: Gulliver may be "identified" with the external object and another agent may be given the appropriate traits and opinions to show that he—and the external object—are ridiculous, as in his disagreement with the Brobdingnag king; or one or more of the other agents may be identified with the external object and Gulliver may display the appropriate traits and opinions to show that the agents—and the external object—are ridiculous, as when Gulliver refuses to enslave the Blefuscudians.

But perhaps the richest of all the conjunctions which effect ridicule is still a third: Gulliver and the subsidiary agents are both identified with the external object so that all three become ridiculous. The attributes of the Lilliputian emperor in the following passages would themselves be a source of satiric delight, but perhaps Swift alone as a satirist was capable of the added fillip resulting from Gulliver's reaction to the gracious expressions of "GOLBASTO MOMAREN EVLAME GURDILO SHEFIN MULLY ULLY GUE, most mighty Emperor of Lilliput, delight and terror of the universe, whose dominions extend five thousand *blustrugs* (about twelve miles in circumference)":[40]

> I swore and subscribed to these articles with great cheerfulness and content, although some of them were not so honourable as I could have wished; which proceeded wholly from the malice of Skyresh Bolgolam the High Admiral: whereupon my chains were immediately unlocked, and I was at full liberty; the Emperor himself in person did me the honour to be by at the whole ceremony. I made my acknowledgements by prostrating myself at his Majesty's feet: but he commanded me to rise; and after many gracious expressions, which,

[40] *Ibid.*, p. 30.

to avoid the censure of vanity, I shall not repeat, he added, that he hoped I should prove a useful servant, and well deserve all the favours he had already conferred upon me, or might do for the future.[41]

By a fourth, less frequently exploited conjunction, neither Gulliver nor the people he is among are identified with the external object, and both co-operate in attacking it. Such conjunction appears most frequently in the fourth book whenever Gulliver agrees with a particular Houyhnhnm opinion of men,[42] but there are many earlier instances, as when Gulliver perceives the insufficiencies of English legal and educational systems contrasted to the Lilliputian,[43] or when, in Balnibarbi, he completely justifies Munodi's practicality by such an observation as the following:

> I could not forbear admiring at these odd appearances both in town and country, and I made bold to desire my conductor, that he would be pleased to explain to me what could be meant by so many busy heads, hands, and faces, both in the streets and the fields, because I did not discover any good effects they produced; but on the contrary, I never knew a soil so unhappily cultivated, houses so ill contrived and so ruinous, or a people whose countenances and habit expressed so much misery and want.[44]

That Swift can sometimes make Gulliver seem ridiculous and at other times represent him as a plausible and competent commentator is, then, not surprising. But our best clue to the peculiar demands of prose fiction organized as satire is the recognition that our attitude to Gulliver can shift from paragraph to paragraph without confusion. Though it is Swift's use of stylistic and rhetorical devices that normally defines one of the four relationships for us, the reason that such frequent shifts are possible without confusion is that, at any given moment after the initial adventures in Lilliput, stylistic or rhetorical clues to how we are to regard Gulliver are not absolutely necessary. Occasionally, in fact, they are not present. We immediately apprehend that Gulliver is to be believed in the following passage, in which, almost directly after his debacle with the Brobdingnag king, Gulliver comments upon a Brobdingnagian writer's notion that Brobdingnagians must originally have been much larger:

[41] *Ibid.*, p. 31.

[42] This conjunction is, however, frequently complicated in the last book, when Gulliver and his master agree and some trait of a Yahoo is simultaneously identified with the object of satire.

[43] *Gulliver's Travels*, pp. 48-54.

[44] *Ibid.*, p. 186.

For my own part, I could not avoid reflecting how universally this talent was spread of drawing lectures in morality, or indeed rather matter of discontent and repining, from the quarrels we raise with nature. And, I believe, upon a strict enquiry those quarrels might be shown as ill-grounded among us as they are among that people." [45]

This, clearly, is an instance of the conjunction in which the subsidiary creation (the Brobdingnagian belief) is identified with the external object, and Gulliver's comments are believable, though immediately before and immediately after this comment he is the butt of ridicule.

But what, in the work, enables us to follow almost effortlessly the frequent shifts from one set of relationships to another? We could not do this when reading either a novel or an apologue. The answer seems to lie in the one set of relationships impossible in a satire: the external object can never be seen as superior both to Gulliver and to the subsidiary agents, or we do not have satire at all. Moreover, where Gulliver and a subsidiary agent disagree, the only relevant satiric relationship is that which ridicules the external object; in a work organized as satire, there would be no point in identifying a particular external object with a fictional creation simply to make Gulliver seem ridiculous, though such a conjunction is frequently employed in novels. In the passage above, the irrelevant consequence of viewing Gulliver as foolish and the Brobdingnagian as correct would be no other than that Gulliver is foolish again. But if Gulliver is right, and the giant author is foolish, so are "the quarrels we raise with nature."

I do not mean to suggest that we ever consciously examine the alternatives and then decide which is the best. Such examination is unnecessary when even the crudest identification of the object is made; the relationships themselves are then so limited in number as to be obvious, and—except in the last book— we never have to select the better of two alternatives; only one is possible. From the instant that such "lectures in morality" are indicated as present "among us" we do not have to conjecture; we *know* that Gulliver is to be believed. After the very beginning of *Gulliver's Travels* the one constant in the pattern of organization is that each encounter between Gulliver and another agent results—with minor exceptions I discuss below—in ridicule of a clearly defined external object. We can hardly get through a few pages of the Lilliput episode without intuitively expecting such ridicule to result from the interaction of Gulliver with other agents in the book.

But if this be true we would expect a confusing ambiguity to result at any

[45] *Ibid.*, p. 140.

point at which the object was ridiculed, whether we regarded Gulliver as foolish or as essentially "correct." And that is precisely what happens from the moment Gulliver leaves Houyhnhnmland and is picked up by the Portuguese sea captain. For, on the one hand, if Gulliver is displaying an absurd instance of human pride as the result of his contact with the Houyhnhnms, we have one reasonably effective culmination of Swift's attacks upon human pride. But, on the other hand, if even the best of sea captains and of men may only be tolerated by one who has seen rational horses, the attack on human pride is at least as devastating. The argument drawn from the virtuous nature of the sea captain is a sword that cuts both ways. If we take the first interpretation, his rescuer's essential goodness makes Gulliver's pride more reprehensible and ridiculous. But, if we take the second, we may argue that Swift has been attacking human pride in its own species and that he might be expected, as one last bitter thrust, to show even the best of men as hardly a justified cause for human pride.

In other words, the difficulties implicit in the ending of *Gulliver's Travels* are not merely the result of a critical chimera. They are the result, instead, of Swift's having shown us the object of ridicule, but then having left us alternatives among the relationships either of which would ridicule that object. For the first time in the pages of *Gulliver's Travels* we are forced to select not the one possible relationship relevant to satire, but the better of two. The ambiguity is a predictable consequence of a conjunction of satiric agents in which either, though not both, may be identified with the clear object of satire in such a way as to ridicule it.[46]

Finally, it is important to note that works organized like *Gulliver's Travels* easily accommodate a number of ludicrous remarks which are not directed against an easily identifiable external object. Opportunities for brief absurd portrayals are inevitable in such a fiction and, to the extent that they do not obscure the satiric pattern, they may contribute to our general expectation of ridicule in the work. As opposed to an action in which, if it is coherent, our

[46] I do not wish to obscure the delineation of the kinds of fiction by engaging in a controversy not absolutely relevant to the grammar of types, but a strong argument as to which alternative is preferable could be made along the following lines. The kind of pride which has been the object of satire most consistently throughout the work has been pride in the human species rather than a form of individual vanity. If we view Gulliver's disinclination to associate with his fellow Englishmen as a final instance of unwarranted pride, then the average Englishmen—and ourselves—are, by contrast, not so bad after all. It is Gulliver, not the Englishmen with whom we are identified, who appears, finally, the fool. This is a very comforting way to look at the end, but it hardly seems a very effective culmination of a long book which has ruthlessly exposed us to ourselves.

pleasure in the whole is not simply a sum of the pleasure we have received from its subordinate parts, our delight in the whole of any satire is essentially the sum of the pleasure we have felt at each satiric thrust.[47] A simple example may clarify this point. When Fielding, in *Joseph Andrews*, first shows Slipslop and Parson Adams together, he is content to indicate almost in passing that Slipslop feels competent to engage in theological discussions with Adams, who cannot understand her arguments because of her ludicrous distortion of the English language. Fielding does not at this early stage of the action portray such a theological dispute for us, despite tempting opportunities to evoke laughter through techniques he employs successfully later in the novel. He could, in other words, easily have made the episode far more amusing with very little trouble. But, had he done so, he would seriously have compromised Adams' ability to "rescue" Joseph from the foolish figure he makes during the London episodes, since the rescue depends on our not having seen Adams as ludicrous in the very early stages of the novel. In turn, unless Joseph is somehow justified after his performance in London he cannot perform his role as comic hero in the rest of the action.[48] Fielding, then, could easily have taken the mildly amusing initial discussion between Adams and Slipslop and transformed it into one of the most humorous episodes in his comic novel. But in doing so he would seriously have detracted from our pleasure in *Joseph Andrews*.

Swift, in contrast, is not faced with any such limitation on the degree of laughter he may evoke at any point. His task as the creator of a prose fiction organized as satire is to wring the last ounce of ridicule possible from every new juxtaposition of his satiric agents. Since our delight stems from the sum of the parts of the satire, he may and does, when a convenient opportunity affords itself, evoke occasional laughter which enriches his satire though it is not directed against a special external object. Though if one hunts hard enough for an external object he can usually find one, Gulliver's protestations of innocence of sexual impropriety with a female six inches high is a particularly fortunate example of a convenient absurdity included for its own sake. And, though again we can uncover or even manufacture an object of ridicule if we wish, the fine brief portrait of a Houyhnhnm female threading a needle is easily explained as another such absurdity easily accommodated in a satiric organization and enriching *Gulliver's Travels*.

[47] This conception was suggested to me by some remarks made by Professor Arthur Friedman, though he would view it as simply a further consequence of the theory of satire advanced in E. W. Rosenheim's *Swift's Satire in a Tale of a Tub*.

[48] This is discussed in detail in chapter two.

The discussion of satiric agents in these past few pages is essentially schematic, but detailed enough to show that the creator of a prose fiction organized as satire must meet extremely exacting demands if his work is to be effective. These demands are not merely different from but incompatible with those which must be met by the creator of either of the other two types of fiction. One cannot create an action which is also a satire any more than he can write an active sentence which is also a passive sentence in English. To carry the analogy a step farther, the observation that the types are mutually incompatible is no more an attempt to dictate to writers what they may or may not do than is the observation that active sentences are not passive sentences.

A child not yet adept at using the principles by which sentences are constructed in his language is, in a trivial sense, original when he says, "the milk was drinks the cat." But when T. S. Eliot writes, "Webster was much possessed by death/ And saw the skull beneath the skin," he employs common English grammatical principles for constructing passive and active clauses joined by a conjunction; in so doing he creates a coherent English sentence that is not merely original but unique.[49] In this sense alone a grammar of a natural language is analogous to a grammar of literary types. *King Lear* is a unique play. To say that it has the form of tragedy is in no way to disparage Shakespeare's originality. To say that tragedies, since they are actions, must be coherent *as* actions is not to detract from the originality of tragedians.

Alternatively, nothing prevented Jonathan Swift from writing an effective work in which one chapter was organized as apologue, another as action, and still a third as philosophical dialogue—that is, a work whose effect did not depend on a strong principle of coherence. But if *Gulliver's Travels* is a coherent satire, we can more fruitfully recognize that all of its components, including ethical judgments, must be incorporated in the work in a manner that satisfies the demands of the type. We need not confuse meretricious novelty with artistic invention to do adequate justice to Swift's creative powers.[50]

Though we began to discuss *Gulliver's Travels* by observing that the statement of the organizing principles of satire seemed rather directly related to a satirist's ethical beliefs but inconveniently remote from his aesthetic accomplishments, the problem at this point is almost reversed. Aesthetic demands on the satirist are exacting and specifiable, but if the artistic requirements discussed in this chapter are in fact those of satire, the demands for positive ethi-

---

[49] For a brilliant exposition of the relation between grammatical principles and unique sentences see Noam Chomsky, *Syntactic Structures* (The Hague: Mouton and Co., 1957).

[50] Cf. note 27.

cal revelation in this type are almost nugatory. This does turn out to be the case.

Any reasonably well educated man in our society will have incidentally learned enough about Jonathan Swift to feel somewhat shocked at the following statements: We cannot infer from *Gulliver's Travels* alone that Swift was a Christian. Though knowledge of the highly particularized objects of satire, especially in the first voyage, would justifiably lead us to presume that Swift's sympathies were with Oxford and Bolingbroke as opposed to the Whigs, we can infer so little from *Gulliver's Travels* alone about Swift's positive political commitments that we could not definitely determine that he was not a republican.

Of course, since we *know* he was not a republican and that he was a Christian, his selection of objects of satire, if not an inevitable consequence of his religious and political commitments, seems entirely consonant with them. If we have read a good deal of Swift's work and have a special acquaintance with the political and intellectual history of eighteenth-century England, it may even seem—and justifiably so—that Swift and Swift alone had the precise set of beliefs, prejudices, and abilities necessary to create *Gulliver's Travels*. But if we knew absolutely nothing of Swift except that he had a written the great satire, we could easily postulate a general set of positive ethical, religious, and political commitments quite different from Swift's which could have led to the selection of the same objects of ridicule. An antimonarchist might have chosen to ridicule precisely the same political and social customs that Swift did. And, even if we consider the particular prejudices revealed in the first and third books, we have no very strong inferential probability about Swift's positive attitudes toward Woods' ha'penny, the Irish question in general, or the defunct Harley ministry, since a republican satirist interested in attacking English institutions might reasonably be expected to employ any *cause célèbre* to facilitate the satiric exposure of those institutions. It is true that the republican satirist would have a completely different set of motives from those of the monarchist for what he attacks, but positive motives are seldom revealed in a prose fiction organized as a satire. Even in the relatively infrequent uses of the satiric conjunction in which both Gulliver and the subsidiary agents are seen as superior to the object, the end is still ridicule of that object. One wonders, for example, if any critic would even be willing to postulate Swift's positive suggestions for the education of women from Gulliver's detailed remarks concerning the admired Lilliputian customs in this regard, though we should all be willing, I think, to infer what Swift finds reprehensible in the education of English women.

Even a slight acquaintance with the history of ideas would prevent us from postulating as a reasonable probability that the man who wrote *Gulliver's Travels* was a republican atheist. But this is to beg the issue, since we are aware that even superficial historical research will reveal many of Swift's commitments; what we are trying to define is the shape that Swift's beliefs necessarily assumed in the type of fiction organized as satire, and that so few positive ethical demands were made on the satirist that a republican atheist as well as an Anglican monarchist might reasonably select the same objects of satire is crucial for understanding that definition.

In order to detach ourselves momentarily from the knowledge we have derived about Swift from many sources, it may be useful, finally, to consider a hypothetical instance. Suppose that a small group of Druids or neo-Druids still exist in twentieth-century England, and believe that only by burning a man alive in a wicker basket once a year can mankind achieve virtue and contentment. One Druid is a professional writer who is also interested in furthering the cause of Druidism. Depending on a variety of circumstances, he may write an action, an apologue, or a satire; if he does write a satire, in the sense that we have defined it, he may very well decide to ridicule statesmen whose opinions and practices he believes are antithetical to Druidism, and institutions or even literary works deemed harmful to the Druidical cause. Whatever his motives, no matter how strong his Druidical commitments, either intuitively or consciously he recognizes that successfully to *further* Druidism in a satire he must fully realize the artistic end of such works: he must effectively ridicule the external objects of satire. To do this he will use whatever deficiencies of the external objects lead to their appearing most ludicrous or otherwise undesirable. If he were writing an apologue he would have to show by fictional example what is admirable about Druidism, but since the demonstration of what is admirable is irrelevant to the artistic end common to satires, it is not only possible but likely that the only clue to the satirist's Druidical commitments will lie in the fact that all the objects have been selected because he believes them to be harmful to the Druidical cause. But many of the men satirized are anti-Christians as well as anti-Druids; others are not even aware of the existence of a neo-Druidical movement, but the satirist interprets— though not in his satire—their acts or beliefs as harmful to Druidical beliefs (e.g., some of them have eloquently expressed a belief that men should not kill other men). It is very unlikely that we should learn anything of such a satirist's positive commitment to Druidism from his satire.

Our hypothetical satirist and our real satirist in accomplishing the artistic end of satires had to include their beliefs in a shape possible in such an organization. The positive shape of belief in this type of fiction is essentially limited to the negative pattern implicit in the selection of external objects. We can infer little from such a negative pattern.

The Special Demands of Apologue:
Rasselas

The organizing principle of the apologue is not an automatic consequence of an especially strong positive moral intention. An ethically discursive or irritatingly "preachy" novel may be a bad novel, but it does not become an apologue by virtue of its unformalized material. There is no reason why the writer of an apologue may not fully share with the satirist an intention to ridicule, nor any reason why he may not do so successfully. Fielding, when he wrote *Shamela*, obviously intended to ridicule *Pamela* and did so successfully by creating a splendid example of burlesque—a particular subclass or "form" of satire. But he was no less successful when, with an intention to ridicule the notion that goodness and greatness were synonymous, he managed, in his final revision of *Jonathan Wild*, to show us by a series of bitingly ironic fictional examples that it is foolish to identify goodness and greatness.

Though all works which are apologues are organized as fictional examples of a statement or a series of closely related statements, the type subsumes a great variety of forms, as different from each other as are the varieties of action which constitute the various forms of novels. The variants which define the several forms of actions are, however, quite different in kind from those which define the subtypes of apologues. These variants can and, in a full treatment of the subject, should be specified. For the purposes of this book, however, a discussion of *Rasselas* as a representative of the type should suffice.

Bertrand H. Bronson eloquently describes the special quality of the narrative progression in *Rasselas* when he remarks, "One by one, in their appointed sequence as the work moves deliberately forward, the rush-lights of hypothetical earthly happiness gleam ahead of us but, when we come close to them, gutter out and leave us in the uncertain, but not unpeopled, dark." [51] Stated in its most prosaic form, the concept obviously illustrated in *Rasselas* is that earthly happiness does not exist. Gwin J. Kolb has shown, in his penetrating study of the structure of *Rasselas*, how deft Johnson was in arranging the

---

[51] Bertrand H. Bronson, ed., *Samuel Johnson: Rasselas, Poems, and Selected Prose* (New York and Toronto: Rinehart and Co., 1958), p. xvi.

sequence of episodes: as each rush-light gutters out, we are made to feel not
merely that another single hypothetical source of human happiness has proved
illusory but rather that there is no happiness.[52] When Rasselas, in Cairo, attempts consciously to make a choice of life, for example, he associates first
with young men of spirit and gaiety who spend all their days "in a succession
of enjoyments." But when his attempt to find happiness in a life devoted to
satisfying the passions fails, Rasselas discovers a "wise and happy man" whose
wisdom—conveniently for the apologue—consists of advocating absolute sub-
jugation of the passions and whose temporary felicity is an ostensible consequence of allowing rationality its proper dominion over the lower faculties.
When the Stoic's daughter and the Stoic's "invulnerable patience" prove
equally mortal and show us that the attempt to deny the dictates of the passions
is as inefficacious a source of happiness as the attempt to satisfy them, we are
made to feel the truth of a concept that is far more general in scope than the
concept that neither Stoicism nor a life of pleasure leads to lasting contentment. Indeed, the generalization made possible simply by the juxtaposition of
the two episodes persuades us that all abstract moral dicta about the behavior
of men have only rhetorical significance and are not conducive to permanent
contentment. The fact that the "wise man's" intellectual convictions are
analogous to some Stoical tenets is less important in *Rasselas* than is the juxtaposition of men who try to find contentment by gratification of their passions
with those who are philosophically committed to subduing them. That we are
made to feel that Stoicism is an unsatisfactory doctrine is relatively trivial for
the artistic end of the apologue. When we are made to feel the inefficacy of
abstract philosophical commitments, we have gone a significant way toward
apprehending that happiness does not exist.

     The economy of means that Johnson employs to make us feel the truth
of his doctrine cannot be too much admired; by including a rhetorically forceful discussion between Rasselas and the eminently qualified guide, Imlac,
immediately before the two episodes we have discussed, Johnson is able to
use those two brief episodes to convince us of a further and still more general
truth relevant to his message. In chapter xv, just before his association "with
young men of spirit and gaiety," Rasselas insists at some length that "wisdom
surely directs us to take the least evil in the *choice of a life*." [53] Although he
is eloquent, Imlac cannot convince the prince that the "causes of good and
evil . . . are so various and uncertain, so often entangled with each other,
so diversified by various relations, and so much subject to accidents which

52 Kolb, "The Structure of Rasselas," *op. cit.* in note 11.
53 *Rasselas*, p. 542.

cannot be foreseen, that he who would fix his condition upon incontestable reasons of preference, must live and die inquiring and deliberating." [54] Rasselas claims that "my birth has given me at least one advantage over others, by enabling me to determine for myself." [55] The failure of Rasselas' two immediately subsequent investigations forcefully substantiate Imlac's contention that even absolute freedom to choose one's mode of life provides no advantage in the pursuit of a phantasmal earthly happiness.

That same deftness in ordering the elements of fiction to convince us that earthly happiness does not exist is perceived throughout *Rasselas*. Imlac's and Pekuah's tales are both narratives constructed as examples of the fruitlessness of the pursuit of happiness, but they do not merely repeat the adventures of Rasselas and his party; each of the narratives makes a direct contribution to the effectiveness with which Rasselas' quest itself convinces us of Johnson's message. Imlac's narrative helps to establish the poet as a qualified guide in the fruitless search; and, even more important, the points of Imlac's tale which Rasselas rejects and, in a sense, seeks to disprove when he insists upon undertaking his own search heighten the reader's expectations about the future course of Rasselas' "adventures," but they also limit those expectations to a concern with what Rasselas will discover about happiness while he pursues it. The reader's interest in a possible change in Rasselas' external condition or even in his moral nature as a result of his discoveries is almost entirely suppressed. The demonstration in each subsequent episode that Imlac and not Rasselas is correct sufficiently satisfies all the expectations aroused by Rasselas' initial refusal to accept the nonexistence of earthly happiness as a universal consequence of Imlac's history. Even Imlac's "Dissertation upon Poetry"—much as it may owe to Johnson's aesthetic convictions—contains precisely the elements to convince us that Imlac is an appropriate guide and it does so within three pages; Imlac is a man who has at least striven to make "Nature" his subject and "to be conversant with all that is awfully vast or elegantly little," but whose task "is to examine, not the individual, but the species." [56] The danger of this mode of establishing Imlac's claim to the virtues appropriate for a guide is that the enthusiasm and obvious pleasure he takes in describing his profession may suggest fruition too strong to be consonant with the impossibility of happiness in the universe. This Johnson handles with precision and wit by telling us *after* the description of the poet's task that "Imlac now felt the enthusiastic fit, and was proceeding to aggrandize his own profession,

[54] *Ibid.*
[55] *Ibid.*, p. 543.
[56] *Ibid.*, p. 527.

when the prince cried out, 'Enough! Thou hast convinced me, that no human being can ever be a poet.' " [57]

Or we may turn to the tale that Pekuah tells when, conveniently, she returns both alive and unraped from her Arab abductors shortly before Rasselas' party has exhausted its possible enquiries into sources of happiness in a world which, for all its Oriental setting, has offered those possibilities of contentment limited to Western culture. The addition of Pekuah's tale adequately extends the apologue to a people with a radically different form of civilization so that, as we are convinced that the passions, reason, the imagination, youth, age, philosophical commitment, and condition in life are equally barren of happiness in the "geographical" world explored by the prince, we are also convinced that these things are equally barren in all societies.

But despite the ease with which we can relate major sections of *Rasselas* to the whole on the hypothesis that it is ordered as a complicated example of the truth of the notion that earthly happiness does not exist, the organizing statement of *Rasselas* is far more complex than might at first appear. This could be shown in either of two ways: we might indicate complete episodes and elements within other episodes that cannot contribute to our feeling that happiness does not exist. Or, as I prefer to do here, we can start with a precise statement of the effect of the whole work on some readers—an effect that is not likely to result from even the most convincing proof that earthly happiness does not exist—and then turn to *Rasselas* to see if a more precise formulation of its central theme better accounts for that effect and enables us better to explain particular episodes and parts of episodes that Johnson chose to include.[58]

My own experience when reading *Rasselas* is a source of surprise to me and yet, I discover, that experience is not idiosyncratic. As each rush-light of hypothetical earthly happiness gutters out, I increasingly feel a profound sense of comfort which is not a likely result of Johnson's demonstration that there is no earthly happiness, though certainly he convinces me of this as well. It is as if he were, without my knowing how, convincing me of something quite positive with each addition to his fictional demonstration that hope is a phantom. Since the very opening sections of the apologue elicit in me that ostensibly perverse response, it cannot be a product of the first long passages which do not seem directly relevant to demonstrating that happiness is non-

[57] *Ibid.*, p. 528.

[58] Which "approach" we use is, of course, a trivial matter; I have chosen the second, since I seldom use it in this book and would like to emphasize that my attempt in this chapter is to present a theory and not a methodology or a discovery procedure.

existent, although those passage do afford insight into the subtle qualifications implicit in the previous fictional examples. The most obvious divergence from the theme that happiness does not exist is in the sequence of events in which Pekuah reveals her fear of ghosts and is allowed by the princess to forego a visit to the pyramids, with the consequence that she is abducted and the princess made temporarily miserable. Johnson does not use these events, as he might have, further to convince us that there is no human happiness but, surprisingly enough, to persuade us that human misery is itself transitory. It is on Nekayah's state of mind that Johnson concentrates. She is first "sunk down inconsolable in hopeless dejection" and blames herself for not having forced Pekuah to accompany her to the pyramids. In Imlac's remonstrance to the princess' self-accusation we might well expect some emphasis upon the notion that even action dictated by virtuous motives may have dreadful consequences, but what is emphasized far more strongly is the consolation of virtue even in face of the most unfortunate consequences:

> 'Consider, princess, what would have been your condition, if the lady Pekuah had entreated to accompany you, and, being compelled to stay in the tents, had been carried away; or how would you have born the thought, if you had forced her into the pyramid, and she had died before you in agonies of terrour.'
>
> 'Had either happened, said Nekayah, I could not have endured life till now: I should have been tortured to madness by the remembrance of such cruelty, or must have pined away in abhorrence of myself.'
>
> 'This at least, said Imlac, is the present reward of virtuous conduct, that no unlucky consequence can oblige us to repent it.' [59]

Although Nekayah refuses immediate consolation and rejects the notion that a time will come "when the image of your companion has left your thoughts," [60] we finally learn that Imlac was right:

> Nekayah, seeing that nothing was omitted for the recovery of her favourite, and having, by her promise, set her intention of retirement at a distance, began imperceptibly to return to common cares and common pleasures. She rejoiced without her own consent at the suspension of her sorrows, and sometimes caught herself with indignation in the act of turning away her mind from the remembrance of her, whom yet she resolved never to forget.[61]

If we had no more evidence than the episodes dealing with the progress of

[59] *Rasselas*, p. 576.
[60] *Ibid.*, p. 579.
[61] *Ibid.*, p. 580.

Nekayah's sorrow, we should have to modify our notion that *Rasselas* is organized as a fictional example of the truth of the statement that there is no earthly happiness. Tentatively—and still rather crudely—we may formulate the statement as follows: there is no earthly happiness, but the consequence is not unbearable human misery.

A lesser artist than Johnson might easily have exemplified such a notion by including a clear set of fictional examples showing that earthly happiness does not exist and then attempted to qualify this conviction in such subsequent episodes as those which deal with the progress of Nekayah's grief. Johnson, on the contrary, has made a set of artistic choices which, from the very beginning of *Rasselas,* contribute to a single fictional example of the now complex statement. The newly formulated statement will enable us to explain more precisely the artistic choices that Johnson made earlier. Note his emphasis, at the very outset, upon the disappointment of Rasselas' old teacher when he is unable to dissuade him from his discontent with the Happy Valley:

> At this time the sound of musick proclaimed the hour of repast, and the conversation was concluded. The old man went away sufficiently discontented to find that his reasonings had produced the only conclusion which they were intended to prevent. But in the decline of life shame and grief are of short duration; whether it be that we bear easily what we have born long, or that, finding ourselves in age less regarded, we less regard others; or, that we look with slight regard upon afflictions, to which we know that the hand of death is about to put an end.[62]

For all Rasselas' unhappiness in the Happy Valley, he is described as the "master of a secret stock of happiness" whose "load of life was much lightened," [63] ironically enough, during his preparations to flee from his "unhappy" retirement in the valley. He spends time in fruitless attempts to escape in order to find happiness, but the time thus spent "passed chearfully away." [64] And even for the unhappy inventor, the wings "which were of no use in the air, sustained him in the water." [65] Immediately after this event, Imlac comes upon the scene, tells his tale of human unhappiness, and displays in his enthusiasm the fact that he is anything but miserable. Wherever we look we find that Johnson has chosen to represent human unhappiness in terms which deftly distinguish it from unbearable misery. The worst fears about Pekuah's fate, for example, not only turn out to be unwarranted, but the tale she tells of her Arab captors is a tale not of misery but of people moderately unhappy.

[62] *Ibid.*, p. 512.
[63] *Ibid.*

[64] *Ibid.*, p. 515.
[65] *Ibid.*, p. 519.

Any complete statement of the idea that is exemplified in *Rasselas* would have to include at least the following qualifications: earthly happiness does not exist, but its absence does not result in unbearable misery in this world for the reasonably virtuous who, in addition, may turn their eyes with hope toward heaven.

Most readers of *Rasselas* will readily perceive the reasons for the additional modifications, especially if they note the arguments about human virtue and Imlac's discourse on the nature of the soul. A discussion of the first modification will suffice to show the special demands of apologue. For this type of fiction alone of the three described will careful modification of a formulated idea allow us to discuss with precision the particular artistic choices made by its creator. If we start with some general notion of the "subject" or "theme" of an apologue, we are unable to account for all the parts of the work, since these parts are relevant in a coherent apologue only to the exemplified statement or statements, formulated in their most precise shape. We may start with the statement that Johnson's "theme" in *Rasselas* is happiness. But the discriminations we can make about how Johnson accomplished the artistic end of *Rasselas* increase in number and precision if we assume that the exemplified theme of the work is that happiness does not exist. This, in turn, is less adequate for explaining Johnson's choices than is the notion that earthly happiness does not exist but that its absence does not result in unbearable human misery. The most precise formulation of the exemplified theme will enable us to make the most precise and numerous set of discriminations about the fictional examples which contribute to their controlling idea.

In contrast to this, if we attempt to account for the artistic choices of a work organized as a represented action by relating its parts to the themes that, hypothetically, they exemplify, we move from precision of statement toward the increasing vagueness of a general label. We might begin with some fairly detailed statement about war or about peace in which we presume Tolstoy would acquiesce. But as we attempted to account for more and more of the qualitative parts of the novel we could do so only by a more general statement until, finally, we would find that *all* the parts are relevant, somehow, to war and to peace, but not to any formulable idea about war and peace. This is not to deny that Tolstoy's novel will make us feel strongly about war and peace; but the necessity of stating the theme as a general subject is the surest sign that.the novel is not organized as a fictional example of the truth of a formulable statement about war and peace or, quite probably in this case, that it is not organized as the fictional example of any statement at all. This distinction between an action and an apologue is in no sense caused by a difference in complexity: the more complex the controlling themes of an apologue, the greater is the need for more precise and qualified statements of those themes. But the most elementary detective story will have "themes" as general as those of *War and Peace* and the themes in the former will be as remote from the principle which explains the choices made to accomplish its artistic end as are those of the monumental novel.

In discussing the way in which the major parts of *Rasselas* contribute to its redefined complex theme, I may inadvertently have emphasized those elements of its structure that are analogous to the structure of an argument. I should not wish to leave the impression, however, that Johnson's fine apologue is a species of philosophical dialogue.

The episodes themselves are obviously related to each other in a rhetorical order. There is no fictional "probability" that Rasselas, after he leaves the haunts of gay young men, will meet a sage committed to controlling the passions; and not only have we no expectation that the sage's daughter will die: we do not even know of her existence until she conveniently expires so that her father's empty philosophy can be exposed for the sake of the enquiring prince. Such relationships are obviously dictated by the requirements for best exemplifying the controlling theme. Probability is as irrelevant to the artistic end of *Rasselas* as consistency of character is to the artistic end of *Gulliver's Travels*. Any attempt even to suggest such probability as one might expect in the crudest action could easily destroy the coherence of the apologue. Nothing could have been simpler for Johnson than to have aroused in his reader mild apprehensions for Pekuah's danger when she is permitted to remain in her tent rather than visit the pyramids; a few words from Nekayah, while she is arguing with Pekuah, about possible marauding Arabs rumored to be in the vicinity would go far in preparing us for the lady's abduction. Since Johnson was not writing a crude action but a highly sophisticated apologue, arousing any serious apprehension about the fate of Pekuah would have been artistically undesirable: the moment that our interest focuses on Pekuah's fate, the vitally important contribution made by the description of Nekayah's journey through sorrow becomes impossible; even that sorrow does not make us nearly so concerned for the princess' well-being as it interests us in the question of whether Imlac's predictions about Nature's healing powers or Nekayah's insistence on the permanence of her grief will be justified. Equally important, if we become strongly concerned with what is happening to Pekuah, she cannot return to tell a tale perfectly calculated to show us that the Arabs, like the former residents of the Happy Valley, lead moderately unhappy but quite bearable lives; if the expectations raised are analogous to those aroused in actions, they can never be satisfied by a perfectly organized part of an apologue. Whatever our ethical prejudices in such matters, had Johnson introduced the kinds of expectations which are a consequence of establishing probability, then artistically if not morally Pekuah would have been better off undone by Arabs than she is as the unharmed narrator of her own little apologue.

Despite these strictures, it is clear that *within* any one of the exemplary episodes Johnson's task was to increase our interest in the agents of apologue to the greatest degree possible short of obscuring the relation of the episode to the controlling theme. To the extent that he failed to do this, his fictional example would be unconvincing; to the extent that he went one step over the line and made our interest in the relationship of characters in the episodes stronger than our interest in what the episode exemplifies, then, no matter how convincing the episode was "artistically," it could no longer convince us of the truth of the now-obscured statement. In fact, if he stepped over the line, we would be thoroughly disenchanted with subsequent episodes which did not satisfy our interest in the relationship of characters; though, if Johnson were to satisfy such expectations, he would necessarily have written an action and the world would have been the poorer by one powerful apologue.

These general statements may seem clearer if we recall the problem of the Stoic. The Stoic's loss of his daughter leaves him grief stricken. The effectiveness of this episode as a part of the apologue depends upon Johnson's ability to make us *feel* that against the impetus of strong and genuine passion high-flown moral commitment is powerless. But he cannot make us feel this unless he also makes us believe momentarily in the genuine power of the Stoic's grief; if he cannot do this, he may convince us irrelevantly only of the Stoic's pretentiousness and not of the gross inefficacy of abstract moral commitment in eliciting happiness. But he may not so portray the Stoic's grief that it arouses our sympathy and turns our attention, as it would in an action, to Rasselas' personal—as opposed to intellectual—relationship with the unhappy teacher; if it had this effect, we should expect the subsequent episodes either to reform or to punish the prince for his unfeeling response to misery.

Negatively, some of the elements which prevent our reacting to the episode as an action are obvious. First, the rhetorical order of all the previous episodes establishes strong expectations that this episode too will be an example of the nonexistence of earthly happiness; we are predisposed to interpret all relationships as examples of the theme Johnson has suggested in his invocation to all "who listen with credulity to the whispers of fancy, and persue with eagerness the phantoms of hope," and which he has further developed in the Happy Valley. Second, the dead daughter is not merely traitless; she has not existed in *Rasselas* until after her convenient death. Third, the Stoic himself has (with an exception discussed below) revealed no traits before his daughter's death except those directly relevant to the rhetorical force with which he propounds his doctrine.

These factors allow Johnson considerable leeway in emphasizing the genuineness of the rhetorician's grief without grave danger of unduly interesting readers in his fate. Somewhat less obvious but at least equally important is Imlac's reaction to the prince's attachment to "the wise and happy" man:

> 'I have found, said the prince at his return to Imlac, a man who can teach all that is necessary to be known, who, from the unshaken throne of rational fortitude, looks down on the scenes of life changing beneath him. He speaks, and attention watches his lips. He reasons, and conviction closes his periods. This man shall be my future guide: I will learn his doctrines, and imitate his life.'
>
> 'Be not too hasty, said Imlac, to trust, or to admire, the teachers of morality: they discourse like angels, but they live like men.' [66]

The attention Johnson has previously devoted to establishing Imlac as guide is justified by the weight his predictions carry in all subsequent incidents. What is most important about Imlac's prediction at this moment is its generality; he does not even know that Rasselas gave the Stoic a purse of gold, which, most unstoically, he received "with a mixture of joy and wonder." Since the genuineness of the wise man's grief is conveyed by careful contrast to the spuriousness of his moral dicta, it is absolutely necessary that we regard his meretricious pretensions as typical of "teachers of morality," since for purposes of the apologue the pretensions of a single moralist are irrelevant. Imlac's brief rejoinder at once reinforces our propensity to find in the episode only its thematic contribution—i.e., we expect to see Imlac's pronouncement justified—and prevents us from interpreting the seer's spuriousness as idiosyncratic.

We may turn now to Johnson's artistry in portraying the moralist's grief. Rasselas is attracted to the moralist when he discourses publicly "with great energy on the government of the passions." The stylistic clue implicit in Johnson's deft "with great energy" as the primary characteristic of the discourse makes the speaker immediately suspect. The suspicion is reinforced by

[66] *Ibid.*, p. 546.

a description of his virtues as those relevant to rhetoric rather than to morality: "His look was venerable, his action graceful, his pronunciation clear, and his diction elegant." [67] But the summary of his lecture which expounds the virtues of "invulnerable patience" does make it seem forceful; when Rasselas asks the privilege of visiting him and he hesitates until the prince presses upon him the purse of gold (which he accepts "with a mixture of joy and wonder"), the contradiction between the moralist's rhetorically forceful professions and his passionate reaction makes the former seem obvious sham. It is then that Rasselas speaks to Imlac, who, by his short pronouncement, defines all teachers of morality as mere rhetoricians. And it is only then that Johnson disposes of the convenient daughter and allows Rasselas his final confrontation with the bereaved moralist, whom he is not allowed to see until he bribes a servant. The necessity for the bribe is a convenient reminder of the specious virtue of the teacher of morality, and, by contrast, the picture of his grief is made more striking. His final words in answer to Rasselas' attempt to console him by philosophical argument are devoid of rhetorical flourishes and, as they strike the only genuine note he sounds in the whole episode, seem momentarily convincing and even powerful: "What comfort, said the mourner, can truth and reason afford me? Of what effect are they now, but to tell me, that my daughter will not be restored?" [68] As a result the reader, as well as Rasselas, is fully convinced of "the inefficacy of polished periods and studied sentences." [69]

Throughout *Rasselas*, the ways in which Johnson succeeds in realizing fictional effects which emphasize rather than obscure the relationship of any part to his controlling theme are varied and impressive indeed, especially since he does not have the freedom of the satirist to attribute any traits he wishes to his agents whenever it is convenient. Swift can make Gulliver seem constantly vivid and alive, for he can invest him with a new set of lively traits at almost any point in the satire. But though Johnson may at points ascribe new traits to the major characters of the apologue (e.g., Pekuah's fear of ghosts), consistency does play a role in their creation. Imlac cannot perform his role as guide if he exhibits intellectual traits inconsistent with those which qualified him for the role in the first place. And yet, though characters must be consistent, they may never reveal traits which commit them to acts or relationships extraneous to the controlling theme. What is revealed about any major

[67] *Ibid.*, p. 544.
[68] *Ibid.*, p. 546.
[69] *Ibid.*, p. 547.

character is, almost of necessity and almost ruthlessly, limited to qualities directly required for their role in the apologue.[70] Nekayah is sufficiently sisterly to wish to accompany Rasselas, sufficiently feminine to explore the possibilities of domestic felicity, sufficiently intelligent to report her findings accurately, and sufficiently kind to grieve over her lost friend. Such traits are, of course, highly general, though they may also be very numerous. The feeling of generality is increased to the extent that the rhetorical relationship of episodes prevents us from inferring particular traits of characters from their relationship with others: Rasselas' contempt for the meretricious teacher of morality does not reveal his emotional reaction to human suffering.

These factors make *Rasselas* a very bad novel, for in writing it Johnson brilliantly satisfied the special demands of apologue. Though it is the inalienable right of any reader to prefer the virtues of novels, it is unreasonable to ask why Johnson did not write a novel which was also an apologue; even he could not do the impossible.

The shape of belief in apologue is obviously defined mainly by the themes exemplified, though we make at least minimal inferences from the examples as well. Unlike the writer of satire, the writer of an apologue is called upon to reveal by fictional example his positive beliefs—which may explain why many writers of prose fiction whose primary intention is to ridicule nevertheless choose to embody their intention in apologue rather than satire. Though both the organizing principle and the artistic demands of apologue suggest the obvious relation between the writer's ethical beliefs, opinions, and prejudices and the form he creates, it is important to interpret that relationship with care. For in an apologue, more than in either of the other two types, the writer is called upon to proclaim his formulated, long-range commitments rather than to reveal a pattern of intuitive judgments. Here he may don his public mask and present us with an ethical image of himself which, if sincere, is nevertheless partial. The limitation imposed by the particular themes he exemplifies in his work is still further straitened by the ease with which he may set his house in order for guests who have, after all, no legitimate concern with how much dust lies under the profound pattern of the Oriental rug.

---

[70] Some forms of apologues—e.g., *Jonathan Wild* and *Candide*—make more use than *Rasselas* does of the qualities which impart vividness to characters, but impose other kinds of restrictions to suppress the expectations appropriate only in actions. The general postulation that the job of the writer of apologue is to maximize our interest in the agents to the greatest degree possible short of obscuring the relation of any episode to its controlling theme is applicable to all forms of apologue.

More Durable Than Brass

Specifying the artistic demands peculiar to satire and apologue, respectively, proves less intricate than explaining the shape of belief in fictions organized as actions. The remainder of this book is devoted to such explanation and to an intensive illustration of that shape especially as it is realized in Fielding's novels. The task is simplified when we understand that the shape of belief in actions cannot be the pattern of ridiculed objects peculiar to satire or the exemplified thematic statement of apologue. We may legitimately expect to discern the shape peculiar to beliefs in actions as some special element or combination of elements which either may or must be included in order to accomplish the artistic end common to actions. From the moment that we conceive of a novelist's beliefs as having a possible formal significance in his novels, we have postulated those beliefs as qualitative parts of his works. If his novel is coherent, then the writer's relevant beliefs, like all other qualitative parts, must be subordinate to the artistic end which informs the work.

I began the previous section by a stricture against interpreting as apologues all works which exhibit strong moral intentions. The positive counterpart to that stricture is that works which exhibit no moral intentions and works in which a moral intention is primary may both be organized as actions.

We have discussed *Pamela* as a coherent action and not, despite its subtitle, as a fictional example of a truth about virtue rewarded. It is extremely difficult to disprove a supposition only presumed to be a theory; negatively, all I can legitimately say is that I am unable—and I know of no published critique which has been able—to relate all the parts of *Pamela* to any statement or series of statements more precise than "virtue rewarded." Such identification of a form with a title or subtitle in no way permits us to account for the artistic choices Richardson made to create a coherent and reasonably effective work; any principle of coherence which does not help us to understand the contributions of all the parts to the whole is not a theory of coherence at all.

Positively, in contrast, when we conceive of *Pamela* as a work which introduces characters, about whom we are made to care, in unstable relationships which are further complicated and finally resolved by removal of the represented instability, we can explain with considerable precision how Richardson employed the variables possible in actions to create a work which is a coherent and effective form of a represented action. Note how the complicated revelations in the first two letters make sense from the moment we conceive of *Pamela* as an action. Clearly revealed in the first letter is an initial instability caused by the death of Pamela's mistress and frank admission of the undesirability of Pamela's returning to her parents, partially because of their indigence, but more significantly because she has been "qualified above my degree" so that "it was not every family that could have found a place that your poor Pamela was fit for." The threat to Pamela's invaluable place caused by her mistress' death is immediately dispelled by her mistress' death-bed insistence that Mr. B. "remember my poor Pamela," and the clear indication that he will do so; she, in turn, regards him as "the best of gentlemen."

But the motherly recommendation has also called special attention to Pamela and, with the discovery of her letter, Mr. B. possesses knowledge of her virtue, her superiority to a common servant, and, perhaps most important, her overflowing gratitude to him for his concern. With the discovery of the letter, too, Pamela engages in the first of a series of ambiguous acts, themselves innocent in origin, which nevertheless exhibit how strongly attracted she is to Mr. B., and which may easily be interpreted as counters in a game of seduction:

> I have been scared out of my senses; for just now, as I was folding up this letter in my late lady's dressing-room, in comes my young master! How was I frightened! I went to hide the letter in my bosom; and he seeing me tremble, said, smiling, 'To whom have you been writing, Pamela?' I said, in my confusion, 'Pray, your honour, forgive me!—only to my father and mother.' He said, 'Well, then, let me see how you are come on in your writing.' O how ashamed I was! He took it, without saying more, and read it through, and then gave it me again; and I said, 'Pray, your honour, forgive me!' Yet I know not for what . . .[71]

Stowing things in one's bosom and demonstrating obvious signs of unmotivated embarrassment may have innocent enough explanations, but they are quite likely to arouse erotic interest in the stower as well.

The second letter is from Pamela's parents; with its arrival our fears for Pamela's virtue are definitely aroused, and our suspicion of Mr. B.'s motives increased. But two other elements are introduced: first, the undesirability of Pamela's losing her virtue is emphasized as even more disastrous than the unpleasant alternative of returning home and thereby relinquishing her slight hold on the only "world" in which she is fit to live; second, her parents' fears are not concerned primarily with Pamela's being raped but with her being willing to reward Mr. B. "with that jewel, your virtue" out of gratitude. There can be no clearer answer to those of Richardson's critics who

[71] Samuel Richardson, *Pamela* (New York: E. P. Dutton and Co., 1949), p. 2.

accuse him of unconsciously including those elements which make *Pamela* seem flirtatious than that on the third page of the novel Pamela's parents see more explicitly than the reader has that their daughter is dangerously "full of *joy* at his goodness, so *taken* by his kind expressions . . . that we *fear*— yes, my dear child, we *fear*—you should be *too* grateful."

It is no exaggeration to say that, after the fourth page of *Pamela*, Richardson could not have written an apologue. When we view *Pamela* as an action, we can easily explain why a substantial section of the tale is represented as occurring after Pamela and Mr. B. decide on marriage: the represented instability of the relationships among all the characters is not removed by the marriage but, instead, new elements of instability result from it. Both Pamela and Mr. B. have formed important sets of relationships with the servants who love Pamela and those who have attempted to abet Mr. B. Both hero and heroine have formed significant relationships with Parson Williams. Both have significant relationships with Lady Davers and with the local gentry who refused to aid Pamela in her distress but who are Mr. B.'s friends and are now to be her own. Both Pamela's and Mr. B.'s relationships with these characters must be resolved if we are to feel that the action is complete, but, in fact, they are further complicated by the marriage. The relationship between the two main characters cannot be stabilized without the resolution of the other relationships. Since Pamela and her husband have revealed a whole set of traits which provoke grave doubts that their marriage will result in a permanently satisfactory state, Pamela actually changes more significantly in the final section of the novel than she does before the change in her external condition. The removal of all represented instability is impossible without such strong indications as Pamela's mixed reactions to the written set of marital injunctions presented to her on the sixth day of their marriage. Her reactions enable us to feel that she can at once love Mr. B. and still retain her own personality and integrity as a human being. Many of the injunctions seem to Pamela just and admirable, but the terms of her future relationship with Mr. B. are partially defined by such remarks as the following: "*Well, I'll remember it, I warrant. But yet I think this rule is almost peculiar to himself.*" [72] Or, "*Good Sirs, I don't know what to say to this! It looks a little hard, methinks! This would bear a small debate, I fancy, in a parliament of women.*" [73]

[72] *Ibid.*, p. 406.

[73] *Ibid.*, p. 408. If one considers the extent to which *Pamela* is a successful innovation, it is not surprising that it is somewhat flawed. The unstable relationships are not resolved when Pamela willingly returns to Mr. B. nor when she becomes his wife. But

But if *Pamela* is organized as an action, what has happened to Richardson's moral intention? Is his ethical commitment limited to his strictures at the end of the novel about the moral applications "which naturally result from the story and characters"? We may, I think, more fruitfully turn to the possibilities implicit in a task Richardson actually had to perform to accomplish the artistic end of his novel. Obviously, he had to make us feel that Pamela was essentially virtuous and deserving of reasonable contentment. But to do this, he had to make us feel also that her return to her parents was only slightly less desirable than her being raped. Less obvious, but equally important, if his novel were to be effective at all he had to portray Mr. B.'s attempts to rape Pamela as monstrous acts but—and here his job was difficult indeed—he also had to make certain that we did not feel that Mr. B. was a monster, since the effect of his work depended completely on his ability to make us desire a marriage between the two. To put this in a more general form: Richardson had to control our reactions to the characters, their acts and thoughts, at every stage of the work with considerable precision if he were to write a coherent action.

In order to move from a statement of particular tasks to a hypothesis about the shape of belief in novels, we may call upon the intellectual assistance of David Hume:

> The poet's *monument more durable than brass*, must fall to the ground like common brick or clay, were men to make no allowance for the continual revolutions of manners and customs, and would admit of nothing but what was suitable for the prevailing fashion. . . . But where the ideas of morality and decency alter from one age to another, and where vicious manners are described, without being marked with the proper characters of blame and disapprobation; this must be allowed to disfigure the poem, and to be a real deformity.[74]

The problem Hume raises about the extent to which a literary work may be judged good if it departs from a high standard of morality is not germane to this chapter, but those "proper characters of blame and disapprobation" are directly relevant. In delineating the subclasses of comic, tragic, and serious actions, we found it necessary to rely on some notion of the relationship between a character's represented ethical desert and the rewards he reaps

---

the synthesizing power *is* exhausted in the representation of the marriage. Had Richardson ended his novel at that point, the whole would have seemed incomplete. Though the final section—especially the auspicious solution of the problem of Sally Godfrey—deftly resolves the action, it is anticlimactic and detracts from the novel's effectiveness.

[74] David Hume, "Of the Standard of Taste." Quoted here from *Criticism*, ed. Schorer, Miles, McKenzie (New York: Harcourt, Brace and Co., 1958), p. 448.

at the end. The crudest cowboy and Indian tale must make us feel that the cowboys are good and the Indians are bad. Despite immediate appearances, the fact that one character is a cowboy and the other an Indian is not sufficient to discriminate between those who deserve to be shot and those who deserve to ride off into the sunset; the ease with which the cowboys are transformed into the bad men in equally crude literary works is attested to by the spate of noble savages and avaricious whites who have left their eighteenth-century haunts to re-infest our popular entertainments. More subtle writers—A. B. Guthrie, for example—have been able to show both whites and Indians as ethically mixed, *but* they had to "mark" them with more subtle but still comprehensible "characters of blame and disapprobation" or of approbation too. To put this in another way, a novelist not merely may but must subtly control our feelings about the characters, acts, and thoughts represented at each stage of the novel if it is to have a coherent effect. In turn, what we feel about the characters, acts, and thoughts represented in a coherent action depends primarily on the way in which they are revealed to us. We may not, of course, react as the "marks" suggest we do. Some people believe it would be desirable if Fielding's Amelia did not recover when she faints for what seems like the ten-thousandth time; others feel foiled each time Mr. B. falls short of success in an attempt to rape Pamela. But such readers, invariably, are also aware that some sort of mark or signal present in the work indicates that they are supposed to regard the fainting fits as charming and exemplary and the attempted rapes as less than admirable.

Such signals of evaluation in any action are a complicated matter indeed. Formal variables which affect our reactions to characters, their acts and thoughts include the author's choices of diction when he describes the activities and thoughts of his characters, the point of view from which a character is presented, the effect of any act upon those characters with whom our sympathies have already been identified. In short, they consist of a host of possible combinations of stylistic, rhetorical, and structural elements which can be summed up in the phrase "devices of disclosure." [75]

To turn to the question asked at the very outset of this chapter, we can begin now at least to see how, in the very act of performing the tasks necessary for a good "history," Fielding might have been able to implement his "sincere endeavor . . . to recommend goodness and innocence" so successfully as to elicit from a man like Coleridge the remark that one could not emerge

[75] I use this phrase much as it is used by Elder Olson in "William Empson, Contemporary Criticism, and Poetic Diction," *Critics and Criticism* (Chicago: University of Chicago Press, 1952), p. 71.

from reading those novels "without an intense conviction that he could not be guilty of a base act." Since each of Fielding's three major novels has a rather wide scope, and since, though their forms may differ in other respects, the effectiveness of each depends heavily upon the efficiency with which it controls our feelings toward the characters, their acts, and their thoughts, Fielding has been forced, as it were, by the artistic end of each action to convey richly varied judgments on each page by means of devices of disclosure.

It becomes possible now to investigate as a probability the notion that the novelist's beliefs, opinions, and prejudices are expressed in the judgments he conveys of his characters, their actions, and their thoughts; to use other terms, they are expressed as Hume's formal "marks"—the signals—which persuade his readers to react to those characters, their acts, and their thoughts in a manner consonant with the artistic end to which all elements in his work are subordinate.

But therein lie two enormous rubs. Presumably one stage of our investigation will necessitate isolating the signals themselves, but the practical difficulties of recovering all relevant devices which convey particular judgments are enormous. We might, for example, find ourselves inadequately treating some of the variables responsible for a single judgment in *Joseph Andrews* as follows: the narrator condemns from behind an ironic mask a character whose action he really approves after that character's act has been approved by another character of whom the narrator, as straight commentator, has disapproved and of whom, as ironic commentator, he has approved. This way madness lies. Though a general proposition that the ethical content of novels, as opposed to apologues or satires, is to be found in formal signals of evaluation may still be true, the critical utility of recognizing that truth is seriously compromised. We should still be unable to make useful discriminations among the ethical effects of different novels and even less likely to make them for all the parts within any single novel. We must be able to find a short cut, even though the same short cut may not be equally applicable to all subforms of actions. In Fielding's novels we will discover that various combinations of classes of ethical agents actually indicate the presence of specifiable kinds of value judgments. The agents, classified according to the roles they play in conveying judgments, can be recognized by an extremely limited number of devices of disclosure, and even extremely subtle judgments can be differentiated by reference to them. It is probable that the total range of utilized devices will be more directly responsible for conveying any subtle judgment, but a combination of agents is sufficient to predict what the devices convey.

Since the ability to define such classes of agents seems to depend directly on the necessity for redundant signals in any comic action, *some* set of classes of agents can probably be found to provide a similar short cut to evaluations in any comic action. If a novelist has made us care about the fates of his agents, there must be a point soon after the beginning of any comic novel at which an act or thought represented as an unwarranted threat to what we have been made to regard as a character's ethical desert will arouse our hostility. The presence of such agents in comic action is the assured consequence of the novelist's leading us *both* to expect and to desire that the unstable relationships will terminate in rewards suitable to the "marked" ethical merits of his represented characters. But when we begin to differentiate such agents in a given novel, we have departed from a concern with demands common to all novelists or even to all writers of comic actions: we are now in that dangerous area in which knowledge that a creature is mammal, *Homo sapiens*, female, and blonde is insufficient; we want to know the special rewards and difficulties which would result from living with her.

A simple list of the descriptive titles of the agents which combine to ensure judgments in Fielding's novels will suffice to indicate at this point how special are the possible combinations: "split commentators"; "fallible paragons"; "nondiscursive female paragons"; "species characters," which, in their more important forms, become "walking concepts"; narrators of digressive tales about their own lives, especially the "strayed lambs" and the "demi-reps"; "male heroes as occasionally privileged commentators"; "those characters who, though carefully evaluated, play only a minor role in evaluating others." Such special classes are not only what we might expect but what we must desire if the general theory is to justify itself in particular discriminations that help us to see what makes the ethical effect of *Tom Jones* the ethical effect of *Tom Jones* and not of *Emma,* that help us to understand what makes Fielding Fielding and Jane Austen something else again.

But now for the other rub. The task undertaken in this book is not simply that of accounting for the ethical effects of novels, but of relating such effects to the beliefs, opinions, and prejudices of novelists, and the theory advanced at this point is completely ambiguous regarding the status of the signals which a novelist must include if he is to accomplish his artistic end. The artistic end, it is obvious, may very well dictate not merely the inclusion of signals but *what* is "being marked with the proper characters of blame and disapprobation." A minimal test of whether we have in fact established a relationship between novelists' beliefs and their novels is whether the following intricate question may be asked with a reasonable presumption of an answer:

What must this novelist have believed to have evaluated characters, acts, and thoughts in such a manner in such a work? If our answer is "nothing," it is a certain sign that, no matter how accurate our description of the signals and their roles in actions, we have established no positive relationship between the ethical beliefs of novelists and their novels. If artistic considerations could have exerted pressure upon Fielding, for example, to make insincere judgments, our answer to the question will be "nothing." If the artistic end of actions is of such a nature that it limits the range of judgments to the most obvious situations, our answer may be "next to nothing." If some conceivable conscious aesthetic *intention*, rather than an artistic end, may exert serious influence on a novelist to compromise or even severely to limit his ethical predilections, our answer may be "worse than nothing." Or, finally, if a given sincere moral intention may be used to *predict* the artistic end of the work, discovery of such an intention may prevent us from asking the question at all since it is applicable to represented actions alone and not to satires or apologues of any variety; we might then have to drop the notion that "actions" in the sense that we have defined them exist at all.

But if we can show that such a question may justifiably be asked with a reasonable expectation of a valid response, in answering it we will, in effect, have converted aesthetically sufficient signals of authorial judgments into ethical statements without danger of distorting the novels, or of rewriting them as apologue or satire, so that we may discuss the novelist's beliefs. The ability to ask and to answer such questions would show that we had established a positive relationship between artistic belief and literary form. Though this clearly has implications for biography and the history of ideas, the end of this book is not to write a biography of Fielding or other novelists, but only to show by a number of means that the question may justifiably be asked and answered—to show its feasibility as a necessary part of a theory about a positive relationship between belief and literary form. This end alone dictates discussion of such problems as the relation of intention and ethical predilection to the dictates of literary form.

But this chapter, intricate as it is, has already performed or failed to perform its own difficult though necessarily dusky task: it has articulated the skeleton of the theory advanced in the whole book. The remainder of this work is occupied with the less onerous task of putting flesh and then clothing upon the bare bones so that they will not rattle. To this end we will proceed to deal in detail and at great length with the subtle and artistically successful judgments conveyed through appropriate signals in the wonderfully rich and, for our purposes, suitably complex novels of Henry Fielding. These will provide an excellent test of the general theory advanced in this chapter; they contain such complicating factors as frequent digressions; though all are comic novels, each one maximizes a very different particular power; the moral content of the works as well as the sincerity of Fielding's moral intentions has been disputed. We shall see what light our theory is able to shed on these matters.

Only then, with our skeleton fully fleshed, will we turn to a careful definition of the status of those "appropriate marks" of approbation and disapprobation to show that they are, indeed, adequate reflections of a novelist's ethical being.

Thus clothed, the bony articulation of this chapter will, I hope, seem more comfortable, and its concluding statement, if still theoretical, will nevertheless seem much more than idle speculation.

The ethical beliefs, opinions, and prejudices of novelists do not shape their novels, but rather have a discernible and vital shape within those novels. An awareness of that shape has important implications for literary criticism, for literary history, and for the many humanistic pursuits that depend upon a relationship between the two.

Chapter Two

From Comment to
Structure

The Split Commentator

This chapter does not exhaust the topic of the narrator's function in Fielding's work, or even in *Joseph Andrews,* the novel chosen for close study. It is concerned primarily with delineating those structural devices, especially ethical agents, capable of conveying judgments crucial to the power realized in each of Fielding's novels. It is necessary, however, to consider the complex character of the narrator, for initially his comments control our attitudes toward characters who usurp evaluative tasks which were originally solely his own; his subsequent comments convey judgments either independently or, far more frequently, in concert with his creations.

In *Joseph Andrews* we first meet the narrator in his role as explicit commentator. Throughout the first chapter, he maintains this role consistently, yet with surprising complexity considering the brevity of the chapter. The complexity is the result of the ironic tone, of the subtle and rapid movement from serious to ironic comment and back again—in short, the result of the fact that, as explicit commentator, the narrator plays two roles almost simultaneously. He is free to, and does, assume the role of either serious or ironic commentator throughout the novel. He can, within certain limitations, drop or assume either at will. The nearly simultaneous use of both roles is typically reserved for special occasions once the pattern is established. As the novel progresses we have many structural clues as to which role he is playing, but in the beginning we have only rhetorical clues to rely on.

The first two paragraphs seem serious enough and there is no reason to doubt that they are. The sentiments are commonplaces not only of Fielding's time but of Fielding's writings, both earlier and later:[1] examples work more forcibly on the mind than precepts; the writer, in describing good men, does a service to mankind by communicating a valuable pattern to the world.

In the third paragraph, however, the serious commentator begins to smile, to introduce us to the burlesque element of the novel. He begins seriously

[1] Nevertheless, Fielding was not always convinced that a worthy example was rhetorically effective. See *The Complete Works of Henry Fielding,* ed. William Ernest Henley (London: William Heinemann, 1903), XV, 330.

enough by praising biographies that give patterns of worthy persons to the world—but then, ostensibly with a straight face, takes unmistakable pot shots at his own age, partially by donning the mask of ignorance and identifying himself with the ignorance of his own times. He admires not only contemporary biographers but also "those ancient writers which of late days are little read, being written in obsolete, and, as they are generally thought, *unintelligible languages* such as Plutarch, Nepos, *and others which I heard of in my youth.*" [2]

We are immediately put on guard by the author's professing ignorance of standard works in a field about which he has been discoursing more or less learnedly for two paragraphs and by the qualification of the ancient languages as "unintelligible." Our "guard" will extend tentatively to the writers in English discussed in the context of assumed ignorance. (The commentator's first two paragraphs prevent our assuming that his ignorance is real and it is important that they do, since, if the narrator cannot be trusted, if we laugh at instead of with him, his function as direct ethical commentator is destroyed. We cannot then take his word for anything and in *Joseph Andrews*[3] we must take his word for a good deal.)

In his description of works in English which are "finely calculated to sow the seeds of virtue in youth, and very easy to be comprehended by persons of moderate capacity," [4] Fielding reinforces our "suspicion" of the works in English that ostensibly fit the formula of the first two paragraphs as they relate to "biography." Knowledge of the works themselves helps, of course, to emphasize the disparity between the exemplary virtue of the first two paragraphs, the romantic, perhaps childish, virtue of John the Great, etc., and the false virtue of Cibber's *Apology* and of *Pamela*. But if we had no knowledge of these works, the commentator's position would still be relatively clear because of the terms in which he describes the "biographies": ". . . John the Great, who, by his brave and heroic actions against men of *large and athletic bodies* . . . . that of an earl of Warwick, *whose Christian name was Guy.* . . . " [5]

In his last two paragraphs the commentator can, from one point of view,

---

[2] Henley, I, 25-26 (*Joseph Andrews*, I, i). Italics mine.

[3] For an excellent discussion of the narrator in Fielding's works see Wayne C. Booth, "The Self-Conscious Narrator in Comic Fiction before *Tristram Shandy*," *PMLA*, LXVII (1952), 163-185. Booth attributes some judgments solely to the narrator which I believe are conveyed by other agents in conjunction with him.

[4] Henley, I, 26 (*Joseph Andrews*, I, i).

[5] *Ibid*. Italics mine.

play it straight. His encomiums on *Pamela* and Cibber cannot be mistaken for real compliments, even though there is no stylistic indication that the commentator does not mean for us to take him seriously. The very incongruity of the comparisons is a clear signal to the reader: the works of Plutarch and Nepos (written in "unintelligible languages") are compared with *John the Great* and *Guy of Warwick* (exemplifying virtues such as "heroic actions against men of large and athletic bodies"), which are, in turn, compared with the *Apology* and *Pamela*.

With our present knowledge of Fielding and his attitudes toward Cibber and the early Richardson, it is easy to assume that the burlesque element is self-explanatory, that the exaggerated encomiums on the two works would automatically appear ridiculous to Fielding's contemporaries. This, of course, is not true. The *Pamela* hailed from the pulpit itself, the widely read autobiography of the poet laureate, were ridiculous only to some of the wits of the time. Fielding himself, in his letter to Richardson, was later to praise *Clarissa* in terms as laudatory as those he uses mockingly here in reference to *Pamela*.

We might assume that the effect of Pamela on Joseph, as described in the last paragraph, is innately funny; that it was, especially for the eighteenth century, ludicrous in itself for a young man "to preserve his purity in the midst of such great temptations" by "keeping the excellent pattern of his sister's virtues before his eyes." [6] There is no evidence, however, that an eighteenth-century audience found it necessary to snicker at Malcolm when he announces to Macduff as one of the virtues that will fit him for kingship the fact that he is "yet unknown to woman." Shakespeare's treatment of Malcolm is, of course, quite different from Fielding's treatment of Joseph, but that is essentially the point. It is the treatment of a general situation, its particularization, that tickles our risibility or stimulates our admiration, seldom the situation *per se*. We do not necessarily laugh *because* a man named Joseph Andrews is maintaining his purity against odds; we are inclined to laugh, even before we meet him, at Joseph Andrews' attempt to maintain his purity because a narrator acting in a subtly defined role as ironic commentator has already affected our attitude toward the pattern on which the as yet uncharacterized young man has molded himself.

A contemporary reader of *Joseph Andrews* would not automatically find a species of high comedy or farce in the following: "And she caught him by his garment, saying, Lie with me: and he left his garment in her hand and fled and got him out." Some might very well disagree with the Biblical atti-

---

[6] *Ibid.*, p. 27 (*Joseph Andrews*, I, i).

tude toward Joseph's action, but their disagreement implies that a scheme of values was implicit in the Biblical narrative; they know what judgments have been conveyed, though they do not share them.

Our introductory impression of the book is of great importance, for it establishes our attitudes toward the characters we are to meet—including our attitude toward that elusive and protean Narrator. Still more important, the pattern by means of which the commentator has tentatively conveyed certain generalized value judgments (Joseph Andrews' attempt to preserve his purity is amusing) is a recurrent pattern. The serious comment juxtaposed to the ironic comment becomes important at many places in the novel. Still in Book I, for example, though far along in it, at a point at which the burden of conveying judgments is no longer solely the narrator's, we find the pattern repeated. Here it is used in a situation with which the structural devices which have already usurped parts of the narrator's evaluative prerogative cannot cope. The last two chapters in Book I deal in part with Mrs. Tow-wouse's discovery of her timid husband in bed with the chambermaid, Betty, who has submitted to Mr. Tow-wouse only because Joseph's virtue will not allow him to allay the desire he has aroused. The situation, treated essentially as farce, leads to no really disastrous results, partially because of Parson Adams' physically restraining the indignant wife. At the end of chapter xvii, the incident concluded, the narrator begins to reassume his role as serious commentator:

> Mrs. Tow-wouse, at the intercession of Mr. Adams, and finding the enemy vanished, began to compose herself, and at length recovered the usual serenity of her temper, in which we will leave her, to open to the reader the steps which led to a catastrophe, common enough, and comical enough too, perhaps, in modern history, yet often fatal to the repose and well-being of families, and the subject of many tragedies, both in life and on the stage.[7]

In chapter xviii, the last of Book I, the serious (though far from lugubrious) commentator becomes an apologist for Betty, toward whom the reader is already sympathetic as a result of her kind treatment of Joseph. The danger is not that the reader will condemn Betty but that, because of the sympathy already aroused in her behalf, the antagonism already directed at Mrs. Tow-wouse, the tendency to reverse the apparent prudish values of the chapters in which *Pamela* is ridiculed,[8] and the farcical manner in which the scene of adultery is treated, the reader will feel no need of apology for Betty's action.

---

[7] *Ibid.*, p. 99 (I, xvii).

[8] The sense in which these chapters are "burlesque" is clarified below.

He may accept it as a direct antidote to the prudery mocked in the London chapters and feel that sexual incontinence, including adultery, is to be regarded in *Joseph Andrews* as relatively commendable. Fielding's problem is more complex than may appear on the surface: he must partially counteract the implications of the ludicrous treatment of the scene without spoiling the fun he has been having at Richardson's expense and without reversing the negative judgment (already conveyed) about overindulgence in chastity.

R. S. Crane has clearly shown how Fielding uses the narrator in *Tom Jones* as one device to maintain a comic tone at moments when our "original comic detachment may give way, temporarily, to tragi-comic feelings of fear, pity, and indignation." [9] In *Joseph Andrews,* the artistic problem is frequently the converse of this. Most often it is scene, as in Betty's discovery in *flagrante delicto,* that is treated as farce; it is, then, the serious commentator, if the commentator is the device used, who must "rescue" his values and keep us from being misled by the tone of the incident portrayed. A series of such "rescues" subtly alters the power of *Joseph Andrews* from mere farce; instead, permanent social and ethical deficiencies, represented as ludicrous, are seen first to delay the expected comic rewards of Joseph, Fanny, and Adams, and, in turn, to be defeated when the relations of all major characters are stabilized.

Though Parson Adams acting as "paragon" can do this without the help of the commentator in certain situations, and has already done so in his dispute with Barnabas, Fielding would have to make him step completely out of character to use him in this manner here. While it is perfectly in character for the good man to restrain Mrs. Tow-wouse in her attempt to mangle the erring Betty, and to calm her down, the very lack of knowledge of the world ascribed to him by the narrator would make it impossible for Adams to present, in discussion with Joseph Andrews or one of the "walking concepts," the sociological explanation which serves as apologia—not absolute justification—for Betty's action. To put such an apologia in Adams' mouth would certainly prevent Fielding from effectively laughing good-naturedly at Adams later when he displays that ignorance of the world which endears him to us as we laugh at him. In *Tom Jones,* in contrast, Allworthy, who performs the function of paragon, can and does convey the appropriate judgment of unworthy acts for which there is some excuse. This is possible primarily because Allworthy is a far less complex character than Adams, and the area which the narrator retains for himself, in which the paragon is in-

---

[9] R. S. Crane, "The Concept of Plot and the Plot of *Tom Jones*," *Critics and Criticism* (Chicago: University of Chicago Press, 1952), p. 642.

competent to perform his function as paragon, is extremely limited. In *Amelia*, where the paragon, Harrison, assumes almost the role of *raisonneur*, assuming even the narrator's role as wit, it happens with great frequency. In the dispute with Barnabas, however, although subtle distinctions are made by Adams, they are all concerned with functions of the clergy and with the practical applications of Christianity—an area in which perhaps no other fictional character ever created has more right to act as paragon.

The "sociological" explanation which at once apologizes convincingly for Betty's adultery and yet greatly qualifies the implications of the comically treated scene, largely by showing that apology is necessary, can be handled at this point in the book only by the commentator playing his dual role. And he plays it briefly but so thoroughly that we cannot miss his point. Finished with the comic presentation of scene, he ends the chapter with the serious paragraph quoted above, in which he promises to "open to the reader the steps which led to a catastrophe. . . ." His opening paragraph in chapter xviii is a comment on Betty's good qualities—good nature, generosity, and compassion—and on the passionate element in her nature to which her position as chambermaid at an inn provides too great a temptation. (Even here, the ironic narrator makes a mocking reference to "the purity of courts or nunneries" which might have controlled Betty's "warm ingredients"; as in the first chapter, however, the satiric thrust is directed outward, away from the situation in the novel to a particular contemporary institution not immediately relevant to the novel; hence, while the whole passage remains light in tone, the ironical thrusts in no way detract from the values explicit in the serious comments of the narrator.) The narrator takes over and half-humorously describes Betty's previous affairs. We find her accosting Joseph, who defends his virtue gallantly and then—moving us away from the semiserious tone— the comic commentator again takes over completely, first in a mock apostrophe on the fortunate ability of men to defend their virtue physically, and second in a purely farcical psychological description of Betty's reactions in terms of the battle of the passions within her.[10] Amusing comment does not simply maintain comic detachment at this point. Actually, the ludicrous was the point from which we began; it is the serious commentator who momentarily intrudes (we have seen the pattern before and accept him in his serious role) to rescue the values of the novel from a purely farcical interpretation; he then returns to his humorous role to resume the tone which was never lost, though seriously qualified.

[10] Some relevant aspects of Fielding's style are discussed in A. R. Humphreys, "Fielding's Irony," *RES*, XVIII (1942), 183-196.

If we turn back now to the first chapter, certain elements in the pattern being established will be more easily recognizable. We begin with a commentator whom we take seriously; when he puts tongue in cheek, we do not lose confidence in him as a serious commentator; when he makes his mocking thrust at Cibber and, more important for his later London episodes, at *Pamela*, his ability to convey serious judgments is not compromised.[11] It is by comparison to the serious aesthetic frame established for "biography" in the first two paragraphs, by their inadequacy as examples worthy of perpetuation, that Cibber's *Apology* and *Pamela* and the "romances" too are seen to be ridiculous, rather than because they have measured up to a set of criteria which the narrator has labeled as ridiculous. As the pattern is repeated we know that, unless we have some rhetorical or structural clue to the contrary, the commentator means what he is saying, though he may, in a moment, begin to poke fun at something which is not apposite to his serious remarks or which is especially funny in the light of his serious remarks. For example, the serious comments on Betty's good qualities mixed with her propensity for bedding double are lightened, but not destroyed, as serious qualification of the preceding comic incident by the commentator's thrust at the virtue of the court.

Another constant element of the pattern is found in the objects attacked by the narrator when he resumes his ironic role—typically, contemporary phenomena which are at best peripheral to the values, or other elements, of the action at the moment they are introduced.[12] In the opening chapter, chivalric romances first endure the commentator's thrust, then Cibber's *Apology*—undoubtedly works which Fielding strongly felt needed attacking, and undoubtedly important in considering his aesthetic predilections, but hardly of direct importance in the value scheme of the novel at that point. In the comments on Betty, the initial comic thrust is at the virtue of the court—again peripheral, though potentially important in the value scheme of *Joseph Andrews*.

The pattern established at the beginning of the near-simultaneous use of

[11] The learned preface adds weight to our acceptance of the serious commentator and to our knowledge that he has tongue in cheek when he talks of classical biography as being written in "unintelligible languages."

[12] An ironic reference to a person or institution outside the fictional world must not, of course, be confused with an episode organized as satire. A great number of such casual references may be accommodated in any comic form; if they become important in conveying appropriate attitudes to represented events, they increase the coherence of the work. An episode organized as satire and included in an action will inevitably affect readers as a digression. (See chap. five.)

narrator as both comic and serious commentator is of importance later in the book. We have seen one example of how it works in a situation in which the other devices that have usurped the commentator's function could not operate successfully, a situation in which the value judgment is complex and about which the reader is expected to form a mixed attitude.

From Comment to Character

Once he has introduced himself in chapter i it is a relatively simple matter for the complex commentator to make use of our knowledge of his character in a number of ways: he can, on the one hand, continue the pattern already set up and, by the almost simultaneous use of his two roles, make barbed thrusts without destroying the validity of interspersed serious comments, or vice versa; he can, on the other hand, maintain either one of the roles for a relatively long time by making use of stylistic qualities to identify his role to the reader or, more important still in the next few chapters, by making use of his previous serious or mocking treatment of any subject. He can, for example, pay as many stylistically unqualified compliments as he wishes to *Pamela* or to Cibber's *Apology* without running the risk of our taking him at his word. At the opening of chapter iii after an initial complimentary description of Parson Adams, we learn: "He was generous, friendly, and brave to an excess; but simplicity was his characteristic: he did no more than Mr. Colley Cibber apprehend any such passions as malice and envy to exist in mankind, which was indeed less remarkable in a country parson than in a gentleman who hath passed his life behind the scenes. . . ." [13] We have no difficulty in making the transition between the serious comments, which are just beginning to establish the character of Adams, and the thrusts at Cibber, which partially derive their destructive power from the implied discrepancy between the serious standard (here Adams' simplicity) and the thing mocked (Cibber's simplicity). Reliance on the commentator, in either or both of his roles, remains an important factor in conveying judgments before the removal to London. With one crucial exception, the burden of establishing characters in chapters ii and iii is his.

Though chapter ii begins with a mock genealogy of Joseph Andrews which continues the biting tone of the first chapter, helps prepare us for the London scenes, and certainly establishes comic rather than serious or tragic expectations for the young man (still uncharacterized), its sting is directed not at Joseph but at "modern biographers" and modern pride in ancestry:

[13] Henley, I, 30 (*Joseph Andrews*, I, iii).

To waive, therefore, a circumstance, which, though mentioned in conformity
to the exact rules of biography, is not greatly material, I proceed to things of
more consequence. Indeed, it is sufficiently certain that he had as many ancestors
as the best man living, and, perhaps, if we look five or six hundred years back-
wards, might be related to some persons of very great figure at present, whose
ancestors within half the last century are buried in as great obscurity.[14]

Still light in tone, his next comments are more or less serious; he resumes
the knowledge of Greek he had dispensed with in the previous chapter, and
slashes at those whose sole claim to honor comes from ancestry.

His comments give way to a half-humorous description of Joseph's occupa-
tion as a boy, his position in the Booby household,[15] his musical voice which
prevents his being a good Jack o' Lent, and his final elevation to footman.
When we consider that Joseph's quest for purity has already been defined as
amusing in chapter i, that his ancestry has been described in ludicrous terms,
that his position in the house of a family known as Booby has been treated
lightly, it is not surprising that we expect the young man to take part in comic
adventures and are prepared even for "burlesque." What is surprising is the
fact that, within the comic frame, his essentially serious characteristics are
revealed and his virtues are not (at this point) portrayed as ridiculous. These
traits are taken seriously enough to survive a descent into absurdity that would
normally destroy a fictional character for even a semiserious role—a descent
that would normally take the young man's virtues, mocked in one frame, and
make them perpetually ridiculous. As it is, Fielding must do some difficult
rescue work after the London scenes, but that rescue work is made possible
later by the care with which he handles tone and value judgment now, when
he introduces us to his character proper.

He trades heavily, first of all, on our acceptance of the validity of the
serious commentator. The role of straight narrator, which he has played for
only a few moments, gives way for a time to that of serious commentator.
Joseph's position as stableboy and jockey is described briefly: "The best
gamesters, before they laid their money, always inquired which horse little
Joey was to ride; and the bets were rather proportioned by the rider than by
the horse itself, *especially after he had scornfully refused a considerable bribe
to play booty on such an occasion.*"[16] As a result of this display of honesty,
Joseph is promoted to attend on Lady Booby, and his virtue is further emphasized when its manifestation in church attracts the attention of Parson Adams,

---

[14] *Ibid.*, p. 28 (I, ii).

[15] The comic implications of the name are obvious.

[16] Henley, I, 29 (*Joseph Andrews*, I, ii). Italics mine.

who is further pleased by Joseph's answers to questions put to him concerning religion.

Despite her comic name, Lady Booby is as yet uncharacterized; hard as it may be to realize with our knowledge of her future actions, the promotion is not represented as ridiculous. Similarly, since Parson Adams is only a name at this point, his approbation of Joseph does not necessarily raise Joseph greatly in our opinion. The narrator has mildly qualified the attitude we have formed toward the pure young man, but, as serious commentator, has not yet emphasized the serious nature of the virtues he has ascribed to him.

He does this, however, at the beginning of the next chapter, not by devoting more space to Joseph, but by lengthy serious comments on the man who has approved his virtue, Parson Adams. The commentator is still in complete control, but he is in process of creating a character who will be able implicitly to convey judgments that do not depend on comment at all.

In spite of the occasional aside directed at contemporary institutions, the commentator is at his most serious in his initial description of Adams. The areas in which Adams *may* become ridiculous are carefully defined, but not even the most loving kind of ridicule is offered the good parson at this time by the commentator. He is described as an excellent scholar, a man who knows many languages, and who "had treasured up a fund of learning rarely to be met with in a university."

> He was, besides, a man of good sense, good parts, and good nature; *but was at the same time as entirely ignorant of the ways of this world as an infant just entered into it could possibly be. As he had never any intention to deceive, so he never suspected such a design in others.* He was generous, friendly, and brave to an excess; but simplicity was his characteristic. . . .[17]

The traits italicized define the area in which we may expect Adams to get into situations with which he is incompetent to deal and which, in keeping with the basic tone of the book, will probably turn out to be amusing—with qualifications. The plethora of good traits assigned to Adams, and soon displayed in action, leaves a wide margin in which the good parson's word is to be trusted, his remarks taken seriously, his actions seen as more or less exemplary. As long as our faith in the serious commentator is to be maintained, he must keep faith with us. As long as Adams is foolish only in ways the narrator has led us to expect, he retains our complete faith in his competence to act wisely. If Fielding wishes to cross the line of definition (as he does, for example, with Adams' vanity about his sermon on vanity) he must cross it after we have

[17] *Ibid.*, p. 30 (I, iii). Italics mine.

had ample opportunity to witness Adams' general competence; all we need do, then, is add another limitation to the character's competence rather than shatter all notions of it. At this point, however, Adams' virtues are accented; ridicule is carefully avoided, since the general ironic tone makes us prone to it in any event, and Adams must not only help the commentator rescue the values of the London incidents but must also assume serious commentative functions later in the novel.

This does not mean that we do not meet the ironic commentator almost immediately after (or even during) his serious counterpart's description of Adams' virtues, but here again his sharp sword does not cut the web spun by the serious commentator; it is directed elsewhere. Immediately after the commentator has described Adams and made the thrust at Cibber, he resumes as follows:

> His virtue, and his other qualifications, as they rendered him equal to his office, so they made him an agreeable and valuable companion, and had so much endeared and well-recommended him to a bishop, that at the age of fifty he was provided with a handsome income of twenty-three pounds a-year, which, however, he could not make any great figure with, because he lived in a dear country and was a little incumbered with a wife and six children.[18]

The obvious irony involved in the meager reward for Adams' virtue and qualifications, the ironic understatements that on twenty-three pounds a year Adams could not "make any great figure" because he is *"a little incumbered with a wife and six children"* direct our hostile laughter not at Adams but at the munificent bishop.

Once the bare bones of Adams' character are articulated, we immediately see the good man in action, questioning Joseph. He is amazed at such learning in a footman and, after discovering how Joseph was educated,[19] asks him if he doesn't resent his lack of a liberal education. Joseph's emphatic "no" involves a certain amount of philosophizing: ". . . 'He hoped he had profited somewhat better from the books he had read than to lament his condition in this world. That, for his part, he was perfectly content with the state to which he was called; that he should endeavor to improve his talent, which was all required of him, but not repine at his own lot, nor envy those of his betters.' "[20] The serious commentator need make no remarks about Joseph's

[18] *Ibid.*

[19] Some of the topical asides now ascribed to Joseph (e.g., his explanation of why he could not enter a charity school), though conveyed by the narrator, follow the pattern of mocking thrusts already described.

[20] Henley, I, 31-32 (*Joseph Andrews*, I, iii).

theorizing; he can now use his new creation to do the job for him so that, at one stroke, he gives significance to Joseph's virtue, tentatively establishes Joseph's "philosophical" acceptance of his position as one of the acceptable parts of the value scheme of the whole novel,[21] and reinforces by example what the serious commentator has previously told us about Adams.

It is Adams, not the serious commentator, who evaluates Joseph's remark, though it was the serious commentator's word that indicated the degree of credit we are to give to Adams' evaluation: " 'Well said, my lad,' replied the curate; 'and I wish some who have read many more good books, nay, and some who have written books themselves, had profited so much by them.' " [22] The narrator has momentarily delegated his role as serious commentator to Adams, but he now reassumes his own evaluative prerogative in creating other characters, though he makes good use of our absolute sympathy with Adams' goodness—Adams' foibles have not yet been exploited for purposes of ridicule —as a touchstone by which we can form our attitudes to the new characters he creates. Our attitudes toward these new creations are a result of the inter-action between what the serious commentator tells us about their traits and what he tells us about their attitudes toward and treatment of Adams.

Immediately following the passage quoted above, the serious commentator begins to sketch the characters of the Boobys: *"Adams had no nearer access to Sir Thomas or my lady than through the waiting-gentlewoman;* for Sir Thomas was too apt to estimate men merely by their dress or fortune; *and* my lady was a woman of gayety, who had been blessed with a town education, and never spoke of any of her country neighbors by any other appellation than that of the brutes." [23] The commentator's method is readily apparent: the few traits of the Boobys—all unflattering—that he chooses to describe for us are ascribed as causes for their poor treatment of the good man. Fielding makes good use of his agents even as he creates them. In portraying the Boobys according to their treatment of Adams, the commentator reinforces Adams' ability to characterize others. He informs us that the unpleasant Boobys "both regarded the curate as a kind of domestic only, belonging to the parson of the parish, who was at this time at variance with the knight." [24]

The judgment of the next character introduced is more complex. Our laughter at Slipslop's expense is never hostile as our laughter at Lady Booby

---

[21] Extreme manifestations of Stoicism are ridiculed later in the novel; such ridicule does not reflect on Joseph's moderate statement here.

[22] Henley, I, 32 (*Joseph Andrews*, I, iii).

[23] *Ibid.* Italics mine.

[24] *Ibid.*

is hostile, but neither is it the sympathetic laughter we engage in at the expense of Adams' foibles. We laugh at Slipslop without hating her;[25] we grow fond of her without admiring her, except, of course, as an artistic creation. She, too, is introduced by a description of her relationship with and attitude toward Adams. The perpetuation of the pattern is surprising in its consistency, but less surprising, perhaps, when we realize its flexibility. Slipslop's attitude toward Adams has the ingredients necessary to stimulate the desired complex reaction in the reader:

> Mrs. Slipslop, the waiting-gentlewoman, being herself the daughter of a curate, preserved some respect for Adams: she professed great regard for his learning, and would frequently dispute with him on points of theology; but always insisted on a deference to be paid to her understanding, as she had been frequently at London, and knew more of the world than a country parson could pretend to.[26]

Her irrelevant qualification for arguing theology with the learned Adams is particularly ridiculous in the light of previous thrusts at the court and, immediately before, at Lady Booby, who had been "blessed with a town education"; nevertheless, Slipslop's partial respect for Adams and her professed regard for his learning, while they do not mitigate her essential foolishness, do prevent us from classing her with the Boobys. The vanity displayed in her attitude toward Adams contains no serious threat to the good man's livelihood or well-being, as the Boobys' treatment of him does. This is made clear by the nature of the arguments, and by the way in which Slipslop mangles the language. Adams, because he cannot understand her, does not really dispute with her—his doing so might provide some comic scenes but might also make him ridiculous at a point at which Fielding goes out of his way to prevent our laughing at him. As it is, we laugh at the "mighty affecter of hard words," see that she is vain and foolish in her dealings with Adams, but are aware that she does not threaten him in any way and has, if anything, feelings of good will toward him insofar as she is capable of feeling good will.

Parson Adams, toward the end of the chapter, tries through Slipslop to persuade Lady Booby to provide Joseph with an education which would qualify him "for a higher station than that of a footman." Slipslop's mangled refusal, involving unconscious ridicule of the ignorance of gentlemen, particularly London gentlemen, is amusing and in keeping with the tone of absurd-

---

[25] We come close, though, in the scenes in which she displays her own hostility to Fanny.

[26] Henley, I, 32 (*Joseph Andrews*, I, iii).

ity, soon to become dominant in the London chapters; but Joseph and the serious commentator have the final word before the removal to London and the temporary disappearance of Adams before the first adventures of the book: "However, Andrews behaved very thankfully and gratefully to him for his intended kindness, which he told him he never would forget, and at the same time received from the good man many admonitions concerning the regulation of his future conduct, and his perseverance in innocence and industry." [27] Adams showed us that Joseph's virtue was not to be considered ridiculous; now Joseph is able use the credit he has gained from the good parson's words seriously to compliment Adams before his own departure and to leave us with a picture—in no way portrayed as ridiculous—of Adams giving him serious advice.

By removing Adams from the scene now, by keeping him entirely apart from the subsequent London chapters after he has been established in the role of serious evaluator of people and actions, Fielding has left a bridge by means of which Joseph can be rescued after the latter fulfills the destiny promised in chapter i—that of a young man in a ridiculous struggle to keep his virginity. By his refusal to laugh now at Adams' foibles, despite the fact that laughter is our general expectation from the first chapter, the narrator has seen to it that Joseph's virtue is not made ridiculous *per se*. The result is that, after it is seen as ridiculous in one kind of frame, the "burlesque," it can be moved later into another kind of frame; it is then subtly modified so that it constitutes a positive antidote to the standards ridiculed in the London scenes, but an antidote which does not act simply to reverse the values seen as absurd. Over-indulgence in virginity is ridiculous, but in the scheme of values in *Joseph Andrews* promiscuity never becomes virtuous; sexual incontinence is no virtue, but loss of chastity does not indicate that its loser is a villain.

London: Old Friends in a New Frame and the "Situation Character" Introduced

The London episodes continue from chapters iv through xi; allusions to *Pamela* are strongly resumed with the appearance of Pamela and Mr. Booby toward the end of the novel. It is, however, in the earlier chapters that Joseph's ordeal, promised in the first chapter, takes place. Fielding makes use of the situation, already characterized as ridiculous, of a young man using Pamela Andrews as a model for the defense of his virtue. In the later chapters it is not Joseph who is portrayed as ridiculous; his honest virtue, his healthy

[27] *Ibid.*, p. 34.

love for Fanny, his willingness to defend the heroine against the rudeness of
Beau Didapper are then, though still in a humorous frame, seen as admirable.
The ridiculous pretensions of Pamela and the dangerous arrogance of Lady
Booby temporarily threaten the expected resolution; defeated, they give in-
creased force to the desirability of the union of Joseph and Fanny blessed by a
courageous Adams.

But even in chapters iv through xi, although the double attack on Joseph's
virginity by Lady Booby and Mrs. Slipslop is emphasized, the ridicule directed
at Joseph is actually of shorter duration than one might suppose: long comic
scenes between Mrs. Slipslop and Lady Booby, comic analyses of Lady Booby's
passion, the introduction of Lady Tittle and Lady Tattle, receive much of
our attention.

The fact that, by the end of the novel, Joseph's virtues become a standard
by means of which his sister's virtues are mocked indicates how carefully
Fielding must have handled his materials and manipulated our attitudes, since,
at this point in the novel, ridicule of virtues similar to those the "hero" possesses at the end is itself the tool by which Pamela's ethical deficiencies are revealed. That he has been able to achieve this is a testimony to Fielding's
artistry.

Before we even learned of the Boobys' impending removal to London, the
city had been tentatively categorized for us so that we do not approach it without prejudice. In the very creation of the two female characters who are to
take the greatest part in the London incidents our attitudes toward the city
has—whether we remember the source of our bias as we read is unimportant
—been formed: it is her being "blessed with a town education" that causes
Lady Booby to refer to her country neighbors by no "other appellation than
that of the brutes," that prevents her from having any social intercourse with
Adams except through Slipslop. And it is as a result of the fact that "she had
been frequently at London" and therefore "knew more of the world than a
country parson could pretend to" that Slipslop engages in her incomprehensible
arguments about theology with the learned, bewildered Parson Adams. London is their world, and it is a world removed not only geographically but also
in tone and value from the world in which we have seen Adams and Joseph
act in semiserious roles; it is no accident that before he again meets Adams,
Joseph leaves the metropolis—where we never see the two men together in
action.

To add to these distinctions of tone and value, to help isolate London as a
separate world which only accidentally, and always negatively, impinges on
that wider, freer world of "the road"—where even the ridiculous and the

vicious take more direct, less insidious forms—the mocking thrusts of the ironic commentator are woven into the very texture of the book. We can see now how these thrusts, ostensibly relevant only to actual objects outside the novel, can be employed to affect its value scheme at a later time. Note, in the passage quoted previously on page 79, how, in the very act of establishing Adams' character, the thrust at Cibber, "a gentleman who hath passed his life behind the scenes," has tentatively suggested (London does not have to be mentioned by name) an essential difference between Adams' world and the "behind the scenes" world we enter in these chapters.

What is more important, however, is that when we enter that world, by virtue of which both the predatory females claim their distinction, we do not have to make any shifts in our judgments of either of them. The tentative hostility already directed at Lady Booby is reinforced by our hostile laughter and need in no way be counteracted later; similarly, while we learn more about the lusty elements in Slipslop's nature, they do not surprise us; we do not particularly care whether she is successful or unsuccessful in her attempt on Joseph's virtue; her love-making advances are couched in the same malapropisms as her disputes with Adams—she remains ridiculous and our attitude toward her is entrenched rather than modified.

As a result of fulfilling rather than modifying our expectations about the two female predators whom Joseph frustrates, Fielding is able to modify the implications of our laughing at Joseph, who, though he has fulfilled the expectations established by the commentator's promise in chapter i, steps slightly out of the character established in chapter iii in that what was previously seen as commendable is now exaggerated to the point of the ridiculous. Ridiculous or not, even when we laugh at him most, Joseph retains more of our sympathy than either of the two women he frustrates, largely because our initial attitudes toward the two women are reinforced. Joseph may appear ridiculous, but we are glad that the arrogant Lady Booby cannot have her wish; he may misinterpret Slipslop's advances, but the spotlight is focused on her vanity, on her malapropisms, so that she, rather than Joseph, becomes the object of our laughter.

It is easy to underestimate the importance of this in the whole scheme of the novel unless we realize that, if Fielding intended the London scenes only as destructive burlesque of *Pamela* unconnected to the rest of his novel, he has not made as much of his "satiric" tools as he might have. By keeping our sympathy with Joseph stronger than with those he frustrates and by focusing his attack on characters other than Joseph and on incidents which have only the most tenuous analogy to those in *Pamela*, Fielding makes the burlesque secondary to an exposé of the ridiculous that takes our attention away from Richardson's work. No one knew better than the Fielding who wrote the *Champion* of Tuesday, December 25, 1739, and was to write *Jonathan Wild,* the destructive effect to be achieved in satire by an absolute reversal of values: what is condemned is what you really mean most to praise; what you praise is to be most condemned. More important still, the author of *Shamela* was well aware that, for a full destructive attack on Richardson's values—or what he took to be Richardson's values—nothing could match the effectiveness of directing sympathy toward that which Richardson attacks and great hostility toward the virtuous embodiment that Richardson admires.

> Well; at Dinner Mr. *Booby* was very civil to Mr. *Williams,* and told him he was sorry for what had happened, and would make him sufficient Amends, if in his power, and desired him to accept of a Note for fifty Pounds; which he was so *good* to receive, notwithstanding all that had past; and told Mr. *Booby,* he hop'd he would be forgiven, and that he would pray for him.
>
> We made a charming Fool of him, i'fackins; Times are finely altered, I have entirely got the better of him, and am resolved never to give him his Humour.[28]

Think what we will of Mr. Booby, booby that he is, how can we help feeling sorry for him?

I do not mean to imply that there is only one effective way of satirizing *Pamela,* or that the exposure of the ridiculous in *Joseph Andrews* is ineffectual: we certainly can see that the predatory Lady Booby may be meant as the female analogue of Mr. B. in *Pamela* just as Joseph is the male analogue of Pamela; the humor then derives from the treatment of the reversed situation. And yet, laugh as we will at Lady Booby, are we laughing at Mr. B. or at *Pamela* itself? How do the discussions between Mrs. Slipslop and Lady Booby make us laugh at *Pamela* or at Joseph Andrews? As we laugh at their vanity, at the essential similarity of their desires despite the nugatory difference in their modes of attack on Joseph, is not Fielding exposing the ridiculous in areas far more central to the whole of *Joseph Andrews* than to a burlesque of *Pamela?*

Fielding is essentially accurate when he tells us, of *Joseph Andrews,* that while he has "sometimes admitted this [burlesque] in our diction, we have carefully exclude it from our sentiments and characters; for there it is never properly introduced, unless in writings of the burlesque kind, which this is not

[28] Henry Fielding, *An Apology for the Life of Mrs. Shamela Andrews* (Los Angeles: Augustan Reprint Society, Publication No. 57, 1956), pp. 47-48.

intended to be." [29] This does not imply that Fielding had in mind such distinctions as those made in the present work among satire, apologue, and action when he wrote this sentence or when he wrote *Joseph Andrews*. But the distinctions are useful in explaining why, despite the special qualities which distinguish the London episodes from most of the others in the novel, we do not regard them as digressive in anything like the degee we do Mr. Wilson's tale later in the novel.[30]

According to these distinctions, any true burlesque is a subtype of satire. That is, it is a work organized to ridicule an external object, in this case a particular literary production or a type of literary production. Viewed in this way, the burlesque London scenes are extremely deficient. Fielding has not only failed to exploit all the resources of relevant ridicule; he has included an inordinate number of elements irrelevant to ridicule of *Pamela*. Judged merely as works organized to ridicule Richardson's novel, *Shamela* must be regarded as infinitely superior to the later *Joseph Andrews*. But, just as Johnson's treatment of the Stoic in *Rasselas* is deficient as satire but constitutes an excellent episode in an apologue, Fielding's satiric deficiencies disappear when we consider the London episodes as parts of the rich comic action. The form of *Joseph Andrews* easily accommodates any number of occasional mocking remarks about characters who exist apart from the fictional world of the novel. Such remarks no more constitute episodes organized as satires than Fielding's compliment in *Tom Jones* to his favorite mantua-maker in the Strand constitutes an episode organized to present a fictional example of what makes good mantua-makers. As parts of the action such ironic thrusts frequently help ensure an appropriate ethical response to portrayed characters and events, as some of the remarks about Cibber coöperate in characterizing the "behind-the-scenes" world of London and those who derive their prestige from it—the Boobys and Slipslop. More extensively and directly the "burlesque frame" of the London chapters performs the same service. The attempts of Lady Booby and of Slipslop on Joseph's virtue, in fact the whole sequence of events that lead to Joseph's dismissal, when viewed apart from any consideration of *Pamela*, make perfectly comprehensible contributions to the complication of relationships among characters about whose fates we have been made to care. They are well-organized parts of the action. The "burlesque frame," except for one passage, consists of no more than a choice of diction (including the names of characters) that so successfully alludes to

[29] Henley, I. 19 (*Joseph Andrews*, Preface).
[30] See chapter five.

Pamela as to give us a hilarious contrast between the standard by which sexual and other activities are regarded in *Joseph Andrews* and in the work which immortalized the hero's sister.

To sum this up, in the subtype of satire known as burlesque, of which *Shamela* is a perfect example, the artistic end is the ridicule directed at the work parodied. In *Joseph Andrews* the ridicule of *Pamela* is incorporated as part of the language of the novel in such a way as to make a vital and spirited contribution to both our expectations about and our desires for the represented characters; even the episodes in which the allusive language is most strongly operative are organized not as parts of a satire but as parts of an action.

Nevertheless, the framework is there; when Fielding does concentrate on Joseph's fondness for his virginity, some of our reactions depend upon allusions to *Pamela*—i.e., upon our understanding the language—since the pungency of the humor depends at least in part, on the reader's knowledge of Richardson's novel. (Joseph's letter to Pamela would make rather slim comedy to a reader who had never heard of *Pamela;* but the scenes which concentrate on the analysis of Lady Booby's passion, on Slipslop's hilarious attempt on Joseph's virtue, on Lady Booby's fear of Slipslop's knowledge of her attempted indiscretion, would be as pungent or as ridiculous if *Pamela* had never been written.)

Since Joseph, unlike the females who appear in the burlesque scenes, is to be seen in a new light in the new London world, it is useful to see him in a new dress, to show him developing new characteristics which, while not incompatible with his virtues, are ridiculous (they have already been "defined" as London has been "defined") and better fit him for his role as buffoon. Since these ridiculous elements constitute no more than a superficial change in taste, an acceptance of certain aspects of London fashion, they can be doffed at the moment he rejects and leaves London without doing violence to his character, as easily as they were donned when he entered the city and accepted its fashions.

As soon as he entered the city he began to "scrape an acquaintance with his party-colored brethren, who endeavored to make him despise his former course of life." "His former course" is the life whose predominant ethical tone is set by Parson Adams, the life in which we have seen Joseph's virtues as semiserious. The London life to which he is partially converted is associated with the ridiculous pretensions of Slipslop and Lady Booby. And his "party-colored brethren" do succeed, apparently, in converting Joseph: "His hair was cut after the newest fashion, and became his chief care; he went abroad with it all the morning in papers, and dressed it out in the afternoon." He "led the opinion of all the other footmen at an opera" so that "they never condemned or applauded a single song contrary to his approbation or dislike." (If we had no other knowledge of what amounted in Fielding to almost a monomania against opera, its inclusion as a London pastime comparable to spending much of the day in curling one's hair would make his position obvious.) He is "forward in riots at the playhouses and assemblies." He is "outwardly a pretty fellow." He has, indeed, changed so from the virtuous country footman who aroused the good parson's interest that "when he attended his lady at church (which was but seldom) he behaved with less seeming devotion than formerly. . . ." Nevertheless, he cannot be converted to the more serious vices of the town and will not learn to "game, swear, drink, nor [indulge in] any other genteel vice the town abounded with."

By ascribing to Joseph the nonserious vices of the footman-fop, he has made him temporarily ridiculous. The superficial follies of London, which can easily be dropped, are not the "vices" which constitute the main analogue to *Pamela*, the focal point of the "burlesque episodes." It is the very virtues Joseph has retained, especially his refusal to indulge in—that magnificent euphemism—"any other genteel vice the town abounded with," which enables Fielding to incorporate ridiculed virtues of *Pamela* in such a way as to ensure an appropriate reaction to sexual and other activities and attitudes of characters in *Joseph Andrews*. By dressing his character in a set of superficial and removable London follies, Fielding has set his very virtues in a ridiculous frame—one perfectly appropriate for incorporating such ridicule; when the removal of the frame, in combination with other rescue devices, restores dignity to the young man's virtues as he returns from the footman-fop to the "Joey" we originally met, he can perform his role in the comic adventures on the road. The rescue is complete enough to permit his "virtue" ostensibly mocked here to become a standard of virtue later in the book.

It is the footman-fop whom we see walking in the park with Lady Booby, inciting Tittle and Tattle to live up to their names and eliciting from his lady the cry, " 'Aye, there is some life in this fellow.' " The foppery which distinguishes the new Joseph from the boy praised by Adams has won him another kind of advocate in a ridiculous, isolated London world: "She plainly saw the effects which the town air hath on the soberest constitutions."

Immediately after the death of Sir Thomas Booby, Lady Booby, nearly naked, invites the newly dressed and curled London Joseph into her bedroom, and at this point Fielding has the first real fun with Joseph's virtue. Much of the humor of the scene evolves from Joey's seriously construing the transparent, hypocritical veil in which Lady Booby couches her proposals; so, after quizzing Joseph about whether his virtue of secrecy (" 'a very commendable quality, and what I am far from being angry with you for' ") would persist in a "hypothetical" love affair with a lady, she ends by asking, " 'Can you keep a secret, my Joey?' " In spite of the new London spirit the Lady has discerned in him, "my Joey" interprets the question as being a general inquiry into his character as footman: " 'Madam,' says he, 'I hope your ladyship can't tax me with ever betraying the secrets of the family; and I hope, if you was to turn me away, I might have that character of you.' " [31] If Joseph ever steps out of character it is not in the passages in which he waxes eloquent about life in formal language; he does this from the time we meet him and continues doing it after the burlesque scenes. His sharpness, occasional wisdom, and eloquence are part of the character of Joseph Andrews, though they are not characteristics one might expect of the generalized concept "footman." It is in the London scenes that we depart from the character of Joseph Andrews we have met before and will meet again. The departure, brief and in the isolated frame of London values, will not bother us when the footman again becomes Joseph Andrews.

Joseph's obtuseness in the scene, his inability to comprehend his mistress' devious purpose, elicits further humor as, in all honesty, his remarks become, in view of his lady's uncomprehended purpose, the quintessence of tactlessness. When the veil in which her intentions are couched has been withdrawn farther and farther until intention and lady have both reached the point of approximate nudity, and the lady with some justification bursts into a fury at Joseph's blindness, Joseph defends himself as follows:

> "Madam," said Joseph, "I would not have your ladyship think any evil of me. I have always endeavored to be a dutiful servant both to you and my master." "O thou villain!" answered my lady, "why didst thou mention the name of that dear man, unless to torment me, to bring his precious memory to my mind?" (And then she burst into a fit of tears.)[32]

Joseph's very "innocence," ridiculously as it is portrayed, turns the tables so that our laughter is directed at the hypocritical lady. The reader, it is presumed, is not quite so innocent as Joseph and is aware that the remarks he makes in all innocence could not better deflate the lady if they had been contrived for that purpose by a shrewd antagonist.

We see this pattern, too, when Slipslop attacks the hero's virtue. His innocence makes her just as angry as it made her mistress and, though her in-

---

31 Henley, I, 37 (*Joseph Andrews*, I, v).
32 *Ibid.*, p. 38.

tentions are not veiled, the parallel to her lady's attack adds greatly to the
humor of the scene; the similarity of the operation of the "passion" of lust
in lady and maid adds to our laughter at the expense of the proud Lady Booby:

> "Yes, madam!" replied Mrs. Slipslop with some warmth, "do you intend to
> result my passion? Is it not enough, ungrateful as you are, to make no return to
> all the favors I have done you; but you must treat me with ironing? Barbarous
> monster! How have I deserved that my passion should be resulted and treated
> with ironing?" "Madam," answered Joseph, "I don't understand your hard
> words; but I am certain you have no occasion to call me ungrateful, for, so far
> from intending you any wrong, I have always loved you as well as if you had
> been my own mother." "How, sirrah?" says Mrs. Slipslop in a rage; "your
> own mother? Do you assinuate that I am old enough to be your mother? . . ." [33]

Poor Joseph! To emphasize the situation of the comic martyr the narrator
uses, for the first time in the novel, a stylistic device which he later employs
frequently for comic purposes, the mock-heroic[34] simile in which Mrs. Slipslop
is compared to "a hungry tigress" and "a voracious pike," Joseph to a lamb
and "a roach or gudgeon." The epic simile is terminated by the prosaic ringing of her mistress' bell, which forces her to leave her prey.

Joseph has, however, between the two attempted seductions, written a
letter to his mock-exemplary sister which, while revealing him at his most
naïve and ridiculous, prepares us for the dropping of the "burlesque" frame
by revealing his rejection of what London stands for and his honest desire to
see Adams again. His naïveté is in some ways at its best in the letter. He seems
honestly to believe that his mistress has been distracted by the death of her
husband, and if he is slightly puzzled by her grief, easily finds in a wonderfully inapplicable platitude an explanation of the lady's actions: " 'None of
the servants expected her to take it so to heart, because they quarrelled almost
every day of their lives: . . . and I have heard her ladyship wish his honor
dead above a thousand lives [sic]; but nobody knows what it is to lose a friend
till they have lost him.' " [35] Nevertheless, the light is beginning to break
through even to Joseph, though his inability to recognize that the lady and

---

[33] Ibid., pp. 41-42 (I, vi).

[34] In "Henry Fielding's Theory of the Comic Prose Epic," University of Wisconsin
Studies in Language and Literature, No. 30 (Madison: University of Wisconsin Press,
1931), Ethel Margaret Thornbury more accurately suggests that Fielding does not
employ the mock heroic but a comic analogue of epic paraphernalia. In a doctoral dissertation, From Artistic Judgment to Ethical Statement (Chicago, 1960), I implied
that the distinction was empty. My failure to comprehend the important point resulted
from a deficiency in my own understanding, I hope since remedied.

[35] Henley, I, 39 (Joseph Andrews, I, vi).

Slipslop are sisters under the skin prevents his admitting it: " 'Don't tell any-body what I write, because I should not care to have folks say I discover what passes in our family; but if it had not been so great a lady, I should have thought she had a mind to me.' " [36] He asks Pamela to try to get him a job, since " 'If madam be mad, I shall not care for staying long in the family,' " but signifies his intention, if he does not hear from her, to return to "my old master's country-seat, if it be only to see Parson Adams, who is the best man in the world. London is a bad place, and there is so little good fellowship that the next-door neighbors don't know one another." [37] Here, for a brief moment, the insistent male virgin is back with Parson Adams, is attacking what the novel attacks—is again on the side of those angels who have never undergone the misfortune of a temporary descent into absolute absurdity.

In the adventure with Slipslop, our attention is centered on her ridiculous antics, to the parallel between her attack on Joseph and her lady's. Our atten-tion then is completely withdrawn from Joseph to scenes in which Slipslop and Lady Booby have a go at each other, other scenes in which the comic commentator has a field day with mock-heroic apostrophes to love, with in-terspersed thrusts at Cibber and Richardson, with comic analyses of the Lady's psychological state, and with Slipslop's and Lady Booby's false and wavering condemnations of Joseph's lack of virtue. But there follows one more in-terview with Joseph, terminated by his unfortunate "tenderness for his virtue" and ending in his discharge. A final letter to Pamela employs the absurd qualities in Joseph a little longer and, at the same time, indicates that he is potentially virile: " 'But I am glad she turned me out of the chamber as she did, for I had once almost forgotten every word Parson Adams had ever said to me.' " [38] Even the commentator shows some concern at the beginning of the chapter for his protagonist's future reputation: "The disconsolate Joseph would not have had an understanding sufficient for the principal sub-ject of such a book as this if he had any longer misunderstood the drift of his mistress; and indeed, that he did not discern it sooner, the reader will be pleased to impute to an unwillingness in him to discover what he must con-demn in her as a fault." [39] The reader may or may not follow the commen-tator's injunction—it will not matter. No explanation can give us the kind of retroactive knowledge that, in other comic actions, can sometimes make us say, "We've misjudged the man—he was not a fool; we didn't know why he was acting that way." Joseph has been ridiculous and, no matter what

[36] *Ibid.*
[37] *Ibid.*, p. 40.
[38] *Ibid.*, p. 57 (I, x).
[39] *Ibid.*, p. 56.

we learn about him later in a re-reading of the apposite scenes, he remains
ridiculous in the London episodes. The craftsmanship employed in creating
his "burlesque frame" enables Fielding to switch frames again so that Joseph
appears in a new light, judged by another, though not a retroactive, set of
laws by which his virtue is not judged ridiculous. The contrast between evaluations in the two frames helps establish the values of the novel and prevents
us from simply reversing Richardson's ridiculed standards.

The removal begins immediately after Joseph's final letter to Pamela—
and it is not initially a geographical removal: "Joseph having received his
little remainder of wages, and having stripped off his livery, was forced to
borrow a frock and breeches of one of the servants (for he was so beloved
in the family that they would all have lent him anything)...."[40] The serious
commentator's remark reminds us of another world in which we have seen
Joseph and, in the next chapter, as Joseph leaves London, he expends much
of his time in stimulating that memory.

We are immediately told about Fanny and again our old standard for
measuring character is reintroduced as Parson Adams is further entrenched
in the exemplary and evaluative roles we have seen him perform previously:

> This young creature [Fanny] (who now lived with a farmer in the parish)
> had been always beloved by Joseph, and returned his affection. She was two
> years only younger than our hero. They had been acquainted from their
> infancy, and had conceived a very early liking for each other, which had grown
> to such a degree of affection that Mr. Adams had with much ado prevented them
> from marrying, and persuaded them to wait till a few years' service and thrift
> had a little improved their experience, and enabled them to live comfortably
> together.
>
> They followed this good man's advice, as indeed his word was little less than
> a law in his parish; for as he had shown his parishoners, by an uniform behavior
> of thirty-five years' duration, that he had their good entirely at heart, so they
> consulted him on every occasion, but very seldom acted contrary to his opinion.[41]

It is a familiar world now and one in which we can expect future actions to
take place. And yet the ingredients of the love of Joseph and Fanny, approved
by Adams, certainly do cause a backward glance at the previous scenes:
"Though her modesty would only suffer her to admit his eager kisses, her
violent love made her more than passive in his embraces, and she often pulled
him to her breast with a soft pressure, which, though perhaps it would not

[40] *Ibid.*, p. 58.
[41] *Ibid.*, p. 59 (I, xi).

have squeezed an insect to death, caused more emotion in the heart of Joseph than the closest Cornish hug could have done." [42]

Lest we miss the application, the narrator's remark that Fanny could not write and therefore did not correspond with Joseph definitely directs our attention back to *Pamela* and its letter-writing heroine and, by implication, to the ridiculed standard. This is a different Joseph, perhaps, from the one mocked; but if his healthy manhood has been restored, he has not become a roué, and his slightly impatient chastity is not mocked in the new frame. When we compare the values of the two frames and look at the Tow-wouse–Betty incident it is clear that even George Sherburn's mild statement, in reference to *Tom Jones*, to the effect that "Undoubtedly Fielding underrated chastity as a moral virtue," may be too strong to apply to the value scheme of *Joseph Andrews;* the negative view of Richardson exaggerates because, as with most undesirable notions in *Joseph Andrews*, its absurdity is stressed; the positive values of the nonallusive frame subtly modify our notions of the place of sexual propriety in the world of the novel.

One addition to the value scheme, though it is employed very briefly in the London chapters, is subsequently developed into a most important device for conveying judgments and, in its fullest development, is one of the techniques used most frequently by Fielding. The commentator has begun to dramatize his own comment by briefly sketching characters who are formulated by reference to a single trait defined by and used for a single situation. We may tentatively refer to these skeletal figures as situation characters, though later in their more fully developed state, they become what I refer to as walking concepts.[43]

In chapter iv, just as Joseph has acquired enough London folly to evoke Lady Booby's compliment to his new "spirit," they are seen walking arm in arm through Hyde Park. The commentator points out that, though "women of figure" may indulge "in all those innocent freedoms" without sullying their virtue, their reputations are likely to suffer. And this, of course, is what happens to the not-so-virtuous Lady Booby:

> . . . and so it fell out to Lady Booby, who happened to be walking arm-in-arm with Joey one morning in Hyde Park, when Lady Tittle and Lady Tattle came accidentally by in their coach. "Bless me," says Lady Tittle, "can I believe my eyes? Is that Lady Booby?" "Surely," says Tattle. "But what makes you surprised?" "Why, is not that her footman?" replied Tittle. At which Tattle

[42] *Ibid.*, p. 60.
[43] See chapter four.

laughed, and cried, "An old business, I assure you: is it possible you should not have heard it? The whole town hath known it this half-year." [44]

Our sympathies are not really directed toward Lady Booby because, among other reasons, the "innocent freedoms" are not so innocent. But, in using the characters he has sketched, Fielding incorporates in the novel another ridiculous element of London life—gossip. In his footnote indicating that when the two ladies spread the rumor, they had not known about it before, the commentator collaborates with his creatures in appropriate ridicule. But without his help we could make no mistake in our—at this point—admittedly unimportant judgment of them. He does not need to tell us anything about them in order to use them as instruments for evaluation.

This may at first glance seem to contradict the contention that it is in the treatment of character and situation rather than in character and situation *per se* that we get our initial clues as to how we are to evaluate them, and that further treatment provides an expansion or contradiction of our original attitudes. In actual practice, it does not contradict it: particularization or lack of particularization still directs our attitudes. The fact that one has murdered a man is not *per se* an evaluation of the person who does it: it may be an action enforced by society, which is the real culprit (*An American Tragedy*), or it may be partially explained by a political motive which is defined as at least in part, "good" (*Man's Fate*), or it may be justified by the victim's character (*From Here to Eternity*). There are innumerable ways in which a novelist or dramatist can treat a murderer as essentially a good man. But if we meet a character briefly in a book, hear him referred to by the epithet "murderer," and are given no qualification of his action—if we see him only in his unqualified role as murderer—a value judgment has already been made of him. A "murderer" is not the same, in terms of artistic evaluation, as a man who has murdered someone. Extensive treatment of any "murderer" is prone to transform him into "a man who has murdered someone": describing characteristics not connected with his murdering propensities automatically mitigates his action, and requires more subtle evaluation in the treatment of character. (To take a simple example, in the Sherlock Holmes novel *A Study in Scarlet*, our sympathies with the "murderer" are transformed once he is captured and we learn about his past.)

To move from murder to gossip, in creating Tittle and Tattle Fielding is able to use brief, limited treatment of characters good for only one situation —or, as in later instances, a few very similar situations—so that evaluation of

[44] Henley, I, 35 (*Joseph Andrews*, I, iv).

their characters is extremely simple no matter how complex the judgment they help to convey. The names are, of course, evaluatively loaded, and in their short dialogue the characters are seen only in acts connected to their designations. The names, the "handles," useful as they are in designating this pair, are not always necessary for creating situation characters, many of whom have no name at all, as is the case of the hypocritical prude, the legal wit, the avaricious coachman of chapter xii. These characters—rough approximations of those E. M. Forster calls "flat characters" [45]—are invariably self-explanatory: since they represent only one trait or possibly two, their actions and words, limited to the situation that called forth their creation, simply display the traits they embody. We meet them only once and usually they exhaust their usefulness in conveying appropriate judgments of institutions, manners, people of the world in which the action takes place.

The Unconscious Protagonist Adrift in a Sea (or Coach) of Situation Characters

That Tom Jones and Booth have their crosses to bear in the novels of which they are the respective male protagonists, no one could deny. But as artistic creations they are never treated as Fielding treats poor Joseph. Made fun of by the commentator before we meet him, he is finally given credit for some virtue and sense by Parson Adams, only to be removed to an urban world in which the Parson's judgment is invalid and he is reduced to a joke; removed from London, restored to the world where Adams' judgments are impressive, his virtue no longer ludicrous, the poor footman is immediately reduced by his creator to little more than an unconscious lump, and in this ignominious role he is called upon to perform evaluative services important to the novel.

No sooner does he leave London than, after an intrepid struggle, he is robbed, stripped naked, and left unconscious in a ditch. He then has the misfortune to be picked up by a coach driven, staffed, and occupied by situation characters and deposited at an inn run primarily by their more complex brethren.

The postilion, who, though a situation character, is one of the few "good" situation characters in the book, stops the coach on hearing Joseph groan. The passengers' reactions are all uncharitable, to say the least, each objecting in terms that display the trait which characterizes him. The business-is-business coachman objects first: " 'Go on, sirrah,' says the coachman; 'we are con-

[45] E. M. Forster, *Aspects of the Novel* (New York: Harcourt, Brace and Co., 1927), pp. 103-112.

founded late, and have no time to look after dead men.' " [46] Even after the
legal necessity for picking up Joseph is pointed out, "The coachman objected,
'That he could not suffer him to be taken in unless somebody would pay a
shilling for his carriage the four miles.' "

The hypocritical prude, on learning of Joseph's plight, displays her own
brand of virtue: " 'O J—sus,' cried the lady, 'a naked man! Dear coachman,
drive on and leave him.' " [47] Her apparent prudish virtue extends not only to
abhorring the sight of naked men, but also to alcohol. When Joseph is finally
dressed in Robin's greatcoat and, nearly frozen, placed in the coach, the "wit"
asks her if she could not "accommodate him [Joseph] with a dram"; the
prude "answered with some resentment, 'She wondered at his asking her such
a question, but assured him she never tasted any such thing.' " [48] The prim
pose is shattered when the robbers hold up the coach and one drinks "some of
the best Nantes he had ever tasted" from her silver bottle.

Similarly delineated, "a young men who belonged to the law" overrules the
coachman's and lady's objections not because he is charitable but because he
is a lawyer:

> "He wished they had passed by without taking any notice; but that now they
> might be proved to have been last in his company; if he should die they might
> be called to some account for his murder. He therefore thought it advisable to
> save the poor creature's life, for their own sakes, if possible; at least, if he
> died, to prevent the jury's finding that they fled for it." [49]

And even in his attempt at wit before the arrival at the inn, he maintains his
unflattering legal character: "The lawyer likewise made several very pretty
jests without departing from his profession." The prude makes no objection
to his bawdy innuendoes.

The other negative situation characters in the scene are even less fully
drawn: the uncharitable gentleman, the man of wit, the lady's fastidious footman, each self-explanatory, unsympathetic.

The good-natured postilion is the only one who shows Joseph any kindness,
stopping the coach at the first sound of a groan and giving him his own coat.
As a kind of good-natured delinquent he functions in a slightly more complex
manner than the negative situation characters in that his ethical tone is established by contrast to the others. Rebuked for swearing by the passengers,

[46] Henley, I, 63 (*Joseph Andrews*, I, xii).
[47] *Ibid.*
[48] *Ibid.*, p. 65.
[49] *Ibid.*, pp. 63-64.

whose lack of charity makes his swearing a virtue, his good nature is emphasized by his statement " 'That he would rather ride in his shirt all his life than suffer a fellow-creature to lie in so miserable a condition.' " The commentator's single statement informing us that the "lad . . . hath been since transported for robbing a henroost" incisively points to the discrepancy between the terrible unpunished sins of omission by the passengers, all his moral inferiors, and the severely punished minor infraction of the law which can never detract from the postilion's moral superiority over the others.

Joseph has been reduced to a cipher in this scene, although at first we see him gallantly defend himself against the thieves because his honesty will not permit him to surrender borrowed clothes without a struggle. While Joseph's traits have little to do with the passengers' reactions to him as an unconscious lump, our sympathy with him—by this point in the novel great indeed—makes the passengers' treatment of him seem still more culpable. While there is no apparent mitigation of the situation characters' lack of charity, the scene must be treated carefully if Fielding is to emphasize the ludicrous aspect of ethical deficiencies; it is probably for this reason that, when Joseph emerges from his comatose state, we find ourselves laughing at him again. We cannot really believe him in danger of death when his real modesty is as exaggerated as that affected by the prude, when he elects to freeze to death rather than ride naked in a coach. Since his modesty, unlike the prude's, will have no deleterious effects on anyone but himself, our laughter at his expense is far different from that at the prude's. So long as we do not think Joseph in any real danger, we can laugh—hostilely, of course—at the vanity and hypocrisy of the passengers and crew of the coach; otherwise their inhumanity would arouse real fear for Joseph and the kind of hostility directed toward them would be consonant with a serious instead of a comic power. Joseph's reputation can by now defend itself and, as he appears, consciously, very briefly, the author can afford to use him for an occasional thrust at *Pamela*.

By reducing Joseph to a lump and placing him in a coach full of situation characters, Fielding has presented in dramatic form the moral tenor of the comically represented world which Joseph's and Adams' goodness will have to battle before the road is behind them and Joseph can receive his merited reward of the highly desirable Fanny. The comically treated moral turpitude (modified by an occasional flash of real goodness) presented in microcosm in these scenes is developed at length as the Trullibers, the men of false promise, the practical jokers, the men of "faith" without good works, prove hurdles to the peregrinating pair.

When we reduce each of the situation characters to his limited component, their ethical characterization may seem oversimplified and shallow, but in swift comic interaction they appear vivid, animated, and convincing vehicles for their artistic purpose; if they are "flat characters" this does not derogate from Fielding's artistry, since it is by simplifying them, reducing them to a single function, yet presenting them in an animated, witty fashion that he is able to present a world in which value judgments are complicated indeed, where morality is never reduced to an aphorism. Each of them is simplified; what their interaction reveals is highly complex.

Such creations, considered in isolation, are susceptible of misinterpretation: what the author attacks seems so clear that his position can be exaggerated. Some cautionary modifications about using these creations in crossing the bridge from fiction to ethical belief is in order.

First, situation characters, though not always walking concepts, are, for specifiable formal purposes, simplified; there is, therefore, no justification for an inference that a writer who has created them in a coherent comic novel believes that some people (as opposed to some fictional characters) are all good while others are all bad.

Second, since situation characters are often used, in interaction with protagonist, heroine, or paragon, to represent moral turpitude (treated ludicrously) or reprehensible aspects of mankind which present threats to the major characters, it is tempting to infer that the author's view of the world is pessimistic. The obvious antidote to this is consideration of the major characters: if the people in the coach, the Barnabases, and the Trullibers seem to predominate in sections of the fictional world, Adams, Joseph, and Fanny combat them, sometimes with fists as well as words. Situation characters influence our reactions to the ethical deserts of the major characters, and the judgments conveyed about them are more central to Fielding's attitudes.

Third, when situation characters are not directly confuted by the paragon, the protagonist, the commentator himself, or by the values conveyed in digressive narratives, Fielding may confound them by a "good example" whose simplification consists, as it does in the postilion, in a corrective contrast to traits or institutions attacked. These good characters—used infrequently— may be interpreted safely only by limiting their application to the specific institution or trait they are supposed to correct; the postilion's good nature emphatically indicates that a poor man who breaks the letter of the law *may* be morally superior to gentlemen who distort its spirit. It is a complacent belief in the opposite of this that Fielding represents as undesirable. (We must not forget, either, that the lady's footman is as "bad" as any of the gentlemen in the coach.) Any attempt to go beyond this on the evidence of the postilion—

to decide, for example, that Fielding thinks poor people are morally superior to rich ones—is to ignore the character's role. In other words, we may ask, "What must Fielding have believed to have created a situation character as an integral part of a comic action?" But the answer is that the mere creation of such a character has no specifiable relation to a novelist's ethical beliefs.[50]

The End of the Beginning

The characters we meet when Joseph is deposited at Tow-wouse's inn bear some relation to the situation characters we met in the coach. They seem to define themselves according to simple recognizable traits, to establish the hostile values which Joseph and Adams must fight against. We can sum them up, it seems at first, in a phrase that contains its own evaluation: the uncharitable virago of a landlady, the henpecked landlord, the good-natured serving wench, the money-grubbing doctor, the clergyman whose Christianity consists of meaningless words. But we soon see that they are extended, given wider treatment, act a more complex role in the value scheme. A phrase becomes inadequate to describe Betty; it would reduce her individualized characteristics to the lowest common denominator rather than represent the active principle which informs and limits her character. Far from being represented as the mere embodiment of an undesirable trait, her attempted rape of Joseph and consequent affair with Tow-wouse call into play some of the most subtle manipulation of evaluative techniques in the novel.

The innkeeper may remain henpecked in the presence of his wife, but we learn that he has long pursued Betty; his final success destroys the adequacy of the phrase. Even Mrs. Tow-wouse, though she never contradicts our original summary, is not a labeled character. The traits which lead to our original evaluation of her because of her treatment of Joseph, though they certainly influence us, do not totally define our attitude toward her as injured wife.

More important for our present purposes, though, Barnabas, proud advocate of a meaningless brand of Christianity, is developed so that the embryonic summary phrase is only a starting point. The original definition by and for a single situation is the focal point for the development of a character who becomes an articulate spokesman for the position he represents. The position is complicated and, as it has numerous manifestations, he can take part in several kinds of situations. His articulated argument is fully answered by Adams, the paragon, in an ostensibly digressive dispute which establishes values very high in the hierarchy of judgments made in the novel. It is not, however,

[50] A more fruitful form of this question, however, leads to interesting answers. See chapter four.

only the refutation of his articulated position as a walking concept that conveys judgments; but also, just as we have seen positive credit extended to a character by Adams' praise (a function of the paragon) and negative values attached to other characters because of his condemnation, Barnabas' praise acts largely as condemnation, his condemnation largely as praise, in the value scheme. A fairly complex use of this evaluative function is seen in connection with the ostensibly dying Joseph's rhapsody. He begins by invoking Pamela:

> "O most adorable Pamela! most virtuous sister! whose example could alone enable me to withstand all the temptations of riches and beauty, and to preserve my virtue pure and chaste for the arms of my dear Fanny, if it had pleased heaven that I should ever have come unto them. What riches, or honors, or pleasures, can make us amends for the loss of innocence? Doth not that alone afford us more consolation than all worldly acquisitions?" [51]

Where are we? Certainly we know that Joseph is not going to die (the surgeon, as situation character, has said that he is and this alone suggests that he is not) and we can afford to smile at his rhapsody. And yet, by virtue of his invocation to Pamela are we thrown back into the London frame of absurdity so that the sentiments of the rhapsody themselves are ridiculed? As the rhapsody continues, though, we are forced to pause before immediately switching frames again: the fact that Fanny's arms will never hold him is mourned; so we know Joseph's mocked prudishness is not present; sorrow at her loss is great, but resignation to the divine will is possible:

> "These [innocence and virtue] can make me face death without fear; and though I love my Fanny more than ever man loved a woman, these can teach me to resign myself to the Divine will without repining. O thou delightful, charming creature! if heaven had indulged thee to my arms, the poorest, humblest state would have been a paradise; I could have lived with thee in the lowest cottage without envying the palaces, the dainties, or the riches of any man breathing." [52]

This sounds much like the Joseph we met before the London scenes, the Joseph whose perceptive speech to Adams explaining why he did not resent his station in life met with the good man's approval. Nevertheless, the fact that these rhapsodic sentiments are expressed when death is not really probable allows us to smile. That the whole is prefaced by an invocation to the ridiculed Pamela might make us laugh not only at Pamela but at Joseph also. Any doubts are immediately resolved: "Barnabas thought he had heard

[51] Henley, I, 70 (*Joseph Andrews*, I, xiii).
[52] *Ibid.*, pp. 70-71.

enough, so downstairs he went, and told Tow-wouse he could do his guest no service; for that he was very light-headed, and had uttered nothing but a rhapsody of nonsense all the time he stayed in the room." [53] Joseph's credit is established and the fun at the expense of Pamela can now be seen in the new frame, which is maintained with some consistency through the rest of the book and exploited fully when we meet the young lady at the end of the novel: it is no longer through Joseph's definition as a male analogue to his sister that the ridiculed ethical standard of *Pamela* is incorporated; it is rather Pamela's unworthiness as the muse of Joseph's rhapsody, her lack of real virtue as compared with Joseph's conception of her, that provides a positive standard for controlling the reader's reaction to the acts and thoughts of characters.

Thus, in Joseph's rhapsody, partially through the use of a situation character, comic tone is maintained and we continue laughing—Joseph is not going to die and his speech is pathetic only if he is. But the protagonist's sentiments not only escape ridicule but are firmly established as serious positive values in the novel by the absolute condemnation of those sentiments by a walking concept. As a result of these new judgments, the mechanism for occasional references to *Pamela* is firmly entrenched on a new footing. To accomplish all this Fielding has not had to rely on his serious commentator; the subtle judgments are conveyed without his help.

As Book I progresses, Adams makes his re-entry under attack by the hostile world which already has negative qualities attached to it. We see him, not in the lively role he is to play later, but as quiet, dignified, refusing to trade jests or even to argue with the ignorant surgeon; his long argument with Barnabas exposes the unpleasant clergyman without help from the dormant commentator—who, from here to the end of the novel, is invoked for special purposes but always now in subtle interaction with created agents—and the novel and its readers are both ready for the road.

Tom Jones and *Amelia:* A Frame of Comparison

Though the three novels of Henry Fielding are comic actions, each evokes a special variety of comic power; each action is the realization of a substantially different variety of a similar form. It is an error to assume that in *Tom Jones* Fielding extended the principles underlying the form of

[53] *Ibid.*, p. 71.

Joseph Andrews, but did it better; or that in *Amelia* he tried to write a novel which had the same power as *Tom Jones,* but did not succeed. Nevertheless, since each is a comic action, we should not be surprised that judgments are conveyed within them in quite similar ways though they are employed for different ends.

In Fielding's first novel, owing to certain special complexities of form (e.g., the allusive London episodes), the chronological establishment of evaluative devices is far more tortuous and inaccessible than in either *Tom Jones* or *Amelia;* on the other hand, because of certain other elements in the work (e.g., the less important characters are introduced, evaluated, then completely dropped), the manipulation of the devices when established is far less complex in *Joseph Andrews* than in Fielding's last two novels. Once we see how the agents are *established* in *Joseph Andrews* we have no trouble in understanding how they are established in *Tom Jones* and *Amelia;* if we understand how the agents are *used* in *Tom Jones* and *Amelia,* we shall not mistake their simpler use in *Joseph Andrews.*

In *Tom Jones,* although the narrator takes over from the commentator at an earlier stage (the "story" beginning with chap. ii) with frequent short and occasional long instrusions in his role as commentator, as in *Joseph Andrews* he first establishes, through direct comment, a character who conveys complex judgments. Unlike Adams', however, Allworthy's competence to evaluate is limited only by his propensity for refusing to think evil of anyone unless he is forced to (defined by the commentator as an asset rather than a weakness of character) and by his limited possession of relevant facts. Although the area of his competence is thus far more extensive than that of Adams— his hesitancy in thinking evil of people is not equated with Adams' ignorance of "the world"—any indicated limitation of his knowledge of facts acts automatically as a limitation of any single judgment of a situation: when Adams refutes Barnabas, that false Christian is permanently deflated, never again to appear in the plot; when our attitude toward Lady Booby is established by her contempt of Adams, the attitude is entrenched, not modified, when the lady again appears; but when Jenny Jones is lectured by Allsworthy, since he is to meet her again and to learn considerably more about her, his final "word" on the interesting young woman is the result of a series of judgments, each correct only insofar as the facts are known; his expulsion of Tom Jones is correct—even exemplary—action in light of the facts as he knows them at the moment of the action; our greater knowledge of the facts is not matched by Allworthy until the end of the novel, when his final evaluation is almost a summation of many values established in the novel and Blifil is rightfully expelled as Tom had been wrongfully cast out earlier.

Though the progressive rather than, as in *Joseph Andrews*, the episodic nature of the plot does delay our final acceptance of Allworthy's judgments of situations to the extent that we are aware that his knowledge of the facts is limited, the wide general area of competence ascribed to him by the commentator facilitates his extensive use as evaluator in the early stages of the novel. He may be wrong in particular situations; we have faith in his general statements. We see him, therefore, quite early in the novel (our protagonist is still in diapers) lecturing on continence, distinguishing between love and lust, discussing the extent to which monetary considerations are important for marriage—in short, establishing the general values by which we will judge characters and actions as they later appear.[54]

The commentator, important and ubiquitous as he is in *Tom Jones*, need not do for Jenny Jones' ostensible sin what he did for Betty's in *Joseph Andrews*: Allworthy is almost immediately competent to deal with the nuances of appropriate excuse and partial condemnation. Even our sympathy for Jenny is reinforced by her own appreciation of Allworthy. And, yet, even when we consider only his role as ethical spokesman, the commentator carries a great share of the burden during the first book of *Tom Jones*—and later as well. Typically the commentator evaluates actions and characters in the early sections when Allworthy's limited knowledge of the facts makes it impossible for him to do so, as in the long discussion of Doctor Blifil's motives in pulling the wool over Allworthy's eyes; to make certain that we do not misunderstand Allworthy's worthiness at points at which suspicion might hinder the exercise of his ability to convey judgments, as when general opinion fastens the blame for Tom's birth on him and the commentator says, "we think proper to give him [the reader] a very early intimation that Mr. Allworthy was . . . absolutely innocent of any criminal intention whatever," or as, when he fails to divine Blifil's attempt on his sister, we are told "that Mr. Allworthy must have had the insight of the devil (or perhaps some of his worse qualities) to have entertained the least suspicion of what was going forward." And even after he has told us about Allworthy at length and shown him in action, the commentator continues to expand on his virtues, to particularize him as exemplary as at the beginning of chapter x.

In *Joseph Andrews* a complex commentator assigns to one character, at a

[54] Discussed in detail in chapter three.

relatively early stage of the novel, a limited evaluative role; the ethical quality of other characters, including the protagonist, is defined mainly by their actions or attitudes toward him or vice versa. This character is, however, almost immediately moved off-scene—or rather, the other characters are moved from his world to an absurd London world. In this new frame, attitudes toward two of the major characters are essentially entrenched while we find ourselves laughing at Joseph. Restored to a semblance of grace, he is transported to a world of situation characters—later developed at length into walking concepts—to rejoin Adams and be judged by another set of standards.

In *Tom Jones* the assignment is almost immediate, and Allworthy participates as soon as we meet him in making complex evaluations. The commentator uses his own credit to make certain that he maintains our confidence. Allworthy is fallible only so far as he is not conversant with all the related facts, and his *obiter dicta* rather than his judgments of particular situations are used to establish a frame of positive values through which we later see the protagonist's and other characters' actions. Though our attitude toward Miss Deborah is similar to our attitude toward Slipslop, in relation to characters as important to the future action of the book as Jenny Jones is, original judgments are modified as Allworthy learns more about the characters. The walking concepts—Thwackum and Square—are not introduced until a point at which the protagonist is out of diapers and Allworthy is thoroughly defined and entrenched in his role as paragon, though his limitation—again lack of knowledge of the facts about the two men—delays their absolute refutation. The lack of knowledge sets up a complex interaction between Allworthy, a paragon, though fallible; the walking concepts (whose extreme articulated general principles are disputed by Allworthy); and a protagonist whose feelings and actions meet with the approval of the values established by Allworthy's *obiter dicta*, though the latter's lack of knowledge of the facts leads him temporarily to credit the walking concepts and to discredit the protagonist.

In *Amelia*, however, the situation is reversed. The commentator, far more serious in chapter i than in either of the other two novels, does not cede his prerogative to a "good man" until Book II, and even then he does it slowly and indirectly though finally more unreservedly than in any other book. He maintains complete control in his early chapters using walking concepts rather to characterize ethical deficiencies that threaten the Booths than as characters who are to play active roles in the subsequent action.[55] Though the direct

[55] These characters appear in digressive episodes organized as semi-independent apologues. See chapter five.

comment is more profuse than we have seen it in this connection previously, we soon recognize that we are in the world of situation characters that peopled the coach in *Joseph Andrews* and, in the prison scenes, even the comment is reduced somewhat. The protagonist is introduced into and imprisoned by the twilight world of Justice Thrasher, Constable Gotobed, Blear-eyed Moll, Murphy the crooked lawyer, and their ilk. No paragon is established to evaluate Booth for us; the commentator does this himself. To establish the initial frame of values, however, he does rely on a favorite device: two situation characters, Robinson and Cooper, are developed so that they fully articulate the positions they represent, just as, in *Joseph Andrews*, Barnabas articulated the principles which informed his being. They have no Parson Adams to dispute with them and thus to show them, and the reader, the error of their ways: they have only Booth to contend with and he, alas, agrees with them that action is inefficacious, neither good nor bad, though his "determinism" is predicated on the idea that men are motivated solely by the passion uppermost in their minds at any given moment rather than by any belief in a neo-stoic Fortune or in a divine grace independent of men's actions. Though the commentator indicates that Booth's belief is mistaken, he gives us sufficient explicit indication that he is essentially a good-natured and intelligent man so that we still take him seriously; nor does his philosophy at this point suffer the fate of the philosophy of the walking concepts: Cooper's position, rhetorically if not logically, is deflated by the simple act of making him a thief, while Robinson's portrayal as a liar and a crooked gambler leaves only Booth's deterministic philosophy enough credit to be regarded as an error in belief which has serious consequences as the novel progresses—a belief from which Booth must be converted and one which is thoroughly, though only rhetorically, revealed as foolish by Harrison when he appears on the scene. While the commentator has seen to it that Booth's weaknesses and false belief prevent our mistaking him for the kind of general "good man" represented by Adams or Allworthy, he comes out well enough in the world of situation characters and walking concepts to be acceptable temporarily as commentator in limited kinds of situations: when Miss Matthews tells her own tale (when the commentator does bow out for a while, he lets Booth and Miss Matthews narrate their own adventures), Booth has enough credit to emphasize the ludicrous aspects of her character. After Fanny's "betrayal" of the widow whom Heppers is to make believe he is courting, she is in turn betrayed by "this faithless woman" and laments the friendships of women: "At this remark Booth, though enough affected at some parts of the story, had great difficulty to refrain from laughter."[56] More important, when telling his own tale, he is given enough credit so that we firmly believe in the virtue of the Amelia he describes and, equally important, he establishes Harrison as potential paragon. And, even during Booth's narration, Harrison's generalizations about parental rights to decide their children's marriages are established as positive values.

Each of the three works is organized as a comic action in the sense defined in the first chapter of this book. In each of the novels we are led both to expect and to desire a conclusion in which the characters with whom we have been made to sympathize receive their ethical deserts. One clue to the special power of any comic action is always to be found in the special quality or qualities the novelist maximizes when he represents a character, act, or thought as a hindrance to the achievement of those deserts. In this respect the three novels differ significantly.

From the beginning to the end of *Tom Jones* we are made to expect that *all* the characters, except those who appear in digressions, will receive their ethical deserts, but at the same time we are made to feel that things need not have worked out as well for them as they do.[57]

In *Joseph Andrews* we expect that all the major characters involved in the initial unstable relationship will receive their ethical deserts, but, while we are in no sense allowed to believe that good things invariably happen to good people, the operative power realized in the nondigressive episodes is quite different. It consists rather in casting the most ludicrous light possible upon any character, act, or thought which has been represented as a hindrance to the expected and desired stabilization of relationships at the end. Whatever, even momentarily, unjustifiably delays a sufficiently prosperous Parson Adams from performing the marriage ceremony over Joseph and Fanny is shown as strongly as possible in an absurd light. The evocation of laughter is, as a result, of far greater consequence in *Joseph Andrews* than in any other of Fielding's novels. In this way it is possible to explain how Fielding was able to assert that only the Ridiculous "falls within my province in the present work," while at the same time he was fully conscious of the many demands of a "comic epic" in prose. Partly for this reason, too, relatively important characters who have been "serious" threats to the well-being of Adams, Joseph, and Fanny sometimes emerge relatively unscathed, though circumvented, without our feeling at the end a lack of comic completion. Trulliber

---

[56] Henley, VI, 48 (*Amelia*, I, viii).

[57] The description in text is merely a translation of R. S. Crane's theory into the particular terms employed in this book.

is certainly represented as considerably less admirable than Black George. But some relatively mild punishment for the latter is prerequisite to the conclusion of *Tom Jones*. Though a Trulliber, a Lawyer Scout, a Beau Didapper, a Pamela and her husband receive suitable comic punishment, all that is necessary for a satisfactory conclusion of *Joseph Andrews* is that they be both circumvented and revealed as ludicrous. In its ability to maximize such a comic power, also, we may understand the special virtues of *Joseph Andrews'* episodic plot, or the wisdom of including in the London episodes a set of standards for sexual conduct, presumed to be those in Pamela, which are displayed as completely absurd.

The power of *Amelia* is somewhat more difficult to explain in detail. Though we have sufficient assurances early in the novel that all will be well, the emphasis as each obstacle arises differs radically from that of *Joseph Andrews*. Incidental laughter may be evoked during the episodes which lead to any of the Booths' assorted domestic infelicities, but they culminate in scenes of "sensibility." The actual infelicity is represented in such a manner as to draw from us the last possible tender tear over the heroine's distress. Yet what distinguishes *Amelia* from some other works of sensibility is a still different emphasis which always accompanies the evocation of distress. Some agent or agents are always available to make certain that we do not simply feel the full force of the distress but also understand how the acts and beliefs of agents of the social order represented in the novel have caused the distressing situation.

One aspect of *Amelia* terminates in what we might roughly call "relief" when its ethically deserving heroine receives her desired and expected reward after considerable suffering. That we have expected her to achieve a happy life does not destroy our sense of relief, since the anguish she has felt, and we have felt for her, has been fully exploited. This aspect of *Amelia's* power is simply a concomitant of the discrepancy between our expectations and desires for the Booths and the degree to which Fielding has succeeded in conveying his heroine's temporary distress. But this accounts for only part of the work's special power. What accompanies any relief we may feel is a sense of comprehension, different in kind from that derived simply from understanding motive or even ethical comment in any novel. This is the result of Fielding's success in conveying, by a number of means, at each stage of the action the social causes that delay the final removal of the instability among relationships of all the characters.[58]

---

[58] Despite brilliant parts, the effect of the *whole* of *Amelia* is less than his earlier novels, and it has justifiably received less acclaim. The deficiency is partly the result of

Amelia is not organized as a fictional example of social disorders, however, any more than *Tom Jones* is organized as a fictional example of the statement that things do not always turn out well for the deserving. What I have dubbed "comprehension" is merely one important aspect of the power of the novel. This will not cause the reader of the present work any difficulty if he recalls the distinction made previously between moral intention and form. There is no doubt that Fielding would have wished the reader who finds Trulliber's brand of Christianity ludicrous to laugh at that brand of Christianity in eighteenth-century England. He may not merely have intended us to discover in the non-Christian society represented in *Amelia* an explanation of evils current in England in his day, but to stimulate such discovery might have been his primary intention in writing *Amelia*.

To implement that intention he could have written a satire in which the evils were made the objects of ridicule. He could have written an apologue in which he demonstrated by fictional example that the miseries of his country were the result of its failure to practice a meaningful Christianity. Or he might have chosen, as he did, to write a work in which he represented characters and made us care about them; showed them making a series of choices which complicated their relationships; and, finally, resolved those relationships in a satisfactory manner.

---

the representation of some scenes in a manner consonant with a serious, not a comic, power. These detract from the expectation—the defining mark of the comic—that all will turn out well. But the impossible number of alterations necessary for a possible ending in which Amelia is raped and Booth killed indicates that the basic power of the novel is comic. Some effects that Fielding tried to accomplish in this early "novel of ideas" might better have been realized in a serious action, but his genius inclined strongly to the comic.

Chapter Three

The Fallible Paragons

If thou dost delight in these models of perfection, there are books enow written to gratify thy taste; but, as we have not, in the course of our conversation, ever happened to meet any such person, we have not chosen to introduce any such here.[1]

... in the full blaze of his majesty rose the sun, than which one object alone in this lower creation could be more glorious, and that Mr. Allworthy himself presented—a human being replete with benevolence, meditating in what manner he might render himself most acceptable to his Creator, by doing most good to his creatures.[2]

The Ostensible Contradiction

Despite protestations against unlikely paragons in life or literature, Fielding includes in each of his major novels one character who is represented as a positive ethical norm—a standard of virtue against which are measured the acts and thoughts even of those characters to whom our sympathies are strongly attached. Straying, in Fielding's novels, is the business of his male heroes, who, though represented as essentially good and recognized as such by the paragons, do sin, and occasionally sin mightily. Joseph Andrews is burlesqued as footman-fop; Tom Jones, who shares Allworthy's views and echoes his casual pronouncements with some frequency, becomes involved in shady adventures which nearly prevent his winning Sophia; Booth, who is honestly pleased that he had no "very profane oath" from Harrison's flock, sleeps with Fanny Matthews, almost ruins his family by gambling, and seriously doubts the truth of Christianity.

If the male heroes are not "models of perfection," neither are Allworthy, Harrison, or Adams, despite the fact that each becomes a standard of virtue in the novel in which he appears. For though these do not sin, they err: the first casts Tom Jones from him and draws Blifil to his bosom; the second leaps to an erroneous conclusion and imprisons the much-imprisoned Booth despite the potentially dreadful effect of his action on Amelia and her children; the last is harmlessly vain and has pretensions to Christian Stoicism. If the paragons

[1] Henley, IV, 195 (*Tom Jones*, X, i).
[2] *Ibid.*, III, 27-28 (I, iv).

are, in one sense, models of *human* perfection, they are also humanly fallible; but, since the areas in which we may expect them to err are carefully indicated, Fielding can make frequent use of them as *raisonneurs* without compromising their contributions as characters to the artistic end accomplished in each of the novels. Indeed, the very discrepancies between their ethical competence and their human fallibility can lead, as they do in *Tom Jones* and *Amelia*, to important complications of the plot.

It is to the fallible paragons that Fielding's narrators most unreservedly cede the right to make responsible ethical comments. Hence it is to this class of agent especially, although not exclusively, that we must look for help in answering a question of serious import to the present enquiry: "What is it likely that Fielding must have believed to evaluate as he did such actions, characters, and thoughts in such works?" However, it is not from reading the paragons' comments as occasional essays that we may expect to derive the most fruitful knowledge about Fielding's beliefs, opinions, and prejudices. It is rather the role that the fallible paragons play in determining our feelings toward characters, actions, and thoughts that makes such inferences possible.

A Number of Lies and a
Truthful Inference

Lest the following detailed discussion of how the fallible paragons are created and how they are used in Fielding's novels obscure one of the purposes of defining them as a class, it may be useful to preface it with a single concrete example of the kind of inference we may make even with the limited knowledge provided in the previous chapter.[3] The set of judgments conveyed in connection with the discovery that Tom Jones had persistently lied when he denied Black George's participation in shooting Western's partridges is a convenient example.

Thwackum and Square belong to the subdivision of the class of species characters which I have described as "walking concepts": their acts, thoughts, and speeches are consistently related to an obvious label which is blatantly ridiculed; they are articulate defenders of the ethical beliefs from which their labels are derived.[4] Allworthy is a fallible paragon. Tom, the straying hero,

---

[3] See chapter two for the initial definition of "walking concepts." They are discussed in detail in chapter four.

[4] I am to some degree anticipating the necessary discussion of objections raised in chapter one but not answered until chapter six. This commits the reader only to keeping in abeyance such concerns as whether the artistic end of a novel may dictate the judgments implicit in the "signals," or whether a particular aesthetic *intention* may dictate ethical judgments.

has been so represented that our sympathies are with him more than with any other character, but the definition of his moral status is still largely *to be* determined by other agents.

The relevant judgments begin when Blifil, in revenge for a bloody nose, reveals that Black George did indeed have a hand in shooting Western's partridges and that Tom has persistently lied about the matter. Thwackum immediately prepares to apply birch: "At this the fire flashed from Thwackum's eyes, and he cried out in triumph—'Oh! ho! this is your mistaken notion of honor! This is the boy who was not to be whipped again!' But Mr. Allworthy, with a more gentle aspect, turned towards the lad, and said, 'Is this true, child? How came you to persist so obstinately in a falsehood?' " [5] Tom's answer justifies the lie to Allworthy, who "declared privately he thought the boy deserved reward rather than punishment," [6] but both Square and Thwackum violently disagree with him:

> Thwackum, whose meditations were full of birch, exclaimed against this weak, and, as he said he would venture to call it, wicked lenity. To remit the punishment of such crimes was, he said, to encourage them. He enlarged much on the correction of children, and quoted many texts from Solomon, and others; which, being to be found in so many other books, shall not be found here. He then applied himself to the vice of lying, on which head he was altogether as learned as he had been on the other. [7]

What Thwackum can derive from his religion, Square can inevitably derive from "the rule of right":

> Square said he had been endeavoring to reconcile the behavior of Tom with his idea of perfect virtue, but could not. He owned there was something which at first sight appeared like fortitude in the action; but as fortitude was a virtue, and falsehood a vice, they could by no means agree or unite together. He added, that as this was in some measure to confound virtue and vice, it might be worth Mr. Thwackum's consideration whether a larger castigation might not be laid on upon the account. [8]

But Allworthy cannot be swayed by "the religion of Thwackum or with the virtue of Square." [9]

[5] Henley, III, 119 (*Tom Jones*, III, iv).
[6] *Ibid.*, p. 120 (III, v).
[7] *Ibid.*, pp. 120-121.
[8] *Ibid.*, p. 121.
[9] *Ibid.*

Two walking concepts, then, have argued, according to the principles from which their labels are derived, that lying is a vice and must be punished; they propose severe castigation for the hero, the character to whom our sympathies are strongly attached. The paragon, however, not only prevents further castigation of Tom but refuses to interpret the act of lying as inevitable vice; he asks "how came you" to lie, and the answer he receives causes him actually to admire the act.

Considerations similar to those justifying for Allworthy Tom's persistence in falsehood are involved in the condemnation of Black George: "Towards the gamekeeper the good man behaved with more severity. He presently summoned that poor fellow before him, and, after many bitter remonstrances, paid him his wages, and dismissed him from his service; for Mr. Allworthy rightly observed that there was a great difference between being guilty of a falsehood to excuse yourself and to excuse another." [10] Indeed, it is Blifil's ability to counterfeit generous motives for his actions that enables him to maintain the approbation of Allworthy. When the former freed Sophia's bird, for example, the paragon "was sorry for what his nephew had done, but could not consent to punish him, as he acted rather from a generous than unworthy motive." [11] Allworthy's propensity to be fooled by villains defines in large part the area of his fallibility. Since the reader has far more reason than the paragon to distrust Blifil's motives, he will in no way excuse the act that causes Sophia such pain; but the principle by which the paragon has judged the merit of Blifil's action remains unimpeached.

Attempts by Blifil and the two walking concepts to disparage Tom to Allworthy meet with consistent failure as long as they are confined to revelations of ostensibly culpable actions. When the hero's affair with Molly is discovered, Allworthy listens to Thwackum and Square and gives "a patient hearing to their invectives," but then answers "coldly: 'That young men of Tom's complexion were too generally addicted to this vice.' " Though he is angry with Tom's incontinence, he is "no less pleased with the honor and honesty of his self-accusation." [12] Square begins to meet with success, however, the moment he begins to challenge Tom's motives: "You now plainly see whence all this seeming generosity of this young man to the family of the gamekeeper proceeded. He supported the father in order to corrupt the daughter, and preserved the family from starving, to bring one of them to shame and ruin.

[10] *Ibid.*
[11] *Ibid.*, p. 153 (IV, iv).
[12] *Ibid.*, p. 188 (IV, xi).

This is friendship! this is generosity! As Sir Richard Steele say [*sic*], 'Gluttons who give high prices for delicacies are very worthy to be called generous.' " [13]

Since Fielding has indicated what Tom's motives were, the reader is in no danger of misunderstanding the hero. But to Allworthy, who never read *Tom Jones*, Square's arguments must be partially convincing: "The goodness of Allworthy had prevented these considerations from occurring to himself; yet were they too plausible to be absolutely and hastily rejected, when laid before his eyes by another. Indeed what Square had said sunk very deeply into his mind, and the uneasiness which it there created was very visible to the other. . . ." [14] The uneasiness, however, momentarily stops short of conviction. Allworthy, ostensibly on his deathbed, remarks that Tom has ethical qualities which make him deserving of happiness, but lacks the "prudence and religion" necessary for achieving it. And it is, of course, "goodness, generosity and honor," unrestrained by prudence, which lead to Tom's drunkenness when he learns of Allworthy's probable recovery and which subsequently lead him to battle Blifil, who again taunts him with the accident of his birth.

A single word of truth about the motives for Tom's drunkenness and for his battle with Blifil would obviously bring forgiveness, perhaps even elicit quiet admiration, from Allworthy. Unfortunately for Tom, though happily for the plot of *Tom Jones*, Fielding had a wonderful gift for creating agents appropriate for their roles at each stage of the comic action. Allworthy's propensity to be deceived by characters who counterfeit generous motives—his "fallibility"—makes it almost inevitable that he will believe Blifil's account of Tom's ostensible misdeeds. This propensity is reinforced by the fact that the "truth" must apparently be forced from the successful schemer, who even pretends to intercede for Tom with such plausible effect that the paragon does not know "whether I should blame or applaud your [Blifil's] goodness, in concealing such villany [*sic*] a moment. . . ." [15] The combination of modesty and reluctance to insist on the ceremony due his position—both emphasized as important elements in Allworthy's character—further conspires to prevent him from asking "how came you to. . . .": "Many disadvantages attended poor Jones in making his defense; nay, indeed, he hardly knew his accusation; for as Mr. Allworthy, in recounting the drunkenness, etc., while he lay ill, out of modesty sunk everything related particularly to himself, which indeed

[13] *Ibid.*, p. 189.
[14] *Ibid.*, p. 190.
[15] *Ibid.*, p. 314 (VI, x).

principally constituted the crime; Jones could not deny the charge." [16] Tom is not exiled from Paradise Hall because of drunkenness and brawling, but because the motives which led to his misconduct have been misrepresented.

A significant number of random judgments conveyed in the course of the novel excuse an apparently bad act, as when Tom, acting in the kind of situation in which Fielding's heroes become competent to evaluate directly,[17] exculpates a highway robber because his crime was committed for the sake of his hungry family. If we then ask what Fielding must have believed to have so evaluated such characters, actions, and thoughts, the answer is obvious: when he wrote *Tom Jones*, Fielding must have been deeply committed to the notion that action should be judged according to the motives that led to it.

This is one minor and not very startling inference. Yet even this inference is important for a biography of Fielding. It enables us to understand how frustrating Mandeville's ostensible similarity to Fielding must have been to the novelist and why it was inevitable that the latter strongly attacked the cunning physician. For Mandeville's neat dialectic, designed to trouble the subtle schools by defining the very springs of action as selfish, must inadvertently, if only temporarily, have confounded the practical moralist accustomed to making judgments by those selfsame springs. To a man less profoundly committed than Fielding to judging actions according to the motives of the men who performed them (though he might indeed wish to disparage the notion that private vices are public benefits), the artful reduction of human motives to uniformly selfish passions need not have been disconcerting: Tom Jones lies and has therefore engaged in an unvirtuous action; a young woman has lost her virginity without benefit of clergy and, though we may sympathize with her plight, she might well use her coffin as a desk, complete her journal, and die; a man has stolen and should be punished by hanging.

But when a man is committed, intuitively or consciously, to determining the ethical caliber of a variety of acts by reference to the motives that led to them, then his inability to refute the Mandevillian reduction becomes a measure of his inability to justify his judgments. One possible justification would be to deny the potency of the passions and to emphasize the power of reason to curb them and to motivate action. In a *Champion* essay[18] written long before *Tom Jones*, Fielding had informally explored the possibility that reason might control the passions; but even here the power of the former is

[16] *Ibid.*, p. 316 (VI, xi).
[17] See pp. 182-207.
[18] Henley, XV, 177-181.

seen as so circumscribed as to be well-nigh nugatory. In fact, if we ignore the
expressed faith in the power of religion to control the passions—a faith which
Fielding shows little evidence of sharing before the writing of *Amelia*—
Barrow's statement of the relative efficacy of reason and the passions might
be Fielding's:

> Doth it [content] result from a well-governing and ordering our passions?
> Then it is plain, that only a pious man is capable thereof: for piety only can
> affect that; it alone, with the powerful aid of Divine grace, doth guide our
> passions by exact rules, doth set them upon worthy objects, doth temper and tune
> them in just harmony, doth seasonably curb and check them, doth rightly correct
> and reform them.
>
> This no bare reason (which naturally is so dimm and so feeble in man) can
> atchieve: much less can unreasonableness do it. . . .[19]

With little faith in the efficacy of reason and, indeed much dissatisfaction
with an ethic predicated on the notion that rational denial of the dictates of
passion leads to good action (he ridiculed Adams' Stoic pretensions in *Joseph
Andrews*, and in *Tom Jones* took pains to include the adventures of the Man
of the Hill as a sort of negative analogy to Tom's moral state),[20] Fielding
would have found it impossible to refute Mandeville by disputing the potency
of the passions. Without a burning faith in the "powerful aid of Divine
grace," he might still have justified the kinds of judgments he was prone to
make by assuming that there are benevolent as well as selfish passions. Allworthy's initial reaction to the discovery of the foundling in his bed is not
ascribed to reason, principle, or even religious rule: "He stood sometime lost
in astonishment at this sight [the infant Tom]; *but, as good nature always
had the ascendant in his mind, he soon began to be touched by sentiments of
compassion* for the little wretch before him." [21] Reason, of course, appears
in *Tom Jones* in the guise of the prudence that Tom lacks. Allworthy, the
paragon figure, on his deathbed, explains to Tom that insufficient prudence
may prevent him from attaining the happiness he deserves; yet the presence
or absence of prudence has no implications for judging Tom's deserts. Similarly, and more strikingly in the light of arguments that Fielding's religious
views were not greatly altered during his adult years, the religion Tom lacks

---

[19] Isaac Barrow, "The Profit of Godliness," *Works*, ed. James Hamilton (3 vols.;
London: Thomas Nelson, 1847), I, 23.

[20] R. S. Crane, "The Concept of Plot and the Plot of *Tom Jones*," *Critics and
Criticism* (Chicago: University of Chicago Press, 1952). And see my discussion of this
episode in chapter five.

[21] Henley, III, 23 (*Tom Jones*, I, iii). Italics mine.

does not alter Allworthy's view of the hero's deserts and does not play a major role even in that slight moral regeneration which helps to put Tom in possession of happiness. This is *not* to say that Allworthy, Tom, or Henry Fielding were Deists or even that they were not *good* Christians of one variety. But if Fielding had shared not merely Barrow's view of the relative potency of reason and the passions but also the religious conviction which the eminent divine had expressed in the passage quoted above, it is unlikely that he would have evaluated such characters, actions, and thoughts as he did in *Tom Jones*. On the other hand, I should not wish to assert that Fielding, had he been asked about the passage in question, would necessarily have denied Barrow's description of the role that divine grace and the rules of religion play in controlling the passions. There is evidence enough that Fielding, the practical moralist and the practical Christian, made many attempts to reconcile his view of such matters as the role that "Fortune" plays in human affairs, the principles by which he actually made judgments, and his convictions about human nature with his general belief in Christianity.

To have evaluated actions, characters, and thoughts as he did in *Tom Jones*, Fielding must have been deeply committed to judging action according to the motive of its agent; he must have identified motives largely with the passions; and he must have reconciled the practical judgments he made with his conviction about the springs of action by assuming that passions were not uniformly selfish but that some were benevolent, others maleficent. At the same time, Fielding, like Allworthy and Tom, must have thought of himself and been thought of as a perfectly orthodox Christian; there could have been little doubt in his mind that his mode of making particular judgments, his view of what led to human happiness or misery, his convictions about human psychology, were intellectually reconcilable with Anglican teaching. But he had not yet made that intellectual reconciliation.

Had he done so, *Tom Jones* would not have been the *Tom Jones* we know, though the resultant differences in evaluations of characters, actions, and thoughts would not necessarily have made it a better or a worse work than it is. For Fielding did not embody his moral judgments or beliefs in an apologue; *Tom Jones* is not organized as a fictional example of the truth of a formulated statement. To achieve the artistic end of his "history," he need only have made us happy that Tom marries Sophia, is reconciled with Allworthy, is not Jenny Jones' son, and so on; though the moral effect of the work would differ with alterations in either the characters, actions, or thoughts which were judged, or with alterations in the judgments of the characters, actions, and thoughts in the *Tom Jones* we know, the artistic end need not have been compromised by the change in belief which led to the changed evaluations.[22]

But it is one thing to exculpate a highway robber in a novel, and another to decide to let one go free or to hang him in everyday life, and this is precisely the kind of decision Fielding was called upon to make with increasing frequency after he wrote *Tom Jones*. For a man of Fielding's sensitivity and moral concern it was no light thing to hang a Bosavern Penlez; nor, as his own apologia for his decree in that case indicates, could he rest content with a purely legal justification for his decision. We should certainly not expect that a division of the passions into good ones and bad ones would provide Fielding with a satisfactory intellectual justification for deciding matters of life and death; if the passions control action, it must be hard to condemn a man to death because one of the bad ones happened to dictate an illegal action. Furthermore, he was faced daily with a responsibility to a society which had made him magistrate; one can see, even in his apologia for hanging Penlez,[23] that Fielding *had* to judge action as much by its consequences as by the motives which led to it. It would be surprising if Fielding, though admittedly neither abstract philosopher nor theologian, had not tried mightily to reconcile his intuitions about what constituted good and bad, and the socio-ethical implications of the legal decisions he was called upon to make in situations where his customary mode of making judgments was inapplicable, with the dictates of the religion he had, with obvious sincerity, professed throughout his mature years. And it would have been amazing if such an attempt were not reflected in the particular judgments of the actions, thoughts, and characters represented in *Amelia*, even if the novel had embodied no moral purpose. In fact, *Amelia* was "sincerely designed to promote the cause of virtue, and to expose some of the most glaring evils, as well public as private, which at present infest the country." [24] If we ask the controlling question of this inquiry about *Amelia* and answer it with some precision we may isolate important changes in Fielding's beliefs; we need not become partisans either of those who argue that Fielding's beliefs were virtually unchanged throughout his life or those who use evidence of change to infer radical conversion from Deism to Christianity.

---

[22] The relation of the judgments conveyed in a novel to its artistic end and to the moral intentions of the author is a very complicated matter. It is discussed in some detail in chapter six.

[23] Henley, XIII, 257-288.

[24] Henley, VI, 12.

Almost at the beginning of *Amelia,* we do indeed discover that particular forms of "determinism"—each of which would seriously compromise human responsibility for evil action—are judged ridiculous; the Stoic belief in capricious fortune and the Methodist belief in preordained grace which need not be reflected in action become mere labels for species characters.[25] The Mandevillian reduction is admired in passing only by the ethically undesirable Fanny Matthews. But Booth's clearly formulated deterministic notions, whose error he perceives only at the end of the novel, are closely analogous to those we have inferred were held by the Fielding who wrote *Tom Jones.* As is not the case with Fielding, however, the erring hero's belief that men are motivated by good or bad passions has led him to doubt the truth of the Christian religion; when Booth is converted by Barrow's sermons, Harrison, the paragon figure in *Amelia,* does not argue that the passions should not be regarded as the springs of action, but rather that the church's recognition of the potency of the passions and its equipment for controlling them argue for the truth of Christianity. Furthermore, a series of judgments, attributed primarily to Harrison, indicates that social evil is largely the result of the magnification of private vices in the public world of a non-Christian society.

The complexities of Fielding's attempt to reconcile ethical judgment of action, social inequities, and legal opinion with Christian belief are discussed below.[26] Here we need only stress that one inference drawn largely from a paragon figure's judgment of a number of lies has put us in firm possession of one fact. This, in turn, makes possible coherent speculation; and, finally, further consideration of the signals that enabled us to derive the first inference will allow us partially to determine the validity of such speculation.

On Recognizing Paragons

Early in *Joseph Andrews,* the narrator insisted on Adams' goodness in a series of direct statements and, almost immediately, began to use Adams as an agent important in determining our attitudes toward the acts, thoughts, and general nature of other characters. Considerable subtlety in the attitudes evoked toward Slipslop and the Boobys is made possible by their treatment and opinions of the good man; his opinion of Joseph, on the other hand, plays an important part in determining our reactions to the hero. Once Adams has praised him and the commentator's remarks have confirmed the justness of Adams' opinion, Joseph in turn becomes a semi-independent

[25] See chapter four.
[26] See pp. 147-149, 189-190, and 260-262.

ethical agent. The result is that his immediate praise of Adams reinforces
our respect for that character's ability to judge as *the* good man, the paragon.[27]

Adams, Allworthy, and Harrison are defined and maintained as paragons
by roughly the same means. Praise from the narrator, the male hero, the
heroine, and minor nonspecies characters (often previously judged by the
paragon himself) is liberally sprinkled throughout the novels and is especially
abundant at moments when, for the sake of the artistic end of the novel, it
is important for the paragon's judgment to be accepted without question.

Next in importance to the remarks of the commentators are those of the
hero of each novel, since he is the character to whom our sympathies must be
strongly attached.

When Joseph, for example, is only a short way out of the woods of burlesque, Adams discovers the battered footman in bed at Tow-wouse's inn and,
refusing to leave him there, offers what money he has. Though his action
alone would be sufficient to maintain his character as that of a good man,
still more is required to maintain his status as *the* good man of the novel.
Joseph reacts as follows: "This goodness of Parson Adams brought tears
into Joseph's eyes; he declared, 'He had now a second reason to desire life,
that he might show his gratitude to such a friend.' " [28] Again, after the
mock-heroic description of the attack of the dogs on Adams, we learn that
"Joseph answered, with great intrepidity, that they had first fallen on his
friend . . . whilst his veins contained a single drop of blood, he would not
stand idle by and see that gentleman (pointing to Adams) abused either by
man or beast." [29]

After the burlesque scenes Adams accompanies Joseph and Fanny on their
journey. The result is that, although there are constant indications of mutual
approbation, the hero's explicit praise of the paragon is less conspicuous than it
is in either of the other two novels. In *Amelia* and in *Tom Jones*, however,
since the heroes are separated both geographically and morally from the paragons for long stretches of the action, frequent and sometimes lengthy expressions of faith in the good men are more important. In *Tom Jones* the hero's
expressions of faith begin early in the novel and reappear throughout. Punished for refusing to betray Black George, Tom persists in denying that he
had a partner in his crime. To his own consternation he convinces Allworthy
of his innocence: "Tom's guilt now flew in his face more than any severity

[27] See chapter two.
[28] Henley, I, 80 (*Joseph Andrews*, I, xv).
[29] *Ibid.*, p. 273 (III, vi).

could make it. He could more easily bear the lashes of Thwackum than the
generosity of Allworthy. The tears burst from his eyes, and he fell upon his
knees, crying 'Oh, sir, you are too good to me. Indeed you are. Indeed I don't
deserve it.' " [30] Sometimes Tom invokes the name of the good man in order
to refute the arguments of another character; the effect is not only to justify
his own argument by the highest authority in the book but to maintain Allworthy as the highest authority. Tom "once ventured [in arguing with
Square] to make a jest of the rule of right; and at another time said he believed there was no rule in the world capable of making such a man as his
father (for so Mr. Allworthy suffered himself to be called)." [31]

This dual effect of self-justification and of insistence on Allworthy as paragon results also when Tom defends his actions directly to Allworthy, invokes
the latter's goodness, and wins his concurrence:

> "Indeed, my dear sir, I love and honor you more than all the world: I know
> the great obligations I have to you, and should detest myself if I thought my
> heart was capable of ingratitude. Could the little horse you gave me speak, I
> am sure he could tell you how fond I was of your present; for I had more
> pleasure in feeding him than in riding him. . . . You yourself, sir, I am con-
> vinced, in my case, would have done the same: for none ever so sensibly felt the
> misfortunes of others. What would you feel, dear sir, if you thought yourself
> the occasion of them? Indeed, sir, there never was any misery like theirs." [32]

After Tom's description of the misery of the Seagrims, "Mr. Allworthy now
stood silent for some moments, and before he spoke the tears started from his
eyes." [33]

Tom's remarks to and about Allworthy not only determine the reader's attitude toward Tom's own immediate action and thought but also help to assure
that Allworthy's future acts, thoughts, and even his *obiter dicta* will remain a
positive measure of what we are meant to react to as ethically desirable. Even
when the action draws to its comic conclusion and the paragon is made aware
of the great error of judgment that led him to banish Tom, the latter—in the
only kind of situation in which his judgment must be more valid than Allworthy's—refuses to accept his uncle's self-accusation:

> "O, talk not so!" answered Jones; "indeed, sir, you have used me nobly. The
> wisest man might be deceived as you were; and, under such a deception, the
> best must have acted just as you did. Your goodness displayed itself in the midst

---

[30] *Ibid.*, III, 112-113 (*Tom Jones*, III, ii).
[31] *Ibid.*, p. 123 (III, v).
[32] *Ibid.*, pp. 133-134 (III, viii).
[33] *Ibid.*

of your anger, just as it then seemed. I owe everything to that goodness, of
which I have been most unworthy. Do not put me on self-accusation, by carrying your generous sentiments too far. Alas! sir, I have not been punished more
than I have deserved; and it shall be the whole business of my future life to
deserve that happiness you now bestow on me; for, believe me, my dear uncle,
my punishment hath not been thrown away upon me: though I have been a
great, I am not a hardened sinner; I thank Heaven, I have had time to reflect
on my past life, where, though I cannot charge myself with any gross villainy,
yet I can discern follies and vices more than enough to repent and to be ashamed
of; follies which have been attended with dreadful consequences to myself, and
have brought me to the brink of destruction." [34]

The role of the hero in defining the paragon becomes most complicated in
Amelia, since the initial remarks that determine Harrison's ethical status are
not the narrator's but Booth's; the ethical status of the latter has initially,
though only initially, been determined without reference to the paragon. Before Booth introduces Harrison into his narration to Fanny Matthews, the
hero has been partially defined for his ethical role by his interaction with some
"walking concepts," to whom he is seen as vastly superior, and by direct comments from the narrator. Even before he tells his tale to Fanny, Booth has
been used as a minor commentator so that, when he tells his tale, we credit
those of his statements—including direct ethical comments—which do not
involve his theory of the predominant passion, itself defined as invalid by the
narrator's comments. On the other hand, Booth almost immediately creates
in Harrison an ethical paragon as capable as an Allworthy of judging the
actions Booth describes to Fanny and the actions he engages in subsequently.

Though initially against the marriage of Amelia and Booth, Harrison, as
described in Booth's narrative, is soon won over, and Booth refers to him as
"one of the best of men." [35] In describing him, Booth actually replaces Harrison's name with the epithet, "the good man" [36] or "our worthy friend." [37]
Before long, Booth, not content with mere flattering description of Harrison's
role in the earlier adventures of Amelia and himself, emphasizes the doctor's
amiable characteristics in what threaten to become digressive encomiums:

"Of all mankind the doctor is the best of comforters. As his excessive good-
nature makes him take vast delight in the office, so his great penetration into the
human mind, joined to his great experience, renders him the most wonderful

[34] *Ibid.,* V, 346 (XVIII, x).
[35] *Ibid.,* VI, 82 (*Amelia,* II, iv).
[36] *Ibid.,* p. 84 (II, v).
[37] *Ibid.,* p. 92 (II, vi).

proficient in it; and he so well knows when to soothe, when to reason, and when to ridicule, that he never applies any of those arts improperly. . . ." [38]

Or, still more striking:

"Nothing, however, can be imagined more agreeable than the life that the doctor leads in this homely house, which he calls his earthly paradise. All his parishoners, whom he treats as his children, regard him as their common father. Once in a week he constantly visits every house in the parish, examines, commends, and rebukes, as he finds occasion. This is practiced likewise by his curate in his absence; and so good an effect is produced by this their care, that no quarrels ever proceed either to blows or lawsuits; no beggar is to be found in the whole parish; nor did I ever hear a very profane oath all the time I lived in it.

"But to return from so agreeable a digression . . . ." [39]

Far more than Joseph Andrews and more even than Tom Jones, Booth tends to make general statements based upon specific characteristics of the paragon. He describes his reactions to Harrison's leaving to attend "a young lord" in his travels as follows:

"By this means I was bereft not only of the best companion in the world, but of the best counsellor; a loss of which I have since felt the bitter consequence; for no greater advantage, I am convinced, can arrive to a young man, who hath any degree of understanding, than an intimate converse with one of riper years, who is not only able to advise, but who knows the manner of advising. By this means alone, youth can enjoy the benefit of the experience of age, and that at a time of life when such experience will be of more service to a man than when he hath lived long enough to acquire it of himself." [40]

Though the heroine in Fielding's novels less frequently expresses her admiration for the paragon, her plaudits are, in some ways, even more effective in helping to maintain the good man as *the* good man in each novel; she does not occupy the inconstant moral position of her mate, or mate-to-be, but is herself a sort of "non-discursive" paragon, a fit reward for the morally regenerate hero. Her direct moral comment is strictly limited to that defined by other agents—particularly by the fallible male paragons—as appropriate for a desirable woman to make. Though infrequently argumentative, even when her moral position is that approved by the paragons, she comments, when she does so at all, to great effect.

This is least obvious in the case of Fanny, who, though her virtues are

[38] *Ibid.*, p. 115 (III, ii).
[39] *Ibid.*, p. 164 (III, xii).
[40] *Ibid.*, pp. 167-168.

legion, has such decided limitations as a conversationalist that her admiration
for Adams, unlike his approval of her, is expressed in a brief remark or gesture rather than in extended encomium. Much as she wishes to marry Joseph,
she accepts Adams' notions about the impropriety of haste. Encouraged by
Fanny's vehement "O Joseph! you have won me; I will be yours forever," [41]
the hero asks Adams to marry them immediately, but the latter rebukes him
and makes a speech about the importance of the banns. Though Fanny will
be Joseph's forever, she will do so only with Adams' consent: she "agreed with
the parson, saying to Joseph with a blush, 'she assured him she would not consent to any such thing [marriage by license], and that she wondered at his of-
fering it.' " [42] Her affection for the good man is briefly displayed by the
strength of her concern for him: Adams' being thrown from a horse "afforded infinite merriment to the servants, and no less frightened poor Fanny,
who beheld him as he passed by the coach; but the mirth of the one and
the terror of the other were soon determined when the parson declared he had
received no damage." [43]

Sophia and Amelia, both more articulate, are less laconic about their admiration for Allworthy and Harrison, respectively. Sophia has suffered greatly as
a result of Allworthy's inability to understand that Blifil is a villain; yet, when
the paragon urges Tom's suit on her, she prefaces almost every remark she
utters with a testament to his extraordinary goodness:

> "Sir," said Sophia, with a little modest hesitation, "this behavior is most kind
> and generous, and such as I could expect only from Mr. Allworthy. . . ." [44]

> "I am convinced, sir, you are too good and generous to resent my refusal of
> your nephew." [45]

> "You speak now, Mr. Allworthy," cries she, "with a delicacy which few
> men are capable of feeling!" [46]

> "Let me beseech you, let me conjure you, by all the goodness which I, and
> all who know you, have experienced. . . ." [47]

Sophia's short-lived reluctance to marry the sinning Tom provides an exciting last barrier to the fine comic resolution of the book, but we must not resent

[41] *Ibid.*, I, 184 (*Joseph Andrews*, II, xiii).
[42] *Ibid.*, p. 185.
[43] *Ibid.*, p. 389 (IV, xvi).
[44] *Ibid.*, V, 337 (*Tom Jones*, XVIII, ix).
[45] *Ibid.*, p. 338.
[46] *Ibid.*
[47] *Ibid.*, p. 339.

her temporary refusal or her marriage to Tom will seem less desirable, and the force of the comic ending substantially reduced. Both our desire for the marriage and our acquiescence in Sophia's delay depend in part on the ethical status of the hero and heroine as measured by the scheme of values by which characters, actions, and thoughts have been judged in the novel. Allworthy's expression of his desire to have Sophia marry Tom and Sophia's tributes to Allworthy as paragon emphasize the judgments on which they agree: their accord on limiting the right of parents to a negative voice in regard to their children's potential mates, and on some other aspects of marriage as well, strongly reaffirms the judgments which have emerged from such scenes as that in which Tom argues with Broadbrim[48] and that in which he confronts the elder Nightingale. Each of these points of agreement serves to strengthen the desirability of the marriage of Sophia to Tom and, simultaneously, to justify the heroine's temporary rejection of Tom's suit.

If Sophia retains her faith in Allworthy as the good man, Amelia must doubt the goodness of all men in order to accept the notion that Harrison has had Booth imprisoned for debt. She cries, "Dr. Harrison! . . . Well, then, there is an end of all goodness in the world. I will never have a good opinion of any human being more." [49] When corrected by Harrison for stating that "all mankind are almost villains," Amelia insists to the paragon himself on his own goodness, much as Sophia did to Allworthy in the passage quoted above:

"Indeed, my dear sir," cries Amelia, "you are the wisest as well as the best man in the world." [50]

"But you understand human nature to the bottom," answered Amelia; "and your mind is the treasury of all ancient and modern learning." [51]

"Well, sir," cries Amelia, "I must admire you and love you for your goodness." [52]

When the worthy blesses the worthy in this manner, we can hardly regard the latter as anything but a paragon. Each Harrisonian dictum eliciting such encomium has received the strongest single vote of confidence possible to the novel, for the heroine who *is* good and can recognize good intuitively has been represented as learning from the only other ethically unexceptionable charac-

[48] See chapter five.
[49] Henley, VII, 64 (*Amelia*, VII, x).
[50] *Ibid.*, p. 145 (IX, v).
[51] *Ibid.*, p. 146.
[52] *Ibid.*

ter in the novel the proper intellectual justification for a particular ethical judgment.

In *Amelia*, more than in either of Fielding's previous novels, the paragon is maintained as such because, as a couple, the hero and heroine allow him to make important decisions for them. It is Harrison who decides, despite Amelia's initial objections, that it would be dishonorable in Booth not to fight with his regiment in Gibraltar:

> " 'Do you hear that, sister?' cries Miss Betty. 'Yes, I do hear it,' answered Amelia, with more spirit than I [Booth] ever saw her exert before, 'and would preserve his honor at the expense of my life. I will preserve it if it should be at that expense; and since it is Dr. Harrison's opinion that he ought to go, I give my consent. Go, my dear husband. . . .' " [53]

Though the paragon's opinion cannot prevent Amelia from enduring a number of exemplary weeping spells and fainting fits at her husband's departure, it is sufficient to convince her of the right course of action and reconcile her to it.

When Fielding's narrators, heroes, and heroines regard one character in each novel as the good man, the latter's judgments of actions, thoughts, and other characters must inevitably become those most closely identified with the ethical standards of the novel, except at points where those judgments are represented as resulting from the paragon's fallibility. But, quite naturally, other characters also recognize the good man's excellence and, especially in the last two novels, their testimony reminds us both of the paragon's specific ethical pronouncements and of his ethical superiority at moments when we might forget either or both. In *Joseph Andrews*, Adams and his judgments are constantly at hand, with the single exception of the burlesque London episodes;[54] so such interpreted testimony is of little importance. Obvious fondness for Adams is expressed by two casual parishioners who chance to meet him: " 'Tom,' cries one of the footmen, 'there's Parson Adams smoking his pipe in the gallery.' 'Yes,' says Tom, 'I pulled off my hat to him, and the parson spoke to me.' " [55] The least admirable character recognizes his honesty: "so good was the credit of Mr. Adams that even Mr. Peter, the Lady Booby's steward, would have lent him a guinea with very little security." [56]

[53] *Ibid.*, VI, 110 (III, i).
[54] The importance of Adams' isolation from London is discussed in chapter two.
[55] Henley, I, 89 (*Joseph Andrews*, I, xvi).
[56] *Ibid.*, p. 107 (II, ii).

But in *Tom Jones*, Allworthy is not seen during much of the middle part of the action, though his ethical standards measure the acts of the exiled Tom. Testimony from outsiders is important and receives particular emphasis when the hero is geographically and morally separated from the paragon. Such testimony begins, however, before Tom's exile: although Allworthy's diatribe against incontinence is directed at Jenny Jones, the lickerish young woman responds with a statement that to "know you, sir, and not love your goodness, would be an argument of total want of sense or goodness in any one." [57] As soon as Tom does begin his peregrinations, we conveniently discover that Allworthy's reputation is well known; Partridge confides to the landlord of an inn that Tom " 'is the heir of Squire Allworthy.' 'What, the squire who doth so much good all over the country?' cries my landlady." [58]

The casual though emphatic reintroduction of the paragon's name and goodness keeps us in touch with the moral center of the novel at a moment when the hero has just performed an act stemming from that natural goodness which Allworthy has recognized as essential to his character (he has just rescued Mrs. Waters while the Man of the Hill sat stoically by) and followed it by an action which, with qualifications, is condemned by the paragon's code (he has slept with the lady). But the most important use of the reintroduction of the paragon's name occurs in the London scenes, when Mrs. Miller, Allworthy's greatest devotee, makes a series of judgments about Tom and Tom's actions the validity of which depends heavily on her being a spokesman for the absent paragon. Mrs. Miller's praise of Allworthy helps to maintain the latter in his role as paragon and simultaneously identifies Tom with his uncle's goodness. Having heard the tale of the impoverished Andersons, Tom gives Mrs. Miller his purse for them. Mrs. Miller "burst into a kind of agony of transport," and cried, " 'Good heavens! Is there such a man in the world?' But recollecting herself, she said, 'Indeed, I know one such; but can there be another?' " [59] From previous references we are aware that the "one such" to whom Tom is compared is Allworthy. But we are not allowed to miss the significance of Mrs. Miller's simultaneous praise of Allworthy and her identification of Tom with him; Nightingale, not an ungenerous young man himself, discusses the Andersons' plight and, referring to the paragon by name, makes the following suggestion. " 'Suppose, madam,' said he, 'you

---

[57] *Ibid.*, III, 39 (*Tom Jones*, I, vii).
[58] *Ibid.*, IV, 184 (IX, vi).
[59] *Ibid.*, V, 71 (XIII, viii).

should recommend them to Mr. Allworthy? Or what think you of a collection? I will give them a guinea with all my heart.' " [60]

But Allworthy need not be approached on this occasion; Tom has already played his part, and Nightingale's relative parsimony contrasted with Tom's generosity emphasizes the latter's ethical kinship with the explicitly-alluded-to Allworthy, the highest ethical praise the novel can bestow. The praise is most timely, since Tom is at his lowest moral ebb at this moment. In forcing us to regard Tom as essentially good despite his sordid role as Lady Bellaston's cully, Mrs. Miller and Nightingale unwittingly coöperate in maintaining Allworthy, long absent from the novel's pages, as the moral touchstone of the novel and, at the same time, they momentarily attach the weight of Allworthy's ethical excellence to Tom precisely when his imperfections loom largest. Since *Tom Jones* is not punitive comedy, such scenes mitigate our disapprobation of the hero and thereby help to achieve the artistic end of the novel.

Even the characters who tend to disparage Allworthy at various points, if they are meant to retain any of our sympathy, at some point must give him his due. Partridge may honestly think that the paragon is Tom's father, but he is obviously sincere when he says, "and when my wife died (for till that time I received a pension of £12 a year from an unknown hand, which indeed I believe was your honor's own, for nobody that ever I heard of doth these things besides). . . ." [61] And even the irascible Squire Western grudgingly acknowledges the good man's influence: ". . . Western promised to follow his advice in his behavior to Sophia, saying, 'I don't know how 'tis, but d--n me, Allworthy, if you don't make me always do just as you please; and yet I have as good an esteate [*sic*] as you, and am in the commission of the peace as well as yourself.' " [62]

The recognition of the paragon's superiority by minor characters is somewhat less important in *Amelia*, but is nevertheless present. Mrs. Harris, despite her desire to see Amelia marry a rich man and despite her initial aversion to Booth, gives way before Harrison:

> He concluded with saying that Amelia's happiness, her heart—nay, her very reputation—were all concerned in this matter, to which, as he had been made instrumental, he was resolved to carry her through it; and then, taking the license from his pocket, declared to Mrs. Harris that he would go that instant and marry her daughter wherever he found her. This speech, the doctor's voice, his look, and his behavior, all which are sufficiently calculated to inspire awe,

[60] *Ibid.*
[61] *Ibid.*, p. 318 (XVIII, vi).
[62] *Ibid.*, p. 345 (XVIII, ix).

and even terror, when he pleases, frightened poor Mrs. Harris, and wrought a
more sensible effect than it was in his power to produce by all his arguments and
entreaties. . . .[63]

Atkinson's disbelief in Harrison's ability to perform an ignoble deed is as
strong as Amelia's, and, when asked to name the man responsible for Booth's
arrest, " 'One I am ashamed to name,' cries the sergeant; 'indeed I had
always a very different opinion of him; I could not have believed anything
but my own ears and eyes; but Dr. Harrison is the man who hath done the
deed.' " [64] Even as morally culpable a character as Fanny Matthews recognizes that Harrison is "one of the best men in the world . . . and an honor
to the sacred order to which he belongs." [65]

Fielding's commentators are anything but inarticulate admirers of the
paragons. At the beginning of *Joseph Andrews*, Adams' virtues are delineated
and immediately used in the evaluation of Joseph; the areas in which he is
likely to be foolish are briefly indicated and then ignored until later in the
novel, when even a strong touch of ridicule cannot compromise his ability
to function as a paragon in the areas in which his judgment is unchallenged.
But the commentators' introductory praise of the paragons is only a small
part of the story. Actually, the coöperation between commentator and paragon in conveying authorial judgment is so complex that I can only touch upon
it here.

Note, for example, the subtle effect of the commentator's apology for
Adams' unheroic flight from the attacking dogs:

> Nor let this be any detraction from the bravery of his character: let the
> number of the enemies, and the surprise in which he was taken, be considered;
> and if there be any modern so outrageously brave that he cannot admit of flight
> in any circumstance whatever, I say (but I whisper that softly, and I solemnly
> declare without any intention of giving offense to any brave man in the nation),
> I say, or rather I whisper, that he is an ignorant fellow, and hath never read
> Homer nor Virgil, nor knows he any thing of Hector or Turnus; nay, he is
> unacquainted with the history of some great men living, who, though brave as
> lions, aye, as tigers, have run away, the Lord knows how far, and the Lord
> knows why, to the surprise of their friends and the entertainment of their
> enemies.[66]

While the commentator succeeds in maintaining a comic tone at a moment

[63] *Ibid.*, VI, 96-97 (*Amelia*, II, vii).
[64] *Ibid.*, VII, 64 (VII, x).
[65] *Ibid.*, VI, 79 (II, iii).
[66] *Ibid.*, I, 269 (*Joseph Andrews*, III, vi).

when Adams' fate might alarm us, and although serious defense of Adams' courage—which we have seen mainfested previously and will see manifested again—is unnecessary, Fielding does convey a judgment about physical courage generally. The commentator's remarks, supererogatory *as* a defense although pertinent as an element in maintaining the non-serious tone of the novel, act as a vehicle by which Fielding conveys the general applicability of the particular judgment to—at the very least—the world of the novel. If we consider the description of the battle in isolation, the commentator's defense of Adams may seem insignificant, and the point he makes is lost in the flurry of Joseph's battle with the dogs and the ensuing troubles with the practical-joking lord. But if *Joseph Andrews* has been successful up to this point, the reader has already been affected by the incident in which Adams disputes with a "man of courage," delivers a long speech on the subject, and then dashes off to save Fanny. The very terms of reference employed in the commentator's comic defense of Adams are strikingly similar to those employed by Adams in the earlier episode. The "man of courage" had disinherited his nephew because he believed him to be a coward; he insists that he "would have all such fellows hanged." Adams does not agree: "Adams answered, 'That would be too severe; that men did not make themselves. . . .' He said, 'A man might be a coward at one time, and brave at another. Homer . . . who so well understood and copied nature, hath taught us this lesson; for Paris fights and Hector runs away.' " [67] The echoing by the commentator—whatever its immediate artistic purpose—of the paragon's previous remarks re-emphasizes and generalizes the judgment initially conveyed by the paragon.

The effect of such echoing may be more readily discernible in a situation devoid of comic paraphernalia. In *Tom Jones* the lengthy sermon Allworthy delivers to Jenny Jones on the heinous nature of her supposed offense draws attention both to the religious and the secular consequences of unchastity. On the latter head Allworthy says the following:

> "There are other consequences [than divine displeasure], not indeed so dreadful or replete with horror as this; and yet such as, if attentively considered, must, one would think, deter all of your sex at least from the commission of this crime.
>
> "For by it you are rendered infamous, and driven, like lepers of old, out of society; at least, from the society of all but wicked and reprobate persons; for no others will associate with you.
>
> "If you have fortunes, you are hereby rendered incapable of enjoying them; if you have none, you are disabled from acquiring any, nay, almost of pro-

[67] *Ibid.*, I, 157 (II, ix).

curing your sustenance; for no persons of character will receive you into their houses. Thus you are often driven by necessity itself into a state of shame and misery, which unavoidably ends in the destruction of both body and soul." [68]

After some further discussion of love as a rational passion and Allworthy's assuring Jenny that "I have talked thus to you, child, not to insult you for what is past and irrevocable, but to caution and strengthen you for the future," the paragon promises that " '. . . . I will take care to convey you from this scene of your shame, where you shall, by being unknown, avoid the punishment which, as I have said, is allotted to your crime in this world; and I hope, by repentance, you will avoid the much heavier sentence denounced against it in the other.' " [69] This charitable speech is delivered soon after the beginning of the novel. The commentator has heaped unqualified encomiums upon the head of the good man and we have seen him act toward the foundling in a manner consistent with the commentator's evaluation. Jenny's ostensible fall, however, calls for one of the first really complex judgments to be made in the novel, and its importance is proportionate to the number of times that signals in the novel must control the reader's attitude toward characters who participate in unchaste activities: Tom's affairs with Jenny Jones, Molly Seagrim, and Lady Bellaston, for example, must be represented so as to ascribe to each of the participants the appropriate kind and degree of blame if Fielding is to accomplish the artistic end of *Tom Jones*. If we see Tom as a confirmed sinner, punitive comedy or artistic chaos must result; if we see Jenny, under the name of Mrs. Waters, as unforgivably lewd in sleeping with Tom, Fielding cannot use her as he does in the comic resolution of the novel.[70]

Significantly, when the first unchaste act is revealed, the commentator temporarily bows out of the picture and the judgment is conveyed largely by Allworthy—religious, practical, severe, yet sympathetic and flexible enough to temper disapproval with tolerance. Jenny's virtues, though they do not negate, radically qualify the heinousness of unchastity. Though the commentator does not make the relevant judgment, his later echoing of the paragon's sentiments reinforces Allworthy in his role as the good man of the novel and, at the same time, tends to generalize the paragon's judgments:

So far from complying with this their inclination [the "mob's" desire to see Jenny go to Bridewell], by which all hopes of reformation would have been

[68] *Ibid.*, III, 37-38 (*Tom Jones*, I, vii).
[69] *Ibid.*, p. 39.
[70] See pp. 153-157.

abolished, and even the gate shut against her if her own inclinations should ever hereafter lead her to choose the road of virtue, Mr. Allworthy rather chose to encourage the girl to return thither by the only possible means; for too true I am afraid it is, that many women have become abandoned, and have sunk to the last degree of vice, by being unable to retrieve the first slip. This will be, I am afraid, always the case while they remain among their former acquaintance; it was therefore wisely done by Mr. Allworthy, to remove Jenny to a place where she might enjoy the pleasure of reputation, after having tasted the ill consequences of losing it.[71]

There is no remark in this passage which has not been emphasized in All-worthy's address to Jenny, but the passage does lend the commentator's weight to the paragon's judgment. Since, however, Allworthy's role as paragon has been clearly defined before he makes his speech to Jenny, and the sinner's reaction to his lecture has sufficiently emphasized this fact, the added weight is supererogatory if intended only to determine our feelings toward Allworthy and Jenny at this point. Nevertheless, though the commentator's remarks do not amplify those of the paragon, they do extend their significance by reiterating them outside the dramatic frame in which they initially appeared. Though Allworthy's lecture did indeed consist of general comments upon the plight of fallen women, since attention was focused upon the interaction between Allworthy and Jenny, the effect of the paragon's statement is limited primarily to determining our reaction to Jenny herself. The commentator's brief echo of Allworthy's *obiter dicta*, however, interprets the latter's judgment as a truth both important for and generally applicable to the world of the novel.

If the commentators are the paragons' friends during their moral ascendancy, they also remain true to them when the light of their virtues is temporarily eclipsed by questionable judgment or humanizing weakness. Remaining true may take the simple, though adequate, form of insisting on the paragon's goodness when he is represented as riding his hobbyhorse: "Indeed, if this good man [Adams] had an enthusiasm, or what the vulgar call a blind side, it was this: he thought a schoolmaster the greatest character in the world, and himself the greatest of all schoolmasters, neither of which points he would have given up to Alexander the Great at the head of his army." [72] Or it may take the form of a fairly complex explanation which justifies the paragon for

[71] Henley, III, 46 (*Tom Jones*, I, ix).
[72] *Ibid.*, I, 263 (*Joseph Andrews*, III, v).

an ostensible error of judgment and maintains his status as paragon despite his human fallibility:

> Upon longer acquaintance, however, and more intimate conversation, this worthy man saw infirmities in the tutor which he could have wished him to have been without; though as those seemed greatly overbalanced by his good qualities, they did not incline Mr. Allworthy to part with him: nor would they indeed have justified such a proceeding; for the reader is greatly mistaken if he conceives that Thwackum appeared to Mr. Allworthy in the same light as he doth to him in this history; and he is as much deceived if he imagines that the most intimate acquaintance which he himself could have had with that divine would have informed him of those things which we, from our inspiration, are enabled to open and discover. Of readers who, from such conceits as these, condemn the wisdom or penetration of Mr. Allworthy, I shall not scruple to say they make a very bad and ungrateful use of that knowledge which we have communicated to them.[73]

Similarly, the reader is warned against condemning Harrison: "Nay, I am aware that the esteem that some readers before had for the doctor may here be lessened; since he may appear to have been too easy a dupe to the gross flattery of the old gentleman. If there be any such critics, we are heartily sorry, as well for them as for the doctor. . ." [74]

Though, as characters, Fielding's good men err, the commentator, as well as other agents, is always at hand to make sure that, no matter how drastic the consequence of their errors, when they speak *ex cathedra*, as it were, their word will be the law of the novels in which, though fallible, they remain paragons.

A Paragon without an Apologue

It should not be assumed from the foregoing remarks that the relationship between paragon and values is a simple one—that, for instance, to discover Fielding's beliefs or opinions on a specific point we need only find the appropriate page, cite one of Allworthy's remarks, and be done. The fact that the paragon's voice, if not his presence, seems ubiquitous may tend to support such simplification: Joseph, separated from Adams, does confess in his letter to Pamela that he had almost forgotten the good man's teachings when Lady Booby made her final assault on his virtue in London; Mrs. Miller compares Tom's good action to Allworthy's at a moment when the

[73] *Ibid.*, III, 124-125 (*Tom Jones*, III, v).
[74] *Ibid.*, VII, 208 (*Amelia*, X, iv).

hero is at his lowest moral ebb; even in Gibraltar Booth receives a witty letter in which Harrison informs him that Amelia has been disowned and instructs him how to accept his misfortune.

Nevertheless, if we were to regard the paragons' remarks simply as species of topical essays from which we could cite Fielding's beliefs, we would finally conclude nothing much more specific than that Fielding was indeed for good and against evil. At best, we might discover what we all know now is true of Shakespeare, that Fielding was for order and against chaos. It is true that Fielding's paragons are more direct in the expression of significant ethical opinions than are other agents, and that, with the exception of opinions carefully indicated as resulting from their fallibility, the paragons' statements are consistent with Fielding's own views.[75] Yet those statements are primarily important as signals which contribute to, though they are not the sole cause of, our attitudes toward characters, actions, and elements of thought in a manner consistent with the artistic end which informs each novel. Merely to cite the paragons' statements as species of Fielding's opinions is, therefore, to ignore the most important evidence of Fielding's beliefs contained in his novels and, inevitably, to fail to account for the ethical effect of those novels on as sensitive a reader as Coleridge, who believed that one cannot read Fielding's novels without feeling "an intense conviction that he *could* not be guilty of a *base* act." [76]

Even if we ignore the less accessible evidence derived by inferring what Fielding must have believed to have evaluated such actions, characters, and thoughts in such works, the paragons' *obiter dicta* represent so fragmentary an expression of Fielding's views on most ethical questions as to be misleading. Both from Allworthy's statements and from his actions we know that Allworthy's goodness is manifested in good works, in charity. His "death-bed" speech indicates that he is not easily shaken by the blows of fortune, but accepts his lot with what we may term a moderate Christian Stoicism. But it is primarily in connection with the episode of the Man of the Hill that we find a series of judgments of Stoicism—a negative, though complex, evaluation of its most exaggerated tenets as leading to a morally deficient way of life, though one with meretricious attractions sufficient to tempt men who are neither fools nor villains. Even in this episode, however, the paragon's voice is not absent: the explicit arguments with which Tom tries to refute the hermit echo Allworthy's earlier refutation of the elder Blifil's attacks on

[75] The complicated relationship among moral intentions, value judgments, and the artistic end of any novel is discussed in detail in chapter six.
[76] Quoted from Henley, V, 374.

charity; Tom's instinctive dashing to the aid of the screaming woman directly reflects the particular qualities which Allworthy, ostensibly on his deathbed, had judged to be Tom's adequate claims to happiness, and that instinctive dash is in itself the final refutation of the hermit's formulated ethical position. It does not, however, constitute an absolute rejection of the hermit as a man; Tom still regards him as a friend and, earlier in the episode, their mutual and lengthy rejection of the Jacobites adequately defined the attitude we are meant to have toward the lost cause. Despite the paragon's ubiquity, the remarks he makes are not adequate indices to Fielding's beliefs.

In isolating the ethical functions of the paragons, in separating those functions from the sum total of traits, speeches, and acts which makes Adams, Allworthy, and Harrison appropriate for the important roles they play *as characters*, we are aware that we, and not Fielding, have isolated and separated them for the specialized purpose of this enquiry; if at any point we assume that the purpose of this enquiry is coincidentally equivalent to Fielding's purpose in writing his novels, the results of the enquiry itself become sadly compromised. The purely ethical voices of the paragons are generally as tactfully unobtrusive as they are ubiquitous. If on occasion they speak at some length—Adams refutes Barnabas, Allworthy lectures Jenny Jones, Harrison praises God and rushes everyone off to church—their direct ethical comments are, both quantitatively and qualitatively, far less important in determining the reader's feelings about characters, actions, and thoughts than are the more subtle forms of judgments they convey through their direct participation in the events of the novels.

The relative subtlety and complexity of the ways in which a paragon may define the ethical caliber of other characters are revealed in Allworthy's relation to the foundling, and to Deborah and Bridget, who have their own opinions about the propriety of encouraging fornication by showing charity to the illegitimate fruits thereof. Allworthy rises from his nightly prayers to discover the foundling in his bed. The narrator informs us that he "stood sometime lost in astonishment at this sight; but, as good nature had always the ascendant in his mind, he soon began to be touched with sentiments of compassion for the little wretch before him." [77] Though one need not be a paragon in life or literature to feel "sentiments of compassion" for a sleeping infant, Fielding is quick to demonstrate that such sentiments are far from universal in the world of *Tom Jones*.

Allworthy rings for the meticulous Deborah, and when the commentator

[77] Henley, III, 23 (*Tom Jones*, I, iii).

explains with undisguised sarcasm that she delays her appearance in Allworthy's room because of her "strict regard for decency," though "her master, for aught she knew, lay expiring in an apoplexy, or some other fit," [78] we are unlikely to be prepossessed in her favor. Indeed, when Allworthy, already described as "the favorite of both nature and fortune," [79] meets "Mrs. Deborah Wilkins, who, though in the fifty-second year of her age, vowed she had never beheld a man without his coat," [80] any disagreement about decorum, morality, or anything else will inevitably be decided in Allworthy's favor. A disagreement does occur immediately upon Mrs. Wilkins' becoming aware of the foundling:

> "My good sir! what's to be done?" Mr. Allworthy answered, she must take care of the child that evening, and in the morning he would give orders to provide it a nurse. "Yes, sir," says she, "and I hope your worship will send out your warrant to take up the hussy its mother, for she must be one of the neighborhood; and I should be glad to see her committed to Bridewell, and whipt at the cart's tail. Indeed, such wicked sluts cannot be too severely punished. I'll warrant 'tis not her first, by her impudence in laying it to your worship." [81]

Allworthy at this point has said nothing about the lack of charity displayed in Deborah's statement; because of the way in which both characters have been represented, the contrast between Allworthy's prepossession with the infant and Deborah's prepossession with the punishment of the infant's mother is more than sufficient to determine the appropriate judgment of Deborah as a character and of the ethical notions embodied in her statement. Nevertheless, Deborah's remarks do momentarily shift our attention from the disparate attitudes toward the foundling to the judgment of its mother. Allworthy rejects Deborah's uncharitable view of the sinner, thus helping further to categorize the ethical caliber of Deborah's opinions, while his direct defense of the mother begins to prepare us for that complex evaluation of Jenny Jones which, though sufficiently defined to enable her to play her role effectively at her every appearance, is not complete until the very end of *Tom Jones*. Allworthy's rejection of Deborah's views is brief but explicit: "I can't think she hath any such design. I suppose she hath only taken this method to provide for her child; and truly I am glad she hath not done worse." [82]

The incorrigible Deborah, as spokesman for virtue, continues, however,

[78] *Ibid.*
[79] *Ibid.*, p. 20 (I, ii).
[80] *Ibid.*, p. 24 (I, iii).
[81] *Ibid.*
[82] *Ibid.*, p. 25.

to express her grisly ethic, now extending her judgments from mother to child:

> "I don't know what is worse," cries Deborah, "than for such wicked strumpets to lay their sins at honest men's doors; and though your worship knows your own innocence, yet the world is censorious; and it hath been many an honest man's hap to pass for the father of children he never begot; and if your worship should provide for the child, it may make the people the apter to believe; besides, why should your worship provide for what the parish is obliged to maintain? For my own part, it goes against me to touch these misbegotten wretches, whom I don't look upon as my fellow-creatures. Faugh! how it stinks! It doth not smell like a Christian. If I might be so bold to give my advice, I would have it put in a basket, and sent out and laid at the church-warden's door. It is a good night, only a little rainy and windy; and if it was well wrapt up, and put in a warm basket, it is two to one but it lives till it is found in the morning. But if it should not, we have discharged our duty in taking proper care of it; and it is, perhaps, better for such creatures to die in a state of innocence than to grow up and imitate their mothers; for nothing better can be expected of them." [83]

Though Deborah expresses views which the novel defines as evil, the role she performs as a character would be seriously compromised if *she* were to achieve enough stature to be regarded as evil. She is essentially a comic creation, much as Slipslop in *Joseph Andrews* is a comic creation, though she mangles morality rather than the English lexicon, and is excessively prudish, while Slipslop is lecherous. The very fact that she does present such arguments to a character like Allworthy helps preserve her character as ludicrous rather than evil, and, since our knowledge of his character is sufficient to ensure that she will be unable to accomplish her purpose, we have no trepidation about the infant's immediate fate. But if Allworthy were to argue with her, as Tom does later with the Man of the Hill, or to lecture her at length as he does a receptive Jenny Jones, he would so dignify her blather as to characterize Deborah herself as evil and as a potential threat to Tom at a stage of the action when it is obviously inappropriate to introduce this kind of complication. And indeed, once Fielding had judged Deborah as evil rather than ludicrous, she would be thoroughly inappropriate for the role she plays in the discovery of Jenny Jones as Tom's ostensible mother, since our fear for Jenny would then be so strong as to make even Allworthy's lecture to her seem unduly severe. The way in which Fielding does refute Mrs. Wilkins' ethic (which, when later expounded more moderately by an ethically more

[83] *Ibid.*

dangerous Blifil, will already have been defined as unworthy by its identification with Deborah's remarks) is by subtly representing Allworthy as attaching no weight to it at all: "There were some strokes in this speech which
perhaps would have offended Mr. Allworthy had he strictly attended to it;
but he had now got one of his fingers into the infant's hand, which, by its
gentle pressure seeming to implore his assistance, had certainly outpleaded the
eloquence of Mrs. Deborah, had it been ten times greater than it was." [84]
From here on we have a measuring rod other than Allworthy—though it
was defined as such by him—with which to gauge the moral respectability of
other characters: they either take the foundling's hand with Allworthy or
reject him with Deborah. Any character prejudiced against Tom on the score
of his birth will be villain or fool.

With the very introduction of the foundling into the novel, then, a series
of important judgments is made and conveyed. Deborah Wilkins is a fool
whose ethical comments make her ludicrous rather than wicked; nevertheless,
her later attack on Jenny Jones will tend to elicit sympathy for the sinner.
The mother of the foundling is not necessarily evil and her motive in placing
the infant in Allworthy's bed is quite possibly good. Our sympathy has been
strongly attached to the foundling; unless later judgments suffice to negate
those already made, our sympathy will remain with him and with those who
wish him well, and our hostility will be aroused toward those who threaten
or disparage him.

The agents who effect these judgments include the commentator, but in
a decidedly limited role. Allworthy, already tentatively established as paragon,
is more directly responsible for our reaction to Deborah, the foundling, and
the foundling's mother. But Allworthy, as paragon, effects these judgments
without making a single comment on the proper way to receive illegitimate
children discovered in one's bed, on the impropriety of Deborah Wilkins'
remarks about the foundling, or on the fact that she is ludicrous rather than
evil.[85]

Once made, these judgments become part and parcel of the world of the
novel. We need not even remember that they have been made for them to
affect us, since they immediately influence our subsequent reactions to character, thought, and action and these in turn influence the judgments which
follow. How these judgments become part of the world of the novel is made
clear by Bridget's initial reactions to the foundling. Though Mrs. Wilkins
expects her mistress to concur in her own opinion of foundlings and the way

84 *Ibid.*
85 *Ibid.*

to treat them, Bridget initially joins her only in intemperate castigation of the mother and to this extent alone allies herself with Deborah's undesirable ethical position. Our subsequent discovery that Bridget is Tom's mother obviously explains her actions and attitudes at this point. But, though our feelings about Bridget must be such that we will not be horrified to discover that she is Tom's mother, the discovery itself does not define her role as an ethical agent in the incidents in which she appears, for she is, after all, dead when we learn about her peccadillo. Though they seem obvious once the truth is out, the hints of the commentator are not strong enough to cause immediate suspicion:

> Her orders [for the care of Tom] were indeed so liberal, that, had it been a child of her own, she could not have exceeded them; *but, lest the virtuous reader may condemn her for showing too great regard to a base-born infant, to which all charity is condemned by law as irreligious,* we think proper to observe that she concluded the whole by saying, "Since it was her brother's whim to adopt the little brat, she supposed little master must be treated with great tenderness. For her part, she could not help thinking it was an encouragement to vice; but that she knew too much of the obstinacy of mankind to oppose any of their ridiculous humors." [86]

Since the narrator carefully explains that such grumbling "accompanied every act of compliance with her brother's inclinations," we are not quite certain whether her tender treatment of the infant or her concurrence in Deborah-like lack of charity defines her true feelings. To the extent that we accept as true her own explanation of her motives for treating the infant well, she fails to capture our sympathies just as, apparently, the infant failed to capture hers. Her "liberal orders" regarding the child, however, are emphasized; hence, in the light of the commentator's hints about her attitude toward her brother, her action seems disproportionately kind to have stemmed from enforced compliance with Allworthy's desires.

More important, in the italicized portion of the quoted passage, there can be no doubt that the commentator's remarks are meant to be sarcastic; the "virtuous reader" who could indeed condemn Bridget for her kindness to the foundling would be himself condemned by the judgments previously conveyed in the novel. Yet there is no stylistic indication that the commentator is sarcastic. We beg the issue if we simply assume that our recognition of the sarcasm is the result of the general moral sensibility which we share with Fielding since we are actually trying to discover how he conveys that moral

[86] *Ibid.*, pp. 30-31 (I, v). Italics mine.

sensibility with which we may agree or disagree; it is manifestly absurd to assume that everyone who has read or will read *Tom Jones* has the same moral code as Fielding's. A reader who shared the sentiments expressed in the italicized passage would still recognize that they were sarcastic in intent.[87]

Actually, this knowledge is largely the result of the conflict between the judgments already conveyed in the novel and those explicitly made by the commentator in the quoted passage. The complicated interplay of commentator, paragon, and Deborah has already determined those attitudes toward the foundling and its mother which are to be regarded as desirable and those to be regarded as culpable. Allworthy, as paragon, is the most important of the agents conveying those judgments. The propriety of regarding the paragon as a "structural device" should emerge if we recognize that once the paragon has been instrumental in evaluating an ethical position, that evaluation cannot normally be overruled without artistic chaos ensuing. This must be so even though the commentator was himself instrumental in defining the paragon *as* paragon. The discrepancy between the judgments previously made and those expressed by the commentator in the italicized passage defines the commentator's remarks as sarcastic; if we had not seen the commentator previously united with Allworthy and the angels and if we had no stylistic clues (these are far less common in "ironic" passages than one might think), we should have to regard the commentator as ethically *wrong*. It is possible for the commentator to be ethically wrong only when he is himself a character participating in the action (e.g., Pip in *Great Expectations*). In such circumstances he may create an agent morally superior to himself who is therefore capable of measuring the moral acceptability of the commentator's own remarks. Once the commentators in Fielding's novels, however, have defined a character as paragon, any real discrepancy between the ethical judgments of commentator and paragon must lead to absolute confusion.

The commentator may, of course, comment upon the paragon's remarks or acts and generalize them. But if any statement of his contradicts judg-

---

[87] The presence of signals of authorial judgments would be simple enough to prove if we could find an example of a judgment with which most contemporary readers would disagree. Whenever I think I have found such a judgment, however, I discover that respectable commentators would disagree with me, not with Fielding. I find myself disliking Amelia, for example, at points where it is clear that I am to admire her. I know what Fielding wants me to feel and, indeed, what I must feel if I am to appreciate the novel; I cannot manage to accommodate the novelist, however. *De gustibus non est disputandum.* A modern biographer like Miss Godden, who unreservedly admires Amelia, would undoubtedly find my sensibilities inadequate. Where the judgment conveyed is one we share readily, however, we are likely to feel that we, rather than Fielding, have made the evaluation.

ments already conveyed by the paragon, such a statement is automatically to be regarded as ironic unless the judgment contradicted is the result of the paragon's defined fallibility, as when Adams lectures Joseph on stoically accepting the fact that Fanny is, at the moment of the lecture, probably in the process of being ravished. Even these latter instances, however, are not exceptions to the notion that the commentator cannot overrule judgments conveyed by the paragon since, in such instances, the paragon's fallible statements do not directly convey the appropriate judgment. That is, Adams' lecture to Joseph does not define Stoicism as desirable; the commentator may subsequently attack the "philosophy" without contradicting any judgment previously conveyed, even though he does contradict the paragon's statement.

The relation between paragon and judgment is, therefore, far from simple; to attempt to determine Fielding's beliefs by regarding the paragon's statements as isolable topical essays is to make impossible the accomplishment of one of the ends for which the class was defined in the first place.

Good Men, Heroes, and Crustier Paragons

We have seen that Adams is so impressed by Joseph Andrews' virtue that he makes an unsuccessful attempt to persuade the Boobys to arrange for the footman's education, which he is personally willing to take charge of.[88] Adams' sympathy with the hero, however, takes many forms in the course of the novel. It is manifest in so simple a gesture as his display of willingness to defend Joseph by force:

> The only difficulty that remained was, how to produce this gold before the justice . . . nor was there any great likelihood of obtaining it from him [Joseph], for he had fastened it with a ribbon to his arm, and solemnly vowed that nothing but irresistible force should separate them; in which resolution, Mr. Adams, clenching a fist rather less than the knuckle of an ox, declared he would support him.[89]

Or, perhaps even more heroically, he defends Joseph by force of argument when everyone else condemns him:

> "What," says the lady [Booby], "I suppose he [Beau Didapper] would have kissed the wench [Fanny]; and is a gentleman to be struck for such an offer? I must tell you, Joseph, these airs do not become you," "Madam," said Mr. Booby, "I saw the whole affair, and I do not commend my brother; for I can-

[88] See chapter two.
[89] Henley, I, 80 (*Joseph Andrews*, I, xv).

not perceive why he should take upon him to be this girl's champion." "I can commend him," says Adams: "he is a brave lad; and it becomes any man to be the champion of the innocent; and he must be the basest coward who would not vindicate a woman with whom he is on the brink of marriage." [90]

It little matters that Adams' wife takes up cudgels for the enemy: the voice of Joseph's champion is the ethical voice of the novel, and it is incorruptible.

In *Amelia*, Booth has the difficult task of quoting Harrison's praise of Booth, but he manages nobly:

> "I cannot express, nor would modesty suffer me, if I could, all that now passed. The doctor took me by the hand and burst forth into the warmest commendations of the sense and generosity which he was pleased to say discovered themselves in my speech. You know, madam, his strong and singular way of expressing himself on all occasions, especially when he is affected with any thing. 'Sir,' said he, 'if I knew half a dozen such instances in the army, the painter should put red liveries upon all the saints in my closet.' " [91]

Harrison's "strong and singular way of expressing himself" suggests some of the artistic problems Fielding had to solve in order to use paragon figures successfully in his novels. Some discussion of the special kinds of ingenuity he employed to solve those problems may afford at least random insights into the quite different kind of substructure which informs each action.

Adams has so many foibles and eccentricities that, although he is represented as directly participating in most of the important scenes in *Joseph Andrews*, the emphasis on his virtue and his frequent use as an ethical commentator do not reduce him to a mere mouthpiece for the expression of ethical opinion. The very fact that his fallibility is such that he may actually be ridiculed for a particular expression of ethical opinion prevents our becoming cloyed with his virtuous ubiquity, and his frequent demonstration of amiable foibles which do not compromise his judgments prevents his role as a positive ethical measuring rod from obscuring the traits which make him one of Fielding's most colorful characters. When a character is defined as thoroughly good and he is, in addition, thoroughly articulate, there is danger of his degenerating into an inadequately represented character. But, although Adams himself evinces no sense of humor, so much of the fun of the novel centers about the good man that the narrator can safely keep all wit as his own province.

The problem is more difficult and perhaps, in minor ways, less satisfactorily solved in *Tom Jones*, where Allworthy has no sense of humor, is never ridi-

[90] *Ibid.*, p. 366 (IV, xi).
[91] *Ibid.*, VI, 81 (*Amelia*, II, iv).

culed,[92] makes many subtle ethical distinctions, and plays so prominent a part in establishing the initial values in the novel that his forcefulness as a character is threatened. Ironically enough, his importance as an agent of the controlling action is so great that if he seriously fails as a character his role as ethical commentator is fruitless. That threat is, for the most part, successfully avoided by the expedient of dispensing with his direct services during the long middle section of the novel. Indirectly, however, his ethical voice becomes conspicuously, though not irritatingly, ubiquitous because of the coöperation of other characters, particularly Mrs. Miller, in deriving their right to judge from him, and then in making judgments in his name.

We might state as almost axiomatic, when we compare Allworthy and Adams, that the more general, various, and subtle the evaluations the paragon is called upon to make directly, the fewer the mitigating foibles and intellectual limitations he may possess; with fewer limitations he runs a greater chance of degenerating from a character to a barely embodied ethical voice. The more danger he runs of degenerating in this fashion, the less time he may safely spend "on stage." And yet, in *Amelia*, Harrison is called upon directly to evaluate at length a greater variety of action, thought, and characters than is Allworthy himself. Furthermore, though he is never ridiculed, Harrison is almost continuously present and plays a major role even in the early adventures narrated by Booth. He alone of Fielding's paragons is called upon by the hero and heroine to settle ethical questions. Despite his formidable task, however, Harrison remains one of the more convincing characters, perhaps the most convincing, in *Amelia*. Fielding's success seems to be the result partially of his transferring to his paragon much of the wit and sarcastic bite he had hitherto reserved for his commentator, and partially of his endowing the paragon with the conscious and articulate awareness that paragons may be boring.

Significant differences may be observed by comparing Allworthy's and Harrison's rectifications of their mistakes about the heroes of the two novels. When Allworthy is finally reunited with Tom, a very effective scene, Tom's sufferings, only partially due to his own imprudence, are almost at an end and his essential goodness is again recognized by the mistaken paragon. No one, I think, would ask for any mitigation of the solemn treatment of the reunion:

---

[92] Some critics find Allworthy's "deathbed" actions ridiculous in light of the later revelation that his illness was in fact trivial. Except for the irrelevant facts that the major characters, the reader himself, *and* Allworthy were *unavoidably* mistaken, I do not find a grain of justification for the notion that Fielding pokes fun at his fallible paragon.

"After Allworthy had raised Jones from his feet, where he had prostrated himself, and received him into his arms, 'O my child!' he cried, 'how have I been to blame! how have I injured you! What amends can I ever make you for those unkind, those unjust suspicions which I have entertained, and for all the sufferings they have occasioned to you?' " [93] Tom, who will have none of Allworthy's self-accusation, recognizes his own guilt as the main cause of his difficulties; we accept the hero's self-accusation as accurate because, if for no other reason, Allworthy, touched as he is, agrees with it: " 'I am rejoiced, my dear child,' answered Allworthy, 'to hear you talk thus sensibly; for as I am convinced hypocrisy (good Heaven! how have I been imposed on by it in others!) was never among your faults, so I can readily believe all you say. You now see, Tom, to what dangers imprudence alone may subject virtue (for virtue, I am now convinced, you love in a great degree).' " [94] Allworthy, in analyzing Tom's virtue at length, emphasizes the difference between the kind of error Tom has made through lack of prudence and the kind of evil action which is the consequence of villainy. The emotional force of the reunion tapers off, to be replaced by a moral discourse that makes explicit the ethical standards by which we should already have judged Tom's actions; it stresses both Tom's innate goodness and his responsibility for his own misfortunes in such a manner that, while we feel he is deserving of Sophia, we do not blame the heroine for temporarily refusing his hand and, in so doing, momentarily delaying the happy resolution of the novel. The resolution itself is enhanced by the final complication which, when finally overcome, satisfies not only Tom, Allworthy, and Western but also fulfills Sophia's wish to please her father whenever the results of such compliance would not be disastrous. Indeed, the very tapering off of the emotional force of the reunion between Allworthy and Tom helps to ensure that the effect of the final resolution will not be weakened.

In *Amelia*, Harrison has made a similar mistake about Booth and has actually had him imprisoned for debt. But their reunion differs greatly in emotional force from that of Tom and Allworthy:

"So, captain," says the doctor, "when last we parted I believe we neither of us expected to meet in such a place as this."

"Indeed, doctor," cries Booth, "I did not expect to have been sent hither by the gentleman who did me that favor."

"How so, sir?" said the doctor; "you was sent hither by some person, I suppose, to whom you was indebted. This is the usual place, I apprehend, for

[93] Henley, V, 345 (*Tom Jones*, XVIII, x).
[94] *Ibid.*, p. 346.

creditors to send their debtors to. But you ought to be more surprised that the gentleman who sent you thither is come to release you. Mr. Murphy, you will perform all the necessary ceremonials." [95]

In *Amelia*, strangely enough, scenes of "sensibility" are far more frequent than in Fielding's earlier novels; the tender, tearful scene is reminiscent of Richardson, though frequently devoid of that facility for representing emotional intensity which enabled the latter—though sometimes barely—to skirt the maudlin. It is particularly interesting under these circumstances that the paragon, even when he takes part in scenes of emotional intensity, is so represented that he does not become an agent of sensibility. In *Tom Jones*, Allworthy's feelings and states of mind are expressed not only by his own comments and actions but also by the commentator's description of them; Harrison analyzes at length, but is rarely analyzed in *Amelia*. His feelings are expressed only indirectly in action (he frees Booth, arrests Murphy, etc.), or, more directly, in that "strong and singular" language to which Booth has previously called attention.

The creation of this crustier paragon has enabled Fielding partially to succeed in the herculean task of marrying the novel of sensibility to the "novel of ideas" in a work which is not merely a pastiche of unformalized elements from each type. The ascription of the couple's difficulties to their causes in an insufficiently Christian social order and in Booth's non-Christian acquiescence in psychological determinism commits Fielding to the solution of artistic problems far different from those he handled with consummate success in *Tom Jones*. While *Amelia* is not a variety of apologue but a very complex kind of action in which, because of Fielding's particularized moral intention, elements of thought play a more important role than they do in *Tom Jones*, it is nevertheless true that each incident which deters Booth and Amelia from the happy married life they achieve at the end is related by complicated varieties of ethical comment to intellectual and moral deficiencies in the England of his time. If Fielding is not entirely successful in accomplishing the artistic end on which the achievement of his moral purpose depends, the fault does not lie in his use of Harrison as a paragon. As a result of his creation of Harrison, a character neither as unworldly nor as eccentric as Adams, Fielding could draw on the services of a moral agent whose ethical beliefs were consistently unexceptionable and who had the intellectual subtlety and competence to argue cogently with an articulate nobleman about the historical necessity for the spiritual decay of society and, in general, to comment on the action in such a way as

[95] *Ibid.*, VII, 119 (*Amelia*, VIII, x).

to convey the connections between the state of society, intellectual error, and the difficulties of the highly characterized Booths. As a result of transferring the wit, irony, and semidetachment of the narrator in *Tom Jones* to the paragon in *Amelia*, he could use Harrison as direct commentator far more frequently than he could Allworthy, and could do so without the risk of reducing the paragon to a mere ethical voice.

Either an Allworthy or an Adams could have explained to Colonel Bath that dueling is undesirable. But, of the three, Harrison alone is capable of the sarcastic aphorism, which he wields as deftly as Bath does his sword:

> "I am of the Church of England, sir," answered the colonel, "and will fight for it to the last drop of my blood."
>
> "It is very generous in you, colonel," cries the doctor, "to fight so zealously for a religion by which you are to be damned." [96]

Harrison alone of the three paragons can prevent prolonged comment from overwhelming his forcefulness as a character without help from the narrator or from a manipulation of event which removes him from the scene. Some slightly caustic pleasantry is always at his command:

> "But why should I mention those places of hurry and worldly pursuit? What attention do we engage even in the pulpit? Here, if a sermon be prolonged a little beyond the usual hour, doth it not set half the audience asleep? as I question not I have by this time both my children [Booth and Amelia]. Well, then, like a good-natured surgeon, who prepares his patient for a painful operation by endeavoring as much as he can to deaden his sensation, I will now communicate to you, in your slumbering condition, the news with which I threatened you." [97]

Even Booth's conversion to Christianity—news to Harrison, who was unaware of Booth's defection—leads not to rejoicing but to a pithy intellectual refutation of Booth's former doubts. A refutation most notable, perhaps, in connection with Fielding's own views, because of its absolute acceptance of the basic premise—men act primarily from their passions—which had originally led Booth astray, and because of Harrison's deft use of the basic assumption as, rhetorically, the most telling proof of the truth of Christianity. The refutation constitutes the final intellectual solution to the most serious problem which has confronted the protagonist from the beginning of the novel; yet it is brief and unemotional, and terminates in typical Harrisonian aphorism: " 'But we will defer this discourse till another opportunity; at present, as the

[96] *Ibid.*, p. 134 (IX, iii).
[97] *Ibid.*, VI, 157 (III, x).

devil hath thought proper to set you free, I will try if I can prevail on the bailiff to do the same.' " [98]

Though very similar in some respects, the relations of paragons and heroes differ considerably from novel to novel. Adams never loses faith in Joseph's essential goodness. His initial judgment of Joseph's character, a judgment important in determining our attitude toward the hero, is temporarily modified only in the burlesque London episodes in which the paragon's *name* alone is employed as a measuring rod; elsewhere Adams is Joseph's champion. In *Tom Jones*, on the other hand, Allworthy's misunderstanding of Tom's motives leads to the latter's exile, a most important complication of the controlling action. After Allworthy has initially directed our sympathy to the infant foundling and our hostility to those hostile to him, it is his further task largely to define the ethical caliber of the hero. Typically, the judgments of Tom's actions as a boy and very young man—i.e., up to the moment of his exile— result from Allworthy's interaction with Square and Thwackum.[99] Disreputable as some of Tom's subsequent actions are, they never compromise the "goodness, generosity and honor" which Allworthy found in Tom—a situation possible only when a man's "goodness, generosity and honor" are measured by his motives rather than by his actions.

But though Harrison finds much that is admirable in Booth, commits an error of judgment which results in the hero's arrest for debt, and rectifies his error, the reunion of the two does not (as it does when Allworthy and Tom are reunited) represent the final approval of the hero by the strongest moral voice in the novel. Released, Booth is still in that state of intellectual error in which we first met him. The emotional intensity of the near father-son relationship which characterizes Tom and Allworthy's reunion is conspicuously absent when Harrison, with a caustic comment, has Booth released. Most important, though Tom's adventures, if judged by the same standard, would seem more culpable than those of the harrassed Booth, the latter is judged by a code which is not only more rigid but also significantly different from that which defines Tom as consistently deserving of happiness, which imprudence may only prevent him from attaining. Booth's imprudence, his acquiescence in the dictates of his passions (carefully defined as controllable), leads to Harrison's temporary rejection of him for causes not at all based on mistaken judgment. The hero is judged as morally culpable, as so nearly unworthy of the paragon's desperately needed aid that only the latter's affection for Amelia can induce him to rescue Booth for the second time:

[98] *Ibid.*, VII, 313 (XII, v).
[99] See pp. 113-115, 185, and 190.

The doctor fetched a deep sigh when he had heard Amelia's relation, and cried, "I am sorry, child, for the share you are to partake in your husband's sufferings; but as for him, I really think he deserves no compassion. You say he hath promised never to play again, but I must tell you he hath broke his promise to me already; for I had heard he was formerly addicted to this vice, and had given him sufficient caution against it. . . . You know I would go to the utmost verge of prudence to serve you; but I must not exceed my ability, which is not very great; and I have several families on my hands who are by misfortune alone brought to want. I do assure you I cannot at present answer for such a sum as this without distressing my own circumstances." [100]

Touched by Amelia's despair, however, Harrison decides that he "will distress them [his circumstances] this once on your account, and on the account of these poor little babes." [101] Amelia falls on her knees in thanksgiving, and the worthy blesses the worthy.

Tom's peccadilloes and his general imprudence lead him into a state of temporary misery; they never make him undeserving of happiness. Booth's lapse —and certainly Tom's degeneration into a cully must be considered to be as serious as Booth's gambling—is judged by the paragon to have made him unworthy not only of absolute happiness but of desperately needed aid. Fielding, when he evaluated Tom Jones, could not have had the same beliefs, opinions, and prejudices that he did when he evaluated William Booth. Though honorable and generous, Booth is judged by Harrison in relation to others in society who have not so clearly participated in causing their own misfortunes. Booth has committed a bad act in gambling when he should not have; whatever his motive, the act was sufficiently wrong to compromise his claim to happiness.

Booth's temporary inability to control the passion uppermost in his mind and his conviction that this is the situation of all men have led him to reject Christianity. He has done this even though Christianity has been defined, largely through Harrison's agency, as the one force capable of subordinating the "bad" passions and appealing to the "good" ones. Indeed, the efficacy of Christianity in exerting such an influence is indicated in *Amelia* as greatly increased if the whole society is Christian.[102] The absolute and sustained admiration of Booth for Harrison and his custom of asking the pargon's advice on ethical matters while rejecting the religious assumptions which give rise to it lead us to expect a meeting of the two men. Such a confrontation is clearly foreshad-

[100] Henley, VII, 301-302 (*Amelia*, XII, iii).
[101] *Ibid.*, p. 302.
[102] See pp. 158-159.

owed in the following exchange: " 'I have often told you, my dear Emily,' cries Booth, 'that all men, as well the best as the worst, act alike from the principle of self-love. Where benevolence therefore is the uppermost passion, self-love directs you to gratify it by doing good, and by relieving the distresses of others; for they are then in reality your own.' " [103] Amelia, whose moral position, like that of all Fielding's heroines, is almost identical with the paragon's, though, unlike his, it is not intellectually formulated, cannot argue with her husband and remain an exemplary wife; she can, however, register her disapproval: " 'I have often wished, my dear,' cries Amelia, 'to hear you converse with Dr. Harrison on this subject; for I am sure he would convince you, though I can't, that there are really such things as religion and virtue.' " [104] Booth does finally converse with Harrison, although Barrow rather than the doctor convinces him. Harrison is not particularly sympathetic with Booth's initial doubt:

> "Very well," answered the doctor, "though I have conversed, I find, with a false brother hitherto, I am glad you are reconciled to truth at last, and I hope your future faith will have some influence on your future life." "I need not tell you, sir," replied Booth, "that will always be the case where faith is sincere, as I assure you mine is. Indeed, I never was a rash disbeliever; my chief doubt was founded on this—that as men appeared to me to act entirely from their passions, their actions could have neither merit nor demerit." "A very worthy conclusion truly!" cries the doctor; "but if men act, as I believe they do, from their passions, it would be fair to conclude that religion to be true which applies immediately to the strongest of these passions, hope and fear; choosing rather to rely on its rewards and punishments than on that native beauty of virtue which some of the ancient philosophers thought proper to recommend to their disciples." [105]

The explanation by the paragon in Fielding's last novel would have more easily enabled the younger Fielding to thumb a virtuous nose at the author of *The Fable of the Bees*: the passions which, for the creator of *Tom Jones*, seemed to be the springs of human action have, for the writer of *Amelia*, become divine instruments capable of being directed by Christianity, but by no other force. Harrison's opinion of *Tom Jones* as cully might indeed have been unprintable.

[103] Henley, VII, 237 (*Amelia*, X, ix).
[104] *Ibid.*
[105] *Ibid.*, p. 313 (XII, v).

Paragons and Lesser Folk

Typically, in *Joseph Andrews*, at the end of an incident or of a short series of incidents in which a lesser character appears briefly, Adams' opinion of the character's act or statement conveys emphatic judgments; Adams' summary terminates the incident, the lesser agent disappears from the novel, and Joseph and Fanny either are one step closer to or are apparently prevented from that virtuous marriage with which the novel concludes. Occasionally Adams does change his mind about a minor character, as he does about Slipslop. On good terms with her, essentially, at the beginning of the novel, he protests in no uncertain terms when the lickerish wench casts aspersions on Fanny:

> . . . she acquainted Adams with his having left his horse, and expressed some wonder at his having strayed so far out of his way, and at meeting him, as she said, "in the company of that wench, who she feared was no better than she should be."
>
> The horse was no sooner put into Adams' head but he was immediately driven out by this reflection on the character of Fanny. He protested, "He believed there was not a chaster damsel in the universe. I heartily wish, I heartily wish," cried he (snapping his fingers), "that all her betters were as good." [106]

Undaunted, Slipslop pursues her attack not only on Fanny but on Adams himself for rescuing the heroine from her would-be ravishers when he "should have rather prayed that she might have been strengthened." [107] Though Adams now knows more about the maid than he did formerly, and though the incident provides us with some fine comedy and some fine blows at class arrogance, Slipslop remains for us essentially the same unadmirable, though delightful, comic creation she has been since her first appearance in the novel.

Adams' judgment of Barnabas is more typical. The latter, whose Christianity is of the purely verbal sort, is enraged by Whitefield's attacks on luxury among clergymen.

> "Sir," answered Adams, "if Mr. Whitefield had carried his doctrine no farther than you mention, I should have remained as I once was, his well-wisher. I am myself as great an enemy to the luxury and splendor of the clergy as he can be. I do not, more than he, by the flourishing estate of the Church, understand the palaces, equipages, dress, furniture, rich dainties, and vast fortunes, of her ministers. Surely those things which savor so strongly of this world become not

[106] *Ibid.*, I, 182-183 (*Joseph Andrews*, II, xiii).
[107] *Ibid.*, p. 183.

the servants of one who professed his kingdom was not of it." [108]

Adams now begins to state his own objections to Methodist doctrine:

"But when he [Whitefield] began to call nonsense and enthusiasm to his aid, and set up the detestable doctrine of faith against good works, I was his friend no longer; for surely that doctrine was coined in hell; and one would think none but the devil himself could have the confidence to preach it. For can any thing be more derogatory to the honor of God than for men to imagine that the all-wise Being will hereafter say to the good and virtuous, 'Notwithstanding the purity of thy life, notwithstanding that constant rule of virtue and goodness in which you walked upon earth, still as thou didst not believe every thing in the true orthodox manner, thy want of faith shall condemn thee?' Or, on the other side, can any doctrine have a more pernicious influence on society than a persuasion that it will be a good plea for the villain at the last day—'Lord, it is true I never obeyed one of thy commandments, yet punish me not, for I believe them all?' " [109]

When Adams finally praises the practical Christianity expounded in *A Plain Account of the Nature and End of the Sacrament*, Barnabas becomes really aroused: "At these words Barnabas fell a ringing with all the violence imaginable; upon which a servant attending, he bid him 'bring a bill immediately; for that he was in company, for aught he knew, with the devil himself; and he expected to hear the Alcoran, the Leviathan, or Woolston [*sic*] commended, if he staid a few minutes longer.' " [110] Asked to cite his objection to the book, Barnabas claims proudly that "I never read a syllable in any such wicked book," [111] with which gem of logic he terminates his role in *Joseph Andrews*.

Since Barnabas never reappears, it is obvious that this lengthy refutation does not serve to determine our attitude toward him for the sake of some role he *is to play*. This is, rather, the first of a series of adventures in which characters hostile to Adams, Fanny, or Joseph profess a brand of Christianity which reduces it to a cipher; in it, as in the rest of the series, the validity of Adams' religion is emphasized and the desire to see him perform the marriage ceremony for his two charges is increased. Adam's sympathetically naïve assumption that his brother clergyman Trulliber will provide the meager funds necessary for the return home of himself, Joseph, and Fanny, for example, leads to a theological dispute:

"I am sorry," answered Adams, "that you do not know what charity is, since

[108] *Ibid.*, pp. 95-96 (I, xvii).   [110] *Ibid.*, p. 97.
[109] *Ibid.*, p. 96.   [111] *Ibid.*

you practice it no better; I must tell you, if you trust to your knowledge for your justification you will find yourselves deceived, though you should add faith to it, without good works." "Fellow," cries Trulliber, "dost thou speak against faith in my house? Get out of my doors; I will no longer remain under the same roof with a wretch who speaks wantonly of faith and the Scriptures." [112]

Adams points out that Trulliber is no Christian, an assertion which Trulliber is willing to refute by doing physical battle with the good parson. The final rhetorical thrust at such Christianity is delivered, unconsciously, by Mrs. Trulliber who, "seeing him [Trulliber] clench his fist, interposed, and begged him not to fight, but show himself a true Christian, and take the law of him." [113] Typically, the Trullibers disappear from the novel after Adams, undaunted by Trulliber's muscular, or his wife's legal, defense of their Christianity, leaves without the required funds: "As nothing could provoke Adams to strike out but an absolute assault on himself or his friend, he smiled at the angry look and gestures of Trulliber; and telling him he was sorry to see such men in orders, departed without further ceremony." [114]

At another point, Adams is puzzled by the attitude of a Christian landlord:

Adams asked him "why he went to church, if what he learned there had no influence on his conduct in life?" "I go to church," answered the host, "to say my prayers and behave godly." "And dost not thou," cried Adams, "believe what thou hearest at church?" "Most part of it, master," returned the host. "And dost not thou then tremble," cries Adams, "at the thought of eternal punishment?" "As for that, master," said he, "I never once thought about it; but what signifies talking about matter so far off? The mug is out; shall I draw another?" [115]

The denial of Christianity in the name of Christianity is occasionally practiced by characters who do not disappear after a single episode but who are either actively hostile to or passively unconcerned about the marriage of Joseph and Fanny, as when Slipslop reduces Christian ethics to a proper appreciation of masculine beauty:

". . . the woman [Mrs. Grave-airs] must have no compulsion in her: I believe she is more of a Turk than a Christian; I am certain, if she had any Christian woman's blood in her veins, the sight of such a young fellow must have warmed it. Indeed, there are some wretched, miserable old objects that turn one's

[112] Ibid., p. 192 (II, xiv).   [114] Ibid.
[113] Ibid., p. 193.   [115] Ibid., p. 115 (II, iii).

stomach; I should not wonder if she had refused such a one; I am as nice as herself, and should have cared no more than herself for the company of stinking old fellows; but, hold up thy head, Joseph, thou art none of those; and she who hath not compulsion for thee is a Myhummetman, and I will maintain it." [116]

Far more typically, however, lesser characters in *Joseph Andrews* appear, temporarily hinder the desired marriage of hero and heroine, are evaluated by Adams, then drop out of the novel.

Complications of a very different order in the relationship of paragon and lesser characters are encountered in *Tom Jones*. A character like Jenny Jones reappears, and the paragon's initial judgment of her makes possible the complicated ethical role she plays during much of the novel; however, modifications of that initial judgment caused by her subsequent actions or by Allworthy's increased knowledge about her previous actions have important implications for the accomplishment of the artistic end of the work.

To a certain extent, Allworthy's initial conversation with Deborah about the foundling and his mother indicates that Jenny is to be viewed charitably.[117] The judgment is sufficiently clear that, partially as a result of the episode in which it was made, the subsequent severity of Deborah Wilkins and the ostensible severity of Bridget Allworthy toward Jenny's sin become indices to the unflattering ethical roles they perform in the novel. The mixture of charity and blame, of condemnation for the sin but recognition that its commission does not define Jenny as evil, is made explicit in Allworthy's long speech to Jenny.[118] The length of the speech, the detailed account of the problems caused by the sin, and the later echo of Allworthy's dictum by the commentator go far beyond what is necessary to influence the reader's attitude toward Jenny when she first appears; they establish a general ethical view important in the world of the novel.[119] Significantly, for example, when Allworthy reprimands Tom for his affair with Molly, the commentator indicates that "it is unnecessary to insert it [Allworthy's remarks] here, as we have faithfully transcribed what he said to Jenny Jones in the first book, most of which may be applied to the men equally with the women." [120]

Nevertheless, what Allworthy learns about Jenny during the "trial" of

---

[116] *Ibid.*, p. 144 (II, v).
[117] See pp. 135-138.
[118] See pp. 130-131.
[119] See pp. 131-132.
[120] Henley, III, 187 (*Tom Jones*, IV, xi).

Partridge, though it does not lead him to change his opinion of the initial sin, forces him to describe the girl in terms similar to those used by Deborah and Bridget:

> At the appointed time the parties all assembled, when the messenger return-ing brought word that Jenny was not to be found; for that she had left her habitation a few days before, in company with a recruiting officer.
>
> Mr. Allworthy then declared that the evidence of such a slut as she appeared to be would have deserved no credit. . . .[121]

Jenny's apparent betrayal of trust, while it turns the paragon against *her*, in no way revokes the charitable judgment of the sin—a judgment already gen-eralized as valid in the world of the novel. When we meet Jenny as Mrs. Waters, it is essentially the charitable view we take, and that view is facilitated by the fact that Sophia is far less troubled by Tom's infidelity than by the knowledge that he has bandied her name about.

When Allworthy again meets Jenny toward the end of the novel, he has been informed that she was Tom's mistress and is soon to learn that she is not the hero's mother. His knowledge of the former fact has confirmed All-worthy in his unflattering view of the sinner; he greets her in anything but a friendly manner: " 'Have you, madam, any particular business which brings you to me?' Allworthy spoke this with great reserve; for the reader may easily believe he was not well pleased with the conduct of this lady; neither with what he had formerly heard, nor with what Partridge had now deliv-ered." [122] Jenny does, of course, have most particular business with the para-gon and, when Partridge leaves the room, she acts as advocate for herself not by pleading her own cause but by serving Allworthy:

> Mrs. Waters remaining a few moments silent, Mr. Allworthy could not refrain from saying, "I am sorry, madam, to perceive, by what I have since heard, that you have made so very ill a use—" "Mr. Allworthy," says she, in-terrupting him, "I know I have faults, but ingratitude to you is not one of them. I never can nor shall forget your goodness, which I own I have very little deserved; but be pleased to waive all upbraiding me at present, as I have so important an affair to communicate to you. . . ." [123]

Jenny then reveals the mystery of Tom's parentage and, in part, Blifil's plot against the hero's life. Western breaks in, and it is only after his departure that Jenny undertakes to defend herself: " 'Indeed, sir,' says she, 'I was

[121] *Ibid.*, p. 89 (II, vi).
[122] *Ibid.*, V, 320-321 (XVIII, vi).
[123] *Ibid.*, p. 321 (XVIII, vii).

ruined by a very deep scheme of villainy, which if you knew, though I pretend not to think it would justify me in your opinion, it would at least mitigate my offense, and induce you to pity me. . . .' " [124] Though he sharply reprimands her for an ostensibly learned justification of common-law marriage, Allworthy is affected by Jenny's defense when she explains her deviations from the path of virtue in terms at once eloquent and reminiscent of the sentiments which had originally led Allworthy to aid rather than punish her: " 'And consider, sir, on my behalf, what is in the power of a woman stripped of her reputation and left destitute; whether the good-natured world will suffer such a stray sheep to return to the road of virtue, even if she was never so desirous. I protest, then, I would have chose it had it been in my power; but necessity drove me into the arms of Captain Waters. . . .' " [125] Describing Tom's subsequent rescue of her from Northerton, she calls Tom "the worthiest of men," and insists that "whatever vices he hath had, I am firmly persuaded he hath now taken a resolution to abandon them." Allworthy applies her remarks about Tom's resolution to her own case:

> "I hope he hath," cries Allworthy, "and I hope he will preserve that resolution. I must say, I have still the same hopes with regard to yourself. The world, I do agree, are apt to be too unmerciful on these occasions; yet time and perseverance will get the better of this their disinclination, as I may call it, to pity; for though they are not, like heaven, ready to receive a penitent sinner, yet a continued repentance will at length obtain mercy with the world. This you may be assured of, Mrs. Waters, that whenever I find you are sincere in such good intentions, you shall want no assistance in my power to make them effectual." [126]

This differs from Allworthy's initial charitable view of Jenny only in that his dispensation has now been extended to additional deviations from the path of virtue. There is no change in Allworthy's opinion of chastity, no real modification of the judgments initially generalized as pertinent to unchastity whenever it appeared in the world of *Tom Jones*. Elements present in the episode in which Allworthy originally confronted Jenny are repeated, even to the detail of her recognition of his goodness: "Mrs. Waters fell now upon her knees before him, and, in a flood of tears, made him many most passionate acknowledgments of his goodness, which, as she truly said, savored more of the divine than human nature." [127] But for all Jenny's acknowledgments, Allworthy's reversion to his initial opinions is an artistically unsatisfactory resolution of Jenny's complicated relationships with the major characters. Her un-

---

[124] *Ibid.*, p. 329 (XVIII, viii).
[125] *Ibid.*, p. 330.

[126] *Ibid.*
[127] *Ibid.*, pp. 330-331.

selfish defense of Tom and the effect of her revelation in reuniting Allworthy and the hero and in making possible Tom's union with Sophia demand more tangible recognition than a tentative promise of Allworthy's future favor contingent upon the fulfillment of her good intentions. If Jenny's unselfish and all-important act is to leave her in so tenuous a position, the emotional force of the final reunions is lessened. Allworthy's recognition of the virtues of Jenny's nonsexual contributions to the hero's fate is, however, dexterously delayed, not omitted; the very delay contributes to our satisfaction when the relationships among all the characters are finally resolved. As the effect of Jenny's revelations becomes apparent, as the extent of Blifil's villainy is recognized, and as the final scenes of reunion come closer to fulfillment, Jenny reaps her reward. No longer a fallen woman who *may* reform, she is seen as one worthy of great reward:

> The poor woman [Mrs. Miller] followed him [Allworthy] trembling; and now Allworthy, going up to Mrs. Waters, took her by the hand, and then, turning to Mrs. Miller, said, "What reward shall I bestow upon this gentlewoman, for the services she hath done me? O! Mrs. Miller, you have a thousand times heard me call the young man to whom you are so faithful a friend, my son. Little did I then think he was indeed related to me at all. Your friend, madam, is my nephew. . . ." [128]

Mrs. Miller's joy is so great that she "now felt bereft of her power of speech." Before she answers Allworthy's query, she poses a series of rhetorical questions, each of which, appropriately and emphatically, reminds us of the happiness made possible for Tom as a result of Jenny's disinterested revelation:

> "And is my dear Mr. Jones then your nephew, sir, and not the son of this lady? And are your eyes opened to him at last? And shall I live to see him as happy as he deserves?" "He certainly is my nephew," says Allworthy, "and I hope all the rest." "And is this the dear good woman, the person," cries she, "to whom all this discovery is owing?" "She is indeed," says Allworthy. "Why, then," cries Mrs. Miller, upon her knees, "may Heaven shower down its choicest blessings upon her head, and for this one good action forgive her all her sins, be they never so many!" [129]

An immediate forerunner of the concluding episodes, this directs us to the happy ending now at hand; it provides the initial satisfaction to be followed by the reunion of Tom and Allworthy and, most important, by the reunion

[128] *Ibid.*, p. 335.
[129] *Ibid.*, pp. 335-336.

of Tom and Sophia. The general ethical judgments made explicit in All-worthy's first speeches to Jenny and to Tom about the evils of unchastity are not changed as Allworthy's attitude toward Jenny fluctuates from poor sinner to "slut" to "gentlewoman." As is frequently the case in *Tom Jones*, the paragon's early *obiter dicta* are reinforced by the particular judgments made later in the novel. Those judgments seldom introduce new ethical principles of any importance.

Harrison's increased knowledge about James in *Amelia*, though, is put to a different use. The paragon's initial opinion of James is based on reports from Booth and Amelia about their friend's generosity and friendship:

> The doctor . . . on what he had formerly heard from both Amelia and her husband of the colonel's generosity and friendship, had built so good an opinion of him, that the was very much pleased with seeing him, and took the first opportunity of telling him so. "Colonel," said the doctor, "I have not the happiness of being known to you; but I have long been desirous of an ac-quaintance with a gentleman in whose commendation I have heard so much from some present." [130]

The reader, aware of James' hypocrisy, remains hostile to Amelia's would-be seducer. Later undeceived, Harrison is shocked by the revelation of James' true nature:

> The good man seemed greatly shocked . . . and remained in a silent astonish-ment. Upon which Amelia said, "Is villany [*sic*] so rare a thing, sir, that it should so much surprise you?" "No, child," cries he; "but I am shocked at seeing it so artfully disguised under the appearance of so much virtue; and, to confess the truth, I believe my own vanity is a little hurt in having been so grossly imposed upon. Indeed, I had a very high regard for this man; for, besides the great character given him by your husband, and the many facts I have heard so much redounding to his honor, he hath the fairest and most promising ap-pearance I have ever yet beheld. A good face, they say, is a letter of recommen-dation. O Nature, Nature, why art thou so dishonest as ever to send men with these false recommendations into the world?" [131]

Harrison's recognition of James' hypocrisy does little more initially than evoke in the paragon a response somewhat similar to that already evoked in the reader. But it is typical of *Amelia* that one of its thoughtful characters should attempt a rational explanation of ethical problems as they arise. In this instance Harrison has his task cut out for him, since Booth has already offered an os-

[130] *Ibid.*, VII, 127-128 (*Amelia*, IX, ii).
[131] *Ibid.*, p. 144 (IX, v).

tensibly cogent explanation of the discrepancies between James' occasional benevolent actions and his disavowal of virtue. In fact, Booth has cited James as an example of the truth of his theory of the dominant passion:

> "The behavior of this man alone is sufficient proof of the truth of my doctrine, that all men act entirely from their passions; for Bob James can never be supposed to act from any motives of virtue or religion, since he constantly laughs at both; and yet his conduct toward me alone demonstrates a degree of goodness which perhaps few of the votaries of either virtue or religion can equal." [132]

While a variety of methods are employed to indicate that Booth's theory is, in general, erroneous, Harrison is the only agent capable of substituting a positive explanation for Booth's ethically dangerous one. The theory Harrison is to offer must accomplish, however, a difficult task: it must replace Booth's explanation, and it must indicate that men are responsible for the evil in the world, at the same time forcing us to regard James as somewhat less culpable than we have hitherto believed him to be. This complicated judgment must be conveyed powerfully; only when it becomes one of the general values of the novel can we comprehend that the evils which beset Amelia are man-made, though her own contribution to her "misfortunes" is slight. One of the strongest modes of emphasizing judgments in Fielding's novels is to represent a heroine in momentary disagreement with a paragon and to have the disagreement culminate in the good woman's recognition of the virtue and wisdom of the paragon's arguments. Since each of Fielding's heroines is represented as morally constant and ethically exemplary, such a culmination represents the worthy blessing the worthiest. It is, in fact, a bitter remark of Amelia's which gives Harrison the opportunity to explain James' behavior:

> "Indeed, my dear sir, I begin to grow entirely sick of it," cries Amelia; "for sure all mankind almost are villains in their hearts."
> "Fie, child!" cries the doctor. "Do not make a conclusion so much to the dishonor of the great Creator. The nature of man is far from being in itself evil; it abounds with benevolence, charity, and pity, coveting praise and honor, and shunning shame and disgrace. Bad education, bad habits, and bad customs, debauch our nature, and drive it headlong as it were into vice. The governors of the world, and I am afraid the priesthood, are answerable for the badness of it. Instead of discouraging wickedness to the utmost of their power, both are too apt to connive at it. In the great sin of adultery, for instance. . . ." [133]

---

[132] *Ibid.*, VI, 127 (III, v).
[133] *Ibid.*, VII, 144-145 (Ix, v).

The general discussion of evil is focused again on James' attempt to seduce Amelia; Harrison argues that the law, the priesthood, and the contemporary code of honor condone adultery; the conclusion of his corrective sermon elicits Amelia's concurrence and admiration:

> "What wonder then if the community in general treat this monstrous crime as a matter of jest, and that men give way to the temptations of violent appetite, when the indulgence of it is protected by law and countenanced by custom? I am convinced there are good stamina in the nature of this very man; for he hath done acts of friendship and generosity to your husband before he could have any evil design on your chastity; and in a Christian society, which I no more esteem this nation to be than I do any part of Turkey, I doubt not but this very colonel would have made a worthy and valuable member."
>
> "Indeed, my dear sir," cries Amelia, "you are the wisest as well as the best man in the world. . . ." [134]

In explaining James' actions the wisest as well as the best man in the world alters what we have previously been made to feel about James only to the extent that we will be satisfied with something less than bloody punishment for him when his plans are frustrated and the Booths live happily ever after. His unenviable life with a Fanny Matthews grown fat and exceedingly tyrannical is, partially as a result of Harrison's re-evaluation of the colonel, sufficient to satisfy the demands of the special kind of poetic justice invoked in *Amelia*. But, at a fairly advanced point in the novel, Harrison has in effect introduced new *dicta*. While he accepts as fact that men do have violent appetites—good as well as bad—he is not led, as Booth is, to believe that actions cannot be praiseworthy or culpable; the responsibility for men's acquiescing in the dictates of their worst passions is, at this point, placed partially on controllable human error magnified in an unchristian society. This explanation receives further emphasis when Harrison, in an incident which functions only as ethical comment on the action, argues at length with the nobleman who believes in the inevitable decay of society. Many of the judgments made subsequent to Harrison's evaluation of James depend upon our ability to accept the notion that, while good men may suffer, evil is the result of responsible human agencies. In some ways Booth contributes mightily to his own misfortunes, but it is social corruption which prevents him from obtaining his commission; social corruption, in turn, is not caused by the dictates of Fortune or the absence of Providence but by men.

Unlike the Allworthy–Jenny Jones incidents, those in which Harrison rec-

[134] *Ibid.*, p. 145.

tifies his misconception about James introduce important new *dicta*—assumptions on which the particular final judgments of character, action, and thought depend.

Nondiscursive Female Paragons

Besides the fallible male paragon, another sort of semi-exemplary agent, the heroine, affects what we feel about character, thought, and action in each of Fielding's novels. Since some detailed consideration of Fielding's heroines as ethical agents is included in chapter five, a brief description of the class will suffice here.

Since, in each of Fielding's novels, happy married life with the heroine is the goal the hero strives for and the reward he receives, it is almost inevitable that the judgments which stress the heroine's desirability will define her as an agent of such a sort that her attitude toward other characters and theirs toward the heroine will help to determine what we feel in reading the novels. To the extent that Fielding's novels are successful, strong feelings of hostility will be directed at those who attempt to harm or even to disparage the heroine. Our reaction to Fanny's abductors is more strongly hostile than to Northerton in his attempt to hang Mrs. Waters; Slipslop comes dangerously close to losing her comic identity when she disparages Fanny, and only the fact that Adams —in his single attack on Slipslop—repulses the lecherous maid with comic gusto maintains her in her characteristic role. Mrs. Fitzpatrick need make only a few sarcastic remarks about Sophia to deflate her own character, her opinions of women's "understanding," and the value of London propriety.[135]

Fanny, exemplarily inarticulate, makes few direct ethical comments, but this is not true of either Sophia or Amelia. The validity of their comments is not limited by carefully defined areas of fallibility, as is the case with the male paragons; but, since they must never presume to match wits with men if they are to remain fit rewards for Fielding's heroes, their comments are relatively few and consequently emphatic. The principle which limits the heroines' discursiveness is clearly defined by Allworthy's remarks about Sophia:

". . . I never heard anything of pertness, or what is called repartee, out of her mouth; no pretence to wit, much less that kind of wisdom which is the result of great learning and experience, the affectation of which, in a young woman, is as absurd as any of the affectations of an ape. No dictatorial sentiments, no judicial opinions, no profound criticisms. Whenever I have seen her in the

---

[135] See chapter five.

company of men, she hath been all attention, with the modesty of a learner, not the forwardness of a teacher. . . . Indeed, she has always showed the highest deference to the understandings of men; a quality absolutely essential to the making of a good wife." [136]

Undoubtedly Allworthy would have been pleased had he known of Amelia's reaction to her husband when, instead of paying Trent, he foolishly "invests" the money obtained by pawning Amelia's clothes; Booth "communicated the matter to Amelia, who told him she would not presume to advise him in an affair of which he was so much the better judge." [137]

But with an intuitive knowledge of right and wrong which corresponds to that which the male paragons can rationally defend, Sophia and Amelia do comment forcefully. Tom's final punishment for his sexual adventures is administered by a righteously indignant Sophia:

"I do not, I cannot," says she, "believe otherwise of that letter than you would have me. . . . And yet, Mr. Jones, have I not enough to resent? After what passed at Upton, so soon to engage in a new amour with another woman, while I fancied, and you pretended, your heart was bleeding for me? Indeed, you have acted strangely. Can I believe the passion you have professed to me to be sincere? Or, if I can, what happiness can I assure myself of with a man capable of so much inconstancy?" [138]

Toward the end of the conversation, Tom explains, " 'The delicacy of your sex cannot conceive the grossness of ours, nor how little one sort of amour has to do with the heart.' 'I will never marry a man,' replied Sophia, very gravely, 'who shall not learn refinement enough to be as incapable as I am myself of making such a distinction.' " [139] In defense of her intuitive feeling about virtue, Amelia can be eloquent: " 'I do not know what you mean by prudery,' answered Amelia. 'I shall never be ashamed of the strictest regard to decency, to reputation, and to that honor in which the dearest of all human creatures hath his share.' " [140] And, though she may not presume to argue with Booth, her dexterous refusal to do so is sufficient to indicate the undesirability of those of his ideas she intuitively rejects, particularly when she summons the name of the male paragon to her aid: " 'I remember,' cries Amelia, 'a sentiment of Dr. Harrison's, which he told me was in some Latin

[136] Henley, V, 256 (*Tom Jones*, XVII, iii).
[137] *Ibid.*, VII, 267 (*Amelia*, XI, v).
[138] *Ibid.*, V, 361 (*Tom Jones*, XVIII, xii).
[139] *Ibid.*, p. 363.
[140] *Ibid.*, VII, 230 (*Amelia*, X, viii).

book: *I am a man myself, and my heart is interested in whatever can befall the rest of mankind.* That is the sentiment of a good man, and whoever thinks otherwise is a bad one.' " [141] Booth absolutely rejects Amelia's statement and attempts to refute it by reference to his own theory of the dominant passion. Amelia, self-disparaging and noncontentious, can neither accept nor argue: " 'I have often wished, my dear,' cries Amelia, 'to hear you converse with Dr. Harrison on this subject; for I am sure he would convince you, though I can't, that there are really such things as religion and virtue.' " [142] Booth's theory, or anything else that the sweet, unargumentative female paragon dislikes, does not have a chance in the world of the novel.

[141] *Ibid.*, pp. 236-237 (X, ix).
[142] *Ibid.*, p. 237.

Chapter Four

Walking Concepts

I question not but several of my readers will know the lawyer in the stage-coach the moment they hear his voice. It is likewise odds but the wit and the prude meet with some of their acquaintance, as well as all the rest of my characters. To prevent therefore any such malicious applications, I declare here, once for all, I describe not men, but manners; not an individual, but a species. Perhaps it will be answered, Are not the characters then taken from life? To which I answer in the affirmative; nay, I believe I might aver that I have writ little more than I have seen. The lawyer is not only alive, but hath been so these four thousand years; and I hope G— will indulge his life as many yet to come.[1]

Specified Traits
and Generalized Labels

While it would be misleading to apply to his general manner of representing characters what Fielding meant primarily as a statement of the proper objects of ridicule, the types of characters defined as a class in this chapter are so closely related to the way in which Fielding conveys absolute disapproval as to make the statement relevant and useful, though only as a starting point, in the delineation of the class. The remarks seem inapplicable to Adams, Tom Jones, Booth, and Harrison, or even to Squire Western, Jenny Jones, and Colonel James: the species in each case is too hard to classify, and the burden of supplying a label is the reader's. While no one would deny that Jenny Jones can be seen as "an erring woman," as a character she is so highly particularized that—at least *apparently* because of this—we can never assume she is meant to represent the species "erring woman"; her actions, speeches, general role in the action would seem to involve traits so particular that it is an effort to see her as typical of a species. Since Tom Jones is benevolent, certain of his actions will certainly stem from this trait, but the sum total of his actions will be seen as typical of Tom Jones, not as typical of a class of benevolent beings.

Oddly enough, the degree of particularization with which a character is represented has less to do than might at first appear with whether we react

[1] Henley, I, 214-215 (*Joseph Andrews*, III, i).

to him as an individual or as a species. Squire Western is in some sense typical of the eighteenth-century squirearchy, although for his role in the novel he is ascribed traits which, while not necessarily inconsistent with those of his class, are not seen as necessarily shared by that class; his reaction to Fellamar's challenge—the very difficulty of classifying that reaction as "cowardice" or "bravery" would seem to support as valid the distinction made in this manner —and his ambivalent relationship to Allworthy are not represented as typical of a species. But a more useful class of species characters can be distinguished if we use other criteria for establishing it. Historical scholarship might well show that many of Western's traits were shared by the generality of country gentlemen of his day: in this sense we may certainly consider Western "typical." It is not with this type of species character that I am concerned.

The case is very different with the creations discussed as situation characters in chapter two. The "typicalness" of these characters is not necessarily historically verifiable and may, as in the case of some of Fielding's Methodists, for instance, be historically invalid: Cooper's assumptions about Methodism might be shown to be atypical of the assumptions of practicing Methodists in the eighteenth century. The "typicalness" of these characters is the result of the manner in which they are represented; it is outside the scope of this study to determine whether Fielding does succeed in describing, as he does for Western, a species extant in the world outside the novel, but it is of the first importance for the way in which values are formalized within his novels that he does represent certain characters as species: they are introduced with an attached label which they are never permitted to lose, no matter how often they appear.

The most primitive form of the situation character is introduced as almost a pure species, possessor of few traits other than his label, as with Tittle and Tattle in *Joseph Andrews*.[2] The two are indistinguishable as characters and are essentially interchangeable; they have names, but these are generic; they speak to each other, but their statements distinguish them only as gossips.

In this pure, nearly traitless state the situation character is for obvious reasons used sparingly in Fielding's novels. He appears for a brief moment, is used to make a point, and, as a character, disappears from the book and the reader's memory, though the judgment he has been called upon to convey contributes to the power of the novel. What reader retains any impression of the "Mr. Counsellor" called into ephemeral existence by Western? Thwackum and Square are fighting for the honor of having been instru-

[2] See chapter two.

mental in inculcating in Blifil the high principles which led him to free
Sophia's bird. Blifil's action is lauded according to their several abstract notions
of virtue until Western adds still another ludicrous frame by which an element of the society represented in the novel judges the action:

> "So between you both," says the squire, "the young gentleman hath been taught
> to rob my daughter of her bird. . . ." Then slapping a gentleman of the law,
> who was present, on the back, he cried out, "What say you to this, Mr. Counsel-
> lor? Is not this against the law?"
>
> The lawyer with great gravity delivered himself as follows:
>
> "If the case be put of a partridge, there can be no doubt but an action would
> lie; for though this be *ferae naturae*, yet being reclaimed, property vests: but
> being the case of a singing bird, though reclaimed, as it is a thing of base nature,
> it must be considered as *nullius in bonis*. In this case, therefore, I conceive the
> plaintiff must be nonsuited; and I should disadvise the bringing any such ac-
> tion." [3]

Though we forget Mr. Counsellor, we cannot read *Tom Jones* without
becoming aware of Fielding's disapproval of any identification of legality and
virtue and of his contempt for the judgments of the species "lawyer." In
contrast to the power of "mere amiable comedy," that of *Tom Jones* is distinguished by the qualification that things need not work out so well for the
deserving as they do for Tom and Sophia. The particularized lawyer, Dowling, threatens Tom, but his skullduggery is frustrated much as it might be
in amiable comedy. Fielding goes a long way toward realizing the *special*
comic power of *Tom Jones* by including characters labeled "lawyer"—an
entire species, unrepentant, undefeated, and, however ludicrous, a permanent
threat to the deserving.

The most primitive form, "situation characters," is not the most important
form of the species: any one of the characters in the coach scene in *Joseph
Andrews* is more complex than Tittle or Tattle. In their most complex and
important forms—which I shall distinguish by the name "walking concepts"—they appear in a variety of situations, possess a sizable number of concrete traits, and are successfully infused with animation. The courting of
Bridget Allworthy by Thwackum and Square; the latter's reaction to the
embarrassing discovery of his affair with Molly Seagrim; Colonel Bath's
acting as his sister's nurse; or even the less detailed Cooper's efficiency at picking pockets certainly are particularized elements of character that we do not
normally associate with a species character. But what enables Fielding to use
even a complex character in such a manner as to make the reader constantly

[3] Henley, III, 155 (*Tom Jones*, IV, iv).

aware that it is meant as an implicit commentary on a whole species is not the number and the concreteness of traits that separate a character like Jenny Jones from that of the prude in the coach in *Joseph Andrews;* instead, it is the manner of selecting and subordinating the traits: for species characters, the traits, the actions seen as caused by the traits, no matter how concrete or complex, are consistently related to a generalized trait (prudery, gossip, etc.); a broad, though simply formulated, idea (virtue must square with the rule of right); or, closely connected with the latter, a simplified code of behavior (honor consists of dueling with anyone who may conceivably have insulted you). It is in this sense that we classify Western with "individual" characters, and Bath—whose traits are, like Western's, multiple and concrete—with species characters.

The distinction—an important one in isolating methods of conveying judgments—may seem suspect since, in some sense, Jenny acts always as "the erring woman" just as Bath acts always as the man of honor; but this objection is easily disposed of. What we are interested in is the way in which *Fielding* represents his character: the initial label and relation of action to the label must be the author's; if the reader himself must delineate the species to which the character belongs, if the author does not attach the character's traits to his label, the character does not fall into any of the subclasses dealt with in this chapter.

This stipulation is not arbitrary if our interest is primarily to isolate the methods by which Fielding conveys value judgments in his novels. If a "label" is clearly indicated by the author (the "labels" are either self-evaluating or are evaluated almost immediately upon the introduction of the character), all subsequent actions of the character immediately act as a comment on the class the label represents (if one labeled "Methodist" is a pickpocket, the author will be seen as attacking the honesty of Methodists). Thus we have a built-in ethical commentator in any species character; complexity of evaluation resides in the interaction of species characters, seldom in the evaluation of any one which, for the author's purpose, must always be immediate and clear. In contrast, when we supply the label ourselves, when we sum up Jenny's traits as those of "the erring woman," we do so only after we have witnessed her actions, thoughts, and statements in a variety of situations evaluated by various means. By the time we can generalize about her, we have reached the end of the novel; therefore we cannot make use of *our* generalization about her as we can of Fielding's about Thwackum or Square or Bath or Cooper. Jenny's final good action is not necessarily a comment on all fallen women (e.g., Molly Seagrim is not affected by it); any generalization about fallen women drawn from Jenny's case must be indicated as a general truth by some other value device, as when Allworthy, in his role as paragon, makes general comments drawn from Jenny's problems on the plight of fallen women.[4]

The ways in which concrete traits are pointedly related to the initial label of the species character vary greatly but are consistent in one respect: they prevent us from detaching the character from his class, from interpreting his actions, traits, and statements as applicable merely to the character. Fielding's artistry is manifest in the way in which he exploits the dichotomy between specified traits and generalized label in the creation, especially of the most complex, of these species characters. For example, the traits ascribed to Colonel Bath and the use made of these traits in his actions and speeches are such that some admirers of Fielding would probably rank the Colonel high among Fielding's comic creations; yet the label "false honor" is so indelibly written on the Colonel's sword that none of his actions or statements fails to act as an attack on those who identify honor with the *code duello*.[5]

Making the Label Stick

Situation characters are hanged once, permitted to kick their feet grotesquely a few times, and then are decently buried. Not only such characters as Tittle and Tattle but their slightly more particularized cousins, such as those who comprise the *dramatis personae* of the first coach scene in *Joseph Andrews* or some of the prison inmates in *Amelia*, appear so briefly and their role is so plainly confined within bounds supplied by their general labels that there is no necessity for Fielding's continued insistence on their species. Even some walking concepts (situation characters who act as articulate spokesmen for the position represented by their own labels), usually the most complex of the species creations, occasionally have roles so limited that relabeling never presents a problem: the "man of courage" in *Joseph Andrews* meets Adams on the road, strongly asserts what Adams, as paragon, defines as an exaggerated notion of courage, and then drops from the novel after Fielding—making use of self-contradiction, a typical device by which situa-

---

[4] See chapter three.

[5] I do not mean to imply that it is historically true or that Fielding thought it historically true that all believers in the *code duello* were Colonel Baths. Just, however, as Cooper's propensity for picking pockets is a rhetorical device to attack the honesty of Methodists, the presentation of Bath as a species character discredits any who share the broad label, though not the specific traits, ascribed to Bath; for rhetorical purposes, they are subsumed under the species for which Bath is articulate spokesman and representative, and Bath's concrete foibles reflect discredit on the whole species.

tion characters are deflated—shows him evincing considerably less courage than his own exaggerated conception calls for.

In general, though, the walking concepts must periodically be reattached to their labels or else their particularized traits and the actions stemming from those traits remove them from the category of species character. It is almost a necessary corollary to what I have already said that the attention devoted to relabeling at any given moment is directly proportionate to the importance of the concrete trait or action ascribed to the character or characters at that moment; the greater the emphasis on the concrete trait, the more necessary it becomes to emphasize the label if the character is to remain a species character.

The desire of Thwackum and Square to marry Bridget Blifil, for example, is of minor significance for the progression of the action. Any expectation that either will succeed in marrying her is immediately scotched by the narrator, who informs us that "she [Bridget] was well enough pleased with a passion of which she intended none should have any fruits but herself. And the only fruits she designed for herself were flattery and courtship . . . [Bridget] rather inclined to favor the parson's principles; but Square's person was more agreeable to her eye, for he was a comely man." [6]

Since Fielding is careful to prevent our attaching much importance in terms of future possibilites to the desires of either man, the narrator's analysis of the "passion" of Thwackum and Square, itself fairly general in nature, is important in its relation to the action only as it partially explains the men's past attitude to Jones, sets up expectations of their future enmity toward him, and implants another of the mild clues about the lickerish element of Bridget's nature which are important in preventing us from feeling tricked when we discover Tom's parentage. The most concrete characteristics introduced involve Square's relations with women: Bridget reacts to his good looks, and the narrator describes him as "a jolly fellow, or a widow's man." Though these traits become important later, it is sufficient to subordinate them to the species Square represents when they are made use of in action; for his purposes here, as he has only described their relation with Bridget, the narrator need only *indicate* briefly the way in which the two men reconcile their ignoble behavior with the labeled positions for which they have been (and will soon be again) articulate spokesmen in order to remind us of the species they represent:

We would not, however, have our reader imagine that persons of such char-

[6] Henley, III, 128 (*Tom Jones*, III, vi).

acter as were supported by Thwackum and Square would undertake a matter of this kind, which hath been a little censured by some rigid moralists, before they had thoroughly examined it, and considered whether it was (as Shakespeare phrases it) "Stuff o' th' conscience," or no. Thwackum was encouraged by reflecting that to covet your neighbor's sister is nowhere forbidden: and he knew it was a rule in the construction of all laws that "*Expressum facit cessare tacitum.*" The sense of which is, "When a lawgiver sets down plainly his whole meaning, we are prevented from making him mean what we please ourselves." As some instances of women, therefore, are mentioned in the divine law, which forbids us to covet our neighbor's goods, and that of a sister omitted, he concluded it to be lawful. And as to Square, who was in his person what is called a jolly fellow, or a widow's man, he easily reconciled his choice to the eternal fitness of things.[7]

Although Square emerges from the narrator's comments with some hitherto unknown and, at the moment, unimportant traits, Fielding pays a shade more attention to keeping Thwackum labeled. This is necessitated neither by greater complexity inherent in the species Thwackum represents nor by the fact that he plays a more complex role in the action; one might even argue that, since Square acts as a kind of *deus ex machina* at the end, his role is more significant. But it is Thwackum who, in the pages immediately preceding chapter vi and in the passage following the one quoted, receives, as Tom's chastising tutor, most individual attention; Square's innings are still to come. It is Thwackum, for example, rather than Square who, in the passage following the previous quotation, most nearly emerges from treatment by narrational summary into scenic treatment:

In this [degrading and vilifying Tom] Thwackum had the advantage; for while Square could only scarify the poor lad's reputation, he could flay his skin; and, indeed, he considered every lash he gave him as a compliment paid to his mistress; so that he could, with the utmost propriety, repeat this old flogging line, "*Castigo te non quod odio habeam, sed quod Amem.*" I chastise thee not out of hatred, but out of love." And this, indeed, he often had in his mouth, or rather, according to the old phrase, never more properly applied, at his fingers' ends.[8]

Even very slight distinctions in the degree of specificity with which a species character is represented in any given scene are matched by proportionately greater attention to the conception which provides his initial label.

More important, however, is the contrast between Fielding's emphasis on

[7] *Ibid.*, pp. 126-127.

[8] *Ibid.*, p. 127.

the label when a species character's individualized traits are made use of in incidents of direct importance in the progression of the action, and those, like the one discussed above, which affect the relationships of major characters in lesser degree.

We can clearly see the difference in the intensity of treatment in the episode in which Square is ignominiously revealed to Tom as Molly's lover. The hero's sense of loyalty to Molly has been an important element in retarding his commitment to his newly admitted love for Sophia. Considerations of "honor and prudence" which have heretofore prevented him from such an admission are dispelled by Honour's relating to him the tale of the muff. We are told that "The citadel of Jones was now taken by surprise. All those considerations of honor and prudence which our hero had lately with so much military wisdom placed as guards over the avenues of his heart ran away from their posts and the guard of love marched in, in triumph." [9] Nevertheless, though "Sophia totally eclipsed, or rather extinguished, all the beauties of the poor girl [Molly]," Tom is prevented from acting upon his new feelings because "compassion instead of contempt succeeded to love." This "compassion," in turn, is caused mainly by Tom's conviction that Molly had "placed all her affections and all her prospects of future happiness, in him only." To give maximum effect to the important area of the book in which retarding elements of plot temporarily separate the two lovers, some *éclaircissement* must take place between the two. Their feelings for each other must be represented with sufficient force to suggest, as a definite probability, that the formidable obstacles in the way of their union will be overcome; these must also be strong enough to convince the reader of the desirability of the union if the book is to realize its comic power. The *éclaircissement* does take place, first in the scene of sensibility enacted in Western's garden soon after Tom's discovery of the relations between Square and Molly and later, in stronger terms, just before his expulsion by Allworthy. But the discovery of Square enables Tom to enter into the *éclaircissement* with his loyalties not divided between the two women; though admitting his love to himself and to Sophia does not make a saint of him, Tom's later encounter with Molly is not viewed as an emotionally obfuscating attachment; as a result of the discovery of Square in her bedroom, the encounter is seen as merely another of Tom's imprudent lapses, implicit, as Allworthy has informed us, in his passionate "complexion." It is as vital that Tom's emotional attachment to Molly should be severed, without any reflection on his generosity and sense of fair play,

[9] *Ibid.*, p. 222 (V, iv).

before the *éclaircissement* with Sophia as it is for the severance of his relationships with Lady Bellaston, "Mrs. Waters," and the marriageable widow to
occur before he confronts Sophia with the prospect of marriage.

Square is the agent that Fielding selects to reveal to Tom, albeit against
the philosopher's will, the nature of Molly's love—a revelation which frees
Tom from his scruples at deserting his mistress, yet allows him to preserve his
growing reputation for treating women with generosity and consideration. I
use the term "selects" advisedly, since no probability has previously been established that Square is intimate with Molly. His attempt to woo Mrs. Blifil and
his description as "a jolly fellow, or a widow's man" are sufficient for the
reader to accept him without strain in his new role as illicit lover; and such
sufficiency is all that is necessary to maintain the reader's belief in the non-
serious sequence of events which leads up to and follows Square's discovery.
We are as surprised and almost as delighted as Tom to find the squatting philosopher in Molly's room, and, like his, our delight is neither tinctured by the
slightest regret at Molly's infidelity nor is our pleasure limited to feeling relief at his disentanglement from his relationship with her. Tom has come to
Molly's room to try with some reluctance to break off relations with her; the
young woman bursts into tears and laments her cruel fate when a rug, acting
as a curtain, gets loose and reveals behind it the philosopher Square:

> The posture, indeed, in which he stood, was not greatly unlike that of a
> soldier who is tied neck and heels; or rather resembling the attitude in which
> we often see fellows in the public streets of London, who are not suffering
> but deserving punishment by so standing. He had a nightcap belonging to Molly
> on his head, and his two large eyes, the moment the rug fell, stared directly at
> Jones; so that when the idea of Philosophy was added to the figure now dis-
> covered, it would have been very difficult for any spectator to have refrained
> from immoderate laughter.[10]

The narrator, immediately on the discovery of Square, reminds us of his
general character as "Philosopher," a label still broader in context, though
more concise in form, than the specific philosophical foible from which his
usual label is derived—the man who squares all action to the eternal rule of
right. The narrator does not stop with this partial label, but expatiates for a
paragraph on the difference between philosophic theory and practice, ending
with a characterization of philosophers: "They know very well how to
subdue all appetites and passions, and to despise both pain and pleasure; and
this knowledge affords much delightful contemplation, and is easily

---

[10] *Ibid.*, p. 226 (V, v).

acquired; but the practice would be vexatious and troublesome; and, therefore, the same wisdom which teaches them to know this teaches them to avoid
carrying it into execution." [11] Leaving the philosopher in his ignominious
position, the hero standing dumfounded, and their mutual mistress in despair
on the bed, the narrator relates the events that led up to their present positions
before returning us to the scene. When he does so, however, Square is led
from his exposed hiding place by a laughing Tom and immediately defends
himself; in so doing, and with no lapse in consistency, he squares his action to
the eternal rule of right, thus relabeling himself far more strongly than the
narrator has done at the very moment that he is most vividly portrayed as a
character:

> Square, being now arrived in the middle of the room, in which part only
> could he stand upright, looked at Jones with a very grave countenance, and
> said to him, "Well, sir, I see you enjoy this mighty discovery, and, I dare
> swear, take great delight in the thoughts of exposing me; but if you will con-
> sider the matter fairly, you will find you are yourself only to blame. I am not
> guilty of corrupting innocence. *I have done nothing for which that part of the*
> *the world which judges of matters by the rule of right will condemn me.*
> Fitness is governed by the nature of things, and not by customs, forms, or
> municipal laws. Nothing is indeed unfit which is not unnatural." [12]

In an amusing interchange with Tom, Square reveals a tenderness for reputation which, if it indicates once again his disinclination to drink the hemlock
for the sake of his principles, manages to square the disinclination itself with
his conception of fitness. "Things may be fitting to be done which are not
fitting to be boasted of; for by the perverse judgment of the world, that
often becomes the subject of censure, which is, in truth, not only innocent
but laudable." Tom, delighted at the turn of events, has no intention of revealing Square's amorous activities, but twits Square by ostensibly agreeing
with his defense and pointing out that the philosopher had previously failed
to apply his rule of right to Tom's own case. Square is not at a loss; his conduct in that instance was due merely to Thwackum's misrepresentation of the
case: " 'Why, I must confess,' says Square, 'as the matter was misrepresented
to me, by that person Thwackum, I might condemn the corruption of innocence: it was that, sir, it was that—and that: for you must know, Mr.
Jones, in the consideration of fitness, very minute circumstances, sir, very
minute circumstances cause great alteration.' " [13] Tom's release from emo-

[11] *Ibid.*, p. 227.
[12] *Ibid.*, pp. 229-230. Italics mine.
[13] *Ibid.*, p. 230.

tional responsibility to Molly is nearly complete; any misgivings in the reader's mind about his responsibility for Molly's pregnancy are immediately resolved by her sister's revelation that Tom had not initiated Molly into the world of experience and was not the most likely candidate for the father of her child.

The immediate effect of the episode depends upon the traits and mannerisms that particularize Square's character. But the special comic power of *Tom Jones* is best realized when, without prejudice to the individuality of minor characters, their ethical deficiencies are comprehended as general and permanent evils of the comic world. In selecting Square as agent, Fielding has gone to some trouble to preserve him as a species character, first by the narrator's discussion of him as the prototype of the Philosopher and, more important still, by his painstakingly showing Square himself squaring his action with the rule of right (from which he derives his label). Square undoubtedly performs an important role in advancing the plot, has been infused with enough life to participate in an effective comic scene, and yet, because he vociferously relates his own action to the principle he represents, he has been labeled more prominently than he was before his participation in the scene.

In other situations Thwackum and Square relabel themselves while arguing with each other, as when both are disappointed in the provisions of Allworthy's will. Neither is satisfied by his share of the legacy and each interprets the fact that they have been equally treated to mean that his own merit his been slighted:

> "But [Thwackum says] though the Scripture obliges me to remain contented, it doth not enjoin me to shut my eyes to my own merit, nor restrain me from seeing when I am injured by an unjust comparison." "Since you provoke me," returned Square, "that injury is done to me; nor did I ever imagine Mr. Allworthy had held my friendship so light as to put me in balance with one who received his wages. I know to what it is owing; it proceeds from those narrow principles which you have been so long endeavoring to infuse into him, in contempt of everything which is great and noble. The beauty and loveliness of friendship is too strong for dim eyes, nor can it be perceived by any other medium than that unerring rule of right which you have so often endeavored to ridicule, that you have perverted your friend's understanding." "I wish," cries Thwackum, in a rage, "I wish, for the sake of his soul, your damnable doctrines have not perverted his faith. It is to this I impute his present behavior, so unbecoming a Christian. Who but an atheist . . ." [14]

As each condemns Allworthy acording to the ethical concept from which his

[14] *Ibid.*, pp. 246-247 (V, viii).

own label is derived, the concept is at once prominently displayed and comic-ally deflated by its derogatory application to the paragon, whose conception of right and of practical Christianity has by this point in the novel been estab-lished as exemplary.

In *Amelia*, though Bath's conception of honor is thoroughly and authori-tatively attacked by Harrison late in the novel, the Colonel's initial labeling and relabeling derive from his relations with Booth and Amelia rather than with the paragon. Amelia's attitude, as described by Booth, provides the initial ethical characterization of Bath; she finds him an example of those who "in some parts of their characters, have been extremely ridiculous, in others have been altogether as amiable." [15] Interestingly enough, it is Bath's tendency to spin exaggerated tales—an element of his character not developed at length in the novel—which is orignially seen by Amelia as ridiculous. The closely connected but still distinct conception of honor which soon provides him with his label is not judged by Amelia until later in the novel, when its consequences are too serious to be considered the result of mere singularity. The dramatic introduction of new values as the novel progresses[16] is almost peculiar to *Amelia*; in *Tom Jones*, most of the important values are implicit in the early sections, and are merely expanded and seen in specific operation as the plot progresses; in *Joseph Andrews*, however, many of the important ethical agents disappear after their actions or their labels have been evaluated. There is nothing in the two earlier novels quite analogous to the way in which Amelia directs our initial attitude toward Bath, enabling us to laugh at and yet like him until the *code duello* emerges as an important element in the plot; at this point the initially humorous aspects of Bath's behavior are discovered by Amelia and explained by Harrison as serious evils in society.

But if the precise degree of culpability merited by Bath remains tempora-rily uncrystallized in the novel, his species is defined immediately after Amel-ia's initial description of him. Bath initially labels himself when he becomes an actual, though mild, threat to an amused Booth, who has discovered him per-forming the admirable act of nursing his sick sister. The discovery is inter-preted by Bath as tantamount to an insult, and Booth's protestation that it would be impossible for Bath to "appear in a situation more becoming his char-acter" is only interpreted as a further insult. Booth, in a significant variation on Amelia's initial comments on Bath, is "astonished that it was possible for a man to possess true goodness, and be at the same time ashamed of it." Booth's

---

[15] *Ibid.*, VI, 143 (*Amelia*, III, viii).
[16] See chapter three.

astonishment increases when he is visited the next morning by the Major, who is obviously on the point of challenging him to a duel:

"There were some words of yours," says he, "which must be further explained before we part. You told me, sir, when you found me in that situation, which I cannot bear to recollect, that you thought I could not appear in one more becoming my character; these were the words—I shall never forget them. Do you imagine that there is any of the dignity of a man wanting in my character? do you think that I have, during my sister's illness, behaved with a weakness that savors too much of effeminacy? I know how much it is beneath a man to whine and whimper about a trifling girl as well as you or any man; and if my sister had died, I should have behaved like a man on the occasion." [17]

It is only by indicating that such heroic figures as Brutus and Charles XII of Sweden showed great tenderness for women that Booth is able to placate his irascible friend and to induce him to admit, in characteristically bombastic terms, that he is indeed fond of his sister:

"D-n me, I admire the King of Sweden of all the men in the world; and he is a rascal that is ashamed of doing anything which the king of Sweden did. And yet, if any king of Sweden in France was to tell me that his sister had more merit than mine, by G— I'd knock his brains about his ears. Poor little Betsey! she is the honestest, worthiest girl that ever was born. Heaven be praised, she is recovered; for if I had lost her, I never should have enjoyed another happy moment." [18]

The first threat to Booth has been so easily avoided that, at this point in the narrative he is relating to Fanny Matthews, he can assert that "with all his oddity, there is not a better-natured man in the world than the major."

The ethical dichotomy Booth discovers in Bath's character after his species has been defined is parallel to Amelia's previous discovery. Though both the desirable and undesirable aspects of Bath's character are seen at this point as rather ludicrous, they have serious consequences later in the novel. That we are meant to accept the interpretation of Bath's character as ethically dichotomous is emphasized when Fanny Matthews, the major character least capable of ethical discrimination, refuses to assent to the proposition expressed by Booth and previously by Amelia. She responds to Booth's evaluation of the major by crying, " 'Good natured indeed!' . . . with great scorn. 'A fool! how can you mention such a fellow with commendation?' " Nevertheless, despite

[17] Henley, VI, 146 (*Amelia*, III, viii).
[18] *Ibid.*, p. 147.

the Booths' complex opinion of Bath, the latter does remain a species character: if one aspect of his character is good-natured, the good nature is never
displayed apart from an inevitable reference to the damned code of honor.

Indeed, the very next incident simultaneously displays Bath's good nature
and "all his oddity." He does act as Booth's friend by challenging and wound-
ing the scurrilous Bagillard, who had implied that he hoped to seduce Amelia.
But even in relating the incident to Booth, Bath relabels himself ludicrously by
his assertion that he has done Booth "one of the highest injuries" by taking
"out of your own hands the doing yourself justice." And his species is permanently defined when, on Bagillard's recovery, Bath argues that Booth must
now challenge his wife's traducer. At Booth's demurring on the grounds that
he had forgiven Bagillard when he was apparently on his deathbed, Bath
evinces nothing but scorn: " 'What hath anger,' cried he, 'to do with the
matter? the dignity of my nature hath been always my reason for drawing
my sword; and when that is concerned I can as readily fight with the man I
love as with the man I hate.' " [19] But if, like Thwackum and Square, Bath
remains a species character despite frequent and important appearances, since
his good nature and the few elements of his code of honor analogous to the
"true" conception of honor espoused by Harrison earlier are used in important
ways, it is imperative that Bath be consistently and subtly relabeled. It is Bath,
after all, who asserts the moral truth of Harrison's letter when it is read at the
masquerade. But lest we forget his martial dignity at this point, Bath conspicuously remembers it; when the masqueraders, annoyed by his defense of "religion and virtue," threaten to toss him in a blanket, the bombastic duelist
re-emerges: " 'Me in a blanket?' said the friar: 'by the dignity of man, I will
twist the neck of every one of you as sure as ever the neck of a dunghill-cock
was twisted.' At which words he pulled off his masque, and the tremendous
majesty of Colonel Bath appeared, from which the bucks fled away as fast as
the Trojans heretofore from the face of Achilles." [20]

Still more important is the contretemps innate in Fielding's use of Bath as a
vital second to Harrison's attempt to dissuade James from issuing his challenge
to Booth. Fielding's use of the walking concept in this instance represents a
high point in craftsmanship: Bath continues to be ridiculed, James' intention
is evaluated as more evil than it has been before, since it cannot be justified
even by Bath's notion of honor as a willingness to cut throats, and, with a neat
twist, in the very process of relabeling himself by demonstrating his propensity

[19] *Ibid.*, p. 153 (III, x).
[20] *Ibid.*, VII, 192 (X, ii).

to kill those who affront him, Bath becomes the threat which prevents James from attempting to kill Booth.

One cannot miss the characteristic bombast and elements of the undesirable code implicit in the way in which Bath performs the highly desirable task of forcing James to answer Harrison's questions: " 'D-n me, the question is very transparent!' cries Bath. 'From any other man it would be an affront with the strongest emphasis, but from one of the doctor's cloth it demands a categorical answer.' " [21] The neatest example of Bath's simultaneously relabeling himself while demonstrating his "good-natured" qualities occurs when Bath seconds Harrison's Christian arguments in terms of the very code of honor damned as unchristian by the paragon:

> "Brother," cries Bath, "I hope I shall not make you angry. I lie when I say so; for I am indifferent to any man's anger. Let me be an accessory to what the doctor hath said. I think I may be trusted with matters of this nature, and it is a little unkind that, if you intended to send a challenge, you did not make me the bearer. But, indeed, as to what appears to me, this matter may be very well made up; and as Mr. Booth doth not know of the challenge, I don't see why he ever should, any more than your giving him the lie just now; but that he shall never have from me, nor, I believe, from this gentleman; for, indeed, if he should it would be incumbent upon him to cut your throat." [22]

The joint persuasions of Christianity and the *code duello* prove too much for James, whose reasons for acquiescing in Harrison's request are summed up by the narrator:

> In fact, the colonel was ashamed to avow the real cause of the quarrel to this good man [Harrison], or, indeed, to his brother Bath, who would not only have condemned him equally with the doctor, but would possibly have quarrelled with him on his sister's account, whom, as the reader must have observed, he loved above all things; and, in plain truth, though the colonel was a brave man, and dared to fight, yet he was altogether as willing to let it alone; and this made him now and then give a little way to the wrongheadedness of Colonel Bath, who, with all the other principles of honor and humanity, made no more of cutting the throat of a man upon any of his punctilios than a butcher doth of killing sheep.[23]

Bath easily makes his exit from the novel as an undiluted walking concept; none of our expectations about him is either thwarted or unfulfilled by the

[21] *Ibid.*, p. 308 (XII, iv).
[22] *Ibid.*, p. 311.
[23] *Ibid.*, pp. 311-312.

final description of his being "killed in a duel about six years ago by a gentleman who told the colonel he differed from him in opinion." Nevertheless, if
one consciously looks back at the role he has played in the novel, there seems to
be a discrepancy between the richness and variety of Bath's participation and
the summarizing tag with which he is dismissed. It is precisely because Bath
represents Fielding's most successful and highly developed use of the walking
concept that such a discrepancy is discernible. While a Square may surprise us
by becoming Jones' advocate before his death, the surprise is much akin to
shock, since there has been no indication that such a conversion is probable or
indeed possible. Because Square was conceived of as a mere animated anagram of ideationally dictated traits, Fielding may have felt no artistic pangs
at the lack of psychological preparation for the philosopher's recantation, and
it is this fact that prevents us from feeling absolutely tricked when the results
of the conversion become important for the resolution of the action. Nevertheless, Square's final act complicates his role in the novel without making him
a complex character. But Bath surprises us in a very different manner. Our
introduction to him through Amelia's dichotomous description conditions us
to viewing him as the possessor of traits easily classified as either ridiculous or
amiable. This absolute distinction is immediately reinforced, though the dual-
ity is redefined as "good-bad," in the episode in which he plays nurse to his
sister. Continued emphasis on a strict dichotomy could easily have resulted in
Bath's remaining, like Thwackum and Square, merely an ideational construct
infused with a modicum of animation but incapable of psychological development. But the Colonel is deftly prevented from becoming a simple anagram
of bad-ridiculous and good-amiable characteristics: the undesirable part of the
dichotomy is limited to the cutthroat code of honor, while the desirable elements are displayed, with increasing frequency as the novel progresses, in virtuous activities that do not impinge upon his punctilios. In short, the simple
dichotomy of traits is transformed into a reasonably complex character with
an *idée fixe*, which continually redefines the character as a species. As a result,
Fielding can both have his cake and eat it.

We are surprised at Bath's vociferous approval of Harrison's letter condemning adultery but, primarily because of the adequate preparation made
for such approval in his previous bombastic assertion about what he would do
to any king of Sweden who would dare to pretend that his sister had more
merit than's Bath's own, we are able to accept his defense of women's honor
as a new dimension of his character rather than as a mechanical perversion of
it to satisfy a momentary need of the plot. If it is still more surprising that
later in the novel Bath should swerve from the cutthroat code (which pro-

vides his label) when he attempts to dissuade James from cutting Booth's throat, the surprise is not of the sort, as in Square's or Robinson's conversions, that stems from Fielding's doing violence to his character's consistency; Bath's attitude toward his sister, his summary revenge on Bagillard for aspersing Amelia's reputation, and his admiration for Harrison's diatribe against adultery have provided us with ample preparation for his condemnation of James' actions; indeed, as a fairly effective reminder, emphatic reference is made, during the episode in which James is dissuaded, to Bath's admiration for Amelia, for his sister, and for Harrison's letter.

Bath has in effect emerged as what E. M. Forster terms a "round" character: he can and does surprise us, and the surprise is the result of neither inconsistent nor nearly nonexistent characterization. He never loses his label, however; whenever he surprises us, whenever he takes on a new dimension of character, we are carefully reminded of his commitment to the ridiculed code of honor. As a "walking concept" he incorporates a generalized form of serious ethical deficiency in *Amelia* much as his less complex brethren do, though he performs other services for the novel in a far more complex manner than other species characters. The particularized traits of a Thwackum, a Square, a Robinson, or a Lawyer Scout are almost mechanically subordinate to the evaluative labels which define their species; their closest approximation to creating an illusion of reality must be summed up as "animation," a virtue in some literary works. In creating Bath, Fielding represented a character whose traits and actions are not mere intellectual extensions of the character's label, but are deftly subordinated to that label throughout the novel. As a result, Bath could perform services peculiar to "round" characters, yet could simultaneously be represented as a species, as one norm of a society which threatens to prevent the Booths' experiencing domestic felicity.

Labels as Gibbets

Whether he take a form as complex as that of Colonel Bath or as skeletal as those of Tittle and Tattle, the *sine qua non* for the species character is that he be labeled and, whenever necessary, relabeled. The label itself is frequently accompanied by an immediate and obvious negative judgment. This initial evaluation does not undergo radical change even in the most complex species character and, typically, it undergoes no change of any sort. In the rare instances where the evaluation of a label changes, the change consists rather in intensity than in kind, as when Bath's undesirable but culpably ridiculous threat to Booth is viewed as even more undesirable when it becomes a serious threat later in the novel. Though Bath as a character achieves a measure of complexity, the position from which his label is derived is clearly and consistently seen as unvirtuous.

Typically, then, the label of any species character becomes a gibbet on which he is hanged not only once but at his every appearance in the novel. Though one could isolate innumerable minor stylistic indications that the labeled species is "bad," "ridiculous," or otherwise undesirable, there are five important modes by which the label is judged undesirable almost immediately on the introduction of the character who bears it. Since the shorter the character's stay in the novel, the more necessary it is that his label be emphatically and immediately evaluated, even minor situation characters may be condemned by a number of methods used simultaneously.

The Self-Evaluating Label

The problems implicit in this mode of evaluation have been discussed in chapter two, but a few of its implications should be stressed here. The naming of these characters runs to one of two extremes: either their names are rhetorically loaded, as for Tittle and Tattle, Jonathan Thrasher, Thwackum, and Lawyer Scout; or the character remains nameless but is referred to by catchword descriptions, as are the prude in *Joseph Andrews*, the lawyer at Western's table in *Tom Jones*, and the Stoic at the spunging house in *Amelia*. For a label to *remain* self-evaluating, the character who bears it must never be able to squirm from an extremely confined pigeonhole; hence the self-evaluating situation characters are limited to those who remain nearly traitless, who are only partially dramatized, and who, it follows automatically, play only the briefest and least important roles in the novels. Any extended treatment of these characters, no matter how simple, automatically necessitates the use of one or more of the other evaluative methods.

Evaluation by Self-Contradiction

One could logically argue that for a character to fail to live up to a professed ethical position does not necessarily reflect unfavorably on the position; the man may be unworthy of living up to an honorable ethic; or, as in Adams' despair over the presumed drowning of his son, the failure to live up to the professed creed may be a comic indication that the creed is not a goal fitting for or attainable by men. As logical as these alternatives are, they do not apply to the rhetorical signals by which the label of a species character is judged undesirable. If he is indeed a species character, he is not a Methodist who is incidentally a thief; he has too strongly been labeled Methodist for his thievery not to act as a rhetorical deflation of his religious label. If he is a

Stoic who becomes submerged in despair at the thought of not seeing his wife at an appointed time, so long as the label "Stoic" is constantly forced on the reader's attention, the character's despair makes a mockery of his philosophical position.

The clearness of the signal, the ease with which it can be applied, and its obvious relation to Fielding's conception that the exposure of hypocrisy and affectation is a primary source of the comic make this device the one most frequently employed. Most species characters, even when ridiculed by other means as well, become self-contradictory—that is, debase their labeled positions—at some point in their careers.

Typical is the prude in *Joseph Andrews*, whose delicacy is offended at the thought of riding with the injured and unfortunately naked Joseph, and who resents even being asked if she might not "accommodate him [a cold and shaking Joseph] with a dram," but who is found by the highway robber to possess "some of the best Nantes he had ever tasted." Nor is this method applied only to simple situation characters; "walking concepts" are similarly deflated. "The-man-of-courage" in *Joseph Andrews* would have no scruples at "shooting a man that would not die for his country," and has already disinherited a nephew who "would not exchange his commission and go to the West Indies," but, when Fanny is heard screaming in the bushes, "the-man-of-courage" not only refuses to go to her aid with his loaded shotgun but attempts to dissuade Adams from attempting to rescue her. The Stoic in the spunging house with Booth in *Amelia*, in contrast, argues most convincingly with Booth and even explains the first part of his argument in a manner that certainly would accord with Fielding's own views that by "philosophy, I do not mean the bare knowledge of right and wrong, but an energy, a habit, as Aristotle calls it; and this I do firmly believe, with him and with the Stoics, is superior to all the attacks of fortune." Immediately after his eloquent defense of his philosophy, however, Fortune attacks the Stoic with the news that he is to be removed to Newgate that afernoon; he begs the bailiff for more time and asserts that "if you should remove me now, it would be the most barbarous disappointment to us both, and will make me the most miserable man alive."

Logically the man's failure to become superior to the attacks of fortune need not reflect on the validity of Stoicism but merely on his own ability to live up to its precepts. He is not merely a man who is unable to achieve the Stoic ideal, however: he is the species "Stoic," and his failure—whether fairly or not is irrelevant in this context—indicates the undesirability of the label that defines him.

Evaluation by Relationship
to the Protagonist

As Fielding's novels are constructed, the fallible paragons and
the heroines, who are themselves paragons of sorts, are privileged to disap-
prove of aspects of the heroes' characters or even, as in Allworthy and Harrison, to represent occasional serious threats to their well-being without
incurring the reader's hostility. They receive the former privilege by virtue
of emphatic indications that they are the most desirable ethical embodiments
in the world of the novel in which each appears; the protagonists, no matter
how sympathetic they are, fall below the standard which the paragons represent. It is always in comparison with the paragons that the protagonists are
seen as virtuous or not rather than vice versa. When the paragons actually
threaten the protagonists' well-being, they are shown either to have made an
unavoidable error in the application of correct ethical principles, or actually to
be justified in causing the protagonists some difficulty.

Any other character criticizes or threatens the protagonist, even at moments when he is least virtuous, at his own risk, since to the extent that the
novel is successful its hero retains our sympathy even when he is engaged in
morally culpable activities;[24] if he did not retain our sympathy, we could
not be troubled by his condemned ethical deviations. When a species character
is shown to be a threat to the protagonist as soon as he is introduced, his label
is emphatically judged as undesirable.

All but one of the characters in the coach in *Joseph Andrews* are condemned by their willingness to leave Joseph to die. In this instance, initial
definition of their species is concurrent with the evaluation of their type since
their willingness to keep Joseph from the coach results from the ethical
propensities which label them: the coachman cannot "suffer him to be taken
in unless somebody would pay a shilling for his carriage the four miles"; the
gentleman wishes to "make all haste imaginable, or we shall be robbed too";
the prude would "rather stay in that place to all eternity than ride with a
naked man." The situation of the lawyer is slightly different: he does want
Joseph to be helped, but his motive is fear of the legal consequences of leaving the stricken hero to die; the lawyer's stated wish that "they had passed by
without taking any notice" is more than sufficient to indicate the contempt

---

[24] There are exceptions to this general rule. Mrs. Miller, who acts as an extension
of Allworthy's ethical voice in London, is seen as justified in asking Tom to leave
her house. And Mrs. Whitefield's suspicion of Tom is justified, but only because the
narrator intervenes strongly in her behalf.

we are meant to feel for ostensibly virtuous action dictated by merely legal considerations.

The prude has been evaluated by all three of the modes specified up to this point. First, she has a self-evaluating label. Nameless, she labels herself simply and consistently in every statement she makes before the highway robbery. She hears the groan and calls upon the coachman to stop. Her first quoted words, however, are "O J-sus . . . a naked man! Dear coachman, drive on and leave him!" Even after the lawyer points out the possible legal consequences of failing to help the naked man, she insists that "if they lifted him in, she would herself alight, for she would rather stay in that place to all eternity than ride with a naked man." Her only other remark previous to the robbery extends her ostensible puritanism to alcohol: she is insulted when asked if she might not have a dram for Joseph, who is "almost dead with the cold." As simply defined and nearly as traitless as Tittle and Tattle, the lady, in the very act of attaching a self-evaluating label to herself, simultaneously threatens the protagonist. If the robbery did not expose her as a hypocrite, her prudishness would sufficiently have been indicated as undesirable; her exposure is a final comic thrust.

Since most of the situation characters and walking concepts are fated to emerge as threats to the protagonist's well-being, it is tempting to think of this as the principal method of indicating the ethical caliber of species characters. On closer examination it becomes clear, though, that a threat to the protagonist is not emphatic enough to result in the immediate and unchanging evaluation necessary for a character's use as a species unless the threat becomes evident almost concurrently with the definition of the character's species. For example, our hostility is aroused against Thwackum when he threatens the protagonist not after but immediately before he is labeled:

> In the morning, when Tom attended the reverend Mr. Thwackum, the person to whom Mr. Allworthy had committed the instruction of the two boys, he had the same questions put to him by that gentleman which he had been asked the evening before, to which he returned the same answers. The consequence of this was so severe a whipping that it possibly fell little short of the torture with which confessions are in some countries extorted from criminals.[25]

The actual definition of Thwackum's species begins subsequently, when he tries to argue that Allworthy is wrong to consider Tom's lying as the consequence of a "mistaken point of honor." " 'Honor!' cried Thwackum with some wrath, 'mere stubbornness and obstinacy! Can honor teach any one to

---

[25] Henley, III, 111-112 (*Tom Jones*, III, ii).

tell a lie, or can any honor exist independent of religion?' " The process of definition is not complete until the ensuing argument between Thwackum and Square, but the undesirability of the species has been indicated by our initial view of Thwackum as Tom's tormentor and has been further emphasized by the fact that the position from which his label is derived has been shown to differ radically from the paragon's.

Evaluation by Relationship to the Paragons

Though our strongest sympathies are attached to the protagonists, we are meant to regard the paragons as ethical mentors; Fielding's heroines, however, both interest us in their fates and represent near-perfect ethical embodiments, though they articulate their ethical standards infrequently and only in special situations where it is deemed appropriate for ideal females to express their views. For slightly different reasons, then, a direct threat to the well-being of either male or female paragon automatically stigmatizes the label of the species character making the threat in much the same way as does a threat to the protagonist; normally, the male paragon's reaction to such a threat differs from the protagonist's and from the heroine's in that it entails verbal castigation of the species character who represents the threat. The practical-joking squire and his retinue of situation characters (the captain, the poet, the player, etc.) do not endear themselves to us by their mistreatment of Adams, but their undesirability is emphasized and specifically qualified in Adams' reproving speech to the lot. Similarly, though in a more complex situation, when Bath is relabeled during his argument with Harrison, the former's insults to the paragon are sufficient to deprecate his label, but the deprecation is made complete and unites intellectual justification with rhetorical force when Harrison attacks Bath's code with wit and cogency.

Evaluation by Relation to the Paragon's Ethic

A walking concept need not directly threaten or insult one of the paragons to be seen as ethically deficient, since his own views will be regarded as undesirable to the extent that they deviate from the paragon's. As in the species character who opposes the hero, however, it is only when the opposition between the views of the species character and those of the paragon is emphasized in close conjunction with the introduction or re-introduction of the former's label that the simple "pigeon-hole" evaluation associated with species characters is effected. Although any species character by definition derives his label from a trait, tenet, or complex of attitudes to which the paragon is presumably opposed, the opposition is only occasionally made so emphatic as to provide as immediate and simple an evaluation of a walking concept as self-contradiction does.

Such a judgment is made when the "man-of-courage" in *Joseph Andrews* is corrected at length by Adams, who objects to the former's exaggerated respect for physical courage; the correction is sufficient to disparage the views from which the character derives his label before the character himself receives his *coup de grâce* in being exposed as a coward. In a more complex instance, Thwackum is introduced as Tom's tormentor, but is both labeled and more clearly evaluated while in the very act of arguing vehemently against Allworthy's charitable interpretation of Tom's refusal to reveal his accomplice in the affair of the partridges. At other points Thwackum is re-labeled while disagreeing with Allworthy about Tom, as when, after Tom's relations with Molly Seagrim are made known, the tutor attempts to turn Allworthy against his hero, only to be told that " 'young men of Tom's complexion were too generally addicted to this vice; but he believed that youth was sincerely affected with what he had said to him on the occasion, and he hoped he would not transgress again.' "

Four peculiarities of this mode of evaluating species characters are worth noting. First, it invariably results not only in the rhetorical deflation of a species character but also in at least a fragmentary justification for the rhetorical attack upon him: we not only learn that the views of the "man-of-courage" are despicable, we know how we *should* regard physical courage; we not only learn that Thwackum's opinion of Tom's sexual transgression is wrong, we learn how we should regard that transgression. Second, this method is limited primarily to evaluating walking concepts, since it can achieve special force only when the paragon's articulated views are directly opposed to other articulated ideas. Third, the method is often used when the principles expressed by a walking concept are meant to condemn the protagonist; when used in this connection the method results in a significantly precise indication of the ethical significance of the protagonist's actions. Fourth, the extended use of this method tends to engender a discursive argument between the paragon and the walking concept which transcends the simple problem of evaluating the latter's label; in the extended version the harmful effect of the labeled position and its implications for the whole of the world portrayed in the novel are explored, as when the religious and social implications of Bath's violent code of honor are dissected by Harrison.

The Importance of the Pigeonhole

Fielding was anything but prone to make facile and absolute judgments of human beings. His narrators' outright protestations against the view that men are all good or all bad are emphasized in the creation of such morally complex characters as Jenny Jones, Colonel James, Booth, and Tom; the problems implicit in isolating the ethical judgments made in novels which have pleased generations of readers are indices to the complexity of the novelist's ethical views. It is no accident that attempts to convert value judgments aesthetically sufficient in Fielding's novels into articulated statements are likely to result in distortions: the "man-of-the-hill" episode *can* be misconstrued as a lyrical defense of Stoicism; the narrator's sympathy for Betty when she is caught in bed with Tow-wouse does lend itself to the notion that Fielding espoused sexual incontinence. What signals the appropriate evaluations in each instance is clear, but what is signaled is complex; the reader's sympathies are not haphazardly directed, but are meant to be divided. Perhaps the fact that few readers capable of enjoying *Tom Jones* at all can do so without enlarging their sympathies and losing some of their feelings of self-righteousness points to one aspect of the novel's excellence.

Nevertheless, the species character (as defined above) plays no inconsiderable role in the value schemes of Fielding's novels and, paradoxically, such a character's existence typically depends upon his being placed in a neat ethical pigeonhole: immediately under a tidy little label we find its tidy little evaluation.

To ignore momentarily the aesthetic implications of the paradox, it seems highly probable that any formulated idea or complex of ideas whose treatment is limited to its embodiment in the label of a species character is one which never had or, at least at the time the novel was written, had ceased to have any intellectual appeal for Fielding. Such ideas would not, when embodied in the species character, have represented a serious intellectual threat to Fielding's ethical view of the world, no matter how serious a practical threat they constituted for what he considered virtue in the world.

This statement is not as sweeping a generalization as it might appear to be. If we select at random some species characters from each of the novels—the coach passengers or the "man-of-courage" in *Joseph Andrews*, the lawyer or Thwackum or Square in *Tom Jones*, Robinson or Bondum or Bath in *Amelia*—it becomes evident that not only are the labeled characters judged undesirable, but also the positions from which their labels are derived. These are indicated, by means of cursory rhetorical debunking, as intellectually despicable. There is no valid reason to assume that the form of any of his novels could influence Fielding to represent as intellectually despicable the ideas which he would judiciously reject in the external world.[26] For indicating carefully qualified rejection of actions, characters, and ideas, a rich variety of alternative methods abounds in Fielding's novels, not only *in potentia* but as fully developed and frequently employed ways of conveying judgments. When an idea, a belief, an attitude, or a complex of these is deemed worthy of serious intellectual refutation or qualification before rejection, it is invariably treated in some form other than an embodiment in a species character, though it may receive such treatment also.

In *Tom Jones*, for example, elements of Stoicism are briefly debunked by their temporary association with Square's "philosophy." When the battle between Tom and Blifil is stopped by Thwackum's intervention, "the philosophy of Square rendered him superior to all emotions, and he very calmly smoked his pipe, as was his custom in all broils, unless when he apprehended some danger of having it broke in his mouth." If the Stoic notion of the desirability of becoming superior to passion were treated in this incident only, we would be justified in considering that the notion had little significance for Fielding except as one more trivial affectation of the species, "philosopher." The moment that the "man-of-the-hill" narrates his adventures to Tom, however, the Stoic notion takes on a special *kind* of importance for the novel. With the change in the manner by which the notion is formalized in the plot, new probabilities about the relationship between the element of thought in the novel and the author's general beliefs emerge.[27]

But if the labels of the species characters represent ideas unworthy of serious consideration because of their innate value, walking concepts receive extended treatment, especially in the last two novels; such unworthy ideas are seen as important in almost direct proportion to their intellectual unrespectability. Given the special power realized in each of Fielding's novels, the explanation is relatively simple: the less merit intrinsic in an idea accepted by any segment of the population of the external world or, analogously, accepted by characters in the novels, the more important it becomes to represent the idea as a general and dangerous threat to the deserving. Its importance in these circumstances consists in its absolute lack of merit.

[26] The theoretical implications of making such an *ad hoc* assumption are discussed in chapter six.

[27] The special relationship between Fielding's general beliefs and the judgments conveyed in what I have called "the narratives of the stray lambs" is discussed in chapter five.

In other words, ideas which find expression in Fielding's novels only as they are embodied in species characters differ from ideas embodied in other forms not necessarily in the degree of importance but always in the kind of importance they have both for the novels and for their author.

No character apart from Amelia, Booth, or Harrison plays a more important role in Amelia than Bath does. Not only does he influence the course of events in *Amelia*, but he is labeled and relabeled with appropriate evaluations at many points in the novel. His cutthroat code of honor, which culminates in his own death, threatens Amelia's happiness, Harrison's principles, and Booth's life. An entire chapter is given over to Harrison's refutation of the code, and the single long argument between the male and female paragon figures centers on it. The code is represented as a vicious and dangerous threat to the desirable elements of the social order; the fact that Booth is partially trained and partially impelled to occasional conformity to Bath's code increases rather than mitigates its undesirability. Its importance as a threat resides precisely in its lack of social merit.

This special kind of importance implicit in the embodiment of an idea in a species character, especially in a walking concept, has, in turn, considerable importance for translating signals of judgments conveyed in Fielding's novels into articulated ideas. A shift from formalizing an element of thought by this mode in one novel to formalizing the same element of thought by another mode in a later novel sets up a strong probability that the kind of importance the idea has for Fielding has shifted also.[28]

Such a shift is seen in the treatment of the notion that the proper way to protect oneself from misfortune is to put oneself, by control of the passions and/or physical removal from the world of men, beyond the reach of Fortune's sting. In each novel the notion is rejected, but in a special way.

In *Joseph Andrews* it *is* sharply attacked, but it is embodied not in the label of a species character but as an element of the paragon's fallibility. The discrepancy between Adams' advising Joseph to dispassionately accept the results of Fanny's abduction and his own passionate reactions to reports of his son's drowning and rescue makes us laugh at the good parson. But it is the discrepancy rather than the passionate reactions that we laugh at. Since the traits which earlier defined Adams as a paragon included deep sympathy with human misfortune and passionate involvement in human affairs, his passionate

---

[28] This, of course, holds true only if the mode to which Fielding shifts the constant element of thought does not result in a *kind* of judgment similar to the original; devices other than species characters can, for example, result in "pigeonhole" evaluations; such a shift would not be evidence of change.

reaction (to a serious cause of sorrow and rejoicing) is seen as superior to the fallible principle he advocates verbally but violates in practice. The complexity of this evaluation is such that this particular Stoic ideal is seen as impossible of achievement by the best of men (Adams cannot achieve it), and judged undesirable (it is in opposition to the very actions and beliefs that define Adams as the paragon figure); yet it is represented as having sufficient meretricious attraction to indicate that one who believes in it is not necessarily a fool or a bad man (Adams espouses it).

In the at least equally complex treatment of a similar ideal in *Tom Jones*, the element of ridicule is nearly though not quite absent. The "man-of-the-hill" digression[29] involves a tale of partially self-inflicted misfortunes more variedly disastrous than those which have beset Tom, one possible reaction to such misfortune in the emotional and physical removal of the "man-of-the-hill" from the concerns of mankind, and, finally, Tom's rejection of this reaction in argument and then, more convincingly, in action. The political agreement between Tom and the old man and the carefully contrived temporary identification of their fortunes are emphatic indications that the rejected point of view derives its importance as a threat from its plausibility rather than, as in the ideas which label species characters, from its inanity.

But the same ideal is represented in a very different manner in *Amelia*: it is embodied in the labels of two walking concepts, one treated at length and the other appearing briefly in the novel. Robinson's ostensible acquiescence in the dictates of what he regards as omnipotent Fortune becomes grimly amusing when we discover that he cheats at cards, does passionate physical battle with a prostitute who accuses him of being a cheat, and adheres to his philosophy only in his steadfast refusal to lend money to the hungry Booth. His label is evaluated by the typical modes of self-contradiction and emergence as a threat to the well-being of the protagonist. Its debunking is bracketed with and parallel to that of another "deterministic" position, represented by Cooper the Methodist, which holds that divine grace, and therefore eternal salvation, has nothing to do with good actions. Neither is seen as having anything like the stature of Booth's deterministic notion that men act according to the dictates of their passions; this notion, though ridiculed at points, seems to have superseded the Stoic idea as a plausible (and therefore dangerous) position needing extensive refutation. If we consider the effect of the careful initial juxtaposition of the three "deterministic" positions, it is apparent that the final cursory treatment of the Stoic idea in *Amelia* is not accidental. Fielding still

[29] See chapter five.

felt, when he wrote his last novel, that the attitude to misfortune whose polar extreme is represented by the two Stoics in *Amelia* was of considerable importance; he takes the trouble to attack it twice. His expressed conviction that the concept of Fortune was merely a rationalization of avoidable human error has reduced the intellectual merit of Stoicism to a cipher. When one translates Fortune as Providence and misfortune as human error, the philosophy which advocates a way of life predicated on the earlier view becomes inapplicable; there is no niche for it in the view of the universe. The man of Mazzard Hill could have no place in the world of Amelia; his Stoic imperturbability might indeed have been ruffled had he seen his vestigial remains in the spunging house in Fielding's last novel.

The Undesirable Polar Norm

While I have no wish to quarrel with a traditional view of comedy that assumes that a comic writer reveals in his work a set of values which constitutes a social norm and then shows his protagonist deviating from it, it seems to me that a failure to distinguish between two uses of the term "norm" represents at least a potential source of confusion. If by norm we mean simply that which acts as a kind of measuring rod in the work itself, then the traditional view is applicable to Fielding's novels. But if we attach to the term "norm" the idea of normalcy, if we interpret a "social norm" as that which has been included to represent customary values of a social world outside the novel, I am not certain of the applicability of the traditional view to comic writing in general, nor do I feel that it is a convenient way to describe what occurs in Fielding's novels.

If we limit our definition of "norm" to a standard of measurement, the species characters can clearly be seen as norms, as negative embodiments which help us to measure the ethical significance of the activities, ideas, and attitudes of other characters in the novels. But since the species characters almost by definition embody what is viewed as contemptible, to view them as embodiments of what Fielding considered morally normal in society is to consign him automatically to the role of misanthropist, or at least to the role of extreme pessimist.

Fielding's protagonists deviate from the ethical positions not only of species characters but of paragons as well. This suggests that the protagonist himself represents the closest thing to moral normalcy, defined in the second sense, that we find in Fielding's novels, though this is more clearly applicable to *Tom Jones* and *Amelia* than to *Joseph Andrews*. Initially both Tom and Booth share some of the paragon's traits and possess or soon win his approval;

when brought into contact with species characters, the protagonists invariably reject them, though, indeed, they possess in diluted form the lesser follies, vices, and attitudes which provide the labels for species characters: Joseph Andrews is vain in London, but is no Beau Didapper; Booth duels, but is no Colonel Bath. Those undesirable traits which they may, but not always do, share with species characters cause them to make choices which, in the last two novels, cause them temporarily to lose the paragons' approval, though they retain considerable ethical kinship with them; even at the end, when the ethical approval is regained and Booth and Tom come closest to realizing their ethical kinship with Harrison and Allworthy, they do not become ethically identical with them. They veer between two polar extremes, one of which acts as a threat which never succeeds, the other as a model which is never fully imitated.

And yet, though the species characters represent the undesirable polar extremes—the norms in the sense of measuring rods—there is reason enough to confuse the issue by considering them a microcosmic representation of what Fielding considers normal in society. The rhetorical emphasis afforded by their ubiquity and their oversimplified delineation tends to leave the reader with the impression that the species characters are prototypes of the normal compared to which not only Allworthy or Harrison but even Jenny Jones or Mrs. Miller are to be viewed as exceptional. Though it is easy to conclude that novels which leave us with the impression that the despicable is the normal could have been written only by a man who did not think well of his fellow human beings, it must be remembered that one conscious purpose in each of Fielding's novels was didactic. Fielding hoped to expose the ridiculous in *Joseph Andrews*, to "laugh mankind out of their favorite follies and vices" in *Tom Jones*, and to "expose some of the most glaring evils, as well public as private, which at present infest the country," in *Amelia*. When such intentions are scrupulously carried out, we meet more frequently with the undesirable than with the desirable; when species characters become an important means of carrying out such intentions, this state of affairs is inevitable.

And it is, of course, primarily as artistic embodiments of negative judgments that the species characters are included in Fielding's novels: they control our attitudes toward *undiluted* forms of the vanity and hypocrisy exposed in *Joseph Andrews*; of the "folly and vice" laughed at in *Tom Jones*; and of "the most glaring evils" exposed in *Amelia*. In none of these novels do they have a monopoly on vanity, hypocrisy, folly, or vice, but it is as undesirable *polar* norms that the species characters appear in the novels: social pressure causes Booth to engage in the unchristian act of dueling, but it is Bath's attitudes, assumptions, and actions that simultaneously account for the existence of the social pressure and provide a focal point for the attack on the social evil.

The labeled characters do convey Fielding's negative judgments, but not as mere attachments to something else which is the "real" novel. Such episodes as those in which the coach passengers discuss the naked Joseph, in which Square is discovered in Molly's bedroom, or in which Bath helps prevent the duel between James and Booth indicate that Fielding's consciously didactic intentions, while in no way vitiated, are formalized in his work. The species characters, integral parts of represented actions, contribute to the fullest realization of the special power of each of Fielding's novels.

Chapter Five

The Digressions

First, then, we warn thee not too hastily to condemn any of the incidents in this our history as impertinent and foreign to our main design, because thou dost not immediately conceive in what manner such incident may conduce to that design. This work may, indeed, be considered as a great creation of our own; and for a little reptile of a critic to presume to find fault with any of its parts, without knowing the manner in which the whole is connected, and before he comes to the final catastrophe, is a most presumptuous absurdity.[1]

Reptilian Presumption

The threat of reptilian classification has failed to frighten Fielding's critics, many of whom do indeed find incidents in all three of his novels "impertinent and foreign" to his main design. Others, however, attempt to explain or defend incidents traditionally considered digressions on the basis of their thematic connection to the whole; one recent critic of *Joseph Andrews* has completely escaped saurian classification by denying that the tale of "The Unfortunate Jilt," "The Story of Leonard and Paul," and Mr. Wilson's narration of the events of his life can be considered digressions, since, in exposing the ridiculous, they embody Fielding's stated intention.[2]

I do not know whether it is better to be half a little reptile or a whole one, but I cannot agree about Fielding's digressions with either his severe critics or his complete apologists. As an admirer of eighteenth-century literature who has also imbibed the critical prejudices of his own age, I am only moderately irritated by digressions. And my reactions to most of the incidents traditionally regarded as digressions in Fielding's novels remain unchanged, even after I am made aware of the incidents' ideational relevance to the novels in which they appear. There is little point in defending as nondigressive the incidents which most of Fielding's readers react to as digressions. We serve Fielding's cause better by investigating the formal reasons for that reaction and showing how some incidents, because they are digressions, perform aesthetic services they could not otherwise perform.

[1] Henley, IV, 193-194 (*Tom Jones*, X, i).
[2] I. B. Cauthen, Jr., "Fielding's Digressions in *Joseph Andrews*," *College English*, XVII (1956), 379-382.

The weight of critical opinion in our own day relegates digressions to the same limbo occupied by the *deus ex machina* and other shoddy literary devices and would insist that such services be performed in another manner. This opinion is possibly debatable and had been debated with great heat and at great length by critics writing long before Fielding's time. But to discuss the debate is less fruitful for our purposes than to insist on the judiciousness of Professor George Sherburn's, rather than Fielding's, warning: "Connections between opinions and art need to be specified. . . . Fielding's methods may be wrong, but they are reputable and are understandable. They need to be understood." [3]

The Narratives of the Strayed Lambs

In each of Fielding's three major novels, one character is called upon to tell the story of his life. He does so when the reader's knowledge about him is severely limited; but the manner in which he *has* been represented is such that he has been tentatively judged as sympathetic and trustworthy; as a result, there is no initial reason to distrust either the facts of his narration or his ethical interpretation of the facts. Among his listeners, however, is one of the major characters who has been defined as an ethical agent previously (Adams listens to Mr. Wilson, Tom Jones to the man of Mazzard Hill, and Amelia to Mrs. Bennet); and each of these has been endowed with sufficient ethical credit to reject, amplify, or qualify the narrator's interpretation of the events of his life. The major character, for a reason of his own, shows intense interest in the tale which, if viewed apart from its connection with the novel, is organized as a fairly complete apologue; especially in Fielding's last two novels, it is the carefully controlled representation of relations between the teller of the tale and the major character who listens to it that indicates the applicability the semi-independent apologue is meant to have to the rest of the novel.

Of the three tales, that of the man of Mazzard Hill is most notorious, though in many ways it is both the easiest to understand and, if we do not allow ourselves to assume that a digression is bad by definition and grows worse as it grows longer, is artistically the most successful of the three. Since its length does represent a problem, though, it will be useful to consider another incident first—one which is so brief that it is, as far as I know, nowhere discussed as digression, though it neither satisfies expectations previously estab-

---

[3] George Sherburn, "A Novelist's Opinions and His Art," *Sewanee Review*, LXI (1953), 321.

lished, sets up probability for future action, nor is referred to later in the novel.

Tom's short meeting with Broadbrim the Quaker bears roughly the same relationship to the Strayed Lamb narratives as Tittle and Tattle do to the walking concepts discussed in the previous chapter. It is the most rudimentary version of rather elaborate interpolated narratives which expand, and make general, positive value judgments of special importance to the novel by exemplifying the results of alternative values in negative apologues.

Broadbrim meets Tom when the latter has lost his road to Bristol, where he intends to take to the sea as the result of his loss of Allworthy's favor and probable loss of Sophia. The Quaker, as is customary with narrators of digressive incidents, wins our favor and that of his prospective audience (Tom in this case); Broadbrim does so by being of service to the protagonist:

> These two fellows [would-be guides] had almost conquered the patience of Jones, when a plain, well-looking man (who was indeed a Quaker) accosted him thus: "Friend, I perceive thou hast lost thy way; and if thou wilt take my advice, thou wilt not attempt to find it to-night. It is almost dark, and the road is difficult to hit; besides, there have been several robberies committed lately between this and Bristol. Here is a very creditable good house just by, where thou may'st find good entertainment for thyself and thy cattle till morning."
> Jones . . . was conducted by his friend [the Quaker] to the public-house.[4]

The new friend persists in his good offices when they arrive at the inn; although the dispirited Tom would have preferred solitude and though Fielding soon thereafter uses Broadbrim as a tool with which to poke incidental fun at the Quakers, Broadbrim's motives in conversing with Tom are initially described as charitable: "Though Jones was very unfit for any kind of company, and would have preferred being alone, yet he could not resist the importunities of the honest Quaker, who was the more desirous of sitting with him from having remarked the melancholy which appeared both in his countenance and behavior, and which the poor Quaker thought his conversation might in some measure relieve."[5] His attempt at consolatory conversation, to which Tom reacts politely enough, takes the unfortunate form of lamenting his own lot; Tom's statement, "I am very sorry, sir, for your unhappiness whatever is the occasion for it," is sufficient inducement for Broadbrim to tell the story of his daughter's eloping with a poor man, though he himself had provided her with a rich one. The Quaker's remark to the effect that he

[4] Henley, IV, 21 (*Tom Jones*, VII, x).
[5] *Ibid.*, p. 22.

would have been happier had his daughter been dead elicits a surprised comment from Tom, and this marks the initial point of a widening divergence between the two men.

> "That is very strange, sir," said Jones. "Why, would it not be better for her to be dead than to be a beggar?" replied the Quaker: "for, as I told you, the fellow is not worth a groat; and surely she cannot expect that I shall ever give her a shilling. No, as she hath married for love, let her live on love if she can; let her carry her love to market, and see whether any one will change it into silver, or even into halfpence." "You know your own concerns best, sir," said Jones. "It must have been," continued the Quaker, "a long premeditated scheme to cheat me . . . and I always preached to her against love, and told her a thousand times over it was all folly and wickedness." [6]

The modern reader is inclined to be for love just as he is against evil and therefore to dislike Broadbrim even before Tom's icy dissociation from the Quaker's self-made misery, but no advocate of parentally arranged marriages could fail to recognize that if he approves of Broadbrim he disagrees with Fielding; according to judgments already conveyed in the novel, Broadbrim has condemned himself. The fact that Allworthy had married for love has been emphasized, and we have seen him disparage marriages of pure convenience to the elder Blifil and grow annoyed with the younger Blifil for his dispassionate acceptance of prospects of marriage with Sophia. Though we must not infer from these indications that either Allworthy or Fielding was an advocate of impractical love marriages at any cost, the value scheme clearly does condemn advocates of marriage for purely materialistic reasons; if the earlier parts of the novel have been effective, the reader will be prejudiced against Broadbrim at this point.

But the condemnation becomes far more intense as the Quaker reveals that he had imprisoned his daughter and planned to marry her by force the next morning to a wealthy husband of his choosing. With these revelations, especially because it is Tom to whom they are revealed, the analogy, though not the exact parallel, between Broadbrim's treatment of his daughter and Western's persecution of Sophia intensifies our dislike for the Quaker. But it is Tom's reactions which prove central to the evaluation of Broadbrim. These are understandably violent and, as they involve neither his imprudence nor his lack of religion but rather the judgments he shares with both Allworthy and Sophia, his remarks become, as it were, those of the ethical voice of the novel:

[6] *Ibid.*, p. 23.

Here Jones, starting up, cried, "I really must be excused: I wish you would leave me." "Come, come, friend," said the Quaker, "don't give way to concern. You see there are other people miserable besides yourself." "I see there are madmen, and fools, and villains in the world," cries Jones. "But let me give you a piece of advice: send for your daughter and son-in-law home, and don't be yourself the only cause of misery to one you pretend to love." "Send for her and her husband home!" cries the Quaker, loudly; "I would sooner send for the two greatest enemies I have in the world!" "Well, go home yourself, or where you please," said Jones, "for I will sit no longer in such company." . . . Jones pushed him with some violence out of the room.[7]

Obviously, Tom's meeting with Broadbrim has no effect on subsequent events. Neither are any new general values of importance embodied in the episode, while those which are emphasized in Tom's rejection of Broadbrim are adequately emphasized in later incidents, such as the winning over of the elder Nightingale, or, indeed, in the continued persecution of Sophia in London. Yet the incident is not superfluous.

A clue to some of the special effects achieved by the inclusion of the incident lies not so much in the clear-cut analogy between the skeletally treated relations of Broadbrim, his daughter, and her husband, and the detailed treatment of Western, Sophia, and Tom, as in the differences between the analogous situations. The irascible and powerful squire Western has as his analogue the self-pitying Quaker; the highly desirable and amply treated Sophia has as her analogue an uncharacterized victim whose similarity to the heroine consists, as far as we know, only in that she too has rebelled against an enforced marriage with a rich man; an estate of many thousands of pounds a year is reduced to one hundred in the Broadbrim episode; most important, the (at this point) potentially satisfactory culmination of Tom's and Sophia's difficulties is seen as impossible for Broadbrim's daughter and her husband.

The extension of the condemnation of Western's attitude toward the marriage of his daughter (and of his attempt to enforce his will upon her) to the condemnation of the same attitude in a character of a different social class, religious background, and code of manners inevitably generalizes such condemnation. But what is more important, in connecting such a semi-independent apologue as this to other incidents by representing one of the major characters reacting strongly to the digressive narrator's interpretation of what has happened to him, Fielding creates the illusion that his central characters exist in a "separable" world peopled with men and women who neither influence nor are influenced by the central activities of the novel, though the

[7] *Ibid.*, p. 24.

inhabitants of this world are beset by problems, usually solved unsatisfactorily by them, similar to those faced by the important characters in the novel. Since every novel creates a unique world related to the world outside itself only by analogy, the notion that, in Fielding's novels, the main characters are represented as existing in a peculiarly "separable" world is admittedly tenuous, but it is so important to some of my final conclusions that it warrants further discussion here.

When Richardson's Pamela finally marries her tamed Mr. B., the action has definite implications for every character we have met in the novel, partially because every character has either retarded or aided, desired or disliked, some aspect of the relationship between Pamela and Mr. B. which culminates in their marriage. The action, artistically intense, in one sense affects all those who have participated in it; since this includes the whole of the *dramatis personae,* the limited world we have come to know, largely through Pamela's consciousness, is involved in the resolution. Though, obviously, we are in suspense about the outcome when we read the novel, once we know the resolution we find nothing to suggest that, given the same characters with the same traits, things might have come about differently; that, indeed, in the very world of the novel someone who might easily be Pamela has lost her virginity without gaining a husband. But, in *Tom Jones,* Broadbrim appears, tells his tale of self-induced misery, and departs from the novel: he himself, his shadowy daughter, and his son-in-law—the last two shadowy enough to be Tom and Sophia or any other couple—remain in a limbo of permanent unhappiness in no way lightened by the facts that Tom becomes prosperous, marries his Sophia, and lives happily ever after. Though Broadbrim has been thrown out of a room by Tom, in an important sense neither he nor his rejected family have been participants in Tom's adventures, though ethical problems raised by those adventures have been solved by them in an unsatisfactory manner. Not only Tom but the reader sees that "there are madmen, and fools, and villains in the world" and the latter knows precisely what the important relevant forms are that comprise madness, villainy, and foolishness in the worlds of the novels: though particular forms of the three are defeated by or for the protagonists at the end, we have clear evidence they need not have been defeated and are threats still. This type of narrative plays no mean part in producing the effect best summed up by R. S. Crane in distinguishing *Tom Jones* from the "merely amiable comedy" of *She Stoops to Conquer* or *The Rivals:* "We are not disposed to feel, when we are done laughing at Tom, that all is right with the world or that we can count on

Fortune always intervening, in the same gratifying way, on behalf of the good." [8]

The most important digressive narrative in *Tom Jones*, that of the man of Mazzard Hill, infinitely more complex than Broadbrim's narration, provides some service for the novel similar to those discussed above, while it adds others not provided by the Quaker's rejected interpretations of his own misadventures.

The old man of Mazzard Hill narrates the tale of his entire life, and it is indeed an extensive tale of error and woe involving many value judgments rather than one. Most of these value judgments, made by the old man himself, are emphasized as being correct by the fact that Tom agrees with them. The analogy between Tom's and the old man's misadventures seems obvious and is emphasized when they equate their own misfortunes at a number of points before, during, and after the old man tells his tale; yet this equation is temporary and the points initially established as similar become, at the end of the old man's tale, precisely the ones that establish the differences between the two characters. At no point, however, do we doubt the veracity of the essential facts of the old man's misadventures, which are far more numerous, far more universal in scope than Tom's. When Tom, hitherto rapt and sympathetic, rejects the old man's interpretation of and reaction to the events he has narrated, the old man's suggested solution to the problem of evil in the world is rejected; the world in which it is rejected has, as a result of the old man's tale, been enlarged to include particular manifestations of madness, foolishness, and villainy that Tom does not encounter in his misadventures; as a result, the rejected interpretation is declared invalid for situations other than those the protagonist participates in.

Though Tom is in no way altered by his encounter with the old man, who, in turn, remains unregenerate in his rejection of mankind and in his determination to overcome the dictates of human passions, their meeting presents each character with an alternative way of interpreting and reacting to his own "misfortunes." But at no point during the old man's narration are we in suspense about Tom's reaction to the alternative interpretation presented in the old man's tale; we already know too much about him to think him capable of anything but complete commitment to the fortunes and misfortunes of his fellow men. Fielding's deft manipulation of the relationship between Tom and the old man permits him to embody dramatically important

[8] R. S. Crane, "The Concept of Plot and the Plot of *Tom Jones*," *Critics and Criticism* (Chicago, 1952), p. 638.

ethical comment; it allows him to incorporate the presentation and rejection of what he considers an important attitude toward evil in the external world into the world of the novel at a rhetorically effective moment. Finally, it allows for precise qualification of the rejected attitude; the old man's irrevocable choice is indeed seen as an important threat to the well-being of the world in which Tom's adventures occur; though that choice is never seen as one which Tom is in real danger of making, even at the lowest ebb of his fortune, it is still seen as particularly insidious, since it has been made by a character who is represented not as a bad man, but as a good one gone far astray, not as a man who is completely rejected by the hero, but as one with whom he is in agreement on many points. The alternative presented in the old man's tale is not one which Tom as we have come to know him previously, might have accepted; but it has been irrevocably accepted by a character with whom he can in certain respects identify himself. The acceptance has made ethically unacceptable a man with many virtues.

The deft manipulation of the relationship between the digressive narrator and the major character who hears his tale is at once the means by which the semi-independent apologue of which the tale consists is attached to the novel and by which it is evaluated; as such, this manipulation warrants detailed discussion.

Immediately before Partridge and Tom reach the foot of Mazzard Hill, the hero's fortunes have reached a low ebb; he confesses to Partridge that "it would be cruel in me to suffer you to go any farther; for, to deal plainly with you, my chief end and desire is a glorious death in the service of my king and country." The comic tone is preserved and our attention momentarily diverted from Tom's state of mind by the amusing revelation of Partridge's sympathy with the Jacobites and by Tom's subsequent attack on Partridge's political views. But the moment they arrive at the foot of Mazzard Hill, Tom sees it in a special way which reveals another aspect of his unhappy state of mind: " 'Partridge, I wish I was at the top of this hill; it must certainly afford a most charming prospect, especially by this light; for the solemn gloom which the moon casts on all objects is beyond expression beautiful, especially to an imagination which is desirous of cultivating melancholy ideas.' " [9] So bent is he on pursuing his melancholy humor that when Partridge, with quite enough wit to make us laugh at Tom and refuse to take his melancholy too seriously, objects to climbing the hill for so unpromising a purpose, Tom proposes to go alone and to rejoin his servant in an hour. In this

[9] Henley, IV, 104 (*Tom Jones*, VIII, x).

gloomy frame of mind Tom enters the recluse's house, whose absent owner immediately arouses his curiosity. He bothers the old woman for information about her absent master and even when she "solicited their departure," Tom, with uncharacteristic lack of courtesy, refuses to leave: ". . . Jones purposely protracted the time, for his curiosity was greatly raised to see this extraordinary person. Though the old woman, therefore, concluded every one of her answers with desiring him to be gone, and Partridge proceeded so far as to pull him by the sleeve, he still continued to invent new questions. . . ." [10] Tom's melancholy and curiosity are emphasized again when he has saved the recluse from his attackers and, once the latter's misanthropic suspicions are allayed, he shows himself equally curious about Tom; tentative identification of the two men occurs when the recluse guesses the cause of Tom's unhappiness. The unhappiness itself has initially aroused the curiosity of the recluse: " 'I once more,' replied Jones, 'affirm that you have none; for there can be no merit in having harzarded that in your service on which I set no value; and nothing is so contemptible in my eyes as life.' " [11] The old man expresses his sorrow at Tom's having "any reason to be so unhappy at your years," and in the ensuing dialogue the ostensible kinship between the two is emphasized:

> "Indeed I am, sir," answered Jones, "the most unhappy of mankind." "Perhaps you have had a friend, or a mistress?" replied the other. "How could you," cries Jones, "mention two words sufficient to drive me to distraction?" "Either of them are enough to drive any man to distraction," answered the old man. "I inquire no farther, sir; perhaps my curiosity hath led me too far already."
>
> "Indeed, sir," cries Jones, "I cannot censure a passion which I feel at this instant in the highest degree. You will pardon me when I assure you that every thing which I have seen or heard since I first entered this house hath conspired to raise the greatest curiosity in me. Something very extraordinary must have determined you to this course of life, and I have reason to fear your own history is not without misfortunes." [12]

The old man agrees to tell Tom his story, but, before he does, he explicitly suggests that there is a common element in their backgrounds when he comments, "I must say, in what little hath dropped from you, there appears to be some parity in our fortunes: I hope, however, yours will conclude more successfully." [13]

But as he unfolds his tale it becomes quietly evident that the parity is limited to their misfortunes and to some external aspects of their misadventures;

[10] *Ibid.*, p. 108.   [12] *Ibid.*, p. 112.
[11] *Ibid.*, p. 111.   [13] *Ibid.*, p. 113.

their characters are rather disparate than similar. Tom is imprudent and is
capable, as we soon learn, of as sordid an act as becoming Lady Bellaston's paid
lover; but he could not have rifled his roommate's desk. In short, the recluse
is not merely an older Tom who has made a wrong choice; there are radical
differences of character. Nevertheless, the old man's adventures in London
foreshadow and transcend the sordid London world Tom is soon to enter and
become prey to. More important still, though the implicit differences between
the two men are fairly apparent, the emphasis is placed, before Tom's re-
buttal of the hermit's argument, on random points of similarity between the
two men. Since the old man is himself a severe judge of his youthful in-
discretions, he retains our sympathy. By emphasizing his reactions only to those
points of the old man's tale with which Tom can honestly sympathize and
which bear on his hero's troubles, Fielding is temporarily able to maintain the
illusion of essential similarity between Tom and the old man, who, at one
point, relates:

> ". . . and what made my case still the more grievous was that my paramour, of
> whom I was now grown immoderately fond, shared the same distresses with
> myself. To see a woman you love in distress; to be unable to relieve her, and
> at the same time to reflect that you have brought her into this situation, is per-
> haps a curse of which no imagination can represent the horrors to those who
> have not felt it." "I believe it from my soul," cries Jones, "and I pity you
> from the bottom of my heart:" he then took two or three disorderly turns about
> the room, and at last begged pardon, and flung himself into his chair, crying,
> "I thank Heaven I have escaped that!" [14]

As the old man's tale progresses, however, there is one point at which Tom's
sympathy with him is indicated, briefly and quietly, as being less than complete;
the old man has just quoted Horace in support of his Stoic beliefs, and the
narrator explains: "Here Jones smiled at some conceit which intruded itself
into his imagination; but the stranger, I believe, perceived it not, and proceeded thus. . . ." [15] This is a mild enough indication of dissent, with no immediate elaboration of the reason for it; yet, lest we miss it entirely, it is
heralded by a strange sign: Partridge, whose comments have heretofore been
anything but helpful to the progress of the old man's tale, has suddenly become
the old man's admirer; the latter, after indicating his preference for theology
rather than "heathen" philosophy for reasons not all consonant with his divorc-
ing himself from all humanity, claims to be "afraid I tire you with my rhap-

[14] *Ibid.*, p. 120.
[15] *Ibid.*, p. 137 (VIII, xiii).

sody." " 'Not at all,' cries Partridge; 'Lud forbid we should be tired with good things!' " [16] The unexpected courtesy from Partridge prepares us to beware of what he admires, and the subsequent indication of Tom's disapproval makes certain that we have not missed the contradiction between the old man's praise of Christianity as that which "softens and sweetens" the mind and his advocacy of the unchristian sentiment in the verses quoted from Horace.

Nevertheless, the ostensible feeling of unity between the two men is not shattered at this point—the narrator is careful to point out that the old man has not noticed Tom's smile—and is subsequently intensified as Tom and the old man join in mutual and lengthy condemnation of the Jacobites, for which the latter's account of his joining Monmouth's rebellion provides the opportunity. Only after the old man's account has been lengthened, at Tom's importunity, to include a capsular summary of his travels, which embodies in very general terms his opinion of mankind as "of so low an order in the creation as not to be honored with bearing the marks of the attributes of its great Creator," does Tom begin to quarrel openly with his host.

But this quarrel is not nearly so simple as the one which culminates with Tom's ejecting Broadbrim from the room; Tom never comes actively to dislike the old man, who, in turn, is extremely adept at defending his way of life. In the initial stages of their open disagreement, Tom wonders how the old man "could possibly endure a life of such solitude." But the old man's reply becomes a paean of praise to God, whose works, with the exception of man, are seen as bearing the marks of His attributes, and whose contemplation and worship is viewed as "one single act, for which the whole life of man is too short." This sentiment is expressed in terms so powerful and convincing that one may well wonder why Fielding provides a character whose philosophy and way of life he means to deprecate with such potent ammunition. But it is precisely in embodying nicely qualified negative evaluations that the "strayed-lamb" digressions perform their special service; they are not analogous to an extended version of an argument between, say, a paragon figure and a walking concept. To the extent that the old man is seen *not* as a black sheep, but as a strayed lamb, his solution to the problem of human evil represents a dangerously feasible and important—though rejected—alternative to the protagonist's; his earlier evaluations of London life, his own ingratitude, and the Stuarts are in no way negated by the Stoic notions under attack. Most important, the sentiments expressed in the old man's lyrical praise of God's work,

[16] *Ibid.*

though they border precariously on the verge of dehumanized religious asperity, are not rejected by Tom. It is not a life spent in contemplating God's grandeur and in worshiping Him that Tom reacts to unfavorably; it is the old man's rejection of mankind as a worthy creation of God that he finds objectionable: " 'In the former part of what you said,' replied Jones, 'I most heartily and readily concur; but I believe, as well as hope, that the abhorrence which you express for mankind in the conclusion, is much too general.' " [17] Though with different emphasis, this ground has been covered previously when Allworthy and the elder Blifil argued about charity. Tom echoes the paragon when he argues that the old man is not justified in taking a few examples from "the worst and basest" among men and interpreting their worst traits as a synthesis of human nature. When the old man offers the evidence that "my first mistress and my first friend betrayed me in the basest manner," Tom employs the very terms previously used to create an illusion of considerable similarity between the two men to dissociate himself from the hermit; what was before a point of identification becomes the point of differentation:

> "But you will pardon me," cries Jones, "if I desire you to reflect who that mistress and who that friend were. What better, my good sir, could be expected in love derived from the stews, or in friendship first produced and nourished at the gaming-table? To take the characters of women from the former instance, or of men from the latter, would be as unjust as to assert that air is a nauseous and unwholesome element, because we find it so in jakes. I have lived but a short time in the world, and yet have known men worthy of the highest friendship, and women of the highest love." [18]

Though the argument continues, Tom's disinclination to insult the old man prevents him from pressing it to the end. The Stoic's intransigence does not bring upon him the scorn expressed for Broadbrim; rather, as he grows warmer in his own defense, Tom finds it necessary to withdraw: "The old gentleman spoke this so warmly that as Jones despaired of making a convert, and was unwilling to offend, he returned no answer." [19]

If the incident were to end at this point, while we should have sufficient indication that Tom's arguments are preferable to the old man's, the former's victory would be a scant one. Tom's desire to remain on good terms with the old man, who has forcefully defended his way of life, leaves the latter with laurels a bit tattered but still on his head. The incident, however, does not end

[17] *Ibid.*, p. 151 (VIII, xv).
[18] *Ibid.*, p. 152.
[19] *Ibid.*, p. 153.

here but at the top of Mazzard Hill, to which Tom had originally wished to ascend in order to cultivate "melancholy ideas." Once atop the hill, the definite though polite disagreement between Tom and the old man is obscured, purposefully de-emphasized for the moment; the feeling of unity between the two men is deftly re-established, perhaps with the concomitant effect of temporarily soothing the reader into believing that the way of life chosen by each of the two men is in some way compatible so as to give greater rhetorical force to their final dissociation. For the moment, though, they are seen as united: the old man perceives that Tom's sighs are not so much for his absent home as for his absent love, and even the tone of Tom's reply suggests that the long night they have spent together has culminated rather in friendship and understanding than in disagreement. We are told that "Jones answered with a smile, 'I find, old friend, that you have not yet forgot the sensations of your youth. I own my thoughts were employed as you have guessed.' " [20]

But this further illusion of unity is forcefully ended by the screams of Jenny Jones. Unlike the walking concepts who embody similar notions in *Amelia,* the old man is faithful in practice to his philosophical precepts and, as Tom rushes down the hill "without the least apprehension or concern for his own safety," his "old friend"—who owes his life to Tom's similar efforts previously exerted in his behalf—"sat himself down on the brow, where, though he had a gun in his hand, he with great patience and unconcern had attended the issue." [21]

The width of the gulf between the two men, somewhat obscured by the carefully manipulated representation of their relationship and by their unconcluded abstract argument, is now seen as incapable of being bridged. Tom's choice, made instinctively, leads him away from the hill to further acts of indiscretion, to further encounters with evil not completely dissimilar to those which turned the old man away from the world. But it leads him eventually to rewards impossible for the man of the hill.

If, from one point of view, the whole digression has depicted Tom rejecting a specified alternative to complete participation in the world of men, it is the old man's tale which exemplified that alternative. From another point of view, then, the incident has emphatically depicted a man who has completely accepted and lived up to the alternative; we have seen the steps which have led one who was essentially a good man to make an erroneous choice which, as its consequences in the old man's final ingratitude to Tom make clear, compromise, even negate, his ethical character. The old man's choice, made in

[20] *Ibid.,* p. 161 (IX, ii).
[21] *Ibid.,* p. 163.

the name of Philosophy and Religion, and partially in reaction to his earlier imprudence, acts as a kind of ethical comment on the imprudent choices Tom is about to make without regard to religion or philosophy: he sleeps with Jenny Jones almost immediately after he leaves Mazzard Hill. Tom's imprudence leads to consequences deleterious enough, but his conduct is seen as far less culpable than the kind of "prudence" practiced by the old man.

The value judgments made within this type of digression are obviously of special importance to anyone concerned with Fielding's beliefs and ethical pronouncements. For Fielding to select one particular alternative to the hero's attitude and reaction to evil, to embody it in an extended apologue, and to manipulate the relations between Tom and the old man in such a way as to make the alternative relevant to the central activities of the major characters strongly suggests that he must *consciously* have wished to deprecate the interpretation of and reaction to evil implicit in the old man's tale. Fielding's desire to *make* certain intellectually formulated conceptions, not directly relevant to the relationship among major characters, a part of the world he creates in each of his novels is apparent in the three "strayed-lamb" digressions under discussion. The conceptions made relevant are very different in each, but the ways in which they are evaluated are quite similar.

In the digression just discussed, value judgments are derived directly from either of two sources and indirectly from a third. First, there are the value judgments made by the old man himself at a point when we still accept him as trustworthy, as when he condemns the life of a gambler or his own youthful ingratitude to his father; Tom's role in helping to make these judgments is either passive (his sympathetic silence is sufficient support when we have no indication that we are to regard the old man's views as suspect) or, for special emphasis, active, as when he concurs at length with the old man about the Stuarts. These judgments indicate that evil is pervasive in the world of the novel and emphasize the institutions, social practices, personal faults to be condemned. Second—and more important for this digression than for others—are the judgments derived from Tom's disagreement in thought and action with the old man, as when he argues with him about human nature or rushes down the hill to rescue Jenny from Northerton. These judgments in no way negate those made earlier, but they do negate the general inferences about human nature which the old man has drawn from them. Finally, value judgments are tenuously affected by the fact that their arguments align Tom and the old man with previously established ethical agents; the old man's insistence on being superior to human passion, for example, connects him to a certain extent with Square, who is unreservedly ridiculed for the same belief; he also

shares the elder Blifil's prejudice against charity, and some of the obloquy
heaped upon him, for somewhat similar reasons. Tom's arguments and actions, in contrast, reflect Allworthy's conception of Christian charity. The
effect of this sort of alignment, though, is difficult to ascertain; it is closely
analogous to the effect achieved by the hero's "echoing" the paragon's arguments in new context.[22] The effect of the alignment, possibly the fortuitous—
though not, therefore, unimportant—result of the fact that "good" characters in Fielding's novels inevitably share some views, is to emphasize that here
Tom is to be viewed as efficient ethical commentator. Such alignment becomes
unimportant when the commentator is himself one of the paragons, whose
arguments are, by definition, to be believed unless we are given precise indications to the contrary.

   In Mr. Wilson's tale in *Joseph Andrews*, value judgments are again the
result of the interaction of an important ethical agent with the narrator of
the digressive tale; as in the tale just discussed, the ethical agent initially indicates his interest in the narrator's life and actually requests the tale. The
interaction, though, is far simpler than in the old man's narrative. Mr. Wilson, the strayed lamb, has found his way back to the path of virtue and is trustworthy both in the narration and in the interpretation of the events of his
life. Adams is limited to emphasizing Wilson's own judgments, though this
emphasis is important not only in itself, but occasionally, by indicating a difference in the degree to which Wilson and Adams condemn a given action, it
places that action in a perspective it would not otherwise have had. Simple
emphasis is achieved in a variety of obvious, though often comically effective,
ways: Adams groans repeatedly as Wilson describes his "course of doing
nothing" in London, and is in essential agreement with the strayed lamb when
he points out to him, "Sir, this is below the life of an animal hardly above
vegetation." [23] But when the serious transgressions are described, Wilson's
self-condemnation cannot prevent Adams from reproaching him further;
when Wilson describes how he "debauched" a young woman, his insistence
that "it will never be sufficiently repented of in my own opinion" only mitigates the displeasure of Adams, who fervently hopes that "heaven grant you
may sincerely repent of this and many other things you have related!" [24]

   The purpose of Adams' interspersed comments is clear. What is far less
clear is the purpose of the whole digression, a tale in which a sketchily characterized young man is shown as participating in and almost ruined by a variety

[22] See chapter three.
[23] Henley, I, 232 (*Joseph Andrews*, III, iii).
[24] *Ibid.*, p. 235.

of forms—represented in detail—of the folly, villainy, and madness fashionable in London, from which he finally escapes to a rural paradise only slightly, though significantly, marred by a dog-killing squire. The tale is obviously not represented, as the old man's tale is in *Tom Jones,* as an alternative way of life rejected by the protagonist, who has slept through much of the narration. Although Mr. Wilson's tale does perform services for *Joseph Andrews* closely analogous to those performed by the digressions in *Tom Jones,* the differences between the forms of the two novels are such that the very elements which define incidents as digressions differ from one work to the other.

Some of the digressive narratives in *Tom Jones,* (i.e., those episodes not related to others in the novel and to the whole novel as most of the other episodes are to each other and to the whole) would not seem nearly so digressive if transferred to *Joseph Andrews.* The Broadbrim episode, for example, has a special and clearly marked commentative function in *Tom Jones,* in which most episodes play a fairly direct role in changing the relationships among the major characters. The episodes in *Tom Jones* cannot for the most part be interchanged, since what comes before in some way prepares us for what is to come next; if a compositor were by some accident to interchange the incident in which Tom gets drunk with that in which Allworthy banishes him from Paradise Hall, the reader would immediately be aware that an error had been made; if, however, Tom had met Broadbrim when he first arrived in London, while some rhetorical effects would have been the worse for the change, little violence would have been done to the whole, as the services the incident performs, while not nugatory, are but loosely tied to the chronology of other events in the book. If the episode were omitted, the whole novel would be the loser for its omission, but no expectations raised in previous episodes would be unresolved and no future episode would seem unmotivated because of its exclusion. Furthermore, while there is nothing in his comic scheme of things to prevent Fielding, had he wished, from making Broadbrim cross Tom's path again, there are no expectations raised that he may do so; as a result, his participation in Tom's affairs seems complete when the inn is lost sight of; we do not expect to come across the Quaker again. One may note the difference between the treatment of a character, introduced in a brief episode, who is to be used later, and a character whose role is fulfilled by the end of the episode in which he is introduced, by comparing Tom's meeting with Broadbrim with his meeting with Dowling later in the novel; the sense of finality implicit in the former is carefully avoided in the latter; Dowling's knowledge of Tom's background connects him with past episodes; the emphasis on his present curiosity about Tom raises at least mild questions about the motive for that curiosity; and, finally, the narrator plays very obvious games with future implications: "But we may possibly take some other opportunity of commenting upon this [Dowling's "impulse of compassion" for Tom], especially if we should happen to meet Mr. Dowling any more in the course of our history. At present we are obliged to take our leave of that gentleman a little abruptly. . . ." [25] The omission of any hint about Broadbrim's reappearance, the fact that no unanswered questions have been raised during his single appearance, indicate that he has served his purpose when the inn is left behind; that purpose is so different from that of most of the other characters that the incident, so brief that we do not react strongly to it as "digressive," strikes us as somehow "different"—as an interruption of a pattern we have become accustomed to.

But throughout much of the middle section of *Joseph Andrews*, long and obviously important episodes are interchangeable. It matters little in what order we see Adams argue with Barnabas, the man of courage, the sailor-become-innkeeper, or Trulliber. Nor, I think, would any reader be surprised if, interposed among these episodes, Adams met Broadbrim, heard him tell precisely the same tale he has told Tom, and pointed out the error of the Quaker's ways, since the *dramatis personae* of *Joseph Andrews* typically appear, express a wrong opinion, or commit some wrong action for which they are reprimanded by Adams. This is not to say that the incidents in *Joseph Andrews* could be replaced by others without substantially changing the novel, for, though some episodes can be interchanged, each one makes a precise contribution to the whole; to say that chronological order is not as important in this novel as in some others is not to say that the novel is structureless; we obviously could not react to any incident as digressive in a structureless book.

Though it greatly simplifies it does not significantly distort the relationship of episodes in *Tom Jones* if we think of it as represented by the following formula: [26]

$$A \rightarrow B \rightarrow C \rightarrow D \rightarrow E \rightarrow F \rightarrow \text{etc.}$$

[25] Henley, IV, 347 (*Tom Jones*, XII, xi).

[26] The formula is extremely schematic; I do not mean to imply that the expectations raised in the first episode of *Tom Jones* are made immediate use of in the second, which raises other expectations immediately used in the third, etc. The episode in which Tom first meets Dowling sets up expectations which are not "used" until many episodes later. That which distinguishes it from an episode like the one in which Tom meets Broadbrim is that there *is* an arrow leading *from* the Dowling episode, while there is none leading into or out of the Broadbrim episode; it is the presence or absence of the "arrow," not where the arrow leads, that determines whether an episode interrupts the pattern of relationships.

The arrows stand for possibility, probability, or necessity.[27] An episode like that of Tom's meeting with Broadbrim, represented by Y, can be added with a plus sign to any episode, though not in such a manner that it is tied to any of the arrows:

$$A \rightarrow B \rightarrow C \rightarrow D - [+Y] \rightarrow E \rightarrow F \rightarrow \text{etc.}$$

Any episode added to this formula in the same way that Y is will strike us as "different" and, if it is long, as "digressive" since it interrupts the established pattern.

But this does not account for the ubiquitous, though not universal, reaction to Mr. Wilson's tale in *Joseph Andrews* as digressive. The simplest schematic diagram of the earlier novel adequate for present purposes is:[28]

$$I \xrightarrow{\hspace{3cm}} II \xrightarrow{\hspace{3cm}} III$$

$$\underbrace{A+B+C+D+E+\text{etc.}}\underbrace{F+G+H+I+J+\text{etc.}}\underbrace{K+L+M+N+O+\text{etc.}}$$

The diagram indicates that three major sections of *Joseph Andrews* are not interchangeable; the London incidents must precede those on the road, which, in turn, must precede the incidents in Boobyland, though the episodes of which each of the major sections is comprised are—at least in this admittedly oversimplified diagram—interchangeable. Since, if we represent Mr. Wilson's tale as Y, we can add it anywhere in our diagram without interrupting

---

[27] There are, of course, two kinds of relationships to which these three terms are relevant. It is only as they apply to the sequence of events, not as to how the characters conduct themselves within any episode, that the terms are applicable in this discussion. The reason for this is fairly obvious: It is very *probable* that Tom will act as he does when he hears Broadbrim's tale; it is not the inconsistency of the protagonist that signals a narrative digression; if the arrows were simply to indicate that Tom acts, say, in episode Y in a manner prepared for by his actions in previous episodes, then Y itself—indeed every episode in *Tom Jones*—would be connected to other episodes by arrows. As I am using the terms, however, episode Y has no arrow leading into or out of it; it differs from the Dowling episode, which does not have an arrow leading in but does have one leading out.

[28] In order to simplify matters both here and elsewhere, I define the "plus" sign used in the formula as an arbitrary symbol representing a purely additive relation between the episodes on either side. But if, as I suspect, the schematic formula for the relation among episodes in *Joseph Andrews* is applicable to other important novels of this century, a significant contribution to our knowledge of the development of the novel will be made by anyone who describes the precise contributions made by each episode in an additive series and the relation of the contributions to the "arrows" which connect the three major segments. I may only suggest here that the relations of Y to the episodes connected by arrows in *Tom Jones* provides us with information applicable to the consideration of the very different structure of the earlier novel.

the typical pattern of progression, it is fruitful to explore the possibility that
the ordering and nature of the elements in Y itself make it significantly different from $A, B, C,$ or $D.$

This might seem to be laboring the obvious. For it is obvious that the Mazzard Hill episode in *Tom Jones* and Mr. Wilson's tale in *Joseph Andrews*
have so many common elements that, interrupted progression or not, the elements they share with each other but not with other types of incidents will
account for the frequent reaction to them as digressions. In both episodes a
character newly introduced relates a tale of past occurrences in which the
major character who listens to the tale has had no part, though, in both cases,
he comments on what he hears. The new narrator, the shift in time, the non-
participation of characters already introduced should apparently be sufficient
to make us feel that the incidents are digressive even if they do not interrupt
the pattern of progression normal for the novel. Though, on the face of it,
such an explanation seems sufficient, there is an admittedly irritating sort of
validity in the skeptical view of appearances expressed by Fielding's sailor-
turned-innkeeper, who remarks to Adams, "Symptoms in his countenance,
quotha! I would look there, perhaps, to see whether a man had the smallpox,
but for nothing else." A closer look does elicit enough confusing evidence to
make us cry pox on the question.

First, that the major character does not participate in the events narrated
by the newly introduced character cannot in itself be an indication that the
narration is digressive in *Joseph Andrews;* the major characters' total participation in many episodes consists of listening to and commenting upon the tale
of a newly introduced character who disappears from the novel at the end of
the episode. Possibly, though, this objection might be answered if we assume
that not one but all of the elements enumerated in the previous paragraph must
be present to cause us to react so strongly to the "different" quality of the episode that we feel is a digression. Yet we do not react strongly to Adams' discussion with the sailor-turned-innkeeper about the false-promiser as a digression,
although the sailor, newly introduced, briefly relates the past adventures of the
would-be exciseman, the would-be parson, the would-be gentlewoman, and
of himself, all of whom have been betrayed by the false promises of the
squire who misled Adams.

Even when these elements appear together in an episode, as in Mr. Wilson's
tale, they cannot account for its digressive character. An explanation which
does account—adequately, I think—for our reacting to all three of the episodes conventionally regarded as digressions in *Joseph Andrews* is that, when
the enumerated elements are present in an episode that is not merely long but

contains enough sub-episodes in either an additive or a probable series to produce its own pattern of relationships, we react to it as a digression. Added to
the diagram above, any one of the digressive narrations can be schematically
represented as follows:

$$I \xrightarrow{\hspace{3cm}} II \xrightarrow{\hspace{3cm}} III$$

$$\overbrace{A + B + C + \underbrace{Y}_{} + D + E +} \text{etc.}$$

$$\underbrace{a + b + c + d + e +}_{} \text{etc.}$$

It is unnecessary and would be fruitless to try to ascertain precisely how many
sub-episodes are necessary or how long each must be for a quasi-independent
narrative structure to make itself felt as such; it is clear that as they are connected to the type of narrative structure of *Joseph Andrews* incidents strike
us as being more or less rather than absolutely digressive. Mr. Wilson's tale,
the story of the unfortunate jilt, the tale of Leonard and Paul, will lie at the
extreme end of a pole labeled "digression," and intelligent readers will react
to them as digressions with considerable consistency.[29] In *Tom Jones*, on the
other hand, while Tom's meeting with the Stoic on Mazzard Hill would
clearly be marked as a digressive episode by its quasi-independent narrative
structure alone, Tom's meeting with the Gypsies need contain none of the
elements enumerated above for it to affect the reader as digressive, since any
fairly long episode not connected to other episodes by what the arrows represent in the diagrams will also affect him as such.

The problem of what constitutes a narrative digression is as complex as that
of the nature of literary structure, to which it is integrally bound. But the
simplified explanation is sufficiently complete to clarify why it is possible, without becoming entangled in self-contradiction, to make fruitful distinctions
among narrative digressions—each of which is an apologue of some sort—on
the basis of how they are made *relevant* to the novels in which they appear.
For the explanation offered here does make clear why no "discovery" of the
relevance of ideas implicit in a narrative digression negates the fact that it is

---

[29] When a sub-episode or sub-episodes within a digressive narrative are organically
related to episodes outside the narrative, the digressive effect of the whole tale is miti-
gated, even if the greater part of the narrative is not related to the whole; to the extent
that Mrs. Bennet's narrative puts Amelia in possession of information which influences
her subsequent actions, the narrative will seem organically related to the whole; the
number of details in the narrative that contribute to the communication of the relevant
information, though, is slight indeed.

a "digression." [30] No episode is more clearly digressive than that of Tom's meeting with the hermit of Mazzard Hill; yet not many "organic" episodes in *Tom Jones* have more pertinence to elements of thought important for the activities of the major characters; though recognition of this pertinence is important for a thorough understanding of *Tom Jones*, the pertinence is itself conditioned by the fact that the elements of thought are embodied in a narrative digression connected to the rest of the novel by a subtle manipulation of the relationship between Tom and the hermit.

Connected as they are to quite different structures, Mr. Wilson's tale and that of the hermit of Mazzard Hill make similar use of the elements common to digressive narratives to perform analogous, though never identical, services for the novel.

But the conclusions about what constitutes a digression in Fielding's novels may be further generalized, by reference to the types of prose fiction described in chapter one, as a statement about digressive incidents in all novels. Any episode organized as apologue in a work of fiction which is an action is a digression. [31] Length, the presence of the major characters in the action, the relevance of what is revealed in the apologue to any change among relationships of major characters, may be exploited to increase or decrease the digressive nature of the "foreign" episode.

It is merely a truism, however, that a work must essentially be coherent if we can recognize an episode in it as a digression of the sort defined; coherence is not a *virtue* of any novel, simply a condition of its being a novel. A novelist with sufficient skill may exploit the special qualites of digressive incidents to achieve effects impossible without them. Fielding is such a novelist.

---

[30] While ideational relevance has little to do with whether we react to an episode as a digression, important distinctions among the services particular digressions perform, or fail to perform, result from the manner in which the semi-independent apologues are, or are not, made relevant to the novels in which they appear. It is on this basis, for example, that we can easily distinguish the important narratives of the "strayed lambs" from such interpolated tales as the "Unfortunate Jilt" or the tale of Leonard and Paul. While these also are kinds of apologues, their narrators have not participated in the adventures they relate; these cannot perform services similar to those performed by narratives which depend heavily in an ethical agent's reactions to the narrator's wrong choices.

[31] The fullest general statement would be still broader. A: An episode organized as apologue or satire is a digression in an action. B: An episode organized as satire or action is a digression in an apologue. C: An episode organized as apologue or action is a digression in a satire. I am not familiar with any actual literary productions like B or C. This note predicts that, if such works are written, they will contain episodes which are digressions.

To descend from the theoretical, we can see that, in his role as a strayed lamb, Mr. Wilson has made a series of foolish, even horrendous, choices which have had the consequences of almost engulfing him in vices represented as typical of London; if Joseph's tenderness for his virginity, as it manifests itself in his relations with Lady Booby in the burlesque London adventures, is ridiculed,[32] Fielding makes ample restitution to the cause of sexual continence when, not by discursive invective, but by neat juxtaposition of ethical agencies, he condemns, in one of the most vigorous ways possible to the value structure of the novel, Mr. Wilson's serious participation in those "other genteel vices" with which London is shown to abound.[33] That Mr. Wilson, sketchily characterized as essentially a good man who has found the path which leads, both geographically and morally, away from London and what it has, in precise terms, come to represent (largely by virtue of his own tale) emphasizes the discrepancy between his present and past modes of life; his narrow escape has the effect of establishing the condemned vices as not merely the pursuits of the hopelessly corrupt, but as embedded social institutions capable of corrupting decent men.[34] Nor is Mr. Wilson's tale concerned solely or even primarily with sexual vice. The triviality, hypocrisy, and sexual laxness seen as laughably characteristic of London during Joseph's sojourn there are seriously subsumed in Mr. Wilson's tale, but comprise only a few of the threats which his virtue encounters. Embodied institutions that engender false ethics, philosophical ideas that cater to the whims of spurious virtue, corrupt business practices, disregard of literary merit, and such social aberrations as dueling figure prominently in Wilson's early misadventures.

London, unpeopled and largely undefined, has from the very beginning of the novel been closely associated with the follies and vices of all the major characters, excluding Adams, who appear both in the first and final sections of *Joseph Andrews*.[35] But the association has defined London only as a geographical tag for what is unacceptable and, partially because of Joseph's burlesque adventures, ludicrously rather than viciously unacceptable. As a result of Mr.

---

[32] The mockery, though, is very complex. See chapter two.

[33] The consistent agreement of the paragon figure with one defined as a good man is especially emphatic; Adams' inability to comprehend some of the refinements of the vices Wilson describes—a use of the paragon's fallibility peculiar among Fielding's novels to *Joseph Andrews* (see chapter three)—indicates the absolute degree to which the vice is condemned.

[34] Mr. Wilson does not, of course, escape to an ideal world when he leaves London; the dog-killing squire attests to the fact that rural life is capable of producing its own forms of vice.

[35] See chapter three.

Wilson's straying down paths artistically difficult of access to Joseph or Adams, London has been condemned for specific forms of foolishness and vice, and has been condemned with a variety of unvirtuous characters seen participating in a carefully selected variety of unsavory affairs.[36] As a further result of Mr. Wilson's tale, the scope of Adams' value judgments has, with considerable economy of means, been extended to include what is represented as an insidiously influential urban culture with which he has had no first-hand experience but which seriously affects the world in which he lives. This extension of the area in which Adams' ethical evaluations are seen as applicable significantly though loosely expands the ethical frame in which we see the marriage of Joseph and Fanny as an important ethical victory for the comic world they inhabit;[37] it is not only Lady Booby, Lawyer Scout, Pamela, and their ilk who are seen as eventually overcome by Adams, Fanny, and Joseph, but also the retinue of vicious and foolish characters whose values are indirectly hostile to those that proclaim the two innocents deserving of the particular brand of happiness they win; it is as if they had won this happiness in spite of a hostile world—including the vicious London world depicted primarily in the digression—whose direct agents happen to be Lady Booby, Pamela, Lawyer Scout, et al.

Finally, though most of Mr. Wilson's early difficulties, unlike Joseph's, have stemmed at least partially from his own participation in the vices and follies which threaten his virtue, his discovery of the path from London and what it represents to rural bliss with the former Harriet Heartfree constitutes a perceptible analogue to the struggles and final victory of Joseph and Fanny. But the digressive narrative facilitates more economical expansion of values because the particular forms of obstacles the Wilsons overcome, the terms in which their passion for each other is expressed, and even the minimum material rewards necessary for their happiness are those consonant only with the traits of characters of a different social class from that to which Joseph and Fanny belong. The substance of the obstacles both couples overcome, the

[36] The fate of the Wilsons' lost child, strawberry mark and all, prepares us for the discovery that the Wilsons are Joseph's parents; at the very least, we know we will meet the Wilsons again after Adams, Joseph, and Fanny leave their country retreat. But there is no integral connection between the expectations thus aroused and the strayed-lamb adventures of which Mr. Wilson's tale largely consists.

[37] The ironic fact that the happy ending is brought about partly through Mr. Booby's intercession with a corrupt judge and that he, who stands opposed to what Adams represents, is also the agent who rewards Adams with a living of 130 pounds a year mocks the hostile elements in society, not the virtues of Fanny, Joseph, or Adams. The irony increases the special comic pleasure when they receive their final rewards despite an antagonistic world.

nature of the virtuous passion they feel, and the rewards they desire are just similar enough to suggest that the problem of footman and milkmaid has a wider pertinence; despite the jocular, and probably ironic, sleight-of-hand involved in the discovery that the Wilsons are Joseph's parents, it is appropriate that the last two paragraphs of the novel reveal: "Lady Booby . . . returned to London . . . where a young captain of dragoons, together with eternal parties at cards, soon obliterated the memory of Joseph," while the "happiness of this couple [Joseph and Fanny] is a perpetual fountain of pleasure to their fond parents [the Wilsons]." [38]

The third "stray lamb" digression, Mrs. Bennet's tale, because of its close kinship with those already discussed may be treated more cursorily. Unlike Amelia and Booth, the Bennets have succumbed to difficulties pointedly similar to those faced by the hero and heroine, mainly though not entirely as a result of Mrs. Bennet's indiscretion when faced with precisely the temptation awaiting Amelia.

Though even more clearly than in Mr. Wilson's tale the latter part of Mrs. Bennet's contributes directly to the action, so many details are extraneous to the relationship of major characters that the narrator feels impelled to account for the digressive nature of the episode: [39] "And here possibly the reader will blame Mrs. Bennet for taking her story so far back, and relating so much of her life in which Amelia had no concern; but, in truth, she was desirous of inculcating a good opinion of herself, from recounting those transactions where her conduct was unexceptionable, before she came to the more dangerous and suspicious part of her character." [40] If this establishes a sufficient motive for Mrs. Bennet's verbosity, it does not explain why Fielding imposes her verbosity on the reader of *Amelia* as well as on its heroine. Fielding was as interested in introducing his readers to the least reprehensible, though not unexceptionable, side of Mrs. Bennet's nature as the latter was in showing her best to Amelia before confessing to such unamiable acts as infecting her cuckolded husband with venereal disease. Like Mr. Wilson and the old man of Mazzard Hill, Mrs. Bennet must be a strayed lamb rather than a black sheep; however, unlike Mr. Wilson, who does not stray once he has found

[38] Gaffer and Gammer Andrews conveniently disappear; it is the Wilsons with whom Joseph and Fanny live and on whom they shower their happiness.

[39] Not only does the warning to Amelia relate the narrative directly to the whole, but certain aspects of Mrs. Bennet's character revealed in her tale enable Fielding later in the novel to reduce Mrs. Bennet temporarily to a walking concept in order to attack "learned" women. But both the warning and the preparatory traits account only for a small fraction of the details included in Mrs. Bennet's tale.

[40] Henley, VII, 11 (*Amelia*, VII, i).

the path back to virtue, and unlike the old man, who has irrevocably lost himself in a forest of erroneous philosophy and religion, Mrs. Bennet, we learn
later, is, despite her unfortunate experiences, unable to resist the occasional
meadow a short way off the virtuous path.[41]

That Mrs. Bennet is less than a paragon is hardly surprising. We have seen
previously that the old man of Mazzard Hill is not simply an older Tom
Jones; the way of life chosen by the former is one which is not an aesthetically possible choice for Tom; it is represented as an alternative to Tom's passionate participation in human affairs only in the sense that it is the erroneous
choice made by a character, initially represented as only slightly dissimilar to
the hero, when faced with circumstances pointedly similar to those faced by
the hero. Mrs. Bennet stands in much the same relation to Amelia as the old
man does to Tom: the notion that Amelia might infect Booth with venereal
disease is, of course, ludicrous, and Mrs. Bennet's particular brand of flirta-
tiousness, as it is revealed in the following confession, is not even remotely possible for the heroine:

> "I will—I will own the truth; I was delighted with perceiving a passion in
> him [the licentious lord], which I was not unwilling to think he had had from
> the beginning, and to derive his having concealed it so long from his awe of
> my virtue, and his respect to my understanding. I assure you, madam, at the
> same time, my intentions were never to exceed the bounds of innocence. I was
> charmed with the delicacy of his passion; and in the foolish thoughtless turn
> of mind in which I then was, I fancied I might give some very distant encour-
> agement to such a passion in such a man with the utmost safety. . . ." [42]

The differences between the two women are glaring on the whole, but the
absolutely incompatible elements in their natures which eventually lead them
to quarrel with some violence are not emphasized until after Mrs. Bennet's
narrative has served its purpose as a "strayed lamb" digression. In the narrative, Fielding has carefully arranged matters so that we view Mrs. Bennet's
character in a light just virtuous enough for us temporarily to accept as accurate her own interpretation of the more important episodes in her past life.
When her past actions are most culpable, in much the same manner that Mr.
Wilson and the old man have done, Mrs. Bennet escapes extreme censure by
becoming her own accuser: " 'I know Mrs. Booth will condemn all these
thoughts [expressed in the passage quoted immediately above], and I condemn
them no less myself; for it is now my steadfast opinion that the woman who

---

[41] While impersonating Amelia, Mrs. Bennet gives the licentious lord who had previously seduced her all but "the last favor" in order to obtain a commission for Atkinson.
[42] Henley, VII, 47 (*Amelia,* VII, vii).

gives up the least outwork of her virtue, doth in that very moment betray the citadel.' " [43]

Nor is the direct expression of a potential parity between the narrator of the digressive tale and the narrator's attentive audience—seen previously in the Man-of-the-Hill episode—which momentarily suggests that there is a kinship between the two, lacking here; Amelia, after a characteristic fainting spell, states forcefully: " 'O Mrs. Bennet . . . how am I indebted to you! what words, what thanks, what actions can demonstrate the gratitude of my senti-ments! I look upon you, and always shall look upon you, as my preserver from the brink of a precipice, from which I was falling into the same ruin which you have so generously, so kindly, and so nobly disclosed for my sake.' " [44]

But, while the relations between Mrs. Bennet and Amelia as narrator and audience of the tale are similar to those of the old man and Tom, Mrs. Bennet's tale, unlike either of the two discussed previously, makes use of an analogue between two couples rather than between two individuals. Like the Booths, the Bennets are cast out upon the world as a result of their marriage. Just as Booth, at one stage of courting Amelia, receives a tongue-lashing from Amelia's mother, Mr. Bennet receives one, under somewhat similar circum-stances, from his wife's aunt: " 'She [Mrs. Bennet's aunt] burst in upon us, open-mouthed, and after discharging every abusive word almost, in the only language she understood, on poor Mr. Bennet, turned us both out of doors. . . .' " [45] Unpaid legacies lead to such poverty for both couples that they are forced to the same unhappy expedient to raise money; Mrs. Bennet explains that "as our fund was so very low, we were reduced to some distress, and obliged to live extremely penurious; nor would all do without my taking a most disagreeable way of procuring money by pawning one of my gowns." [46] Pointed similarities between such trivial details are sufficient to establish only the most superficial analogy between the adventures of the two couples. But it is the analogy of circumstance, not of character, that is exploited in these digressions. When the superficial details of the adventures of the hero and heroine of the novel and of the digressive narrative are pointedly similar, the discrepancy between the internal traits of each of the pairs becomes a useful tool for ethical comment, which, in turn, significantly increases both our ex-

[43] *Ibid.*, p. 48.

[44] *Ibid.*, p. 49.

[45] *Ibid.*, p. 34 (VII, v). The inclusion of the phrase "the only language she under-stood" is a thrust at Mrs. Bennet's pride in her learning; this pride is, in her own tale, represented as a weakness of character which contributes somewhat to the undoing of the Bennets as a couple.

[46] Henley, VII, 36 (*Amelia*, VII, v).

pectation and our desire for a happy termination to the heroine's anguish. Equally important, such differences among external characteristics as those of class, education, trade, and manners are exploited to expand the frame in which value judgments are seen as valid.

Mr. Bennet is quite as dissimilar to Booth as Mrs. Bennet is to Amelia. If anything, the curate is less culpable than the hero of the novel, but, unlike him, is finally overcome by the obstacles confronting him. Since, essentially innocent, he does seem to succumb to the caprices of Fortune, it is easy to jump to the conclusion that Mr. Bennet's fate directly contradicts the attack Fielding makes in chapter one of *Amelia* on "laying improper blame on this imaginary being [Fortune]." But such a conclusion would be justified only if the whole of *Amelia* were organized as an apologue to illustrate that a man's weaknesses lead directly to his misfortunes; then we might expect each episode to show how each character's fortunes or misfortunes resulted from his own errors, as the episodes in *Rasselas* illustrate the impossibility of achieving absolute happiness on earth. But to view *Amelia* as such a book is to misunderstand its mode of organization and to oversimplify Fielding's notion of human responsibility for human misfortune. Mrs. Bennet's tale is organized as a complex apologue artfully attached to a represented action, but, while Mrs. Bennet's inadequacies in "this most useful of all arts, which I [Fielding] call the Art of Life" are stressed and their consequences indicated, no faults in Mr. Bennet's character are defined as causal. Neither, however, is he portrayed as the innocent victim of Fortune; on the one hand, his innocence is stressed as little as his guilt and, on the other hand, the circumstances which lead to his misery are carefully revealed as the end product of the operation of responsible and culpable human agencies rather than as manifestations of a capricious force which causes human happiness or misery but which is independent of human control. If Mr. Bennet is not portrayed as obviously responsible for his misfortunes, men and their acquiescence in corrupt social practices are so represented.[47] Poor Mr. Bennet's rather ungracious role in his wife's tale is limited to his use as a tool for the display of the culpable agencies and as an example of how destructive they may be. Mrs. Bennet's culpable flirtation contributes heavily to the couple's misery, but differing forms of

---

[47] In keeping with his notion that life is an art, Fielding does include some minor indications which reflect on Mr. Bennet's lack of prudence: Mrs. Bennet, for example, indicates that during their initial stay in London she and her husband "passed our time . . . a little too agreeably perhaps for our circumstances" so that, in a short time, "we had almost consumed our whole stock." But Mr. Bennet's share of imprudence is stressed so lightly that it can hardly be seen as an important cause of the disaster which overtakes them.

greed, ingratitude, lack of reward for merit, betrayal of friendship, and sexual immorality which—in coöperation with his own faults—almost destroy Booth the soldier, coöperate with his wife's weakness to destroy Mr. Bennet the curate.

Booth, Amelia, and Mrs. Bennet (become Atkinson) are at least moderately happy forever after, but Bennet, miserable forever in that fictional limbo where Mr. Wilson's mistress pays perpetual penalty for her seduction, where Broadbrim's daughter is permanently disowned, where the old man of Mazzard Hill forever contemplates God and refuses to respond to a cry of distress, is a reminder that things need not have turned out so well after all. Mr. Bennet cannot console himself by cursing his stars, since, as he and his wife have helped to show, his stars had nothing to do with the matter.

The Demireps and the Heroines

Two digressive narrations in Fielding's novels, though not as important as those discussed above, bear surface resemblances to the narratives of the Strayed Lambs, and perform relatively important roles in conveying judgments about represented characters, acts, and thoughts. The narrators of these tales, Fanny Matthews and Mrs. Fitzpatrick, are "bad girls" in *Amelia* and *Tom Jones,* respectively. Though both women, and especially Fanny, are important characters in represented actions, their descriptions of their unhappy love affairs are so detailed and extensive that they assume the quasi-independent narrative structure that signals a digression.

Though quite different in detail and in some of the commentative services they perform, obvious similarities make it convenient to place both narratives in the same class; each of the women tells her tale to a character who has known her in the days of her "innocence"—i.e., before her ill-advised attempt at mating; each begins her narration with the events that initiate the disastrous courtship and limits her narrative primarily to events relevant to that courtship and its consequent disastrous marriage or cohabitation. Like the heroines of the novels in which they appear, each of the demireps has ignored the wishes of parent or guardian either in the manner of choosing or the choice of a mate.[48] But in the case of the demireps, both manner and choice

[48] The differences are more striking than the similarities so that if we did not have— as explained below—a number of external indications that we are so to regard them, the differences could not justifiably be interpreted as a formal opposition nor the similarities as a formal parallel which makes the opposition meaningful. Sophia is, of course, not married when she hears her cousin's tale of marital woe induced by a condemned set of "London" values. And Fanny Matthews does not marry Hebbers, though her relations with him are contrasted at certain points to Amelia's relations with her husband; that

are seen—in contrast to the heroines'—as undesirable; each of the demireps has repented of her choice but not of the culpable actions and motives that led to it. The same weaknesses of character which initially led to the wrong choice are manifest in the way in which each of the demireps attempts to rectify her initial error: the abandoned Fanny Matthews, acting according to the dictates of her passions, stabs her seducer; Harriet Fitzpatrick, her faith in her own shallow wit and learning unshaken by the consequences of her former lack of discernment, engages in further disingenuous scheming to run off with a coöperative nobleman.

Each of the narratives presents a clear example of how one ought *not* to go about consummating a covert courtship or marriage. While Amelia is seen as justified in running off with Booth, and Sophia as admirable for fleeing in Tom's general direction from the parental tyranny which threatens to unite her with Blifil, Fanny's and Harriet's tales are represented in such a manner as to limit authorial approval of female rebelliousness to the particular circumstances in which the particular heroines find themselves; the narrative digressions, in effect, destroy any notion that Fielding gives *carte blanche* to any young woman who fancies herself in love. Specific oppositions between the characters of the demireps and the heroines of the novels are used to emphasize inobvious traits or opinions of the heroines which we might not readily view as quite so admirable as Fielding would have us view them.

It is dangerous to argue either that a given number of differences constitutes a formal opposition or that a given number of similarities constitutes a formal parallel or analogue; depending on the kinds of details we look for, we may find more differences between the characters of Tom Jones and Mrs. Miller than between the former's and Blifil's, or more similarities between the adventures of Black George and Tom than between those of Tom and the hermit of Mazzard Hill. To argue on the basis of the number of differences or similarities that an opposition or parallel was intended would obviously be foolish; it is rare indeed that the points of opposition or parallel are clearly self-defining. If, however, as with Tom and the hermit or the Bennets and the Booths, there are external indications that similarities, differences, or both are significant, the points of difference or similarity may be very limited and still effectively constitute a parallel or opposition for commentative purposes.

---

she is willing to sleep with Hebbers without benefit of clergy is itself a point which helps to establish the opposition between Fanny's "passion" and Amelia's. Similarly, it is made clear that Fanny had no reason to think her father would object to her marrying her clever seducer but, having fallen, she is ashamed to see her father again; Amelia, in contrast, is seen as justified in disobeying her capricious mother.

Though the indications that relate Fanny Matthews to Amelia are quite different from those which relate Harriet to Sophia, in both instances they are sufficient to define a very limited number of circumstantial similarities as roughly parallel; the parallel, in turn, forces us to see differences in traits of character and, most important here, attitudes toward courtship and marriage, as significant. Fanny's tale describes in detail how immediate acquiescence in the dictates of the demirep's passions led first to her illicit love affair with Hebbers and finally to her imprisonment for murder. Booth's tale, in the course of which his own interpretation of the role the passions play in human activity is indicated as suspect, follows soon after Fanny's, and, though it relates the events which led to his own imprisonment, is concerned mainly with Amelia. Indeed, the manner of representation is such that, though the tale is told from Booth's point of view, Amelia's character is emphasized at the beginning. Though Fanny has, for example, clearly indicated her passion for Booth and her interest in him, he ascribes the telling of the tale to a desire which Fanny had not only *not* expressed but could hardly have sympathized with: " 'Since you desire, madam, to know the particulars of my courtship to that best and dearest of women whom I afterward married, I will endeavor to recollect them as well as I can, at least all those incidents which are most worth relating to you.' " [49] To Fanny, Amelia—whom we first meet in Booth's tale—is anything but the "best and dearest of women"; as a result when Booth praises his wife's honesty, the demirep offers another interpretation: " 'It is highly generous and good in you,' said Miss Matthews, with a sly sneer, 'to impute to honesty what others would perhaps call credulity.' " [50] It is not only in her reaction to Booth's tale that Fanny, in defining herself as Amelia's rival and detractor, emphasizes the difference between the kind of passion that induced Amelia to run off with and marry Booth and the kind that induced the demirep to form an illicit alliance with Hebbers; her first, rather obvious, intention to seduce Booth is apparent when she begins her own tale with the revelation of her former passion for the hero, and this revelation is accompanied by her own hypocritical comparison of herself with Amelia:

> "I assure you," answered she, "I did all I could to prevent you [from perceiving her passion]; and yet I almost hated you for not seeing through what I strove to hide. Why, Mr. Booth, was you not more quick-sighted? I will answer for you—your affections were more happily disposed of to a much better

[49] Henley, VI, 66 (*Amelia*, II, i).
[50] *Ibid.*, p. 71 (II, ii).

woman than myself, whom you married soon afterward. I should ask you for her, Mr. Booth; I should have asked you for her before; but I am unworthy of asking for her, or of calling her my acquaintance." [51]

The immediate juxtaposition of the two tales of "romantic" passion, the explicit comparison between herself and Amelia made within her own tale and emphasized by her disagreements about Amelia as Booth describes her, are sufficient to force similarities and differences between the characters of Fanny and Amelia and between their respective courtships so emphatically on the attention of the reader as to make them constitute parallels and oppositions. Fanny's tale, clearly organized as an example of the ill effects of "following the blind guidance of a predominant passion" in courtship, helps to distinguish and define what is viewed as the virtuous passion, approved of by no less a judge than Harrison, which causes Amelia and Booth to marry despite the disapprobation of Amelia's weak mother and corrupt sister. The contrast between Amelia and Fanny Matthews as ethical characters is further emphasized when Fielding has them confront each other in the prison and the narrator contrasts the two at length.[52]

The manner in which the matrimonial adventures of Harriet Fitzpatrick and her volatile Irishman are made relevant to the central activities of the major characters of *Tom Jones* is, in some details, closer to the ways in which the "strayed lamb" narratives are made relevant to the novels from which they digress. Sophia, who listens to her cousin's tale, makes a gradual discovery of Harriet Fitzpatrick's culpability, explicitly disagrees with her on certain matters of matrimonial propriety, and, finally, is happy to leave her. The disagreement, however, is slow in emerging, and, before the split between the two, slight—though effective—indications remind us that Sophia is herself engaged in fleeing from home and that her feelings for Tom as well as her disinclination to marry Blifil have caused her to defy parental authority.

Since we have no knowledge of Mrs. Fitzpatrick's character when she meets Sophia, the pleasure of the two women at the fortuitous accident must condition the reader's initial attitude toward the demirep; he shares the pleasure felt by both women when they meet and "with equal joy" pronounce "the one the name of Sophia, the other that of Harriet." The combination of "surprise and joy" is emphasized.[53]

[51] *Ibid.*, p. 43 (I, vii).
[52] *Ibid.*, pp. 182-183 (IV, ii).
[53] *Ibid.*, IV, 249-250 (*Tom Jones*, XI, ii).

During their brief sojourn at a nearby inn, no new elements of Mrs. Fitzpatrick's character are revealed, but in the course of events which lead the
innkeeper to mistake Sophia for Jenny Cameron the heroine's virtues are incidentally but strongly emphasized. Sophia's humility is such that the landlady
misjudges her social position:

> ". . . she is too humble to be any very great lady: for, while our Betty was
> warming the bed, she called her nothing but a child, and my dear, and sweet-
> heart; and when Betty offered to pull off her shoes and stockings, she would not
> suffer her, saying she would not give her the trouble."
>
> "Pugh!" answered the husband, "that is nothing. Dost think, because you
> have seen some great ladies rude and uncivil to persons below them, that none
> of them know how to behave themselves when they come before their in-
> feriors?" [54]

Even the effect of her beauty is represented in terms apposite to her role as
paragon figure: "Perhaps Sophia never looked more beautiful than she did at
this instant. We ought not, therefore, to condemn the maid of the inn for her
hyperbole, who, when she descended, after having lighted the fire, declared,
and ratified it with an oath, that if ever there was an angel upon earth, she
was now above stairs." [55] No unknown Mrs. Fitzpatrick can disparage or
even disagree with a heroine represented in this manner and still retain the
reader's sympathy; Mrs. Fitzpatrick both disagrees with and disparages Sophia
shortly after they leave the inn. Before she does this, though, Sophia is sympathetic to Harriet's woes; when the latter hesitates to confess her reaction to
Fitzpatrick's false display of affection, Sophia helps her out and simultaneously
reminds us of her own temporarily disappointing romantic commitment:
" 'And you was more pleased still, my dear Harriet,' cries Sophia; 'you need
not be ashamed,' added she, sighing, 'for sure there are irresistible charms in
tenderness, which too many men are able to affect.' " [56] But, though Sophia
can share her cousin's penchant for the tender passions, as soon as Mrs. Fitzpatrick begins to interpret the reasons for the failure of her marriage she
meets with less than Sophia's complete approval. At first Sophia's lack of agreement is indicated tacitly; Mrs. Fitzpatrick asks:

> "What is the reason, my dear, that we, who have understandings equal to the
> wisest and greatest of the other sex, so often make choice of the silliest fellows
> for companions and favorites? It raises my indignation to the highest pitch to

[54] *Ibid.*, p. 254.
[55] *Ibid.*, p. 256 (XI, iii).
[56] *Ibid.*, p. 261 (XI, iv).

reflect on the numbers of women of sense who have been undone by fools."
Here she paused a moment; but, Sophia making no answer, she proceeded as in
the next chapter.[57]

Sophia's tacit disapproval does not cause Mrs. Fitzpatrick to discontinue her
narration, but it does lead to her reviving the unflattering appellation with
which she had teased Sophia when they both lived with Aunt Western: " 'You
will easily conceive, my dear Graveairs (I ask your pardon, I really forgot
myself), that, when a woman makes an imprudent match in the sense of the
world. . . .' " [58]

After the quiet revelation of Mrs. Fitzpatrick's mild hostility toward
Sophia, the narrator intrudes to supply the reader with more information
about Mrs. Fitzpatrick than Sophia possesses:

> The married lady seemed less affected with her own misfortunes than was
> her cousin, for the former eat very heartily, whereas the latter could hardly
> swallow a morsel. Sophia likewise showed more concern and sorrow in her
> countenance than appeared in the other lady, who, having observed these symp-
> toms in her friend, begged her to be comforted, saying, "Perhaps all may yet
> end better than either you or I expect." [59]

Harriet's statement is obviously preparation for the arrival of her friend the
peer, and the discrepancy between the demirep's hearty consumption of dinner, as it is emphasized by the narrator, and her own immediately preceding
assertion that she had passed through "a scene the horrors of which can neither
be painted nor imagined," points strongly to a modicum of insincerity in her
protestations of undeserved suffering. Without benefit of the narrator to emphasize it, Sophia is unaware of the discrepancy; unlike the reader's the
heroine's suspicions about her cousin's future plans remain dormant until, in
a number of disputes about Harriet's evaluations of her own past actions,
Sophia has directed our attention to specific marital conduct and attitudes condemned by the value scheme of the novel, has offered positive alternatives to
these, and has lost a good deal of sympathy with her cousin on the basis of her
past performances. The first exchange of remarks between the two women
after Harriet's hearty consumption of dinner develops into a significant argument:

> "The wretch could not bear to see my conversation preferred to his by a man
> of whom he could not entertain the least jealousy. O my dear Sophy, you are a

[57] *Ibid.*, p. 264.
[58] *Ibid.*, p. 268 (XI, v).
[59] *Ibid.*, p. 270 (XI, vi).

woman of sense; if you marry a man, as is most probable you will, of less capacity than yourself, make frequent trials of his temper before marriage, and see whether he can bear to submit to such a superiority. Promise me, Sophy, you will take this advice; for you will hereafter find its importance." "It is very likely I shall never marry at all," answered Sophia; "I think, at least, I shall never marry a man in whose understanding I see any defects before marriage; and I promise you I would rather give up my own than see any such afterwards." "Give up your understanding!" replied Mrs. Fitzpatrick; "Oh, fie, child! I will not believe so meanly of you." [60]

Even values somewhat peripheral to Harriet's tale are disputed by Sophia after this point. When her cousin asks why, despising Fitzpatrick, she should still be angry at learning of his infidelity, this conversation ensues:

> "I don't know, indeed," answered Sophia; "I have never troubled myself with any of these deep contemplations; but I think the lady did very ill in communicating to you such a secret."
>
> "And yet, my dear, this conduct is natural," replied Mrs. Fitzpatrick; "and when you have seen and read as much as myself, you will acknowledge it to be so."
>
> "I am sorry to hear it is natural," returned Sophia, "for I want neither reading nor experience to convince me that it is very dishonorable and very ill-natured; nay, it is surely as ill-bred to tell a husband or wife of the faults of each other as to tell them of their own." [61]

In most of these exchanges, Mrs. Fitzpatrick appeals to her experience and learning as proof for her disputed opinion; thus the quality of both the experience and the learning, as it is rejected by Sophia, is seen to be as suspect as the opinions derived from them.

Sophia's trip to London with Harriet and her peer does arouse in her that suspicion which "seems to arise from the head" rather than the heart and which the narrator is at pains to justify as being "no other than the faculty of seeing what is before your eyes, and of drawing conclusions from what you see" as opposed to the "vast quick-sightedness into evil" characterized as "a vicious excess." Sophia cannot but conclude that "her cousin was really not better than she should be," and, in a complete reversal of their initial reaction of surprise and joy at their meeting, Mrs. Fitzpatrick is "full as desirous of parting with Sophia as Sophia herself could be of going."

But not until their parting conversation is the full extent of the differences in their attitudes toward marriage as an institution made clear. And in that

[60] *Ibid.*, p. 275 (XI, vii)
[61] *Ibid.*, p. 278.

conversation Fielding draws on previous suggestions about the "town" attitudes involved in Harriet's desire to marry Fitzpatrick and about her horror
of leaving London to define the values about marriage implicit in the demirep's tale as those of the London world Sophia is about to enter. In their
parting conversation Sophia, though she makes no claim to the wisdom of
experience in her own right, makes a rhetorically ineffective attempt to warn
her cousin:

> She begged her, for heaven's sake, to take care of herself and to consider in
> how dangerous a situation she stood, adding, she hoped some method would be
> found of reconciling her to her husband. "You must remember, my dear," says
> she, "the maxim which my aunt Western hath so often repeated to us both:
> That whenever the matrimonial alliance is broke, and war declared between
> husband and wife, she can hardly make a disadvantageous peace for herself on
> any conditions. These are my aunt's very words, and she hath had a great deal
> of experience in the world." Mrs. Fitzpatrick answered, with a contemptuous
> smile, "Never fear me, child; take care of yourself, for you are younger than I.
> I will come and visit you in a few days; but, dear Sophy, let me give you one
> piece of advice: leave the character of Graveairs in the country, for, believe
> me, it will sit very awkwardly upon you in this town." [62]

Harriet's parting injunction is a prophecy, soon to be fulfilled, that Sophia's
character will indeed conflict with the ethics, attitudes, and activities of the
town and, as we might suspect, the conflict, when it does appear, centers on
courtship and marriage. The prophecy, however, carries with it an implicit
suggestion that Sophia is as superior to whatever makes her lack of frivolity
"sit very awkward upon her" as she is to the prophetess.

The prophetess herself, in telling her tale, has provided us with a detailed
example of the ethical and aesthetic character of a courtship and marriage in
which both male and female participants act according to what is defined as
London values. These never become more than external threats to Sophia,
whose own values, in contrast with them, are defined as exemplary.

Such definition is more important to the success of the action than may at
first appear. One stroke of comic brilliance appears at the very end of *Tom
Jones*, after Tom has overcome all the adversities of fortune and most of the
consequences of his own imprudence. Reunited with Allworthy, an heir with
sufficient social status to attract Western's backing for his claim to Sophia's
hand, Tom need only gain Sophia's consent to provide a sufficiently happy
ending to the novel. But Fielding momentarily thwarts Tom's and the reader's

[62] *Ibid.*, p. 299 (XI, x).

strongest desire: Sophia temporarily refuses. Not Allworthy himself could
retard the long-awaited consummation at this point with impunity. The momentary retardation does lead finally to a significantly greater degree of
comic pleasure when it is overcome; but it would drastically have diminished
the comic effect if, even in the slightest, the reader were permitted to become
annoyed with the delay resulting from Sophia's moral scruples, for at this
point she must be seen as most desirable. She can be seen in this way as she
punishes Tom only if we have been made to *feel* that her attitudes toward
sexual immorality, toward men, and toward marriage are neither prudish nor
feigned but correct beyond question. Her ride to London in the presence of
the demirep contributes more than any other single episode to assuring us that
Tom's patience and our impatience will be amply rewarded.

Created Relevance

The digressive narratives have an importance to the student of
Fielding's ideas disproportionate to the contributions the narratives make to
the novels. Their special importance is partially a result of their being organized primarily in terms of formulated ideas—i.e., they are semi-independent
apologues—and partially as a result of the fact that, through a complex set of
manipulations (usually of the interaction of the narrator of the digression and
one of the major characters), the controlling ideas of the apologues are made
relevant as ethical comment on the actions of the important characters in the
novel. The incorporation of such narratives into the structure of the novels
suggests, even requires, conscious intellection on Fielding's part.

This is not to deny that such intellection plays an important role in the
creation and use of such ethical constructs as the walking concepts, but these
are almost purely negative constructs and are as likely to embody partially
formulated notions, prejudices, and tentative dislikes as they are to embody
the result of even semisystematic thought; their importance is of a different
nature. On the other hand, concepts implicit in the traits, actions, and speeches
of the contradictory narrators, the fallible paragons, and their literary daugh-
ters the heroines are not always attributable to the result of conscious
thought; these are ethical agents only in part; so far as they participate in the
central activities of the novel and affect essential relationships their traits and
actions may be dictated as much by what Fielding feels is appropriate at any
given point as by some formulated moral belief.

I have argued previously, on the basis of the contrast between the way in
which Allworthy, as paragon, and Thwackum and Square, as walking concepts, regard Tom's "lying," that Fielding's notions about whether actions

were good or bad depended heavily on his attitude toward the motive which led to the action being evaluated.[63] But I should never argue on this basis alone that he was necessarily aware that his creation, Allworthy, did take motivation into account fairly consistently when judging actions. If, on the other hand, Allworthy had actually argued with Thwackum and Square that they had failed to take motivation into account in judging Tom, or if he had advocated such ethical considerations in a lecture to Tom, we should no longer be in doubt. Without such additional internal evidence, there seems to be insufficient justification for an inference that Fielding had *consciously* concluded that consideration of motive was necessary for judging actions; he might not have thought of the matter in these terms at all, though it would be highly improbable that he did not make such judgments—perhaps without intellectually examining the assumptions on which he made them—himself.

It is inconceivable, though, that Fielding could have devised a complete narrative which systematically illustrated how a man was wrong, and related the rejected ethical notions to those indicated as acceptable (at a point in the novel where, ostensibly, his protagonist might have been almost justified in accepting the wrong ones) without conscious examination of the assumptions underlying the digressive narrator's and the protagonist's views. The inclusion of the narrative in the novel indicates that Fielding thought it especially important to reject the organizing idea of the digressive narrative for specific and carefully qualified reasons.[64]

[63] See chapter three.

[64] This discussion of digressions is not meant to be exhaustive. Even so important a digression as the one in which Tom and Partridge are involved with the Gypsies does not conform to the pattern of the narratives I have discussed. It *is* marked as digressive because it interrupts the patterns of "arrows" which normally relate episodes in *Tom Jones*. Furthermore, the episode—though not a tale told by a new narrator but an episode in which Tom and Partridge participate—is organized as an apologue in which a particular kind of marital unscrupulousness is condemned and in which the attitude a just society would take toward the particular form of unscrupulousness is indicated. That the author of *The Modern Husband* and *Amelia* should be seriously concerned with these matters is no surprise; however, despite its intrinsic interest and the dexterity with which Fielding incorporates the apologue in the action, the "gypsy episode"—in contrast to those discussed—decreases the power of *Tom Jones*.

Chapter Six

The Great, Useful and Uncommon Doctrine

I am not writing a system, but a history, and I am not obliged to reconcile every matter to the received notions concerning truth and nature. But if this was never so easy to do, perhaps it might be more prudent in me to avoid it. For instance, as the fact at present before us now stands, without any comment of mine upon it, though it may at first sight offend some readers, yet, upon more mature consideration, it must please all; for wise and good men may consider what happened to Jones at Upton as a just punishment for his wickedness with regard to women, of which it was indeed the immediate consequence; and silly and bad persons may comfort themselves in their vices by flattering their own hearts that the characters of men are rather owing to accident than to virtue. Now, perhaps the reflections which we should be here inclined to draw would alike contradict both these conclusions, and would show that these incidents contribute only to confirm the great, useful, and uncommon doctrine, which it is the purpose of this whole work to inculcate, and which we must not fill up our pages by frequently repeating, as an ordinary parson fills his sermon by repeating his text at the end of every paragraph.[1]

Unlike Fielding, I am not writing a history and I have not yet met my minimal obligations to received notions concerning truth and nature. The skeleton articulated in the first chapter is now fleshed, but it is not clothed. The status of the signals which influence our attitudes toward characters, acts, and thoughts represented in novels still remains ambiguous. Though I have made occasional inferences from them about Fielding's beliefs, the legitimacy of those inferences must remain suspect, since they may have been postulated upon rhetorical signals dictated by purely aesthetic considerations; the signals, then, would have no specifiable relation to the ethical predilections of the novelist who employed them.

If this turns out to be so, there may be no positive relation between Fielding's beliefs and his novels or, more generally, between the beliefs of novelists

[1] Henley, IV, 337 (*Tom Jones*, XII, viii).

and their novels. Or, if there is a positive and specifiable relation between beliefs and novels, such signals of judgments as those described in the past four chapters may not be relevant to it.

It is disquieting but misleading to argue that the proof of the pudding is in the eating and that the way to dispel such discomfort is to worry less about critical assumptions, formulations of questions, or even classifications and to go ahead and solve problems about novelists' beliefs. Unfortunately, as both my introductory chapter and my present dilemma show, nothing could be simpler than to read Fielding's novels in order to arrive at far-reaching solutions which may solve nothing, or to arrive at ostensible answers to questions which have no answers. If it were possible for me to conclude this book with new intellectual biographies of Fielding, Swift, Johnson, and Richardson, no matter how detailed and apparently cogent they seemed, to the extent that they represented answers to foolish questions they would be foolish biographies.[2]

In any event, this book attempts to answer the question, "How may novelists embody their beliefs in novels?" It has advanced the theory that novelists' ethical beliefs, opinions, and prejudices are expressed as the formal signals which control our response to the characters, acts, and thoughts represented in their novels. The dilemma is a direct consequence of the need to show that such responses are not *merely* necessary for the whole work to be artistically effective. It is conceivable that the ethical effect, itself only a consequence of a novelist's having written a good novel, has no specifiable relation to his beliefs. This would be the true case if we could show that in a tragic action our responses were necessary only for the proper evocation of pity and fear,

---

[2] I do not, of course mean to suggest that all or even many biographies are foolish, only that the writing of even good biographies would in no way substantiate the theory advanced in this book. If the theory is correct it explains the shape that novelists' beliefs take in novels and shows that we can make inferences about beliefs from novels. I am not concerned with attacking any "methodology" or with establishing one of my own. I am concerned with showing that theory is generally true and *also* that it is true in detail of Fielding's novels. This concern must be carefully differentiated from an attempt to devise a *method* for discovering beliefs in novels. Such an attempt would be futile, just as any attempt to discover a procedure which inevitably leads to the truth is generally futile in the present state of human knowledge. Much wasted critical heat has been expended in arguments by critics and literary historians who fail to differentiate between proving that a theory is valid and describing how we discover the theory in the first place. The truth is hard to come by; we know of no necessary procedure by which it may be discovered, and we should be ridiculous if we arbitrarily ignored any kind of knowledge which might suggest it to us. I labor the point, since this book is open to the objection that it *rules out* knowledge easily derived from historical studies, and I feel it necessary to insist that it does not.

but that the ethical effect itself was only the further consequence of the degree of pity and fear evoked.[3] The ethical effects of all good tragedies would then be the same. Since we know that writers having widely different ethical commitments can write good tragedies, the ethical effect of tragedies would have no specifiable relation to a tragedian's beliefs.

The force of the dilemma may be felt, then, if one remembers that a test of the validity of the theory advanced is the ability to ask, with a reasonable expectation of finding significant answers, the following admittedly inelegant question: What must the author of this novel have believed to have evaluated as he did such characters, acts, and thoughts in such a work? Only if there is a specifiable positive relation between the signals of evaluation and the author's ethical beliefs will we, in answering the question, have converted aesthetically sufficient signals of authorial judgments into statements which, with a high degree of probability, will represent significant ethical beliefs of the novelist.

The past four chapters of this book have been concerned with defining and describing classes of agents which would facilitate answering the question if we asked it of Fielding and his novels. Important value judgments made in those novels were isolated and later presumably converted into ethical statements on the basis of the interaction of seven classes of agents, each class defined according to the similarity of its members' roles in controlling our reactions to represented acts, thoughts, and characters.[4] Alas, they were justifiably converted into statements only if there is a positive relation between the local judgments responsible for our reactions to represented characters, acts, and thoughts and the novelist's beliefs.

[3] See pp. 253-254.

[4] These classes are the split commentators, the fallible male paragons, the female paragons, the species characters, the narrators of certain kinds of digressive tales, the male heroes, and the characters who, like Jenny Jones or Major James, have important value judgments made about them but do not play a crucial role in evaluating other characters, actions, or thoughts. The classes are not synonymous with "devices of disclosure," and the presence of one of their members is seldom the sole cause of a particular kind of value judgment. The presence of a member of one of these classes or combinations of members of several classes insures the presence of fairly consistent kinds of judgment. The immediate cause of what we feel may at any point be more clearly attributable to the agency of some stylistic or other device of disclosure than to the presence of one of the characters, though the latter's appearance must enable us to predict what those devices of disclosure will make us feel. Another and more obvious condition which must be met is that at least one member of the seven classes listed above must be present whenever an important judgment is conveyed.

It should be clear, then, that I have not directly classified "devices of disclosure," but characters who, though they do indeed disclose and though their ethical function is

It is little wonder, then, that during this investigation the passage from *Tom Jones* quoted at the head of this chapter became a kind of *bête noire* for me; I discovered that I had created, at its insidious suggestion, two ghosts, shades of hypothetical polar critics whose assumptions seemed more easily to accommodate beliefs to literary works. Their assumptions were not so much ignored as rejected in this book. They have argued with me not only about every sentence, phrase, and paragraph I intended to write but in time they began to attack whole chapters after they were written so that, occasionally, the only way in which I could preserve any of my completed work was to get them to arguing with each other—not a difficult task, since their own critical assumptions are irreconcilable. But inevitably I had to rejoin the fray and constantly to risk my critical neck to preserve what I hope is still my critical sanity.

The first of my critical ghosts insisted that Fielding was "not writing a system, but a history" (i.e., what we now call a novel). He pointed out that not only had I made extensive use for my own purposes of a particular critical analysis which relates all parts of the novel to a defined artistic end,[5] but that I had agreed in all essentials both with such concrete analyses and, so far as I was capable of understanding them, with the aesthetic assumptions on which concrete analyses depend. Since I had agreed that all the elements of novels—including what I termed "value judgments"—were dictated by and organized to achieve an artistic end, such judgments may have only the most tenuous relation to authorial beliefs; the answer to my detailed question must be a hearty "Nothing"; though I might define such classes, the judgments whose presence they insured were controlled by the artistic end of the work, and I could make no significant inferences from them. Biographers and historians, this ghost argued, had better confine their activities to biography and history and let literary critics perform feats of literary criticism. As it was not likely that novelists would have to believe anything in particular in order to evaluate characters, actions, and thoughts in a given way, my general question was unanswerable or, worse yet, capable of eliciting a set of thoroughly misleading answers.

---

largely determined by such devices, are not synonymous with them. It should also be clear, though, that, after their introduction, the appearance in later episodes of characters from these classes largely determines what we feel, since relevant elements of what is represented, how it is represented, and the language in which it is represented are involved in determining the class to which an agent belongs.

[5] R. S. Crane, "The Concept of Plot and the Plot of *Tom Jones*," *Critics and Criticism* (Chicago: University of Chicago Press, 1952), pp. 616-647.

The second ghost insisted that neither Fielding nor his contemporaries were aware of the artistic end to which some contemporary critics had apparently related the parts of *Tom Jones* and such critics had, therefore, imposed it on the novel. Fielding would not have known the particular distinctions, made in chapter one of this book, which led to a description of three mutually exclusive types of prose fiction. Unless we were willing—and the second ghost knew I was not—to assume that Fielding was either a liar or a fool, we could not ignore his own statements about the end for which he organized his novels and these statements, similar at least in one respect to those made by his important contemporaries, indicate that his works were organized to achieve a moral end. The second ghost turned frequently to the conclusion of the passage which had initially called him back from the shades and in which Fielding explicitly stated that there is a "great, useful, and uncommon doctrine, which it is the whole purpose of this work to inculcate." Fielding's introductory remarks to *Tom Jones* tell us in no uncertain terms what this doctrine is, but, if they did not, since the work is *saying* something, though perhaps slightly indirectly, we need make no complex set of inferences from a complex set of laboriously defined classes in order to determine what he means. The work is organized to inculcate moral sentiments; consequently, if it is any good at all its morality must be clear. Indeed, most of the literary works we value are organized to exemplify an important moral statement and a series of subsidiary and closely related statements, which we may call the organizing themes of such works; characters and actions represented, simply make us feel the truth of such statements. My general question, he insisted, was therefore foolish, since we need only know what statements the writer has exemplified; our critical task is to explain how he has exemplified them.

I have tried to exorcise these two ghosts in the following section, not from motives of revenge but because, if either is left at large, this book must be regarded as a species of scholarly insanity.

Moralists, Novelists, and Unfallacious Intentions

It is only the mildest hyperbole to assert that those who write about Richardson and Fielding feel impelled to become semi-exclusive partisans of one or the other. Critics as diverse in point of view of time and interests as Samuel Johnson and Ian Watt, for example, seem sensitive almost exclusively to the merits of one of the two novelists. My purpose is not to reconcile, explain, or take sides in the persistent controversy. But in refuting one assumption made by some of their present-day partisans about the conscious moral and aesthetic intentions of the two novelists, I may more decisively lay my two ghosts and simplify the complicated reasons for rejecting both of their polar formularizations of the relation between a novelist's ethical convictions and the form of the novel he writes.

The formularization most difficult for me to deal with, because it is more in accord with my own critical prejudices, is that which presumes that, because Fielding was not "writing a system" but a novel, inferences about his beliefs can at best be minimal; that devices of disclosure making us feel admiration or contempt, sympathy or aversion, for acts and statements of the cowboys or the Indians, the cops or the robbers, the Blifils or the Joneses, may have a purely accidental relation to the writers' ethical convictions, since the purpose of these formal signals is to ensure that the readers' emotional reactions at any given point are consonant with the total effect the whole work is designed to produce.

The second formularization is not so difficult to refute on theoretical as on practical grounds. As an unstated assumption it underlies many critiques which adduce evidence of writers' beliefs from their works in an offhand manner; the ease with which it apparently enables us to relate knowledge derived from studies in biography or the history of ideas to literary works has made teaching procedures dependent upon its validity disquieting favorites in university classrooms. It embodies the assumption that most, possibly all, literary works exemplify themes: literary structure itself is a matter of the relationship of a main theme[6] and subsidiary themes to each other and to the actions which exemplify them. In *Tom Jones*, for example, Fielding's "doctrine, which it is the purpose of this whole work to inculcate," is presumably the organizing theme which the actions of the characters exemplify. If we accept this notion, an attempt to consider local evaluations apart from their relation to Fielding's doctrine would be as fruitless as an attempt to consider the parts of *Rasselas* without reference to Johnson's formally controlling statement about the pursuit of earthly happiness. Indeed, if we accept this view, we must conclude that all literary works are organized as mere variations of the structure ascribed to *Rasselas*; the particular controlling themes and the ways in which they are exemplified account for the differences among literary works.

Accept tentatively the first of the two polar views, which assumes that the judgments conveyed by a novelist are dictated by the form of his work; an

---

[6] I do not imply that the word "theme" is used only in this way; its uses are multifarious.

immediate consequence is that, if we admire *Tom Jones*, we must regard
Fielding's statements of his moral intentions with suspicion; we may write
them off as sops to an audience which expected moral apologia, as evidence that
writers are not conscious of what they have really done, as subsidiary purposes
which fortunately did not prevent Fielding from achieving the requisite
artistic end; or we may simply ignore their existence. More moderate forms
of this polar view seem to underlie some descriptions of the difference between
Fielding's and Richardson's contributions to the development of the novel;
it is common to regard Richardson as primarily and consciously a moralist who
accidentally made important contributions to the new genre, in contradis-
tinction to Fielding, who was a novelist first and a moralist, if at all, incidentally. A well-known American critic states: "Richardson, who, though
not without artistic merit, was primarily a moralist, brought the gift of
psychological insight to the novel; Fielding, despite uncertainties of handling
in *Joseph Andrews*, described and demonstrated the form." [7] There is considerable, though I should argue only ostensible, historical and biographical
support for such a view. Fielding's own famous attacks on *Pamela*, for example, are primarily attacks on the morality he thought the work embodied,
and, since the twentieth-century reader who is at all likely to read *Pamela* is
not likely to share Richardson's views about the importance of virginity,
Fielding's attacks seem apt. On the other hand, although Richardson's objections to Fielding and his work are made on moral grounds, the same reader
who rejected Richardson's morality in the first place may be expected to regard his objections as further evidence that he is primarily a moralist, and not
a very appealing one at that. Since Fielding's moral attack on *Pamela* seems
apt, but Richardson's moral attacks on Fielding and his novels seem irrelevant,
the view that Fielding's work is primarily "art" and Richardson's primarily
morality gains delusive support.

The consequences of adopting such a view are so significant, not merely
for the problem this book tries to solve, but for literary history, that we should
be wary of accepting it. Once assume *Pamela* is a work of morality, once
ignore Fielding's statements of moral purpose or assume that they are supererogatory, and—though we might quibble about definition—we can hardly
object when the same well-known critic concludes that *Joseph Andrews* is
"the first English novel consciously fulfilling an aesthetic theory." [8]

But if, for the sake of argument, we make the far less drastic assumption

[7] Howard Mumford Jones in his introduction to *Joseph Andrews* (New York: Modern Library College Editions, 1950), p. vii.
    [8] *Ibid.*, p. vi.

that both novelists were sincere in their statements of purpose but that such statements may not automatically be interpreted as analyses of the literary types in which their purposes are embodied, we may, simply by selecting arbitrarily from among those statements, not only convict Fielding of being primarily a moralist, but accuse Richardson of writing *Pamela* to fulfill an almost decadently aesthetic purpose. We need not bother to prosecute Fielding at length, since all that is necessary to convict him is to remind the reader of the blatantly moral statements in the opening pages of each of his three major novels. But convicting Richardson of hedonism on the basis of clearly expressed statements from the preface to *Pamela* is important for the remainder of this section and is good sport as well. Among the "desirable Ends" which he claims are "obtained in these Sheets" are the following:

> to Divert and Entertain
> to draw Characters justly, and to support them equally
> to raise a Distress from natural Causes, and to excite Compassion from proper Motives
> to effect all these good Ends, in so probable, so natural, so lively a manner, as shall engage the Passions of every sensible Reader.[9]

Indeed, even in his summary of the ends achieved in *Pamela*, he is unable to resist a parenthetical glance at Pan and assures us: "If these (embellished with a great Variety of entertaining Incidents) be laudable or worthy Recommendations of any Work, the Editor of the following Letters, which have their Foundation in Truth and Nature, ventures to assert, that all these desirable Ends are obtained in these Sheets." [10]

To isolate these remarks from the blatantly moral context in which they appear is to distort Richardson's intentions, but not to a greater degree than we distort them by wrenching his moral statements from their aesthetic context; there is no reason to believe that those nonmoral aims are any less sincere than the moral aims. If we ignore either the moral or aesthetic purposes, we argue from so partial a truth that, whether we try to describe Richardson's role in the development of the English novel or attempt to infer his beliefs from *Pamela*, we will go as far astray as if what we had assumed were absolutely false.

We can see this more clearly if we recognize that one aspect of our well-known critic's argument is quite justified: Richardson did have a blatantly

---

[9] Samuel Richardson's "Introduction to *Pamela*," ed. Sheridan W. Baker (Los Angeles: Augustan Reprint Society, 1954), pp. iii, iv, v.

[10] *Ibid.*, pp. v-vi.

moral intention when he wrote *Pamela*.[11] But, since we wish to know whether the primacy of his moral purpose could have prevented Richardson from writing "the first English novel consciously fulfilling an aesthetic theory," we must still determine in what type of fiction he could have embodied his moral intention and still have achieved the nonmoral aims listed in the preface to *Pamela*. It is sufficient to ask initially whether he could have written a work of prose fiction which achieved those aims and was, at the same time, structurally analogous to *Rasselas*—a work organized to exemplify an idea or a closely related set of ideas.

Such a work is clearly incompatible with those aims. If one writes prose fiction in which he really attempts "to raise a Distress from natural Causes, and to excite Compassion from proper Motives," if he attempts to "support [characters] equally," if he is intensely concerned with literary probability, he has introduced another set of criteria for the selection, ordering, and manner of representing episodes; it becomes virtually impossible for him simultaneously to select, order, and represent those episodes in such a way that they will demonstrate the truth or falsity of a single concept or a closely related set of concepts. If Johnson had aimed at even one of those conditions—to excite compassion from proper motives—he might indeed have made use of an Oriental setting, and of a different character named Rasselas whose attempt to find happiness had failed, and might indeed have caused us to feel distress at that failure, but he could hardly have done so and retained the highly general representation of his protagonist, nor that particular kind of "chance" relation of episodes in which the protagonist and his friends just happen to meet a series of characters who, though barely delineated, happen perfectly to exemplify potential modes of happiness which immediately turn out to be false. He could no longer retain that series of episodes—though their inclusion in the *Rasselas* Johnson wrote is quite effective—in which Pekuah, characterized only as a maid loyal to the hero's sister and afraid of ghosts, is carried off by an unknown Arab so that, ransomed, she may return to tell a tale which conveniently illustrates the lack of happiness in a culture not directly explored by the hero.

No matter how moral Johnson's purpose, no matter how strongly he wishes us to share his opinion that the earthly hope we pursue is a phantom, the moment he decides to make Richardson's nonmoral aims the conditions of his prose fiction, he commits himself in advance to choices among mutually exclusive literary forms and the *Rasselas* we know becomes impossible. His

[11] But, it should be remembered, not in opposition to Fielding, whom we may regard as a self-convicted moralist.

conviction about happiness may—and if the novel he writes is of reasonable scope, undoubtedly will—be expressed in those devices of disclosure which make us feel as we do about the characters, actions, and thoughts represented in his fiction, but the whole work cannot be organized as an exemplification of that conviction.

If we agree that *Rasselas* is an excellent work of its kind, we cannot wish Johnson had made the sorts of changes enumerated above, though these changes and many others would be necessary to fulfill the nonmoral aims of *Pamela*. We must conclude, then, that if two men have equally strong moral purposes when writing prose fictions, but one has assumed certain minimal aims which we associate with novels as conditions of his own work, the forms they create will be so different from each other that similar criteria for excellence cannot be fruitfully applied to both. *Rasselas* is a disjointed novel, but an excellent apologue. If Richardson successfully embodied his moral purpose in a work that achieved his nonmoral aims, he may have produced an excellent novel, but it must be a very poorly constructed apologue. Since both Richardson and Fielding did have moral purposes in writing their novels, and Richardson did have conscious nonmoral aims of such a nature that their successful achievement would automatically result in what we now call a novel, we can hardly agree that *Joseph Andrews* is "the first English novel consciously fulfilling an aesthetic theory."

Unless human nature had undergone a complete transformation since Richardson's time and made it impossible for us to read *Pamela* at all, the villagers who rang church bells on learning of the fictional heroine's marriage to her would-be seducer were hardly likely to have been celebrating their reinforced moral conviction that an able preservation of chastity will be materially rewarded; their reaction to Pamela's marriage to her erstwhile seducer could only result from her creator's successful efforts at drawing characters justly and supporting them equally, at raising a distress from natural causes and exciting compassion from proper motives, and from the fact that he achieved these ends in so probable, so natural, so lively a manner that he did indeed engage the passions of sensible readers. One can hardly imagine bells being rung for the safe return of Pekuah! Only the insensitive, or a shrewd writer of burlesque, could interpret *Pamela* as an exemplification of the notion that a cunning preservation of virtue, defined as virginity, will be rewarded, when its heroine is capable of writing:

> I shall make a fine figure with my singing and dancing when I come home! I shall be unfit for a *May-day* holiday; for these minuets, rigadoons, and French dances . . . will make me but ill company for my milk-maid companions

that are to be. I had better, as things are, have learned to wash, scour, brew, bake, and such like. But I hope, if I can't get work, and can meet with a place, to learn these soon, if any body will have the goodness to bear with me till I am able. . . . It may be a little hard at first; but woe to my proud heart if I find it so on trial! I will make it bend to its condition or break it.[12]

Obviously Pamela does preserve her chastity and obviously she is rewarded; this does not mean that she represents virtue rewarded. The girl represented in the quoted passage as looking almost with horror on her return, although with maidenhead intact, to her milk-maid companions is hardly an appropriate central figure for an apologue; she is a highly characterized fifteen-year-old girl who has emerged from poverty to live on the fringes of a world of great affluence; she is conscious that she has been spoiled for the world in which she was born, but she has a moral sensibility which prevents her from assuming the role of a paid mistress and has but one commodity, her attractive body, with which to gain permanent entrée into the only world in which she is now fit to live.

This is not to say that Richardson did not feel or try to make his reader feel that his harassed heroine was virtuous; on the contrary, unless he can convince his reader that she does act virtuously in the situation in which she is placed, *Pamela* cannot be artistically successful. One of those circumstances is, of course, her understandable desire not to return to impoverished rural life. Fail to take into account the resolution necessary for her to return to this life, and her reluctance to get home when, ostensibly, she is still free to do so, defines her as a kind of Shamela. Fail to take into account that when she has won Mr. B. she has not automatically won herself a place in the only world in which she is now fit to live, and the part of the novel representing her activities after marriage becomes artistically superfluous;[13] if Richardson had actually created a sister to Shamela, all expectations would have been resolved when she won Mr. B., but Pamela must win over her husband's family and friends or she has lost all.

That Pamela is meant to be seen as virtuous is not in question. That Richardson had sincere moral intentions in writing the book is not in doubt. Once admit, however, that we must take into account such considerations as those above when we discuss *Pamela*, that her "problems" and their artistic resolution issue in large part from her character, and that Richardson's conscious

---

[12] Samuel Richardson, *Pamela* (New York: E. P. Dutton and Co., 1949), pp. 62-63.

[13] I am not referring here to Richardson's sequel, but to the original novel, in which Pamela's adventures after her marriage occupy about one-fourth of the whole; her troubles with Mr. B.'s family begin even before her marriage.

aesthetic aims indicate that this state of affairs was not the result of accident, and you have also admitted that, in writing *Pamela*, Richardson is primarily a novelist. The "morality" of the book is no longer as simple or accessible as it might appear, and any attempt to isolate it must depend on a series of inferences about what Richardson must have believed in order to evaluate as he did the characters, actions, and thoughts represented in the work, and especially to evaluate Pamela's actions with regard to the particular choices possible for such a character in such circumstances.

The conditions under which such a work, as opposed to one organized as moral statement or apologue, may effectively embody the writer's moral intention have been aptly described by a distinguished critic:

> It is not that art teaches by precept . . . nor that it moves to action; but clearly
> it inculcates moral attitudes; it determines our feelings toward characters of a
> certain kind for no other reason than that they are such characters. The ethical
> function of art, therefore, is never in opposition to the purely artistic end; on
> the contrary, it is best achieved when the artistic end has been best accomplished,
> for it is only a further consequence of the powers of art.[14]

But committed as we are to the assumption that neither Richardson nor Fielding, when he stated that his purpose in writing his novels was moral, was a liar, a fool, or a slave of his unconscious, and, though we can accept the description of the conditions which make possible the ethical effect of such works, we are forced to make a major reservation about accepting also the description of their ethical function as *"only a further consequence* of the powers of art."[15] If both novelists have embodied their moral intentions in works organized as a represented action, it is a tautology to assert that the ethical effects of those works can only be of the kind possible to such an organization. Such ethical effects will, by definition, be consequent on the powers of art; the ethical function of their works is not merely a *further* consequence of those powers, but may be the *primary* consequence intended by both Richardson and Fielding. For many purposes, it is as misleading to identify the artistic end of a literary work with authorial intention[16] as it is to assume that authorial inten-

---

[14] Elder Olson, "An Outline of Poetic Theory," *Critics and Criticism*, p. 566.

[15] Italics mine. I may have placed too much weight on a casual phrase removed from its context and perhaps the slight disagreement with Professor Olson implicit in the following remarks is illusory.

[16] The identification of authorial intention with artistic end may be useful in discussing works like *Rasselas*, but this is the fortuitous result of Johnson's having embodied a moral intention in a didactic organization; where, as in much of Fielding's and Richardson's work, a moral intention is embodied in a represented action, such a pro-

tion is irrelevant because explicit statements of intention are seldom, if ever, structural analyses of the works which embody those intentions; these appear irrelevant, foolish, or inadequate only if we regard them as misdirected attempts at such analyses.[17]

If we assume that artistic end and authorial intention are identical, we commit ourselves to either of two highly undesirable critical positions. One is that any literary analysis dependent upon critical distinctions not current in Fielding's day must be regarded as imposing a twentieth-century notion of structure on an eighteenth-century work; at best, then, all that any such critique can accomplish is to explain why twentieth-century readers of *Tom Jones* who share the critic's idiosyncratic notions about literary structure hold the novel in high esteem; at worst, such a critique may be regarded as a new version of *Tom Jones* in outline, an absolute distortion of the book's structure, since we know that Fielding's "sincere endeavor"—the "honest purpose" that Lyttelton thought Fielding had attained in "this history"—was "to recommend

---

cedure may cause unnecessary difficulties. Professor Kolb, in "The Structure of *Rasselas*," undertakes "an examination which begins with a fairly precise notion of the end sought in *Rasselas* and then moves to a discussion of the elements incorporated in the work for the purpose of attaining that end. . . ." If we substitute the title *Pamela* or *Tom Jones* for *Rasselas* and try to carry out such an analysis, the moment we begin a "discussion of the elements incorporated in the work" we find it necessary to relate all the parts to an artistic end of which we can derive no "precise notion" apart from a theory which will account for all parts of the work. We might derive from Richardson's introduction and other sources that "the end sought" in *Pamela* was the construction of a "novel" which would have a strong moral effect upon sensible readers, but if we are to discuss the elements incorporated in the work to attain that end we are committed at some point to discussing how he attained one aspect of the end sought: the construction of a novel, that is, the accomplishment of a separate artistic end upon which the strong moral effect was consequent. If we cannot describe how the artistic end was accomplished, we cannot describe how the end sought in *Pamela* was attained.

[17] This is equally true of statements of intent which include even such relatively detailed aesthetic comments as those Fielding includes in his preface to *Joseph Andrews*. To convert Fielding's remarks about "a comic epic poem in prose" into an analysis that would answer the kinds of questions some modern critics might ask would commit us to analyzing how those epics which Fielding had in mind accomplished their artistic ends, to isolating those elements common to all of them, and then to relating the parts of *Joseph Andrews* to the derived inclusive artistic end before analyzing how it accomplished the "new" artistic end of the comic-prose form. Since the results of such an analysis must be translatable into those derived from asking the questions directly of *Joseph Andrews*, such a procedure would be unwarranted. This is not to deny the importance or the value of Fielding's aesthetic comments; it is simply an acknowledgment that a preface designed to impart the special qualities of a new work by differentiating it from and relating it in general terms to works known and respected by general readers is not an analysis designed to answer all questions which interest some twentieth-century critics.

goodness and innocence," but we also know that such a description of the structure of *Tom Jones* as the one used in this work depends on our relating the parts of the novel not to this honest purpose but to an effective comic action of a specified kind.

The obvious refutation of this sort of objection is the common-sense observation that Fielding's and Richardson's statements of purpose, even when they touch upon aesthetic matters, were never intended to answer the kinds of questions that some critics ask. The questions that are asked about literary works reflect different critical interests not wholly determined by the age a critic lives in: Samuel Johnson would have no interest in the present work though David Hume might, since it attempts to give a formal account of relationships men *must* perceive to perform certain intuitive acts that we know they have performed, and still others which, for valid reasons, we must assume they are capable of performing. Men who have read novels with pleasure can generally distinguish between them and, for example, long explanatory essays; they can do this not only with works they can be presumed in some sense to have learned but with works which are new to them: a minimal formal account must explain their ability to distinguish between a countless number of new novels and new essays.

So limited a concept as "represented character" might provide a rough hypothesis about the intuitive distinction between essays and novels; it might even show us why, no matter how original a writer is, he cannot write an essay which is also a novel. But the concept is too narrow to explain certain crude intuitive judgments that even readers with limited education and aesthetic sensibilities are capable of making. For instance, they will recognize that *Pride and Prejudice* (or countless other novels) is incomplete if they read an edition that fails to include the final fifty pages. Many will predict, from the moment Sophia is introduced in *Tom Jones*, that Tom will marry her, even if they understand little else about the novel and do not complete it.

Considerations more complex but akin to these underlie such minimal distinctions as "type," "form," and "unique work." A reader may make judgments barely sufficient to comprehend *Tom Jones* as a represented action when he does not understand its form or its unique power. Or, he may intuitively comprehend *Tom Jones* as a comic form of action (he knows all will go well for some characters) without comprehending the relationship of the qualitative parts that realize the novel's unique power (a degree of comprehension reflected in the attitudes of readers who like the novel but would prefer to do away with introductory essays, narrator's asides, and characters like Broadbrim and Mrs. Whitefield).

A minimal account of the relationships that must be perceived if a reader intuits the whole of a unique work is not a psychological theory of the particular capacities or mechanisms of the mind that enable men to perceive those relationships, though a good account should facilitate formulation of such a theory. The account is as much a paradigm of judgments the writer had to make (and, unlike the reader, realize in an appropriate medium) as it is of readers' judgments. This fact has significance for considerations of literary merit and literary history. A novelist may intuitively make judgments sufficient to create a represented action but not a coherent form (a work in which *what* is represented is barely adequate, but in which the manner, appropriate at different points to different powers, thwarts the realization of any one). Or he may make judgments sufficient to ensure a coherent form of a coherent type but deficient as a unique work (one in which the elements are barely adequate parts of an action represented in a manner that does not thwart a crude power, but in which characters are dull and derivative, their motives uninteresting, and the value judgments trivial).

Better hypothetical concepts than "represented actions," "apologues," and "satires" are necessary for a full paradigm of the judgments that distinguish literary forms. But if we agree only that some readers in Fielding's day and our own have intuited that *Tom Jones* consists of relevant parts, not of English sentences in an accidental sequence, there must be a formal explanation of the common intuitive judgments they have made. Though a twentieth-century attempt to account for that common intuition answers critical questions which Fielding or critics in Fielding's day did not ask, this merely reflects a change in critical interests and should lead to a different description, not a new novel. We may certainly postulate that changes in the manner of representation or among the relationships of character, thought, and action, described by recent critics, would have changed the effect of the novel for an eighteenth-century reader who intuited the wholeness of *Tom Jones* much as it would for one in our own century.[18]

But this argument depends on the condition that artistic end is separable from authorial purpose. If we think of them as identical, all that is necessary

[18] Unless we accept as possible that human beings have changed so greatly since Fielding's time that our reactions have little in common with theirs; we must, in this view, become Elizabethans to read Shakespeare, Augustans to read Fielding. This is an implausible assumption, since people who are neither read all of *Othello* and all of *Tom Jones* with pleasure; the notion that these read a radically different work than did their predecessors would, if true, mean that the same incredible number of details included in a literary work miraculously subordinate themselves into equally coherent and radically

to prove that formal analyses are distortions of eighteenth-century literary structures is to adduce evidence from Richardson's and Fielding's statements which show that their primary purposes were something like "to recommend goodness and innocence," while such analyses as Crane's of *Tom Jones* relate the parts of Fielding's novel to an artistic end other than this. The other critical position open to us, if we wish to deny that such an analysis is distortion and at the same time wish to retain our notion that artistic end is identical with authorial purpose, is that taken by the first of our two ghosts, who arbitrarily denies the validity of evidence adduced from explicit statements of authorial purpose. We are forced either to denigrate with our second ghost the validity of many critical questions, or to join forces with the first, who ignores at will either Fielding's moral or Richardson's aesthetic statements as insincere or misdirected. Do the latter and we have come full circle; we are back once more with Professor Howard Mumford Jones, who sees Richardson, in opposition to Fielding, as primarily a moralist and, with only the slightest quibbling about the term "novel," we can comfortably include as axioms in our histories of English literature that "Richardson . . . though not without artistic merit, was primarily a moralist" but that *Joseph Andrews* is "the first English novel consciously fulfilling an aesthetic theory."

But if we refuse arbitrarily to deny the validity of Fielding's and Richard-

---

diverse organizations each capable of very different but equally coherent aesthetic effects on audiences of different eras. The probability of a sizable body of literature assuming such protean efficiency is zero.

Another different and complicated, though analogous, problem stems from the fact that language itself changes so that syntactic structures and words convey different meanings to twentieth-century readers of *Tom Jones* from those they conveyed to Fielding's contemporaries; the reconstruction of older forms of the language is always necessary before we can understand the works written in them. But except for isolated and short passages in literary works, it is impossible for us to be "fooled" by sentences which, owing to the passage of time, have become homonymic. The king of Brobdingnag, for example, decides that Europeans are "a race of little, odious vermin." His decision is phrased in a sentence which seems perfectly grammatical and meaningful to twentieth-century readers. For the hypothesis to be correct that, as a twentieth-century sentence, this is significantly different from what it was as an eighteenth-century sentence, we should have to make the preposterous assumption that the complicated signals of one language system magically become consistent signals for different meanings in another language system; in other words, that some incredible freak of fate has transformed eighteenth-century language into a perfect cryptogram for a different twentieth-century language.

Many words and some syntactic forms have changed since Fielding's time, but it is only because most have not—because Fielding's and our own language have essentially the same structure—that, except in a few unusual instances, we can historically reconstruct the changed forms without much difficulty.

son's statements of purpose where such evidence is relevant—if we regard these statements, not unreasonably, *as* evidence of purpose, not as analyses of the forms which embody purpose—and refuse also to identify the artistic ends to which, in formal analyses, we find all parts of the works related, with the purpose which has led the author to adopt such a form, our history of literature will be quite different; it will more accurately relate the information we now possess, and more fruitfully suggest areas for further critical and historical investigation.

Our history would take cognizance of the fact that in 1740 and 1742 two very different works were published which, as distinguished from immediately precedent works of prose fiction, we traditionally regard as originals in English of forms which we now classify as novels. It would indicate that neither of the writers of these works seemed to have any notion of freeing himself from the constraint of a moral aim imposed by a critical tradition; on the contrary, there is explicit evidence that the moral effect of their works was a primary consideration for both writers. This does not mean—our history would have to point out—that artistic excellence was an unconscious by-product of their ethical intentions or even that it was a secondary concern; for both writers, though they employ terminology and insist on criteria from different critical traditions, show a surprising awareness that ethical effect is "best achieved when the artistic end has been best accomplished." This surprising conscious awareness is itself suggestive. Many of Fielding's and Richardson's battles had been inconclusively fought or actually won for them before they put pen to paper; the critical issues pertinent to *Pamela* and *Tom Jones* were the concerns of writers of romance and "novels" in seventeenth- and eighteenth-century England, and had been the concerns of critics of "modern epics" since the early renaissance. The exclusion of elements of the marvelous, the inclusion of characters from more-or-less common life, the utility of narrative digressions, the relation of fiction to feigned or actual history—some of these were discussed by men like Cinthio and Tasso in Italy, later by men like Harrington and even Lyly in England; and, still later, Frenchmen like Bishop Huet and the de Scudéries, widely translated into English, argued about these and many other relevant critical matters in detail; furthermore, these matters were weighed and re-weighed, most frequently according to their consequences upon the moral effects of "modern" verse epic, prose epic, and romance. We might do well, therefore, to explore the possibility that when Fielding and Richardson chose to embody their moral purposes in *Joseph Andrews* and *Pamela* rather than in prose fiction organized as apologue or satire, they were not purely unconscious that the kind of art they were creating did not teach by a simple relation of precept and example,[19] but had at least a tentative awareness, conceivably derived from even the popular criticism of their own day, that such art "inculcates moral attitudes," does so in a way impossible for other forms of moral discourse, and does so best only when "the artistic end has been best accomplished."

Given the interests and techniques of criticism in our own age, it is not surprising that some of our most valuable efforts have produced "structural analyses," at their best clear delineations of the conditions which had to be met for the successful accomplishment of the defined artistic end of the work analyzed, and lucid description of how the end was accomplished in that work. Historical and biographical research alone can suggest the importance of the fact that we traditionally date the English novel from the time that two men embodied sincere moral intentions in literary forms which were to influence subsequent writers and were, themselves, to be classified as novels. Formal analyses alone, with no reference to biography or history—by definition irrelevant to its immediate concerns[20]—can describe those forms with relation to the artistic ends the two men accomplished. Meaningful literary history or biography becomes possible not when we confuse the aims of the two activities, as when we identify authorial purpose with artistic end, but when we relate information derived independently from each discipline. From neither alone could we derive or test so important and simple a hypothesis as: "We date the origin of the English novel from the time that two writers chose to embody sincere moral purposes in forms of prose fiction of such a nature that the achievement of their moral purposes became absolutely consequent on the effectiveness with which they accomplished an artistic end—the representation of specifiable kinds of actions, say—which we may value for its own sake."

To separate authorial intention from artistic end does not, of course, commit us to reject such a useful distinction as that made by some critics between mimetic and didactic works; it simply means that we would make the distinc-

---

[19] Both Richardson and Fielding do, of course, consider that parts of their works contain useful examples of conduct and it would be hard to find important literary works of any age that do not. But though we might wish to make love as well as a D. H. Lawrence hero does in a novel, or to make witty remarks as well as an Oscar Wilde hero does in a play, or even to fight as well as a Hemingway hero does in a short story, neither the novel, the play, nor the story teaches as an apologue.

[20] "Irrelevance" must be carefully qualified in this context; see my discussion of discovery procedure (note 2, chap. six). Besides the general utility of ahistorical knowledge in historical analyses, the necessary reconstruction of changed language forms which must precede such analyses is largely a matter for historical investigation.

tion according to how the work is organized, never according to what it is organized *for*. If we do this, we preserve as a possibility, to be substantiated or rejected by historical research, that Fielding's purpose in writing *Tom Jones* was as strongly and consciously moral as Johnson's in writing *Rasselas;* the latter embodied his intention in a form whose parts were related to each other and to the whole in such a manner that we would classify it as didactic; the former embodied his moral purpose in an organization which we should call mimetic; obviously the form that each selected limits the kind of moral or ethical effect his work can have: it is a tautology that represented actions can have only the kind of effect possible to represented actions. If we wish, as we certainly should, to know what caused these men to adopt the forms they did, it is foolish to assume that what caused them to adopt the forms they did was that they intended to adopt them, since this assumption makes inquiry about those causes impossible. Obviously, too, questions about those causes cannot be answered by analyses which describe and explain the effectiveness of the forms, but can be answered only by consideration of biographical, historical, and some critical data.[21]

Since we know that *Tom Jones* effectively accomplishes its artistic end, we may well ask what has happened en route to Fielding's moral purpose, identified in this book with that "ethical function of art" which, as has been explained, "is best achieved when the artistic end has been best accomplished." The notes written in a copy of *Tom Jones* in the hand of no less a critic than Coleridge may be accepted as testimony to the force of the ethical effect of Fielding's novels on a sensitive reader:

> Let the requisite allowance be made for the increased refinement of our manners, and then I dare believe that no young man who consulted his heart and conscience only, without adverting to *what the world* would say, could rise from the perusal of Fielding's "Tom Jones," "Joseph Andrews," and "Amelia," without feeling himself a better man—at least, without an intense conviction that he *could* not be guilty of a *base* act.[22]

Coleridge's intense moral response is no more evidence that Fielding's novels were apologues than is Fielding's clearly stated moral purpose. But the coincidence of the description of response and the description of purpose indicates

---

[21] I include critical data, since we may often make fairly probable inferences about a writer's purpose from the way in which parts of his work are related to the whole. It would not be farfetched, I think, to infer that Fielding had a moral purpose in writing *Tom Jones* from the way in which the Man of the Hill episode is related to the whole novel.

[22] Quoted from Henley, V, 374. Coleridge's italics.

that Fielding's moral intentions were successfully accomplished, not lost, in the forms in which he wrote. Professor Crane has described the artistic end achieved in *Tom Jones* and thereby shown how Fielding fulfilled the artistic conditions which make such an ethical consequence possible. There can be little doubt that this was the consequence that Fielding primarily intended when he wrote *Tom Jones*, in which his "sincere endeavor"—the "honest purpose" that Lyttelton thought he had attained in "this history"—was "to recommend goodness and innocence."

Thus armed, we may proceed to exorcise the two ghosts of hypothetical critics who have haunted this work and, who, while at large, prevent the final clothing of our own articulated skeleton.

To the first, who objected that in a work like *Tom Jones* Fielding was not writing a system but a "history," we may reply that we never doubted it, but made use of the fact that accomplishing the artistic end of such a work depended heavily on how successful its creator was in controlling our sympathy and antipathy toward, our approval and disapproval of, characters, thoughts, and actions at every stage of his work. Such attempts to control are implicit in devices of disclosure; that is, they are embodied in formal signals which are analytically isolable and accessible to useful classification. Admittedly we must be extremely careful about our critical assumptions and recognize that an inquiry which attempts to answer the question "What is it likely that this writer must have believed to evaluate as he did such characters, actions and thoughts in such a manner in such a work?" can yield results based on inference, with a high degree of probability, not a certainty, of being correct. But if we are careful we may expect to learn far more from such a "history" than from, say, an apologue. In the latter, ideas are obviously more accessible —it would be an unsuccessful apologue indeed which obscured the ideas it was organized to exemplify—but, since one or a limited number of such ideas controls the representation of actions, characters, and thoughts in such a work, judgments are severely limited to those ideationally relevant to the controlling concepts. In contrast, a multiplicity of value judgments is demanded in a work like *Tom Jones*; Fielding is forced, as it were, by the artistic end of the work to convey judgments of many kinds on almost every page.

Even a writer who has absolutely no moral purpose in writing a novel with an artistic end similar to that of *Tom Jones* must make such a variety of judgments that, if the novel is of any appreciable length, it would be rare if we could not infer from it his most important ethical beliefs, notions, and prejudices, except in the rare case where his intention is actually to deceive. Given a sincere moral intention on the part of an author, his very selection of characters, actions, and thoughts *to be judged* will make our job that much easier, but only if, paradoxically enough, we are constantly aware that his intention is not identical with the artistic end he must accomplish to embody it successfully. We should never, for example, on the basis of our knowledge that Fielding had a moral purpose, deny the validity of the following passage which relates two digressions to the artistic end of *Tom Jones:*

> Both the story told to Tom by the Man of the Hill and that recounted to Sophia by Mrs. Fitzpatrick, however much they owe to the convention of interpolated narratives which Fielding had inherited, along with other devices, from the earlier writers of "comic romance," are clearly designed as negative analogies to the moral state of the listeners, from which the reader is led to infer, on the eve of the most distressing complication for the hero and heroine, that nothing that may happen to them will be, in comparison, very bad.[23]

What we would insist is that the number of ethical systems Fielding might have embodied as a negative analogy to Tom's moral state is very great; his selection of a form of Stoicism to represent that negative analogy could in no way be dictated by the artistic end of the work, though the decision to include a narrative designed as a negative analogy to the listener's state might be dictated by the artistic end. As our parting shot at our first ghost, we may draw a general conclusion from this observation: whether or not he has a moral purpose, a novelist selects both what he represents and how he represents it; the tremendous multiplicity of characters, actions, and thoughts which he may choose to represent, and the great variety of devices of disclosure from which he may select to control what we feel about them without prejudicing the artistic end of his work, rules out for all practical purposes the possibility that any particular local value judgment will be exclusively dictated by the artistic end of the work, though all such judgments must help to accomplish that end.[24] The artistic end of his work exerts no pressure on a writer to make insincere judgments.

[23] Crane, *Critics and Criticism*, p. 643.

[24] A man who wants to make money writing for television may construct a "western" in which numbers of Indians bite the dust, though their creator does not care about Indians one way or the other; this would confuse us only if the writer constructed an apologue which showed by example that, for instance, the only good Indian is a dead one. But in a work not organized to exemplify a statement about Indians, inferences from the value scheme of such a work would still be possible, especially if we separate artistic end from authorial purpose and determine the latter from available historical evidence.

In any event, the evaluation of Indians in such a case is not dictated by the artistic end of the work—all Indians need not be represented as villains in a work in which a

We may bid our first ghost farewell with a summary: our knowledge that Fielding was writing a "history" does not prevent us from inferring his ethical views from *Tom Jones*, but, on the contrary, enables us to do so with considerable precision. Our added knowledge that he had a moral purpose in writing the book facilitates our job, but if we did not have the knowledge or he did not have such a purpose, it would still be possible to infer his beliefs from his work. The more precise our knowledge of how a writer has accomplished the artistic end of his work, the more accurate will be the inferences we make about his ethical beliefs, notions, prejudices.

Turning to our second ghost, we may begin by agreeing so that we may later try to confound. Not only do we agree that Fielding had a moral purpose in writing *Tom Jones*, but actually share the view of those critics who, like Coleridge, value his novels highly because they successfully inculcate moral attitudes. Furthermore, since we feel that literary works are among the most important creations of men, we are interested not only in the artistic forms of those works or even in the moral attitudes which one work alone inculcates, but in the beliefs and opinions of writers, the function of those beliefs in their works, and the relationship of those beliefs to the history of ideas.

Our rejection of this hypothetical critic stems not from any desire to denigrate ethical criticism of literary works but from a conviction that to regard them all as apologues is precisely the way to make rational inquiry into the ethical nature of literary works impossible or at best trivial. Granted that if all literary works were organized as exemplifications of formulated conceptions, as fictional proofs of statements, the laborious taxonomic activity embodied in this book would be ridiculous; no set of complex inferences is necessary to determine the point Johnson wishes to make when he writes, "Ye who listen *with credulity* to the whispers of *fancy*, and pursue with eagerness the *phantoms* of hope; who expect that age will perform the promises of youth, and that the deficiencies of the present day will be supplied by the morrow,—attend to the history of Rasselas, prince of Abyssinia," [25] and continues his prose fiction with a series of episodes which show that he who listens is indeed credulous, and the hope he pursues is demonstrably phantasmal. Even a tyro critic must recognize that this prose fiction is organized in such a manner that it does make a point. But when even the most sophisticated and learned

---

good many must be sent to their ancestors. In practice, it is suggestive to consider great numbers of such works; the frequency with which all Indians are carefully *not* evaluated as bad hombres in very recent "westerns" might provide future historians with invaluable data about the changing attitudes toward racial minorities in the United States in the twentieth century.

[25] Italics mine.

of critics has some difficulty in attempting to interpret the whole of *Tom Jones* as prose fiction organized to exemplify ethical statements, and when we have at hand an analysis which successfully shows how the parts of the novel are each related to a comic action of a specified kind, we would do well not to predicate our ethical inquiries on critical phantoms.

In rejecting our ghostly critic, we are in no way ignoring as valid evidence Fielding's explicit statements of intention, but simply taking into account an analytically isolable artistic end that controls the conditions under which his moral intention was embodied and defines the kind of moral effect possible to such an embodiment. Indeed, in our discussion of *Pamela*, we have seen that a writer with blatant moral intentions blatantly advertised need have accepted only a minimal number of aesthetic aims to make it impossible for him to write a work organized so that it exemplifies an ethical statement. This reflects not upon the sincerity or accuracy of his statement of intent but only upon the validity of the assumption (partially responsible for one hypothetical critic's argument that *Tom Jones* is an apologue) that a statement of intention is an analysis of the form in which the intention is embodied.

Since the artistic end of *Tom Jones* is of such a nature that the novel does not teach by a simple relation between precept and example, but has an ethical effect dependent upon devices of disclosure which have made us feel in certain ways about characters, actions, and thoughts represented in the novel, if we wish to explore Fielding's ethic as it is embodied in his work, if we wish to relate that ethic to the beliefs of his time or even to the beliefs he himself expressed in his legal writings, we must ask: What is it likely that Fielding must have believed in order to evaluate as he did such characters, actions, and thoughts in such a work? More generally, what is it likely that this novelist must have believed in order to evaluate as he did such characters, actions, and thoughts in such a work?

With my two ghosts at rest, it is now safe to assert that the question may be as fruitfully asked of *Women in Love* as of *Tom Jones*, of *Ulysses* as of *Pamela*. From our answers we may expect to learn more about the ethical beliefs of the writers of such works than if they had written apologues.

From the Whole Plot to Values

No more serious theoretical objection could be made to the classes I have defined, and to the notion of translating aesthetic signals into ethical statements, than that they make possible inferences from only parts of literary works; that is, from purely local evaluations of a kind predictable from particular combinations of members of defined classes. The classes themselves have been so established that the ethical role of any member must always be consonant with the total contribution which, as a character, he makes toward the artistic end of the work;[26] and all important inferences would be made from many rather than from single evaluations in the work. It is nevertheless true that the theory advanced seems to offer no provision for inferences made directly from the "whole plot" or the "whole work" to its author's ethical beliefs, notions, and prejudices. It can be argued that it is from the whole work, not from fragmentary evaluations, that we learn most; it is, after all, the whole works which are responsible for the ethical effect they had on Coleridge or, to take an opposite view, for the absence of the ethical effect of Fielding's novels on F. R. Leavis.[27]

And surely it is the whole of any literary work which modifies our very being and makes us feel, when we have read a masterpiece, that we are not the same men and women we were when we began it. To translate an observation Coleridge made to another context, it is not what a great writer has shown us he believes that matters, it is what he *is* and how his work reflects his being that counts. If a tragedy actually succeeds in evoking in us pity and fear, our moral fiber must be subtly altered, for we have had an experience that is impossible in life: we have been made to feel compassion for a created man suffering nobly under circumstances we are unlikely ever to encounter, and yet we have somehow made his fate our own. Any good tragedy will have such a consequence, and yet good tragedians may, as we know, have widely divergent ethical beliefs, opinions, and prejudices. I am not certain whether an absolute misanthropist or a man who had never wept, if indeed there are such persons, could write a good tragedy, but one can hardly conceive of an ethical commitment which could prevent a sufficiently talented writer from creating an instance of this or any other literary form. If we were to ask what a man must believe to write a tragedy or what he must believe to write a comedy, we could not even reply that he must believe that life is tragic or life is comic. Our answer would have to be, "almost anything."

And yet what a writer believes does matter greatly, and the moral effects of any two tragedies or any two comedies must differ substantially as their authors' beliefs differ. For if we feel pity and fear as a consequence of any tragedy, these emotions have been evoked for the sake of a particular character whose traits have been revealed to us, whose acts have been stamped as

[26] Such consonance is inevitable, since the very devices of disclosure which help accomplish the artistic end by controlling what we feel are the source of the value judgments ensured by the presence of members of the seven classes.
[27] See Crane's discussion in *Critics and Criticism*, p. 646.

noble, whose choices have been subtly marked as wise or foolish. To reverse the coin, perhaps we feel a sense of joy when hero and heroine receive their just reward at the end of any comedy, but what a difference it makes to our ethical being if we are happy for Tom Jones, a one-time cully and occasional fornicator, or for some other comic hero. Considered in this light, the author's ethical predilections are no longer irrelevant to his literary work. For Fielding did have to believe something rather special to cause us both to expect and to desire a happy fate for such a character. And in the very act of making us satisfied with Tom's fate, he indicated the precise degree of disapproval we were to feel about what he precisely indicated as undesirable in Tom's actions. He also indicated the degree and kind of punishment appropriate to those acts. He attributed to the heroine those traits which make her a reward rather than a punishment. He represented other characters who were threats to Tom's well-being and indicated the precise degree of disapprobation we were to feel for their highly particularized traits, thoughts, or acts.

Fielding made scarcely a single artistic choice that did not further modify the ethical effect of *Tom Jones* and, in making each choice, his ethical commitments, intuitive or conscious, not merely were but *had* to be revealed. The demands for such a commitment are, in fact, so ubiquitous that, if a novelist wished to assume a public face and to hide unpopular opinions, he would find it more difficult to do so in a novel than in a letter, a diary, or a philosophical treatise.

Nothing in the present work is meant to suggest that the moral effect of a novel can be accounted for by some of its parts. The distinctions among the forms of fiction made in chapter one, as well as the particular classes of agents described in later chapters have been specifically designed to show that we can determine why it is that the whole of any novel has a particular ethical effect and further to show that such an effect is the direct result of a novelist's success in embodying his beliefs in the form permitted—even demanded—by novels. That is, I have tried to show that a good novelist embodies his beliefs and opinions in such a way that a particularized ethical effect is an assured consequence of his *whole* novel.

The actual phrases "whole plot" or "whole work" are slippery indeed, even when we carefully define either one as a specified artistic end to whose accomplishment all parts of a work contribute; the moment we start making such inferences we tend to make them from catchword descriptions—it is not possible to infer, for example, from "the whole" of Crane's analysis of *Tom Jones*—of that end, from descriptions of recurring literary mannerisms or from descriptions of limited relations of parts. The forms of such descriptions from which I have at one time or another found myself making inferences directly vary from such apparently fruitful and inclusive statements about form as, "The incidents in this work are ordered in a probable or necessary sequence," or "This is a comedy of the kind specified in this article," to such peripheral observations as, "This writer creates some characters who are all good or all bad." Ironically, the danger of making inferences from such statements, even when they are descriptively true, is that doing so prevents us from ascertaining whether the truths they contain are dictated solely by the artistic end of a genre in which a writer, regardless of his ethical beliefs, notions, or prejudices, might reasonably have elected to write. It is obvious that particular value judgments are only parts of works, but they are those parts which reflect judgments the writer has actually made, and we have established it as highly improbable that any particular judgment is made necessary by the artistic end which, of course, it must help to accomplish. If we make inferences directly from descriptively true statements about relationships of larger units in the work, we do succeed in absolving ourselves from the responsibility for trying to convert local aesthetic signals into minor ethical statements before making far-reaching conclusions about a writer's ethical beliefs, but, in absolving ourselves from this responsibility, we make our inferences not from evaluations, which are themselves closely akin to ethical judgments, but from artistic choices the writer has made. Though of great importance, these choices have so tenuous a relation to the writer's ethical beliefs that inferences from them must inevitably be invalid.

To illustrate this is no simple matter, but may clarify the abstract statement of a complicated but important point. Let us assume that, while doing research for a biography of a hypothetical writer, one wishes to clarify the writer's attitude toward an ethic predicated on the assumption that men are not responsible for their own misfortunes, which are to be seen rather as the result of chance or fortune. We know from sources other than his literary works that in 1739 the writer's ethical judgments were based on this assumption, but that by 1751 he had reversed his earlier opinion and was strongly committed to the belief that men are fully responsible for their destinies. For our biography it is important to determine whether he had reversed his opinion before or after he wrote an important work of prose fiction published in 1749. The only explicit evidence we have is ambiguous so that, if we are to solve our problem at all, we must make inferences from the work of prose fiction itself. Apparently we are in luck, since certain descriptively true statements about the whole work suggest an immediate and convincing solution to our problem.

It is a work which consists of fourteen clearly defined episodes; the main character appears in all of them and in each he meets another character purely by chance; indeed, in the last half of the work he accidentally meets in the same order the same characters he had met previously, but these now have precisely the right information to prevent his making a serious error of judgment which he was inclined to make midway through the book. We note further that the traits attributed to the main character not only have no bearing on the ordering of episodes, but have little relation to his error of judgment or to its rectification; there is, in short, no serious causal relation between character and event. The outcome is clearly the result of accidental meetings.

In view of these descriptively true statements it is difficult not to conclude with considerable certainty that our hypothetical writer did not reverse, and was probably not even close to reversing, his opinion in 1749.

Yet, before basing an important section of our biography on our inferences, we might well look more carefully at some of the parts and relationships among the parts of the hypothetical work.

Part I.   "An Errand for Papa"

Episode 1: John Lemuel, a boy from Somerset, is on his way to London to perform an errand for his father. He recalls an argument between his Uncle Toby and his father, during which the former asserted that theory A (the theory held by the author in 1739) was true, while the latter argued for theory B (the theory held by the author in 1751).

Episode 2: Lemuel happens to strike up a conversation with a Mr. Booby, who is also on his way to London. Booby briefly relates a series of events which befell him the previous week and interprets them in such a way that they seem to support Uncle Toby's theory. Booby hires a horse and rides off to London.

Episodes 3-7: In each of these episodes Lemuel meets another character who recounts events which he interprets in such a way that they support Uncle Toby's theory, and each rides off to London ahead of Lemuel. As he arrives in London, Lemuel has become convinced that Uncle Toby is right and that he must act on that conviction.

Lemuel, we note, is characterized as a kind of Everyboy. He is described in sufficient detail to make him credible, but is represented only as polite, openminded, and fond of both Uncle Toby and Father. Considerable artistry is displayed in the order of the tales which the subordinate characters narrate to Lemuel; each proves Uncle Toby's point in a tale which has greater scope and intensity than the previous narrator's. The first characters are from the humbler walks of life, but here again there is a neat progression so that the last narrator is a knight. A progression may be observed also in the relative intelligence of the characters who tell tales. By the time the knight has completed his tale, we are at least inclined, as Lemuel now is, to regard Uncle Toby's judgment as correct. We may now conclude our summary:

Part II. "London"

Episodes 8-14: Lemuel completes his errand and wanders the streets of London. He meets Mr. Booby and thanks him for the lesson he has learned from him, but Booby has changed his mind and explains why his previous interpretation of events was incorrect and why he had misinterpreted them. His new interpretation supports Father's theory. Lemuel bumps into each of the previous narrators in turn. Each explains why his previous interpretation was wrong and, with increasing forcefulness in the respective episodes, explains why theory B is correct. The knight is again the last narrator, and Lemuel leaves London knowing the truth: Father was right and Uncle Toby's theory, apparently more attractive, was a honeyed trap for the unwary.

At this point we may feel somewhat less inclined to rely heavily on the inference we made from what are still descriptively true statements about this sequence of events, for the sequence may as easily be attributed to the apologue form as to the writer's beliefs. Some room for doubt may remain if theories A and B are far removed from considerations of chance and human responsibility—if, for example, Uncle Toby had expounded the theory that women are pestiferous, and Father had insisted that women were men's best friends. But no doubts can remain that our inference was invalid if we recognize that our descriptive statements would still be true if the hypothetical writer had actually designed the work to make the point that men are responsible for their own destinies; Uncle Toby's theory in this work is that chance controls man's destinies, and Father's that men are responsible for their own. In turn, each of the characters Lemuel meets in the first part imputes a series of misfortunes he narrates to chance, and explains in the second part that he has discovered the source of his unhappiness in his own error of judgment or weakness of character. Since the same description of the sequence is as true of the work organized to make the point that women are men's best friends, we must conclude that we were absolutely unjustified in inferring from that statement that our hypothetical writer still believed in the power of chance or fortune in 1749. To the extent that the value of our biography depended upon this inference, it would be worthless.[28]

[28] If the hypothetical writer had actually written an apologue organized to make the second point, the biographer's question would probably not have arisen. But writers of prose fiction are seldom that obliging; when it is important for a biographer to know when a writer changed his attitude toward Fortune, he will have to infer it from a work which makes a point about women, or, more probably, makes no point at all.

There is only one highly unlikely condition which could make our inference valid. If it were true that no writer who believed that men are responsible for their own destinies could write an apologue, then even as inadequate a logician as myself must recognize syllogistic proof that our hypothetical writer had not changed his opinion by 1749. But the major premise will appear preposterous if we remember that only convenience of exposition dictated my choice of a hypothetical apologue to illustrate my point, but that the crucial statement about the sequence will be as accurately descriptive of the sequences of event in a variety of comic forms in which the artistic end depends upon a chance relationship between character and event.[29] For our inference to be valid, we should have to accept the notion that no writer who believed that men are responsible for their own destinies could write such comedy and, conversely, that no man who believed in the power of chance could write that kind of work—frequently classified as tragedy—in which the artistic end usually demands a probable sequence of event and a causal relation between character and action.

Rejecting this notion as improbable does not commit us to the equally unlikely assumption that writers mislead their readers at the dictates of the genre in which they write.[30] A novelist with blatant moral intentions and a deep conviction that men are responsible for their own good or ill fortune will not mislead us if he chooses to write a comedy, akin, say to *Pride and Prejudice*, the effect of which is strongly contingent upon an "accidental" sequence of events; the way in which he discloses what he represents, the evaluations of characters, actions, and ideas he must include to achieve the artistic end of the work inevitably provide signals aesthetically sufficient to prevent misinterpretation. With an accidental sequence of events and classes of agents, as in Fielding's novels, the local interaction of members of those classes will convey to the reader the judgment he is supposed to make of events represented in any part of the sequence. Let a paragon—even for purely formal purposes—explain to a sympathetic but erring protagonist that his attitude toward an event

[29] Note, to take only a few examples, that the resolution of *Emma* depends to a great degree on the death of Frank Churchill's aunt; the resolution of *Pride and Prejudice* depends upon the accidental meeting between Lizzy and Darcy at the latter's estate; the resolution of *The Ambassadors* depends upon Strether's discovery that Chad and Mme de Vionnet are physically intimate. Not one of these events is probable; they are at best possible. This does not mean that they are flaws in the work or that Jane Austen and Henry James necessarily believed that chance controls men's destinies.

[30] They might well lead critics like myself astray, since they did not write their works to solve the problems I happen to be particularly interested in.

represented in an earlier episode has led to his present unhappiness; let a walking concept labeled "Stoic" argue vehemently that his unhappy fate is the result of a caprice of fortune, though his character has been exposed by the protagonist and his moral culpability has been the cause of the heroine's distress, and the reader will be in no danger at all of being misled by the formal sequence of events. Neither will the biographer be misled who, aware that his desire to translate aesthetically sufficient signals into ethical statements is a very special concern, makes inferences only from those parts of whole works —isolable value judgments—which are formal signals of ethical judgments a novelist has actually made to ensure an appropriate response to the whole work, rather than from statements of even the most inclusive and important relationships of parts of the novel interpreted as "the whole work."

We need not go far afield to find examples of how local evaluations prevent ambiguous interpretation of an "accidental" sequence; a brief glance at the complicated ending of *Amelia* will suffice to illustrate the point.[31] The accidental circumstances which lead to the happy ending are such that, treated by a lesser writer than Fielding, we might find them incredible. For our purposes here we need only mention the following: Robinson happens to be in a pawnshop when Amelia pawns her picture; mortally wounded[32] by the hirelings of Bondum, the bailiff who happens to be Booth's own *bête noire*, Robinson happens to be incarcerated in the same spunging house with Booth so that his "death-bed" confession is made to Harrison; that confession reveals precisely the right information to confound sister Betty and lawyer Murphy (who, as it happens, is sometimes employed by Harrison) and to put Booth and Amelia in possession of their rightful inheritance. Add to these coincidences that there is no preparation for Robinson's reappearance after he has served his function as a walking concept in the early prison scenes and that, until he actually speaks to Harrison, there is no suggestion that he is capable of repentance, and we may certainly feel inclined to question the sincerity of Fielding's explicit attacks on men who accuse Fortune of bringing about their own ill-success and, consequently, to question the validity of his assertion that one who calls a man fortunate who has retrieved "the ill consequences of a foolish conduct" "is guilty of no less impropriety in speech than he would be who should call the statuary or the poet fortunate who carved a Venus or who writ an

---

[31] The best example is in *Tom Jones*, but the relation of the local evaluations to the narrative sequence in it is much too complicated for brief discussion.

[32] As it turns out, Robinson's wound conveniently appears to be mortal but does not kill him.

Iliad." [33] The sequence of events in Fielding's novel does not seem to support his statement that "Life may as properly be called an art as any other." [34]

Yet nothing is simpler than to define the events that lead to the happy ending as decidedly not the consequence of chance; nothing more is necessary for such a definition than the remarks of Harrison, who has been firmly entrenched as the paragon figure for some 600 pages by the time he hears Robinson's tale of coincidences. " 'Good heavens! how wonderful is thy providence!' cries the doctor. 'Murphy, say you?' " [35] If from the doctor's cry we infer that we are to regard these events as providential rather than accidental, we are still a long way from being able to see life as an art; neither Booth nor Amelia has been represented as more worthy of the interference of Providence in their behalf than was, say, Mr. Bennet, who was seen as less culpable than, at any rate, Booth. The terms in which Harrison subsequently informs Booth of the glad tidings would alone be sufficient to prevent our inferring that Providence, in Fielding's view, always takes a direct hand in the affairs of the deserving: "The first person who ascended the stairs was the doctor, who no sooner saw Booth than he ran to him and embraced him, crying, 'My child, I wish you joy with all my heart. Your sufferings are all at an end, and Providence hath done you the justice at last which it will, one day or other, render to all men.' " [36] We may be assured that, in Fielding's view when he wrote *Amelia,* apparently fortuitous circumstance is not the result of chance but of Providence; we may be equally certain that injustice was not, in his view, inevitably to be rectified before "the last." But the "happiness" of Amelia and Booth, although it is the result of Providence, is still not in their own control; the denial of chance seems equally to be a denial that men's happinesss is in their own control, and we could hardly infer from this that life is an art which may be practiced well or poorly with expected results. But the strange manner in which Amelia learns that all is well tells us more. Booth does not immediately tell her the good news but delays in such a manner as to wring the last possible tear or smile at the happy conclusion from the reader of sensibility. When the female paragon begs her husband not to borrow money from the Atkinsons, as he has pretended to threaten, Booth asks, "How then shall we live?"

"By our labor," answered she; "I am to labor, and I am sure I am not ashamed of it."

"And do you really think you can support such a life?"

---

[33] Henley, VI, 14 (*Amelia,* I, i).   [35] *Ibid.,* VII, 321 (XII, vi).
[34] *Ibid.*   [36] *Ibid.,* p. 327 (XII, vii).

"I am sure I could be happy in it," answered Amelia. "And why not I as well as a thousand others, who have not the happiness of such a husband to make life delicious? why should I complain of my hard fate while so many who are much poorer than I enjoy theirs? Am I of a superior rank of being to the wife of the honest laborer? am I not partaker of one common nature with her?"

"My angel," cries Booth, "it delights me to hear you talk thus, and for a reason you little guess; for I am assured that one who can so heroically endure adversity will bear prosperity with equal greatness of soul; for the mind that cannot be dejected by the former is not likely to be transported with the latter."[37]

Two walking concepts who believed that the way to outwit Fortune is to become inhumanly dispassionate have already been thoroughly ridiculed in the novel; we are in no danger of mistaking Amelia's tranquillity for the undesirable imperturbability of Stoicism. But those circumstances,[38] defined as providential rather than accidental by Harrison, which make possible the happy ending *of* the novel do not make possible the conditions which constitute happiness *in* the novel; happiness is judged to be in the grasp of the Booths even if Providence had decided not to do them justice till "the last." We are not allowed to forget that the conditions of the happy ending, which maximize the special power of *Amelia,* are not those of the greatest importance for Amelia's well-being:

"Indeed," cries Amelia, "I should almost think my husband and you, doctor, had some very good news to tell me, by your using, both of you, the same introduction. As far as I know myself, I think I can answer I can support any degree of prosperity, and I think I yesterday showed I could: for I do assure you it is not in the power of fortune to try me with such another transition from grief to joy as I conceived from seeing my husband in prison and at liberty."

"Well, you are a good girl," cries the doctor, "and after I have put on my spectacles I will try you." [39]

The worthy has blessed the worthy. That Booth and Amelia become prosperous is important for the artistic end that Fielding accomplished in the novel. The chain of circumstances which leads to their prosperity is judged to be providential and not fortuitous. The chain of circumstances arranged by

[37] *Ibid.*, p. 333 (XII, viii).

[38] The circumstances which maximize that aspect of the special power of *Amelia* which depends upon the discrepancy between her distress and her expected and desired reward.

[39] Henley, VII, 335 (*Amelia,* XII, viii).

Providence is not judged as necessary for happiness. The local evaluations are consonant with Fielding's introductory statements. If we did not have those statements, if we did not try to make sweeping inferences from descriptively true statements about the narrative sequence in *Amelia*, if we asked ourselves "What is it likely that Fielding must have believed to evaluate as he did such characters, actions, and thoughts in such a work?" we could have inferred that he must have believed that men attribute their own unhappiness to Fortune "with no less absurdity in life than a bad player complains of ill luck at the game of chess." [40]

A Speculative Conclusion

The whole of this enquiry has been an attempt to answer two questions. How do novelists embody their ethical beliefs, opinions, and prejudices in novels? And, more particularly, how was Henry Fielding so effectively able to implement moral intentions in his novels that, on the one hand, they evoked a strong moral response in Coleridge and, on the other hand, they led some critics to characterize Fielding as primarily a novelist in opposition to Richardson, whom they view primarily as a moralist?

In a purely negative way it has been shown that no particular set of moral beliefs and no specifiable moral intention determine the form in which a writer includes his beliefs or implements his intentions. The positive analogue to this is that, whatever his beliefs or his moral intentions, a writer of prose fiction may include one and implement the other in a satire, an apologue, or a represented action. Johnson's desire to turn our eyes toward heaven was embodied in an apologue, but the desire might have been accomplished in a satire or an action as well. Fielding's desire to expose some glaring evils of his day might have been effected in a satire or an apologue, but he chose to rely upon the effects of a coherent action to fulfill his purpose.

It is not that these writers had consciously to choose among the three forms, though they might well have done so. Johnson's remarks about Richardson, for example, show that he was aware of moral effects possible only in coherent actions. In *Shamela*, Fielding had written first-rate satire; in *Joseph Andrews*, for all its comic indebtedness to *Pamela*, he carefully limited his ridicule of external objects to the ironic thrusts and verbal allusions which can always be accommodated in a comic action. Accomplishment of such minimal ends as Richardson claims to have embodied in *Pamela* is sufficient to explain why his moral and aesthetic concerns considered together were likely to result in repre-

[40] *Ibid.*, VI, 14 (I, i).

sented action rather than in apologue. In general, though, the degree of consciousness of the implications of aesthetic choice varies radically from author to author. It is beyond the scope of the present work to investigate whether any writer may make all choices intuitively or all choices consciously, though the kinds of discriminations permitted by the critical framework employed in this book might well facilitate such an investigation.

What is more to the point is that the shape which a writer gives to his beliefs and the ways in which he may implement his moral intentions are limited by the mutually exclusive conditions which must be fulfilled if he is to write a satire, an apologue, or a represented action. The rather strict limitation of the shape—though never the content—of ethical beliefs demanded by each of three types in which any moral intention may be embodied has implications for historical studies of works other than prose fictions, since the principles of organization which underlie satire, apologue, and action are applicable to many dramas and verse creations as well.

It is consoling, for example, to assume that once there was an age, in contrast to our own, in which ethical and religious commitments were decorously uniform, but in which, by some ancient magic, a variety of personalities and individual accomplishments flourished unthreatened by the dire conformity that the machine has imposed upon us. A fantasy harmless enough, to be sure. And yet, if it turned out that the religious beliefs of fourteenth-century England were so uniform that detailed studies of theological and other documents enabled us accurately to predict both Geoffrey Chaucer's doctrinal commitments and the details of the ethical standards by which he judged events and people, we would not have one jot more evidence about the forms of his literary works. The most highly detailed account of the religious and moral beliefs of fourteenth-century Englishmen could not justify an inference that their literary works had to be Christian allegories (i.e., a subclass of exempla or apologue), since no religious belief precludes the writing of represented actions or satires.[41] In fact, in the *Canterbury Tales* alone, Chaucer included instances of satire, action, and apologue. Indeed, we might derive from Chaucer convincing arguments that at some point in a critical enquiry it is useful to distinguish satire, action, and apologue according to their artistic ends alone, and apart from a poet's intention. "The Wife of Bath's Tale" is one of the few great examples in English literature of a perfectly organized apologue, a didactic form, employed for a primarily aesthetic end; the apologue would seem to implement no strong moral intent.

[41] I have, throughout this book, referred to all examples which are also prose fictions as apologues. Otherwise the two terms are to be regarded as essentially synonymous.

And if this be true when we postulate an age of doctrinal uniformity, it must be more so when we do not. To return to prose fiction, consider two sentences containing admittedly polar forms of assumptions which underlie some attempts to elucidate literary works by reference to theological documents:

We cannot understand the subtle mystery inherent in Swift's cloudy depiction of Houyhnhnmland without reference to Anglican theology, which neatly solves the mystery for us.

For some two hundred years, readers have enjoyed Joseph Andrews, *but have thoroughly misunderstood the novel because they were inadequately versed in the sermons of Isaac Barrow, whose name happens not to appear in the novel.*

If *Gulliver's Travels* is an apologue organized as fictional exemplification of Anglican theology, and if *Joseph Andrews* is an exemplification of ethical precepts in Barrow's, or other latitudinarians', sermons, the two statements might easily be true. For in an apologue the organizing doctrine or statement must usually be familiar to readers—more familiar than the examples themselves. And it is surely possible to conceive of a circumstance in which a Swift or a Fielding might reasonably presume doctrinal knowledge in their readers which would be lost to subsequent generations.[42] But if this had happened, it would be difficult to explain the appeal that *Joseph Andrews* and *Gulliver's Travels* still make to educated men unless we assume that the latter are not telling the truth, or that each of the works has the protean and highly improbable ability of assuming one coherent form in the eighteenth century and another equally coherent but quite different form in our day.[43] Literary tastes may indeed change so radically that it is difficult for a later age to understand why Elizabethans admired *Euphues* or pre-romantics admired *The Man of Feeling.* But that is another matter altogether.

Our historical investigations might prove more fruitful if we at least held

[42] These and my subsequent remarks should not be interpreted as attempts to disparage historical studies which clarify particular objects of satire. In *Gulliver's Travels*, in which Swift alludes frequently to historical personages and events, it is necessary to understand the allusions if we are to feel the full force of the satire. Where we miss an allusion we are aware that the author means to ridicule an external object, but the object is not clear. A twentieth-century reader might fail to recognize that a ridiculed act was historically performed by Queen Anne, but annotation which simply describes the ridiculed act makes the satire clear. It is quite a different matter, however, when historical criticism postulates as an unrecognized object of satire one which demands that we completely alter the clear signals for ridicule before we can understand the object.

[43] See note 18.

in abeyance the notion common in our day that the justification for such investigations is the degree to which they "illuminate" a literary work—that is, the degree to which they facilitate some new and sensitive reading of works of previous ages. Such excursions into creativity are almost immediately self-defeating. The greater the degree of originality achieved in such a reading, the farther removed it must be from the common experience of generations of intelligent and sensitive readers whose admiration alone gives greater significance to critical efforts than that of a harmless pastime. It would be no reflection upon the critical complexion of our own day if we reverted to the notion of a previous time that literary history or ethical considerations of literary works were themselves valuable disciplines. Their value need not derive from the production of new readings of old masters, but, on the contrary, from a desire to understand how works which have been so important to so many men came about and how they are related to other human concerns.

A study of Swift's indebtedness to Anglican theology is not important primarily because it clears up mysteries inherent in *Gulliver's Travels;* if so used, it may learnedly obscure the simple observations that *Gulliver's Travels* is a satire and that in such works we will always expect all virtues ascribed to the fictional personages to facilitate the ridicule of external objects. But because Jonathan Swift wrote a satire admired and understood by men ages after its creation,[44] we wish to know not only the virtues inherent in the work that elicits such admiration, but everything possible about the beliefs of its author and the relation of his beliefs to ideas current in an age that gave rise to such a satire.

Readers who have laughed as Joseph and Parson Adams and Fanny defeat the ludicrously represented barriers to their happiness, and who have rejoiced in the final success of the peregrinating trio are unlikely to laugh or rejoice in any stronger degree if they learn of Fielding's debt to latitudinarian divines; but because so many men have laughed and rejoiced for so long, it is important to know that some of the beliefs of the man responsible for *Joseph Andrews* were derived from his acceptance of certain religious attitudes common in his day. There is surely no need to reinterpret *Joseph Andrews* as a set of fictional examples of the desirability of those attitudes to justify our historical investigations. It is far more important, even for the history of ideas, to recognize that, at a given point in history, a number of relatively commonplace religious notions were given a special kind of life as

[44] But see note 42.

the value judgments responsible for controlling readers' reactions to represented characters, acts, and thoughts in a relatively new kind of prose fiction we now call the novel.

Insistence on the mutual incompatibility of the modes of embodying belief and moral intention in satire, apologue, and action may seem terribly rigid. And indeed the distinctions are rigid, but the critical discriminations they facilitate are not. The insistence itself represents no more than a repetition of the truism that the moral effects possible to any given type may only be the moral effects possible to that type. If it were feasible for a writer to embody his beliefs and implement his moral intentions in a single work incorporating the virtues of both apologue and action, then we should have every right to accuse Johnson of a lamentable failure to incorporate in *Rasselas* some of the minimal virtues of even the least admirable of actions. Johnson is especially culpable, since he had read novels and was quite conscious of their special virtues. And surely something like this must be the critical fate of *Rasselas* if we attempt to fit all prose fictions to the Procrustean bed of a single kind. If Fielding and Johnson implemented their moral intentions in works which are mere variations of ways in which themes may be exploited, then Johnson is indeed unsubtle, since his characters are puppets and his main theme is always apparent, and Fielding is either unclear or ineffable depending on whether or not one likes his novel. But if Johnson embodies his beliefs and implements his moral intention in ways possible only in an apologue, and Fielding does the same in ways possible only in represented actions, we can account for the peculiar greatness of each work. One may, I think, justifiably ask which is more inflexible, an articulated distinction which helps to explain why *Rasselas* and *Joseph Andrews* have been cherished by many men, or an intuitive use of critical terms current in our day under the misapprehension that they commit us to nothing, though in practice they commit us to an inarticulated assumption that all prose fictions have essentially the same form; *Rasselas*, as a variant of that form, is a bad novel.

Nowhere in this work has coherence been used as an evaluative term. It is not a virtue of any type of prose fiction, simply a condition of its existence. If we can recognize an episode in a work as a digression from it on the basis of the way in which the episode is organized, the whole work must in some sense have a coherent organization. The term "digression" is itself a descriptive, not an evaluative, term. We have seen how deftly Fielding employed narrative digressions organized as apologues to accomplish special effects in *Tom Jones*. Any of the forms may accommodate a number of elements—

though not organized episodes—which would be common to a number of the forms. Swift, for example, in no way compromises the effectiveness of his satire when he evokes laughter at Gulliver's solemn disavowal of an adulterous affair with a woman six inches high, though our laughter may not be directed against any external object. It is almost a mark of Fielding's style to make ironic thrusts at men and institutions outside the fictional world he creates and then to use that ridicule to help ensure an appropriate reaction toward his fictional creations.

The uncomfortable rigidity of the distinctions among forms and the insistence on the implications of those distinctions for the shape of ethical beliefs are not intended as procedures for discovering a writer's beliefs in his works, or as attempts to dictate to novelists what they may or may not do. We may discover the truth about a writer's beliefs in any of the mysterious ways that men discover the truth about anything. The distinctions are merely necessary parts of an attempt to show that we can distinguish three defined shapes that belief necessarily assumes in three kinds of fiction. I have not attempted to show anyone how to discover a writer's beliefs; I have taken what I presume to be the truth about the relation between beliefs and fiction, discovered by any possible means I had, and tried to "prove" that what I discovered is likely to be true. All distinctions are made to show that the theory advanced about belief in fiction is valid. But the theory itself must be judged partially by its explanatory power—by the degree to which it helps to answer questions of general concern in literary criticism, literary history, biography, and the history of ideas. Obviously, among any of a number of theories which seemed to explain equally well the relation of belief to fiction, we would always select as more powerful the one which proved most useful for our general concerns about literary works. The actual distinctions and the number of distinctions made in this book represent an attempt to allow the greatest possible flexibility in making critical discriminations useful for other investigations.

We may glance for a moment at a suggestion, offered casually in this chapter, that we date the first English novels from the time that Richardson and Fielding embodied their beliefs and implemented their sincere moral intentions in represented actions, one serious, the other comic. *Moll Flanders*, among others, will not, in this view, be considered as the first novel in English. Yet we know, of course, that *Moll Flanders* enjoys considerable critical esteem and many readers prefer it to *Pamela* or *Joseph Andrews*. Of course whether we call *Moll Flanders* a novel or not is a trivial matter, but a minimal requirement of any good history of English prose fiction would surely be that it did ample justice to the merits of *Moll Flanders* as a prose fiction but nevertheless took cognizance of such facts as the following: Fielding and Richardson each presume to have done something new and different in his first novel, in a way that Defoe does not; the reactions of many eighteenth-century readers suggest that in *Pamela* and *Joseph Andrews,* though more strongly in the former, something new had actually been accomplished; critics of subsequent generations, even among admirers of *Moll Flanders,* seem to assign Defoe's work an ambiguous position in relation to later novels: virtually all historians of the novel include *Pamela* and *Joseph Andrews* as novels proper, but many discuss *Moll Flanders* as a precursor of the form rather than an instance of it. I do not suggest that any of these observations establish conclusive evidence one way or the other about the form of *Moll Flanders.* But they may support what some readers, including myself, have felt: different though *Pamela* and *Joseph Andrews* are as literary works, they seem to share some important "quality" not present in *Moll Flanders.* It is at least worth exploring the possibility that the shared similarity accounts for the sense of "newness" that Richardson, Fielding, and some of their contemporaries felt about *Pamela* and *Joseph Andrews,* while its absence in *Moll Flanders* led to ambiguous classifications of that work in some subsequent criticism.

On the other hand, a glance at any of the incidental traits or combination of traits of style and manner of representation in the three works seems invariably to lead to the conclusion that Defoe and Richardson are actually closer to each other than they are to Fielding. And even rather intensive examination of those shared surface traits will show *The Unfortunate Traveller* to possess more of them than any one of Fielding's novels does. It is obvious that any history based on distinctions that enable us to see Nash as more central to the development of the novel than Fielding is not very useful. But, different as they are, both *Pamela* and *Joseph Andrews* are organized as actions while *Moll Flanders* clearly is not.[45] And it is, of course, the "whole" literary work more than any of its parts that is responsible for the effect it has upon us. That is, no matter how many traits of style, manner, and attitude are shared by an apologue and an action, we are likely to react to them as far more dissimilar than any two novels, no matter how few traits of style, manner, and attitude the latter share. As far as I can ascertain, no English prose fiction previous to *Pamela* and *Joseph Andrews* is organized as coherent action. If there are some, they were not widely enough known and admired to prevent

[45] Some of the implications of Defoe's adoption of the journal format are discussed in Arthur W. Secord, *Studies in the Narrative Method of Defoe* (Urbana, Ill., 1924).

an eighteenth-century audience's reacting to *Pamela* as being somehow new and different from the prose fiction they were familiar with.

Whether we call *Moll Flanders* a novel is a matter of little consequence for any history of the novel, since, whatever we wish to call it, no history of the genre could fail to discuss it and to distinguish it in some terms or other from coherent actions. But it is of considerable importance that, whatever we decide to call it, we do justice to the merits that have kept it alive for so long a time. It is obviously historically more important than many novels and a greater artistic achievement than most. But if coherence is not necessarily a virtue nor its lack an artistic fault, we might explain more about the effectiveness of *Moll Flanders* and about its contribution to techniques later employed by novelists if we view it as a work which is not coherent than if we strain our ingenuity to discover a principle of coherence for it. We may clarify this by the following analogy: if we come across a sentence in a poem by e. e. cummings which we find effective but inexplicable by any principle of any English grammar, we may do one of two things; we may try to alter the principles of an English grammar so that it will include such sentences; or we may attempt to explain part of the effectiveness of the sentence in question as resulting from a deviation from English grammar. In most cases the latter will prove the preferable alternative, and no admirer of cummings could complain that we have insulted his memory by our explanation.

As in most, though not all, of Defoe's work, *Moll Flanders* does begin with a rudimentary action, not dissimilar in some ways to the episodic action of *Joseph Andrews*, but, though Defoe may wish to restore an earlier character toward the end of the work, the relationships among characters are stabilized before Moll's departure from England. I think it is not an exaggeration to say that after the initial part of the work we would not object to any episode of any kind (i.e., would not find it digressive) so long as the Moll Flanders with whom we have become enchanted is in it. There is nothing to prevent us from calling *Moll Flanders* a novel of character rather than action, but neither is there any magic in such a designation. Since there is no serious sense in which we can relate any substantial number of the later episodes to new revelations of Moll's character or to some consistent internal change which culminates in her conversion, a serious attempt to describe the work's coherence in such terms may, ironically, discover greater deficiencies than would an attempt to describe it as an action. On the other hand, the work's undeniable merits need not be obscured if we recognize that it had only to meet extremely minimal demands of coherence to affect us as, in some sense, a single work (e.g., Moll must appear in all episodes).

The sense in which *Moll Flanders* is a single work is not dissimilar to the sense in which a collection of all the stories and novels in which a single detective hero appears may be viewed as a single work. Many a lover of Sherlock Holmes, for example, has thoroughly enjoyed an occasional inept tale simply because the affection he has developed for the Holmes encountered previously is sufficient to ensure his interest in any tale in which the detective appears.

In meeting minimal demands of this sort, however, *Moll Flanders* will inevitably affect readers as being more "unified" than any collection of tales with a single hero or heroine for a number of reasons. First, Moll does not appear as the heroine of a series of completed actions any more than she appears as the heroine of a single action. Second, merely by showing Moll at various stages of her chronological development from extreme youth to old age, Defoe helps to create an illusion of progression. That illusion is considerably enhanced by the artistic dexterity with which Defoe has employed some sequences of episodes effectively to represent internal change in his heroine, as in the brilliant sequence which begins with Moll pilfering reluctantly to satisfy her external necessities and culminates in her abducting a horse worthless except as it satisfies what has become for her a psychological need to steal. Third, the whole set of narrative devices which suggest that we are reading a journal enhances the illusion that we are reading about an interesting series of events which might possibly have occurred to the fully developed character in whom we have become interested. It is a testament to Defoe's power as a writer that he was able to create a character so fascinating that we do not tire of her no matter where her adventures lead; it is a sign of Defoe's special genius that our interest in Moll Flanders does not flag, though her creator did not to any great extent stimulate our interest, as any novelist does, by consistently arousing expectations not fully resolved until the end of his book. That prose fictions organized somewhat in this manner were not necessarily new in England when Defoe wrote them does not compromise the excellence of Defoe's work, since never before had they been written so effectively. And, although *Moll Flanders* is not organized as a coherent action, the techniques of representation, the creation of a character with psychological depth, and the exploitation of the special stylistic medium employed by Defoe were to have great importance in the novels of some of his contemporaries.

The flexibility of the apparently rigid terminology employed in the present work might also be seen, I think, in considering works like *Humphry Clinker;* for here again we should not need to justify our pleasure in the work by

trying to find for it a new principle of coherence. If we were to consider it
as a work organized as an action with so many digressions of one kind and
another that its total effect was somewhat vitiated, and if we then described
the relatively clear relation between the elements which do tend to vitiate a
single coherent effect and Smollet's ethical (and other) intentions, it would
not be difficult to explain why so many readers have felt greater pleasure from
the work's parts than from the accomplishment of its artistic end. I think that
the discriminations might be useful also in explaining why some modern
readers can derive great pleasure from the sentimental evocations of *Tristram
Shandy* but tend to react with boredom when they read Mackenzie's *Man of
Feeling* in which he takes what had been only the sentimental power of some
previous fiction and embodies it as the controlling theme of an apologue which
shows us by fictional example that tender sensibilities, weaknesses in this world,
are the virtues of the next.

But, of course, such discriminations depend upon the rigid insistence that
no matter what his ethical beliefs or moral intentions a writer may embody
one and implement the other in a satire, an apologue, or an action. If at first
it may appear that apologue and satire demand the greatest degree of ethical
revelation, in the end it turns out to be otherwise. For the beliefs relevant to
apologues are quite likely to be, in some sense, doctrinal and a writer is likely
to reveal his long-range philosophical commitments only. The satirist, no
matter how wide the scope of his satire, need only reveal the negative side of
his beliefs—to show us by ridiculing the men and institutions and beliefs he
scorns; the virtues he describes in his satire have no necessary connection with
his positive beliefs, since their job is to facilitate not ethical statements but
ridicule of external objects.

But it is the novelist, ironically, from whom the greatest degree of ethical
revelation is demanded. Apart from any moral intention he has, he *must*, if
he is to write a good novel, judge characters, acts, and thoughts as a part of
his representation. It is not sufficient for him, as it is for the satirist, to show
us what he does not like in the external world. And he may not limit what
he reveals to the formulated ideas in which he consciously acquiesces. A good
novelist may not even rest content with appropriate marks of approbation and
disapprobation, for he must control our reactions with considerable subtlety
on each page of his work if he is to accomplish its artistic end. A number of
novelists have commented on the fact that readers of their novels sometimes
act as if they knew them personally by virtue of having read their novels.
This is not surprising. When we have read a good novelist's work it is as if
we have had an opportunity to hear him speak to us of his beliefs and also

have been able to observe for years how in fact he reacts to people we have been allowed to know performing actions whose motives have been made comprehensible to us for ends with which we sympathize or which we dislike. And it is not that he *may* do this, he *must* do it if he is to write a novel of any value.

Index

273

Roberto Gonzalez Echevarria
47 Mather St.
Hamden, CT 06517